THE FAR COUNTRY:

A Regional History of Moab and La Sal, Utah

By FAUN McCONKIE TANNER

Olympus Publishing Company · Salt Lake City, Utah

Copyright © 1976 by Faun McConkie Tanner
Olympus Publishing Company
Salt Lake City, Utah

Library of Congress Cataloging in Publication Data

Tanner, Faun McConkie.
   The far country.

   First published (c1937) under title: A history
of Moab, Utah.
   Bibliography: p.
   Includes index.
   1. Moab, Utah—History. 2. La Sal, Utah—
History. I. Title.

F834.M6T3   1976   979.2'58   76-926
ISBN 0-913420-63-8

Contents

List of Figures

Dedication

To my father, William Russell McConkie, "Mr. Moab," son of Moab pioneers, educator, banker, religious leader, civic leader, whose encouragement and help made possible this history.

Special Dedication

To Loren L. Taylor, son of Moab pioneers, editor and publisher, civic leader, whose cooperation and help made possible the first publication of this history.

Preface to the Second Edition

History is a living, dynamic thing. All of our todays have their roots in our yesterdays, and the fruits will be our tomorrows. So long as man lives, the final chapter of history cannot be written.

As events change from day to day, so do our perspectives, our views of the past. Experience, seasoned with time, enables us to view our yesterdays with more maturity and understanding. The panorama shifts and we become dissatisfied. In this lies the hope of the future.

Many events have been written since the publication of the first edition in 1937. It has been my regret that I did not write more extensively of early events and developments. This has resulted in the present rewriting and updating of the first edition. The project has been under way for several years — in fact it is the result of a lifetime of research and study. Fortunately, with a sabbatical leave from teaching, I have been able to push the clock ahead and concentrate more fully on the gathering and organizing of the material for revision. And I have found many primary resources of early history which have, in some instances, changed the previous perspective.

Much more is available in the way of primary resources, and there has been increased responsiveness from many who were interested in a revision. I have been able to complete this project under the direction of Dr. Paul Hubbard, Chairman of the History Department at Arizona State University. His encouragement and help are appreciated.

In addition to those mentioned in the preface of the first edition and acknowledged in the bibliography, I wish to acknowledge assistance from Mr. Samuel J. Taylor, editor of the Moab *Times-Independent*; Mrs. Helen M. Knight (now deceased), director of the Moab Museum;

Mr. A. J. Redd, whose persistence and encouragement led me to include the history of La Sal; Mr. Bert Fireman, executive director of the Arizona Historical Foundation, who has been helpful in securing library loan materials; Dr. Everett Cooley, previously director of the Utah State Historical Society, now curator of the Western History Collection at the University of Utah; Dr. Charles S. Peterson, former director of the Utah State Historical Society, now curator at Utah State University and editor of the *Western Historical Quarterly*; Mr. Chad Flake, curator of the Western Special History Collection, BYU; and their staffs who were most helpful in giving assistance in my search for materials. I wish also to acknowledge the assistance in proofreading, editorial suggestions, and other help given by Dr. John S. Goff, my daughter-in-law Mary K. Tanner, and Charles R. Doss. Special acknowledgment is given to my brother, Wayne R. McConkie, for preparation of the map and its description covering the various positions and events surrounding the Pinhook massacre (chapter 9).

Again, I have sought to be objective with the information available. One must recognize folk history and objective history. Where I have relied on folk history, I have so indicated. I was fortunate in being able to research contemporary newspapers in the Denver City Library and Colorado State Museum and Historical Society, which gave new information about the Pinhook massacre of 1881. I owe much to the helpfulness of those in Colorado who made this material available to me.

In writing the history of a region — or of a relatively small, well-knit community — one is aware of prejudices and criticisms. But history is people and the things people do. A historian cannot manufacture. She has the responsibility of supporting her facts. There are many who have desired that I publish certain statements or accusations, but they themselves refused to be quoted. There are also those who feel that omissions have been made. But the historian must do a credible job in sorting out facts from emotion and folklore.

Moab has, in the opinion of the author and others, moved from a strictly agricultural to an industrialized community, retaining much of the flavor of the past. This in itself is an achievement and is indeed desired. La Sal, too, has undergone many changes. We pay tribute to those who have made this possible.

In this book, I have deliberately refrained from making the spelling of people's names consistent. This is because they have been spelled by earlier historians as the people themselves gave the spellings (e.g., Reece, Reese).

Faun McConkie Tanner

Phoenix, Arizona
January 1976

Preface to
the First Edition

Any attempt at recording history requires considerable research and a careful study of various accounts. In writing the history of Moab, Utah, I have had a sincere desire to present the facts — all of the facts obtainable — correctly to the best of my ability.

The study of history in general has always been fascinating to me, and this book is the result of a genuine interest in western history, particularly of Utah and our own section of the state. Having been born and reared in Moab, I have always delighted in listening to the stories of early settlers. My own grandparents were comparatively early settlers of Moab and did much in building up the community. While yet a child in school, I talked with several early settlers and heard of their experiences in the infant days of Moab. I even kept written notes on some of the accounts and began then to wonder why someone had not written a history of the town.

During my college career, I was a member of a class in social geography under Dr. George H. Hansen, where students were assigned to write a paper on the development of some Utah section, preferably the section in which we lived. Here was a definite outlet for my interest. With the information which I had already collected and additional information obtained from conversation with early settlers of Moab during my Christmas holiday (and available from books), I prepared my paper which became the nucleus for this book.

Later I received considerable encouragement from my major professor in college, Dr. William J. Snow, of Brigham Young University.

I worked out a preliminary manuscript as a result of continued study in which I endeavored to contact all early settlers of Moab. The resulting material was published in the Moab *Times-Independent* by editor-publisher Loren L. Taylor. I asked for corrections and additional materials in this publication, and received some help and suggestions from various people.

Since that time I seriously undertook the work of examining all information, for I intended to use the history as a master's thesis. Much of the research and work of this history was done under the direction of Dr. Snow.

The history, as now presented, is the result of several years' careful study and research. Many of the pioneers who so kindly aided me in my work have passed on. I endeavored to contact as many of the early settlers or their children as possible. From them I obtained all possible information, asking the same questions of each in an effort to establish dates and events. I have obtained information from all available records, and where there has been disagreement as to dates given by various people, I have tried to establish the date either by agreement of the most witnesses, by other publication, or by reason — that is, which date is the most logical in the light of other events.

It is difficult to record a history when no definite records have been kept of all events. However, I have been fortunate in being able to contact many of the people who had a part in the settlement and building of the community and in obtaining several diaries.

I have had no "axe to grind" and have tried to give a fair, impartial account of facts. If there are those who feel I have not given sufficient space to certain people or accounts, or vice versa, I can say only that I have done the best I could in the light of the information I have been able to accumulate.

I have obtained my information from the following sources: *Founding of Utah*, by Levi Edgar Young; *History of Indian Depredations in Utah*, by Peter Gottfredson; "Grand County Teems with Interest," by Albert F. Phillips; "Ore Deposits of Utah," by W. S. Butler; *Utah, the Storied Domain*, by J. C. Alter; *Lost Trappers*, by David Coyner; "The Elk Mountain Mission," by Andrew Jensen; "Early Pioneer of Grand County," by John Bristol; *Utah Since Statehood*, by Orson F. Whitney; "Moab's Third Awakening," by Burl Armstrong; "The Geology of La Sal Mountains of Utah," by Dr. Laurence M. Gould; *Explorations and Surveys for a Railroad Route from the Mississippi River to the Pacific Ocean* (Pacific Railroad surveys), volume 11 (Warren's memoirs); the revised ordinances of Moab; the Moab *Times-Independent*; Salt Lake City's *Deseret News*; and personal diaries of F. A. Hammond and Oliver Huntington (the latter, relative to the Elk Mountain Mission). Information was also gained from the following individuals: J. H. Shafer, George F. Powell, Neal Ray, Ervin Wilson, Hyrum Wilson, Arthur A. Taylor, Addie

10

Maxwell, Tom Trout, J. T. Loveridge, Mrs. Henry Grimm, Libbie L. Lemon, J. H. Johnson, Joseph Burkholder, Annie Shafer, Lydia Ann Taylor, W. L. Taylor, Hyrum Taylor, and June Peirce (son of William Peirce). I also obtained some information from records in the Salt Lake City Historian's Office of the Church of Jesus Christ of Latter-day Saints.

I should especially like to mention and, in a sense, dedicate this book to the following people who have given me the encouragement and help which has made it possible to carry on and complete this record: my parents, W. R. and Nora Johnson McConkie; my husband, Maurice Tanner; Dr. William J. Snow of Brigham Young University; L. L. Taylor of Moab; and all of those who have been so kind in giving of their time and information. The scenic chapter was prepared by my brother, Wayne R. McConkie, who has always been interested in the scenic wonders of the region and who has made a hobby of photography of local scenic wonders. To him I am indebted.

And last, I should like to dedicate this history to all those noble pioneers who endured the hardships of conquering a new land and developing a civilization that we of later generations might enjoy the fruits of their labor.

Salt Lake City, Utah
February 17, 1937

11

Oh, Colorado River, I love you —
    With your valleys wide
Against La Sal Mountains blue
    Where green grass and flowers hide.

Vermilion cliffs steep and sheer
    Shadow streams of water, crystal clear.
In mem'ry's journey dear
    A myriad voices I hear.

Mem'ry, take me by the hand
    And lead me to that Far Country land
Where fantasy, like Wordsworth's daffodils,
    Permits my spirit to wander among the hills
Where trod those ancient years
    Miners, cattlemen, pioneers....

                Faun McConkie Tanner

Chapter 1

The Land and
the Early Dwellers

There is a vast region between the Continental Divide on the east and the crest of the Wasatch Mountains on the west, extending from Yellowstone Park to the Gulf of California, which forms the drainage of the Colorado River — historically and geologically a valley of great interest. The region probably has no more interesting geological counterpart.

The geological structure shows a vast deposit of red sandstone — cut, gashed, and seamed by the Colorado River and its tributaries into fantastic canyons, leaving innumerable flat-topped mountains or mesas like islands surrounded by a sea of canyons and valleys, with an occasional chain of rugged granite mountains protruding through the sandstone.

Throughout the ages since this great basin was formed, the elements of nature have wrought many of the most gigantic and inspiring rock and mountain formations, domes, cathedrals, spires, arches, castles, windows, needles, natural bridges under which the capitol building in the District of Columbia could be placed without its highest point touching the bridge, and canyons of unbelievable beauty.

The deceiving nature of the topography is well described by Dr. Laurence M. Gould[1]:

---

[1]Laurence M. Gould, "The Geology of La Sal Mountains of Utah." Reprinted from *Papers of the Michigan Academy of Science, Arts and Letters* (1926), vol. VII, p. 55.

One's first impression of this plateau country is deceptive. It seems to be a relatively flat surface possessing no marked features of relief; one needs to travel but a short distance across it, however, to be undeceived. It is found to be dissected by a veritable maze of canyons, most of which are steepwalled and present few favorable crossings.

Dr. Gould says that the immense, incisive work of running water over a once relatively flat surface has doubtless been the major factor in the development of the peculiarly deceptive relief of which he speaks.

The Moab district lies in the heart of the great Colorado Plateau — a large physiographic province lying in southern Utah, northern Arizona, southwestern Colorado, and northwestern New Mexico. Crampton[2] indicates the appropriateness of the name when he says, "This is rimrock country; its general surface is flat — a tableland. Approach from any direction and you will soon find yourself on a rim looking down into rather than up at. You can see for great distances."

Towering above Moab, in the east, are the La Sal Mountains, with peaks rising more than 12,500 feet, which are capped with snow approximately nine months of the year. Below timberline are forests of spruce and fir, and at lower elevations, forests of pine — all exceedingly different from the surrounding deserts and canyonlands. Different, too, are the rocks and their geological structure.

Charles B. Hunt,[3] who has done the most recent technical work on the La Sal Mountains, writes:

> In the mountains, the brilliantly colored formations so characteristic of the canyon lands are turned up steeply in huge structural domes at each of the three mountains comprising the La Sals. These domes are formed by the forceful intrusion of igneous rock that was molten, like lava, and pushed upward by the same kinds of forces that cause volcanoes. Most of this molten rock froze before it reached the surface, but molten rock freezes solid at temperatures considerably hotter than Dante's fieriest Hell.... Other mountains on the Colorado Plateau having rocks and structure similar to the La Sals include the Henry Mountains, Abajo [Blue] Mountains, Ute Mountain, and the Carrizo Mountains. But a final episode in the geological history of the La Sals distinguishes them from the others, for they were glaciated during the last period of geologic times, the Quaternary Period. The other mountains either were too low or too dry to develop glaciers. As a result, the high parts of the La Sals have glacial cirques and glacial moraines.

---

[2]Gregory Crampton, *Standing Up Country: The Canyon Lands of Utah and Arizona* (New York: Alfred A. Knopf, 1964), p. 15.

[3]Charles B. Hunt, "La Sal Mountains," Moab *Times-Independent*, July 8, 1965.

Hidden away in the hearts of the mountains or buried in the vastnesses of the deserts are to be found deposits of minerals, metals, and valuable chemicals, oil, gas, coal, oil shale, and hydrocarbon compounds which nature has stored. In addition to these, the fertile valleys are rich in agricultural possibilities.

Within the Colorado River Basin in southeastern Utah lies Grand County with an area of 3,692 square miles — a great empire in itself. This area, bordered by Uintah County on the north, San Juan County on the south, Emery County on the west, and the state of Colorado on the east, is one of the livestock counties of the state. The grazing of cattle and sheep has been a principal industry since the settlement of the region.

Moab and Spanish valleys form one continuous valley which extends fourteen miles southeast from the Colorado River at Moab. The broad floor and the steep, high wall on the southwest and the low wall of the northeast give an appearance to the valley that is different from the rest of the valleys in the area. Baker[4] further describes it:

> Two isolated mountain masses rise above the general level of the Colorado Plateau adjacent to the Moab district. The La Sal Mountains east of the district rise to an elevation of 13,089 feet above sea level, and the Abajo Mountains south of the district to an elevation of 11,455 feet.

Streams which drain the area and supply its water are of three classes: perennial, intermittent, or a combination of these (that is, they are perennial in part of their course and intermittent elsewhere). The perennial Colorado[5] River in summer is normally shallow. After heavy spring rains, it carries larger volumes of water.

Boats have sometimes been used on the Colorado River to transport both passengers and freight between Moab and the junction of the Colorado and Green rivers, or the town of Green River itself. Due to shallow water, numerous sandbars, and the character of the channel, the river is navigable with difficulty, and only by boats of shallow draft.

Principal tributaries of the Colorado River from the east are Castle, Nigger Bill (named for a mulatto who lived in the area), Mill, Cane, Lockhart, Indian, Salt, and Lower Red Lake creeks. Castle and Nigger Bill creeks are fed by numerous springs and are perennial streams. Mill Creek is perennial and in part intermittent. These two streams receive part of their water from springs, but most of it drains from the west slopes of the La Sal Mountains. Cane Creek, with its large tribu-

---

[4]Arthur A. Baker, "Geology of the Moab District: Grand and San Juan Counties, Utah" (New Haven, Connecticut: Yale University, 1931). Doctoral dissertation.

[5]"Colorado" is the Spanish word for "red."

taries, is in part perennial and in part intermittent. Although several springs are found in its smaller tributary canyons, their flow soon sinks below the surface. Lockhart Canyon Creek is fed by several springs, many of which have a high salt content, but the flow from the springs is small, and no water flows in the channel except after rains.

Indian Creek, which begins in the Abajo Mountains, is the largest tributary of the Colorado River within the Moab district. It is perennial where it enters the southern part of the district, but since much of the water is used for irrigation, it carries little or no water in its lower part during the summer months. Together with its large tributaries, Hart Draw, Cottonwood, Davis, and Lavender creeks, which are intermittent streams, Indian Creek drains more than 30 percent of the area, and the rapid runoff after torrential storms sends deep, rapidly moving floods down the main channel.

Salt Creek, a perennial stream, drains the northwest side of the Abajo Mountains, although its flow is small except after rainstorms. Another intermittent stream is Lower Red Creek. Although the flow from none of the perennial streams is large, that of Castle, Mill, and Indian creeks is sufficient to irrigate several hundred acres of bottomland along the valleys.

Water suitable for drinking is limited in quantity. Most of the spring water and the water in many of the flowing streams are suitable for drinking, but large sections of the district have no springs or running water. Water in many of the running streams, such as Castle, Pack, and the lower parts of Mill and Indian creeks, is of course exposed to pollution and should not be used without being boiled or chemically treated. But that in Nigger Bill, Cane, and the upper parts of Indian and Salt creeks can be safely used. Water that accumulates in natural rock tanks after rains furnishes temporary supply. In fact, natural reservoirs may be the only water supply in some areas, and tragedy has befallen many who have set out across the desert without sufficient water and with no knowledge of the location of these natural tanks.

THE CLIMATE of the La Sal Mountain area below 7,500 feet is semi-arid, with precipitation usually less than ten inches per year. There is of course somewhat more precipitation on the higher parts of the region near the mountains. In the lowest part of the area (the canyons), the annual precipitation is seven to twelve inches. In the foothills round the base of the mountains, it is from fifteen to 25 inches.

Monthly mean temperatures at Moab, which probably is typical of the canyon area, range from a January low of 28.8° F to a July high of 77.7° F, and from an absolute low of –18° F (January) to an absolute high of 109° F (July). Monthly mean temperatures at the town of La Sal, which is typical of the foothills, range from a January low of 24.7° F to a July high of 67.1° F, and from an absolute low of –22° F (January) to an absolute high of 94° F (June and July). Corresponding temperatures prevail in the mountains.

Summer storms are usually downpours that last only a few minutes, but these may cause floods in the streams. Often the volume of water is so great that it cascades in sheets over the cliffs. Great damage results from the floods because of their size and sudden occurrence. This is indicated in the size of the creek beds today as compared to those that existed when the area was first settled. Old-timers tell how they could step across Mill and Pack creeks when they first came to Moab, that a fence slat could easily be placed across either creek at almost any point. Today, both creeks are bridged or tiled, and the creek beds are somewhat extensive.

Most of the storms are local in extent, but all of the water quickly drains from the bare "slick" rocks, and the main drainage course is swollen with the sudden onrush. Because of the local storms and their torrential characteristics, the same amount of rain does not fall everywhere in the district within a limited period, and the rainfall for many localities may differ from the average for the region at any given time. During the spring, strong west winds prevail, but more moderate winds from the same direction are normal throughout the year.

Below about 7,500 feet, there are occasional snowstorms during the winter, but the snow rarely lasts on the ground more than a few days. In the mountains, on the other hand, annual snowfall averages more than two feet, and in wet years may be as great as five feet.

Soil in the valleys and canyon floors is rather rich and productive. Early cattlemen came into the valley and to the La Sal area seeking grazing lands. They were attracted by the climate, availability of water, and heavy vegetation. All of those interviewed stated that sagebrush grew tall enough for a man on horseback to ride hidden through the brush, and that grass grew to a horse's belly in Moab, but at La Sal this was almost reversed.

In the midst of the towering red sandstone hills of Grand County is a small pear-shaped valley, some fifteen miles long and two or three miles wide. This is Moab, the county seat of Grand County.

If one were to read certain chapters of the Book of Jeremiah in the Old Testament, one would find numerous references not at all flattering to the Land of Moab, that ancient Syrian kingdom lying near the Dead Sea. Jeremiah must have been greatly displeased with that ancient Moab, for its iniquity provided him with the subject for numerous caustic sermons. One sermon infers that Moab was a pretty bad place and richly deserving of the fate to which it was consigned.

17

Conversely, in a moment of poetic ardor, Rogers, an enthusiastic supporter of the more recent Moab, wrote[6]:

> Here are mountains seamed with veins — yes, arteries of platinum, gold, silver, copper, and other metals useful to man. Here are millions of tons of coal yet untouched by the miner's pick and the richest of oil fields in the entire world but in the infancy of development. Vast areas of luxuriant grasses carpet the hillsides and mesas; great herds of fat, sleek, contented cattle and sheep graze upon those almost limitless natural pastures and bask in the cool, umbrageous shade of pine and aspen groves, where the air is filled with the melody of feathered songsters and redolent with the odor of myriads of wild flowers and the balsamic breath of the forests which gladden the heart and lull the spirit like the perfumes of incense from mystic oriental altars; and bring health and happiness to all who breathe it....Are you seeking health? It is borne on every breeze....Do you desire wealth? It lies in uncoined, unmined, unlimited millions beneath your feet....Have you a desire to dwell in a land where with a minimum of labor you can produce the greatest quantity of cereals and vegetables and the most delicious fruits to be found anywhere? Irrigation and intelligently directed efforts prove that no place on earth excels this heaven-favored region in all of these blessings.

Rogers doubtless has painted his word portrait of paradise and confused it with Moab, but when one considers the red sandstone hills surrounding the valley — and there is beauty to be found in red sandstone, especially in contrast to the beauty of mountains and the green of lush vegetation — one realizes that it does seem a bit like paradise, especially to the travelworn pilgrim who has just crossed miles of desert. Aside from the geological interest of the region, the tourist who delights in the immensity of deep gorges and nature's carving through solid rock may find a paradise here. The valley lies in the center of one of the greatest scenic areas of the West.

The climate and industry of Moab and the surrounding region are greatly affected by the Colorado River and the La Sal (Spanish for "salt") Mountains. The mountains were evidently named by early Spanish explorers, and the reference was made prior to the expedition of Father Escalante and the Dominguez party in 1776, for they used the name with an air of familiarity.

From a geological standpoint these mountains, because they are among the youngest, are unique in the world. They are located a few miles from the Utah-Colorado state line, about half of them within the boundaries of Grand County and half in San Juan County. The moun-

---

[6]Al M. Rogers, quoted in Burl Armstrong, "Moab's Third Awakening," Salt Lake *Herald-Republican*, June 24, 1911.

tains lie within the great desert plateau region justly famous for its cliffs and canyon walls that exhibit with unparalleled perfection great cross-sections of the earth's history.

The La Sals are laccolithic. The entire area associated with the mountains does not exceed a hundred square miles. They are rather far removed from the great mountain systems of our country, yet they possess a number of lofty summits which rival in grandeur and impressiveness of scenery some of the greater and more famous mountain areas of our western lands. According to geologists, some thirty peaks are arranged in three groups.

The upper slopes of the mountains are somewhat precipitous for about three thousand or four thousand feet, while the lower slopes become less abrupt as they emerge into the mesalike lands adjacent to the mountains. The summits of the peaks range in general from about 11,500 feet to thirteen thousand feet in height, while the surrounding mesas are less than eight thousand feet high. Mt. Peale, the highest peak in the group, rises 13,090 feet above sea level.

Westward from the mountains the descent is also precipitous down to the Colorado River which lies fifteen miles away. The river reaches a level of about four thousand feet in the vicinity of Moab. There is, then, a difference in the elevation of some nine thousand feet between Moab and the top of Mt. Peale.

Hunt[7] says the intrusions of the mountains set their age at about the Miocene Epoch of the Tertiary Period, about thirty million years ago. The prevailing rocks of the region are sedimentary, the igneous rocks seem to be confined to the core of the mountains. The Colorado River is an entrenched, meandering stream which has cut a great channel through the rock formations. As stated earlier, the river is a significant influence on the industry of Moab and the surrounding region.

ARCHEOLOGICAL EVIDENCE testifies to prehistoric life in this region. Early man may have been in the vicinity of Moab and La Sal while the glaciers were carving the cirques and depositing the moraines on the La Sals, perhaps some twenty thousand years ago.[8] He hunted elephants and the longhorn bison, but these became exterminated, perhaps because of the hunting, but more likely because feed became scarce as the climate became warmer and drier. At the time of the glaciers, timberline on the mountains was two thousand to three thousand feet lower than it is today. Gradually the forests advanced upward.

---

[7]Hunt, *op. cit.*
[8]*Ibid.*

More recent prehistoric man has been in the West for a long time. For thousands of years the pioneer people (the Desert culture) lived the simple life, hunting and foraging, possessing few material goods. From these archaic beginnings they gradually developed a most sophisticated way of life. By the start of the first century A.D. the Pueblo people, who had a distinctive culture, were living in the Southwest. Those who by then had occupied the canyon country of southeastern Utah and northeastern Arizona and adjacent regions have been called the "Anasazi," a Navajo word meaning "the ancient ones." These people, who lived in separate localities, differed somewhat in their way of life and cultural development, and to these variations names have been assigned, for several regional variants of the Pueblo culture in the American Southwest exist. The northern Pueblo groups in Colorado, Arizona, and Utah, for example, are called Anasazi; the Anasazi are in turn divided into smaller local groups which differ from each other enough to warrant separate designations. Specifically, throughout most of eastern Utah there is the Fremont culture. Nearest to it is the richest and best known of all — the Mesa Verde — the variant found most heavily in San Juan County.

South of the Colorado and San Juan rivers are the Kayenta of northern Arizona, while to the west is the closely related Virgin River branch, and in the whole of western Utah is the Sevier-Fremont variant — the latter much resembling the Virgin River branch but also reminiscent of the Fremont of the eastern half of the state.[9]

Fremont villages were usually small and on eminences; architecture was varied. It is this culture with which we are chiefly concerned in the Moab and La Sal areas. Limits and boundaries cannot be exactly set, but certain characteristics are identifiable.

In the early 1930s, Noel Morris first discovered the Fremont culture along the Fremont River in Utah, and from that time to the early 1940s, little was done in the way of research.[10] However, in the 1950s, there were those who began to recognize that the Fremont were an enigma in need of understanding insofar as American archeology was concerned. As a result, in the 1960s, investigations and excavations into the Fremont culture became of vital interest, and much was done in studying the villages and archeological evidence of these people.

Hansel[11] reports on the ending of an excavation of what was possibly one of the largest finds of Fremont culture (in Paradox Valley)

---

[9]Jesse D. Jennings, "The Aboriginal Peoples," *Utah Historical Quarterly* (July 1960), pp. 216–17.

[10]Dave Hansel, "Ancient Fremont Indian Culture Now Studied in Work at Paradox Valley," Moab *Times-Independent*, Section B, August 20, 1970.

[11]*Ibid.*

which had been carried out by Dr. Larry Leach, professor of anthropology of the University of San Diego, California. The findings indicated at least five different levels of Indian culture dating as far back as A.D. 300, with possibly other and older tribes being in other mounds near by. The five layers contributed to knowledge of the Basket Makers, Pueblo II, Fremont, Utes, and the end, sometime in the 1880s, with the moving in of white settlers, "evidence for the fifth layer of hand-forged square nails which could only have come from the settlers."

Dr. Leach, along with others, indicates that the Fremont culture was the most significant because these people are thought to be members of that culture which "first utilized the 'big three': corn, beans, and squash, in this area." They also hunted extensively, and probably turned to the simpler agricultural way of life when game became scarce.

The findings also indicate that there was a severe drought in the southeastern Utah area where the Fremont Indians seem to have been concentrated the most. Leach states that along with the scarcity of game and the introduction of agricultural foods, the drought, the encroachment of Athabascan-speaking peoples (Navajo, Apache, and so forth) in the 1300s, and the rising level of disease, there was reason for the disappearance of the different races. The dates of course are only tentative, as none of the uncovered material has been submitted to the laboratory for pinpoint dating. Although intensive study is being made, little is really known about the Fremont people at this time.

There are of course other finds outside the Paradox area which have yielded information about this particular culture. Some of these discoveries have been made in the Vernal and Roosevelt areas as well as in Dinosaur National Monument. The findings in the Paradox area indicate that the Fremonts were skilled in a crude form of masonry. They fashioned adobe bricks, round in shape, and then used a mud plaster to hold them in position. However, instead of a squarelike room, they built their walls in circular configurations, similar to the cliff-dwellers found in the Mesa Verde area.

Other materials which have been extracted from the ruins include a supply of hunting points, animal hide scrapers, awls, needles, and various animal bones. The presence of these materials shows that possibly these people used animal skins for their clothing instead of the woven cloth found in so many other Indian cultures.

One of the interesting features is what the Fremonts did with their dead. Actually, little was done. Sometimes a hole would be dug and the body put into it. They would then plaster over the cavity and continue living as before. At other times, the body would be left in its own house and the house burned and caved in over it. Further evidence indicates that some bodies were thrown into a trash heap usually located a short distance from the camp. Whatever means of disposition that seemed best at the time was followed.

After passing through several stages, the Anasazi culture reached a climax in its development during what is called the Great Pueblo period — a golden age which came to a rather abrupt end about A.D. 1300. Agriculture was a fundamental characteristic of these sedentary prehistoric people. Although they enjoyed hunting, they were largely vegetarian, their diet consisting mostly of corn, beans, squash, and, as we see in the La Sal area, berries.

The Fremont culture, which is found in varying degrees all over eastern Utah, seems to have been somewhat distinctive. It is distinguished by locally made plain pottery types, and by the use of calcite as a temper, as well as other traits.[12] Apparently there was a considerable use of wild plant foods and hunting by these people, but they had developed corn of high row numbers. They hunted with the bow and arrow.

The culture of the Fremont does not seem to have been as sophisticated as that of the contemporary Anasazi to the south, but it was well adapted to the way of life which the people in this more northern region pursued. Many features of the culture are reminiscent of Basket Maker II. This makes it a variant of the Anasazi in some respects, but distinguishable.

Mesa Verde has of course been thoroughly classified by archeologists. There have also been some excavations in San Juan, especially in the Beef Basin and Alkali Ridge areas. One study has been made in the La Sal Mountain area.[13] Archeological work in the La Sal Mountains near Moab indicates the presence of a long-lived, simple culture (called Desert culture) in existence before the time of Christ.[14]

The eastern Utah version or variant of the Desert culture is called the Uncompahgre complex. Cliff overhangs and caves were the preferred dwelling places for these people. Their culture, like all Desert cultures, was a highly specialized though simple way of life, geared to exploitation of all of natures' biological resources.[15]

Hunt in her investigations found more than 350 sites in a limited area (five hundred square miles). Of these sites, 119 were higher than eight thousand feet, about half were higher than ten thousand feet. Her findings seem to strengthen the idea of the important ancestral role

[12]John C. McGregor, *Southwestern Archaeology* (Urbana: University of Illinois Press, 1965), p. 310.

[13]Alice Hunt, "Archaeological Survey of the La Sal Mountain Area, Utah," *University of Utah Anthropological Papers*, No. 14 (Salt Lake City: University of Utah Press, 1953).

[14]Jennings, *op. cit.*, pp. 219–20.

[15]*Ibid.*, p. 220.

which the early Basin cultures played in the development of later cultures in both the Plains and the Southwest. She states that it seems highly probable that in prehistoric times, as now, the mountainous part of the area would be occupied only seasonally, and the canyons would be the most suitable part of the area for permanent settlements.

A wide variety of edible shrubs and herbs grows in the nine-thousand-foot range in altitude, an environment favorable to gathering cultures. The shrubs and herbs grow in three distinct vegetation zones: (1) north desert shrub zone of canyons and valleys (four thousand to six thousand feet), (2) piñon-juniper zone (six thousand to eight thousand feet), and (3) mountain zone of aspen-spruce forest and alpine meadowland above eight thousand feet. Each vegetation zone has a distinct variety of bushes whose seeds the Indians ground into flour and made into bread or mush. Her findings indicate that the gathering and drying of abundant berries and roots, which are most plentiful in the mountain zone, may have been a more important activity than hunting game, which was equally available in the lower zones.

This gathering and drying of berries and roots probably explained the amazing numbers of grinding stones found at a high altitude in the mountain areas. Many wild animals, fish, and fowl have been reported in the La Sal Mountain area in prehistoric times. Probably all of these were sought by prehistoric man, for the bones of most have been identified at the sites. It is doubtful that many buffalo were in the La Sal Mountain area because they were not abundant anywhere in the canyon country. The buffalo petroglyph does not appear in the La Sal Mountain area, although it is found along Indian Creek some fifty miles to the south. The natural environment of the La Sal Mountain area was favorable for hunting and gathering cultures.

Hunt believes all of the mountain sites were seasonal camps. Most are small and presumed to represent use by family-size units or other small groups. These are located on tops of high ridges along natural access routes to the mountains and on passes between the mountains.

Since the La Sal Mountain area was located along a natural route of travel between the southern part of the Colorado Plateau and the northern part of the basin and range province, it was subject to many influences from other regions. Almost all of the traits represented in the La Sal Mountain area are also recorded from other parts of the northern Colorado Plateau.

Hunt found that most of the pottery in the La Sal Mountain area resembled the Anasazi types, although much was probably indigenous to the area, judging by the use of local materials. At least five and possibly nine different occupations, lasting over a period of many thousand years, were found to be represented in this area.

Thus the Moab area is rich in the remains of ancient peoples. Barnes[16] tells of some important findings by Lin Ottinger, Moab back-country guide and amateur geologist and archeologist, which could possibly upset current theories concerning the age of mankind on the entire planet.

Searching for mineral specimens south of Moab, Ottinger found traces of human remains in a geological stratum that is approximately a hundred million years old. Some present scientific estimates put the maximum age of the human race at no more than two million or three million years, and even this depends upon defining "human" in a rather loose way.

Looking for azurite specimens on the property of the Big Indian Copper Mine in Lisbon Valley, about 35 miles south of Moab, Ottinger found a tooth that he immediately recognized as human. Further search by his party brought to light several human bone fragments, including an upper jaw section. Looking for telltale indications, bits of charcoal, and the dark brown organic stains that almost always surround ancient or fossilized bones, Ottinger was able to pinpoint the source of the teeth and bone fragments. He carefully uncovered enough of what later proved to be the parts of two human skeletons to verify that he had indeed located the source of the scattered pieces. He then carefully covered the exposure and notified Dr. W. Lee Stokes, archeological and geological authority, at the University of Utah.

Dr. Stokes recognized the implications of the find: that if the human remains were truly "in place" in the Dakota formation — that is, not washed in or fallen from higher and younger strata — then the remains would have to be the same age as the stratum in which they were found. This would be in the vicinity of a hundred million years, depending upon where in the stratum they occurred.

Dr. J. P. Marwitt, professor of anthropology at the University of Utah, was sent to study and develop the discovery site for preliminary examination and to gather specimens for detailed testing. He, with help, carefully uncovered the human bones, removing the sandstone and other material for several inches down, but leaving the bones in place. Parts of at least two separate skeletons were exposed in this preliminary survey. A number of bone shards were screened in the area.

Dr. Marwitt found the discovery to be "highly interesting and unusual" for several reasons. As the bones were uncovered, it soon became obvious that they were "in place," and had not washed in or fallen down from higher strata. The portions of skeletons that were

---

[16]F. A. Barnes, "Mine Operation Uncovers Puzzling Remains of Ancient Man," Moab *Times-Independent*, June 3, 1971, p. 6.

exposed were still articulated (joined naturally), indicating that the bodies were still intact when buried or covered in the Dakota formation.

Furthermore, the bones were stained a bright green by the copper salts that occur in the vicinity, and some of the bright blue azurite balls that were found in and around the bones were partially turned green by reaction with the organic material of the bodies. In addition, the dark organic stains found round the bones indicate that the bones had been complete bodies when deposited in the ancient stratum.

Some unusual features were indicated in the find. For example, while one body seemed to be in the position sometimes used by ancient Indian tribes for formal burials, the other was not, and its upper body was missing — probably carried away by the bulldozer that had earlier removed the rock and other materials above the find during routine mine development work.

Whether or not the bodies are as old as indicated, the bones appeared to be relatively modern in configuration; that is, *Homo sapiens* rather than one of his ancient, semi-animal predecessors. Even though the bones may prove to be no older than other ancient American Indian remains, they are novel in that Dr. Marwitt claimed he had never seen or heard of human bones being so stained and discolored by copper minerals.

The Manti–La Sal National Forest, during part of 1911 and 1912, published a little paper for the information and reports of the area and actvities. In the July 1911 issue[17] the following appears:

> No other forest is as replete with unusual attractions. Within the borders of the La Sal is found a most interesting cliff-dwellers' village which doubtless was constructed many, many snows ago. It is almost intact and doubtless houses many valuable antiquities. This is due to the fact that it is in such an inaccessible locality. At this point a Ranger Station has been surveyed and fitly named the "Cliff Dweller." Near this site is located a natural bridge located off the forest a short distance to the south, but worthy of mention. In the immediate vicinity is also a Mexican settlement. How many people know that at a few hours' ride from this same cliffdweller Ranger Station is located an Indian village. Here live a few renegade Utes and their squaws and goats, in the same manner as their forefathers and keeping up their traditions. Here one can see the same primitive farming methods employed, get an insight into their home life, watch the squaws weave baskets and water bottles, see the papooses make their bows and arrows, and, best of all, one can trade first hand with the Indians — if you have the price.

---

[17]"Echo from the Cliffdwellers of the La Sal National Forest" (Washington, D.C.: U.S. Department of Agriculture, Forest Service, July 1911), p. 8. Microfilm.

In the same edition, there is an account which mentions a mummy found at Cliff Dwelling.[18] The mummy was intact, indicating that people lived here a millennium or more previously. It is reported that homes were built from an elevation two thousand to eight thousand feet high, all along the canyons. They were built near agricultural land. There are pictures of animals and a great number of dwellings to be found in practically every canyon south of Dry Valley (about half way between La Sal and Blue mountains).

Summarizing ancient cultures, one might say that the upper Colorado River Basin of Utah has been exploited for millennia by aboriginal Americans. These were first the foragers of the desert (the Uncompahgre complex of the Desert culture); second, the far better known Anasazi (Pueblo), who either displaced the Desert people or may have actually evolved for themselves; and third, those who followed the disappearance of the Pueblo people.

With the disappearance of the Pueblo cultures by A.D. 1300, there is a gap in knowledge until 1776 when Father Escalante penetrated the area to report for the first time the presence of scattered Ute and Piute bands over the entire area. These bands roved and roamed, never developing any significant strength in numbers or in political organization. They were poverty-ridden tribes and subtribes who were later displaced by the Mormons in Utah and the miners and stockmen in Colorado, finally to come to rest on reservations such as the Uintah Basin by 1870. By virtue of their weakness and their scanty numbers, the basin tribes were subdued and displaced by the white settler, with no significant hostilities except for the "Walker War" in which only a handful of persons were injured or killed.

Today, in addition to the Ute reservations, there are Navajos in the Navajo Reservation in the Utah lands lying south of the San Juan, but these are recent comers.[19]

The Elk Mountain Mission of 1855 found the Utes in the area raising corn, squash, and beans by flood irrigation. In the eighteenth century, Escalante records that he met Tabeguache Utes along the Dolores River east of the La Sal Mountains. No clue has been found to the author's knowledge as to when the Shoshonean peoples first reached the La Sal Mountain area, but in historic times the Utes roamed widely, even into the Plains. In the findings of recent but prehistoric Shoshonean occupation of the area, there was no evidence of white contact, such as glass beads or metal work.

Bands of prehistoric Hopis may have visited the area, as is suggested by the occurrence of a yellow utility ware resembling Awatabi

---

[18]*Ibid.*, pp. 36–41.

[19]Jennings, *op. cit.*, pp. 220–21.

utility ware.[20] It was probably about A.D. 1300, perhaps as early as A.D. 500, that a corn-raising semi-sedentary people of the horticultural and hunting Fremont culture occupied the area. Good evidence of this occupation has been found at some hundred sites that have been studied.

These people, through Basket Maker III times, had a common culture with the Anasazi people who occupied the four corners area,[21] but from then on they developed their own distinctive culture. Dwelling sites of these people in the La Sal Mountain area were found only in canyons. Campsites were found in the piñon-juniper zone, but were virtually absent in the mountain zone. Probably the growing of corn lessened their need for edible berries and roots of the high mountain zone, and game was ample in the piñon-juniper zone.

The Utes of Colorado and the Navajos contacted Spanish culture during the early years of the eighteenth century, and until 1786 at least three tribes were enemies of the Spaniards. Traits were probably introduced which the Indians now consider aboriginal.

The journals of Dominguez and Escalante (1776) furnish us with considerable information about these Indians. Spanish explorers did not specifically locate tribes in the Moab vicinity, but Indian informants indicate that the Wimonuntci tribe was in the Moab-Cortez area.[22] Members of this band of southern Utes are, as previously stated, classified as Uncompahgre, and the La Sal Mountains were the base camp of these people. Their hunting took them well into western Colorado. Some of these Utes and some Piutes were the source of early troubles with the settlers. Thus it might be well to present some of their early differences and some of their customs.

The differences between the Utes and Piutes until about the middle of the seventeenth century were somewhat negligible, for both were rather typical Great Basin tribes with similar language and from the same Uto-Aztecan stock. They were dependent upon the same food resources, which they exploited with similar technologies, although the better watered Ute country was richer in foodstuffs than the Piute range to the south. After white contact, however, the Utes took on a veneer of Plains culture such as the horse and furnishings (saddle, blanket, and so on), tepee, some semblance of large-band organization, the lance and shield as weapons, as well as warfare tactics.[23]

Southern Piutes held much less favored land. Predisposed to wander and visit, these tribesmen were known to have been fewer and

---

[20]Alice Hunt, *op. cit.*, p. 18.

[21]The juncture of four states: Utah, Colorado, New Mexico, and Arizona.

[22]Omer C. Stewart, "Culture Element Distributions: XVIII Ute-Southern Paiute," *Anthropological Records* (January 30, 1942), vol. 6, no. 4, pp. 231–33.

[23]Jennings, *op. cit.*, pp. 211–13.

more impoverished than their Ute relatives. Even though southern Piutes were farmers as early as 1776, they remained weak and scattered and in reality were typical desert gatherers or foragers as seen throughout the Great Basin. They were sometimes referred to as "Diggers" because they dug for roots and food.

Stewart, who has studied the Piute extensively, finds that they were skillful exploiters of a hostile land, adapting their annual diet to seasonal resources of all kinds. They hunted large game, if it was available, by means of traps; small game such as rabbits were taken in nets by means of communal hunts or by single hunters. No animal was safe when they were looking for food; their diet included wolf, coyote, fox, badger, cats, skunk, beaver, ground squirrels, gophers, even rats and mice, and of course they ate fish wherever these could be found.[24] This is substantiated by Frank Silvey who writes of an experience which his family had with prairie dogs. These animals were digging up the oats by the roots and feeding on them at the Silvey place in the La Sal area in the spring of 1883. The Silveys consulted Niels Olson who suggested that they drown the animals. The following account is from Silvey's notes[25]:

> ...[W]e cut many small ditches with our shovels and started to drown the prairie dogs out. About noon a dozen or more Utes [term loosely used] came and helped us, and we got many prairie dogs that day. The Indians took all the drowned prairie dogs with them as they left that evening, and I asked Olson what they were going to do with them. "Eat them," he said....The next day, in company with my father, we visited the Indian camp about two miles away on the ridge east of La Sal. We found they had roasted the prairie dogs, hide, hair, and entrails all night in the hot ashes and coals and now they were eating them, stripping the hide off with their long fingernails. The meat looked good and I was tempted to try some of it, but after seeing them eat the entrails, after stripping the refuse out of them, I balked and did not care to try any. (Brackets mine.)

Vegetable foods ran into the scores — seeds, roots, blossoms, nuts, fruits, and stalks were collected or gathered and eaten. Surpluses were stored and used in winter or other times of scarcity. The Piutes by some standards were less than flamboyant in their lifestyle.

---

[24]Stewart, *op. cit.,* p. 215.

[25]At the Utah State Historical Society in Salt Lake City, there is a large file of Silvey's notes — biography, Works Project Administration notes, a history of northern San Juan County, letters, and miscellaneous materials. Mrs. Becky Walker of the Grand Junction (Colorado) *Sentinel* edited some of these notes, which were then privately published. In this book, footnotes will read only "Silvey, *op. cit.,*" for these are repetitious and interchangeable in many instances.

Early people have left their mark upon the rocks and in their burial grounds. Indian "writings" are to be found in several places on the rocks, Indian manos and matates have been unearthed even within Moab city limits during street excavation projects; skeletons have been found (that of an Indian woman is on display at the Moab Museum); arrowheads and stone weapons have been found in abundance; beans and squash seeds have frequently been located by amateur archeologists. Well known, of course, is the mastodon (Figure 1.1) on the cliff down the Colorado River, dating back to some eight thousand to twelve thousand years ago.[26] There are also other hieroglyphics in the vicinity. All of these indicate that Indian culture was rather extensive in the area many centuries ago.

With the overwhelming evidence of ancient civilizations and peoples inhabiting the vicinity of Moab, one hears the words "petroglyph," "pictograph," and "Indian writings" used frequently and sometimes synonymously. It might be well, in lay language, to explain the difference in the meaning of these terms. Fran Barnes, in the Moab *Times-Independent* of September 23 and 30, 1971, clarifies these meanings for us.

According to the archeologist, "petroglyph" means "rock marking" and is some kind of image or design pecked into a rock surface with a still harder rock point. Commonly, the surface of sandstone, darkened by "desert varnish," was used by earlier Indian cultures for making such images. Time affects the degree of darkness of the varnish, as does its exposure to the desert elements. These elements also affect the clearness of the image.

"Pictograph" means "picture," or (to archeologists) a painted image. Indian pictographs were generally made by literally painting on sheltered rock walls with paints made from mud, clay, colorful minerals, or perhaps natural vegetable dyes. In contrast to the petroglyphs, which are able to survive open desert conditions with virtually no change except for slow darkening, the pictographs tend to be eroded by rain, moisture, or windblown sand, and only those which have been sheltered from these elements have survived the hundreds, or perhaps thousands, of years that have passed since their creation.

The term "Indian writings" appears to be a nonscientific term applied to both petroglyphs and pictographs. The term is misleading because "writing" generally implies the systematic use of graphic symbols for the nonvocal transference of information from one person to another.

---

[26]Dick Wilson, "Moab Spectacular Petroglyph Excites Imagination of Scientific Mind," Moab *Times-Independent*, June 13, 1968.

COURTESY UTAH STATE HISTORICAL SOCIETY

Figure 1.1. The Mastodon Petroglyph

Some authorities on Indian pictography contend that American pictographs and petroglyphs comprise a form of universal language between Indian tribes. Others who have made intensive studies of Anasazi and other "writings" have made a strong case against the universal language theory. Magic may have been involved in some of these, or they may be examples of aboriginal doodling, or they may have ceremonial significance.

Petroglyphs are widespread throughout the western states. Pictographs, because of their more delicate nature, are loss common.[27] Both are more likely to endure in desert areas, and southeastern Utah has an abundance of these archeological novelties. Some sites are famous, such as the petroglyphs on Newspaper Rock (chapter 17) in Indian Creek State Park and the huge pictographs in Horseshoe Canyon. Many remain undiscovered, or at least unpublicized.

---

[27]Fran Barnes, "Petroglyphs in the Moab Area Attract Interest of Residents and Visitors Alike," Moab *Times-Independent*, September 23, 1971.

31

Chapter 2

A Point on the Old Spanish Trail

History is dramatic, and Moab played a part in the historical drama of the imperial struggle between nations for control of land and commerce. This struggle for conquest of the great Southwest is symbolized not in military conflict wherein the soldier is the hero, but in the dreams, courage, and perseverance of the explorer and pathfinder who proved that possession is more effective than conquest.

Distance can overcome government, and disunity can follow failure to overcome this distance. Spain was struggling for survival of its power in the area of its easternmost empire. Two great outposts, Los Angeles and Santa Fe, represented Spain's position. To maintain communication and control, the Spanish must establish a route whereby supplies could be shipped from the coastal port to the inland city. This meant a twelve-hundred-mile course through a spur of the Rocky Mountains, across two swift rivers — the Colorado and the Green — avoiding the Grand Canyon, and through desert stretches. The Hafens tell us[1]:

> Before men and animals could conquer its wearisome length, a mighty river had to be circumvented. Mountain passes, precipitous canyons, and sandy arroyos must be threaded. Gigantic ranges, broken plateaus, and waterless mesas were to be overcome. And the entire course was through an unmapped land

---

[1]Leroy Hafen and Ann Hafen, *Old Spanish Trails* (Glendale, California: Arthur H. Clark Company, 1954), p. 19.

of untamed Indians, intent on exacting tribute from the white intruders.

Envisioned and undertaken in the late 1700s, the short-lived trail reached a day in the 1830s and '40s when annual caravans packed woolen blankets from the Spanish outpost of Santa Fe to trade for horses and mules in Los Angeles. It was never a wagon trail, but is known as the longest, most crooked and arduous pack-mule route in American history. Today no evidence remains to mark the trail, for animals hooves do not leave the deep imprints that wagon wheels do. The course of the trail is recorded, and its route has been traced and marked.[2]

Probably the first whites to discover the fertility of the soil and the excellence of the climate of Moab Valley (also called Spanish Valley and Grand Valley) were the early hunters and trappers whose adventurous lives led them to every nook and corner of the great West. Kit Carson evidently spent a delightful winter trapping beaver on the Colorado (Grand) River in southeastern Utah near the La Sal Mountains. Later he was to play an important part in the drama of history when he carried the first transcontinental mail on the leg from Los Angeles to Santa Fe, bringing news of the gold strike in California. He carried a special booster edition of San Francisco's *California Star* of April 1, 1848, containing an account of the gold discoveries on the American River.[3] On this momentous occasion, according to his account, he crossed the Grand River at the crossing just below the present townsite of Moab.

Crossings on the Colorado at what is now Moab and on the Green at Green River (a small town in what is now Utah) had been found, and persistent thrusts of trappers and traders into the new areas suggest that a northern trail between New Mexico and California had already been in use when the first recorded caravan passed over it from east to west in 1830.

It seems quite probable that the first English-speaking travelers into the territory that is now Utah and the Moab area were James Workman and Samuel Spencer, lost trappers.[4] These men apparently found their way to the valley where Moab is now located. Although the Coyner account is doubtless embellished, there does seem to be some historical acceptance of it.

According to the account of their trip, Workman and Spencer in the summer of 1809 descended the present Colorado River from one of its headwaters to the crossing of the Old Spanish Trail (Figure 2.1) at

---

[2]Dr. Hafen told the author in May 1968 that he had traced the route of the trail and had traveled it.

[3]Hafen and Hafen, *op. cit.*, p. 338.

[4]David Coyner, *The Lost Trappers* (Cincinnati and New York: Hurst and Company, 1894), pp. 165–69.

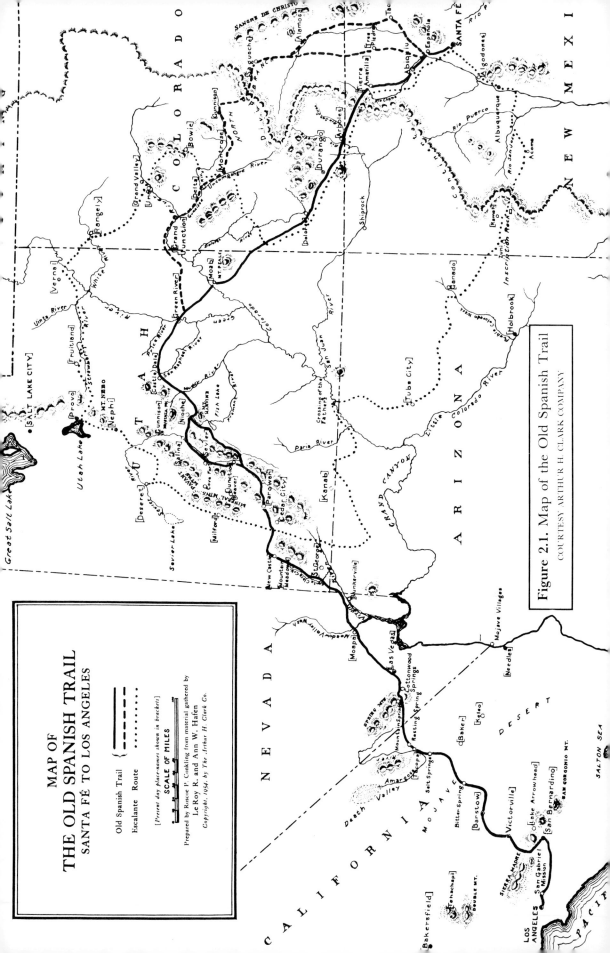

Figure 2.1. Map of the Old Spanish Trail
COURTESY ARTHUR H. CLARK COMPANY

Moab, and journeyed thence with a party of Spanish traders to southern California. They had left St. Louis in the spring of 1807 with a party of twenty trappers, under the leadership of Ezekial Williams, and were all cut off or killed by Comanche Indians, except three men, Williams, Workman, and Spencer. Williams made his way down the Arkansas River and thence overland to St. Louis. But Workman and Spencer struck for Santa Fe, presumably on the drainage of the Rio del Norte (Rio Grande), but by mistake came down the Gunnison and the Grand (now Colorado). Their narrative was preserved by Coyner, an early-day western newspaper correspondent. Near what is now Moab, the lost trappers met a Spanish caravan, en route from Santa Fe to Los Angeles. Coyner's report says[5]:

> Having descended this river for several hundred miles, still believing it to be the Rio del Norte, and wondering why they had not reached Santa Fe, they came to a place which seemed to have been used as a crossing [now assigned to Moab]. There were a great many signs of horses and mules, but they were old, and all pointing an eastern course. Indeed the signs were all so numerous that Workman and Spencer conjectured there must have been several thousand. Without the least hesitation the trappers resolved to follow this great trail, and to take the way the signs indicated the last caravan had gone. They felt confident that this trail had been made by the Spaniards and not by the Indians. They traveled it two days, when they met a caravan of Spaniards (about forty or fifty) on the trail, but going the opposite direction. (Brackets mine.)

From these travelers they learned that the river was the Colorado (Grand) and that they were about five hundred miles from Santa Fe. The report continues[6]:

> The caravan [was] en route from Santa Fe to Los Angeles, a town in Upper California, near the coast of the Pacific, in which region of country they expected to be engaged in trading until the following spring when they expected to return to Santa Fe with horses and mules.... Workman and Spencer determined to join the company and go to California where they would spend the approaching winter and in the spring return with them to New Mexico whence they hoped some opportunity would present itself of getting back to the United States.

Although the first party to journey the entire distance over substantially the route that became the Old Spanish Trail was led by

---

[5] *Ibid.*
[6] *Ibid.*

William Wolfskill and George C. Young in the winter of 1830–31, no one person (or two persons) can be given credit for the opening of this historical travel route. This was a folk trail, conquered segment by segment over a period of many years and by many forces. To honor those who made the trail possible, one must remember the Spanish fathers bent on saving pagan souls, Mexican traders bartering for Indian pelts and slaves, prospectors in search of wealth, Indians who coveted the whites' horses and guns, and trappers seeking beaver pelts. This was a new trade route, which like so many things American, was born of individual enterprise seeking commerce.

The trail was only another step in the daring and dreams of Spanish conquistadores and their sponsors, who within half a century after their arrival in the New World had penetrated the interior of North America as far as Kansas and had mapped the Pacific coastline to Oregon. Here was a land ready for the taking, and Spain, fully aware that occupancy determined ownership, began its program of aggressive colonization at least a century before its European rivals — England and France — made settlements.

Now if Spain could but span the twelve-hundred-mile stretch between its coastal settlements and the missions of New Mexico, it could dominate a vast empire. This concept gave birth to the Old Spanish Trail.

Economic dependence on importations of food and supplies by colonists gave further impetus to the overland route. And the padres felt the need of communication with their people. They in fact were pioneers of this and other trails and routes as they carried their message to their "children."

For over two centuries Santa Fe had been tied to Mexico City by a long tenuous line. Over it came the initial implements and weapons to subdue the country, the household utensils, the church paraphernalia, the presidio ammunition that supported the white settlers through the struggling decades.

Much of the territory northwest of New Mexico had long been familiar to the Spaniards who, in seeking furs and Indian slaves, had followed the trails leading into the country of the Utes. Further explorations by American fur gatherers had extended their knowledge of New Mexico, for contacts between the groups were frequent.

Among those advocating the opening of a route from New Mexico to California, none was more enthusiastic than Fray Silvestre Valez de Escalante. He believed that a westward course to California by way of the Hopi villages was not practicable because of the hostility of the Hopis and the geographical difficulties. He believed that a route through the Ute country north of the great river was much more feasible, and thus the Dominguez expedition was organized with Escalante as its principal promoter and chief chronicler. This was in 1776, and the route as far as the final crossing of the Dolores River in western Colorado was the course which became the Old Spanish Trail. However, their route did not lead them through Moab, for they turned eastward to find the Sabuagana Utes and to make a wide detour that would take them far from the direct course which they had originally planned. Thus they left for others the honor of opening the shorter route that would become the Old Spanish Trail. This would lead northwestward from the Dolores River to the La Sal Mountains and the Colorado River crossing near the present site of Moab, northwest to the town of Green River, and on to the Sevier River.[7]

The individual who braved the desert stretch and pioneered to the Moab crossing the route which was to become the regular course of the trail is not known. It may have been Manuel Mestas or the Arze-Garcia party of 1813, but to date no records have been found to establish the matter with any degree of certainty. The Spanish who traded in furs and slaves or the American mountain men may have worked out the trail along the southeastern base of the Wasatch Plateau (through Castle Valley) where, avoiding the badlands of the San Rafael Swell, they turned to the Green River.

Although the Old Spanish Trail is more perfectly preserved in history and legend than in fact, we do know of its historical importance, with much evidence being found to substantiate its existence. Covering a period of development probably beginning with Juan Maria Rivera (who in 1761 partly broke the trail) to Wolfskill and Young (who in 1830 took the first caravan across it), it was a vital link to traders and trappers. It has been called in various sections the Santa Fe Trail, the Mormon Trail, the Southwestern Route, the Durango Trail, and the Los Angeles Trail.

This trail was used extensively by fortune hunters whose eyes were on the golden west, and often in part by travelers crossing the West diagonally. Subsequently, it and its bypaths became famous for cattle thieving or driving, bandit flights, Indian slave trading, trapping, and hunting.

After the first Spanish contact with the Indians of the Great Basin by the Escalante party, traders followed the trail to barter with the Indians and found these primitive people anxious to procure horses. The horse was prized as a mount for the hunt, a burden carrier, and a reserve food supply. In exchange for these valued animals, the Indians gave their well-tanned buckskin, furs, and dried buffalo meat.

---

[7]Hafen, *op. cit.*, p. 68.

When the Spaniards offered to trade horses and white man's goods for children, the Indians found a new field of commerce open to them. Thus the slave traffic became a major activity on the trail as the annual caravans crept across the basin. The Indians could raid the camps of their enemies, or even of their neighbors, and trade the captives to the whites. Strong bands attacked weak ones. The destitute and hungry Piutes and Diggers of the Nevada desert country were most commonly raided and carried away. Sometimes these unfortunate wretches sold their children to sustain their own miserable lives. Hundreds of these native children and women from weaker tribes, purchased or kidnapped along the route, were fattened and sold in the markets of Los Angeles or Santa Fe, for the Spanish traders, consulting their own selfish interests, frequently found it simpler and cheaper to do the raiding of Digger camps themselves, and thus eliminate the middleman in the slave traffic.

Although a ban was issued September 13, 1778, prohibiting settlers and Christianized Indians from visiting the Utes for trade and barter, this prohibition was probably an attempt to protect the wild Indian from unscrupulous traders and unjust prices to maintain friendly relations with the border tribes. The order was ineffectual. Unlicensed traders continued to visit the Ute country for barter.

A Spanish law of 1812 prohibited Indian slavery, but the order seems to have been ignored. The expedition of Mauricio Arze and Lagos Garcia in 1813 tells of Indians killing horses and mules because the Spanish refused to buy Indian slaves.[8] The practice continued to flourish under the regimes of Spain, Mexico, and the United States.

Major Powell entered the Desolation Canyon area of the Moab country July 8 in the 1870s, according to an item in the Moab *Times-Independent* of July 3, 1969.

Near Flaming Gorge alongside the settlement of Green River he saw the inscription "Ashley, 1825." This would be William H. Ashley who took his fellow fur trappers through that part of the Green River in boats covered with buffalo hide.

Another traveler of that northern section of the Green River was William Manly, who had taken a group of California-bound prospectors down the canyons in 1849. Both of these parties left the Green River at the junction of Yampa, and Powell was the first to scientifically negotiate the remainder of the wild unknown river. This untamed northwest corner of Grand County joins with three other counties — Emery, Carbon, and Uintah — in approximately the middle of Desolation Canyon.

[8]William J. Snow, "Utah Indians and Spanish Slave Trade," *Utah Historical Quarterly* (July 1929), pp. 196–218.

When the Utah territorial legislature enacted an 1852 measure against slave trade, a momentous step was taken toward putting an end to this practice by the Mexicans. However, this greatly angered Chief Walker's band of Utes who dealt widely in the practice. Daniel W. Jones[9] tells how in 1853 the Utes camped on Provo Bench (hillside) with some Indian children for sale, which they offered to the Mormons. When the Mormons refused to buy the children, Chief Walker's brother Arapine became enraged, saying that the Mormons had stopped the Mexicans from buying these children and did not have the right to do this unless they bought the children themselves. He seized one of the children by the heels, dashed its brains out on the hard ground, and threw the body toward the whites, telling them they had no hearts or they would have purchased the child and saved its life. This same Arapine subsequently became a specific part of the history of Moab.

Facts would thus indicate that almost continuously, from Escalante's expedition until after the Mormons came, wandering Spaniards entered these valleys not only for furs, but to traffic in Indian slaves.

The Spanish Trail came into existence before whites resided in Utah. It was extensively used for a time, but has now reverted to its primitive state. Early settlers in the valley tell of evidences of a well-traveled trail through the valley when they came. There were shod horse marks on the rocks at Blue Hill (above Moab) which Lester Taylor, according to his son Don, saw there when he first came into the valley about 1877. A Mexican told him that it would take at least a thousand shod horses to make those marks. Since the horses of the Indians were not shod, the valley was doubtless known and used by the Spanish and other traders of earlier days. There are also traditional tales among many of the Mexicans in this region of trips their fathers and grandfathers made through the valley.

Many of the early settlers told of the trail through the valley, evidence of the crossing, and so on. They outlined the course of the trail from several kinds of evidence, and their outline follows that shown on maps of the trail.

ANOTHER BIT OF evidence that the valley must have been a rendezvous for trappers and traders is the fact that there was a well-defined racetrack a quarter-mile long on what is now known as Taylor Flats in the vicinity of Moab. This track was wide enough to accommodate about six horses abreast and was likely used by traders and trappers as well as Indians.

---

[9]Daniel W. Jones, *Forty Years among the Indians* (Salt Lake City: Juvenile Instructor's Office, 1890), p. 53.

40

The first wagons to pass over the segment of the Old Spanish Trail in which we are interested were those of a small expedition sent out by Brigham Young in 1854 under the direction of William D. Huntington. This was to be a trading expedition to the Navajo Indians and to explore the southern part of the Utah Territory. Oliver B. Huntington (brother of William), who a year later was to be a part of a mission to the same area, in his personal diary[10] refers to this expedition and cites the report that William submitted to the editor of the *Deseret News* (a Salt Lake City, Mormon-owned newspaper) under the dateline "Springville, Utah County, December 21, 1854" and headlined: "Interesting Account of a Trip to the Navajos, and of the Ancient Ruins in That Region":

> Sir: On the thirteenth of October last, by request of Governor Young, I left this city, in company with eleven white men and one Indian, to explore the southern part of our Territory, and, if possible, to trade with the Navajos for sheep, goats, and horses, as they have an abundance of these animals; and besides, are quite a manufacturing people, making all their blankets, leather, bridlebits, etc., many of which were executed with most curious workmanship. They also work iron, gold, and silver into a multitude of forms, and articles for the warrior, husbandman, and tradesman.
>
> On the seventeenth, we left Manti with our full fit-out of men and animals, and with five good wagons. We never felt more gloomy and doubtful, or undertook what appeared to us a more hazardous work, during an experience of twenty years in this church. A wild, mountainous, and dreary desert, hitherto almost entirely unknown, lay before us, and what was still more formidable, Indian Walker and his allies had decreed that we should never pass, and with twenty Spaniards had posted themselves on our route, and their rallying smoke was in full view. Still, we unanimously resolved to go ahead, and our enemies fled before we reached their position, the Spaniards their way, and Walker his, leaving our path perfectly open. In this, and many other instances in our tour, we publicly acknowledge our wonderful protection and deliverance by the hand and power of God.
>
> We followed Gunnison's trail to within thirty-five miles of Grand River, which, according to our calculation, is three hundred fifty miles from G.S.L. [Great Salt Lake] City. This road, so far, was a tolerably good one, but the country has little or no wood, grass, or water. There is a beautiful valley on Grand River, twenty

---

[10]Personal diary of Oliver B. Huntington, official clerk of the Elk Mountain Mission, is at the Special Collection, Brigham Young University, Provo, Utah.

miles long, and from five to ten wide; it has good soil, and grazing range, is very well timbered and watered, and is about fifty miles from the Elk [La Sal] Mountain. From here we traveled one hundred ten miles to St. John's River [San Juan] over a very rough and mountainous region, difficult to pass over even with pack animals, being covered with dense forests of cedar. It is forty miles from St. John's River to the nearest Navijo [*sic*] town.

The Navijos met us with very hostile feelings, as they are at war with the whites, and, three days before we arrived, had exasperation. By the persuasion of two friendly Indians with us, our guide and interpreter, they listened to an explanation of our business. We were finally enabled to form a treaty, and did some trading with them, while they were doing some tall stealing from us. They were highly excited, but the chiefs were more cool, appeared quite friendly, and wished us to come again and trade. Trade is the best letter of introduction a white man can take among Indians. Their great captain wished us not to go among their towns and villages, as there were some that could not be controlled, and he did not want to fight us. He said we had come a very great way, and he wished us well; and sent to his town and brought out an abundance of corn, meal, flour, bread, beans, dried pumpkin, dried squash, pine nuts, with sheep and goat meat of the fatest [*sic*] quality, to fit us out for our journey home....

The second wagons to pass over this shortcut route were not to come until 1855, when Mormon missionary-colonists made their way to the site of Moab on the Colorado River to found the Elk Mountain Mission — called by Brigham Young to establish a mission among the Ute Indians in the area of the Elk (now La Sal) Mountains in southeastern Utah.

These 41 men under leadership of Alfred N. Billings,[11] equipped with fifteen wagons, set out from Manti in the San Pete Valley on May 21, 1855. They followed Captain J. W. Gunnison's road over the Wasatch Mountains (then spelled Wahsatch) and through Castle Valley to Huntington Creek. Oliver B. Huntington, official clerk of the company, records in his journal the first wagon to cross the trail on the section east of Huntington Creek[12]:

Thursday, May 31: Took the right Spanish trail and traveled over a good country for a road without water until two o'clock p.m., when we came to a large gulch in rocks with nearly perpendicular banks a hundred feet high. We camped at the head of this gulch,

---

[11]See next chapter for detailed account of this mission.

[12]The journal is in the archives of the LDS Church Historian's office, Salt Lake City, Utah.

where we found a little water standing in the rocks. By further search Levi Greg Metcalf found two other pools down about a mile, from which we drew water to give all the stock a few quarts each. We got down about sunset, and at half past nine we started again and traveled over good ground until daybreak, when we came to other pools of standing water more convenient. Here we again watered all our stock, giving them all they wanted, and we thanked God with all our hearts. Traveled during the day fifteen miles and during the night fifteen miles....

Friday, June 1: Left our morning camp about one o'clock. Had a crooked and sandy road some of the day. Traveled ten miles and camped near the head of a small cottonwood creek on Gunnison's trail.

It was some three years later that Colonel W. W. Loring's wagon expedition took the same shortcut route along this section of the Old Spanish Trail.[13]

The first official American explorer to find his way over a considerable stretch of the Old Spanish Trail was John C. Fremont.[14] Returning from the second of his five famous expeditions into the West, Fremont followed the trail from near Cajon Pass to a little beyond Parowan, Utah.

Dr. J. S. Newberry and Captain J. N. Macomb in their official expedition of 1859, as shown on their map drawn by C. H. Dimmock,[15] diverging from the trail on the upper Chama, reentered it where it crossed Florida River and followed almost the route of present U.S. Highway 163. They reached the trail again at La Sal and marked its course to the Colorado River. After crossing at the present site of Moab, the trail, as drawn by Dimmock, took a northwest course to cross the Green River near the present site of Green River, Utah. Here the great north branch of the trail also came from the east.

Perhaps it will never be known how many used the Old Spanish Trail, or even the names of well-known traders, mountain men, and explorers who traveled or rendezvoused here. But we do know that the valley of Moab was important to the settlements of Spain and Mexico and to those rugged individuals who sought wealth in the West.

[13]Hafen, *op. cit.*, p. 307ff.

[14]*Ibid.*, p. 285.

[15]J. N. Macomb, "Report of the Exploring Expedition from Santa Fe, New Mexico, to the Junction of the Grand and Green Rivers" (Washington, D.C., 1876).

Chapter 3

Mormon Mission at Elk Mountain

The 1854 trading-exploring expedition, under the direction of William D. Huntington and Jackson Stewart, had been instructed to leave a cache of food and supplies in Grand Valley for those who were to follow. That these instructions were followed is related in the official journal of the Elk Mountain Mission, 1855, when Oliver B. Huntington, clerk, recorded:

> *Sunday, June 10:* The jumping off place is a perpendicular ledge, twenty-five feet high, down which William Huntington and Jackson Stewart, the year previous, let five wagons with their loads by ropes, taking their wagons to pieces....

> *Tuesday, June 12:* Here we found the cache of three wagons and a plow made by the party led by W. D. Huntington the fall previous....

> *Monday, June 18:* Brothers Clark A. Huntington, Levi G. Metcalf, and Moses Draper went with four horses and two yoke of cattle to the caches of wagons, tobacco, lead, etc., made the year before. They found the wagons, a little tobacco and lead, and ten spades, but all the other property amounting in value to three hundred dollars, the Indians had found and taken.

Once the Church of Jesus Christ of Latter-day Saints was organized and the *Book of Mormon* published (1837), it became incumbent upon the Saints to carry to the American Indians the knowledge of their ancestors (as related in the *Book of Mormon*) and to teach them "the gospel." According to the *Book of Mormon*, Indians are descendants of an early migration of Israelites from Jerusalem to America before the destruction of the Holy City. Missionaries were sent among Indians in the eastern part of the country as early as the period of Joseph Smith, founder of the church. During the period of persecution (when Smith and his brother were ultimately slain) and expulsion from the states of Missouri and Illinois, the work was not too actively pursued, since work among the Indians involved the learning of a strange language and learning to live with people of an unfamiliar culture. But after the westward trek of the Mormon pioneers and the establishment of the Saints in "Deseret"[1] (later Utah), and after a successful program of colonization had been effected, the responsibility to their Indian (Lamanite) brethren took precedence over other matters, and missionaries were "called" to teach the Indians. The three most significant missions established in the mid-1850s were those in southern Utah, the Salmon River (in northern Idaho), and the Moab region — the Elk Mountain Mission.

The Saints knew that, furthermore, if effective colonization was to take place, the enmity of the Indians for this encroachment upon their lands must be overcome — the Indians must become friends of the Saints and welcome, rather than oppose, the settlement of the area.

When the General Conference[2] of the Mormon (LDS) church convened in Salt Lake City in April 1855, this question of Indian "troubles" in connection with the endeavor to establish settlements in the southern part of Utah Territory, which had been discussed at some length by the church authorities, culminated in a decision to establish a mission in the Elk Mountains (now La Sal Mountains).

Many historians believe that one of the main purposes of the Elk Mountain Mission was that it was to be a part of the "Mormon corridor" or "outer cordon" — settlements along one of the principal routes into Utah. Larsen[3] says of this:

> An outer cordon was thrown around the basin, intended
> to control strategic points on the principal routes of entrance and
> exit from the intermountain country. These included San Bernar-

---

[1]The name given the Great Salt Lake Valley and surrounding regions by the Saints upon entrance to the valley. The word was coined in the *Book of Mormon*, with the literal translation of "honeybee."

[2]The Saints gather twice a year in Salt Lake City for these conferences where they are addressed by the General Authorities of the church.

[3]Gustive O. Larsen, *Outline History of Utah and the Mormons* (Salt Lake City: Deseret Book Company, 1958), pp. 61–62.

dino and Las Vegas on the west end of the [Old] Spanish Trail...
and the Elk Mountain Mission on the southeast approach of the
Spanish Trail....

Lamar,[4] with others, concurs in this and points out that Brigham
Young concentrated on making a route, a Mormon "corridor to the
sea." By 1855 some twenty communities were already established in a
direct line from Salt Lake City to Cedar City, a distance of 265 miles.
These were connected by a good wagon road, and the road itself was
being extended to the Pacific Coast. He says that since Brigham Young
was a superb strategist, he saw that the Saints must control certain key
points as an outer shell of defense and that this motivated the development of San Bernardino; the seizing of Fort Bridger at South Pass; the
placing of a colony in Carson Valley, Nevada; and the sending of Saints
into the Salmon River area of Idaho and down into southeastern Utah
toward what is now Moab.

These tactics were not of course aimed exclusively at non-
Mormon Americans. Church leaders were very much aware that they
were surrounded with backward and starving Indians and were thus
forced to build protective walls and cattle stockades in nearly every new
colony to keep their livestock from being raided. Even with this protection, they often were forced to send out expeditions to chastise thieving
or murderous bands of Indians. But Mormon theology dictated that the
Indian deserved civilizing and saving. The Elk Mountain Mission, then,
was a part of this proselyting program, however simple or complex it
may have been.

The members of the mission were told that it was their responsibility to educate and convert to Christianity a tribe of Utah Indians who
occupied a region in southeastern Utah. Oliver Huntington wrote in his
personal journal:

> On the twenty-second of April I was blessed under the
> hands of E. L. Benson and Zera Pulcipher and set apart to go to
> the Elk Mountain Mission on or near Grand River in the south
> of Utah territory among the Utah Indians to make a fort and
> open the way for a settlement. Another settlement to be formed
> at Vagos Spring on the road to south California. Five other mis-
> sions were appointed to different tribes.

This would indicate that their work was more extensive than just among
the Indians, for they were to open the way for a permanent settlement.

---

[4]Howard Roberts Lamar, *The Far Southwest (1846-1912)* (New Haven and
London: Yale University Press, 1966), pp. 321-22.

The 41 men who were called at the General Conference of April 1855 to constitute the Elk Mountain Mission were:

Andrew Jackson Allred	John L. Ivie
Martin Behunin	Richard James
William Behunin	D. Johnson
Alfred N. Billings (president)	William P. Jones
Robert Brown	John Lewis
Archibald Buchanan	John Lowry, Jr.
William P. Carroll	John McEwan
John Clark	Levi Greg Metcalf
John Crawford	Stephen R. Moore
Sheldon B. Cutler	Byron Pace
Moses Draper	Christopher Columbus Perkins
Edward Edwards	Ethan Pettit (Pettet)
Alma Fairchilds	William G. Petty
William Freeman	Joseph S. Rawlins
William Hamblin	John Shelby
William R. Holden	William W. Sterrett
James W. Hunt	Peter Stubbs
Clark A. Huntington	Ephraim Wight
Lot E. Huntington	Clinton Williams
Oliver B. Huntington	Thomas Wilson
James Ivie	

The men were set apart[5] for this mission, and on May 7, 1855, those of the missionaries who were ready left Salt Lake City for Manti (in what is now Sanpete County), which had been chosen as the place of rendezvous. Oliver Huntington records in his journal that they were to have left on May 6 but were delayed a day. He gives no reason for the delay, but records their arrival at Manti:

> We arrived at Manti without accidents on the seventeenth of May, 1855. There we found the people very kind, more so than in the city. I swapped my light wagon for a heavier one and everything I wanted nearly I got by asking for as I had no money to buy with and everybody was willing to do all they could to help on the mission. The company all being well together and well fitted up we started on the twenty-first of May and traveled to Six Mile Creek and camped for the night. Here we were more fully organized, Joseph S. Rawlins being chosen Wagon Master and O. B. Huntington clerk of the mission.

---

[5]A Mormon practice whereby those with ecclesiastical authority lay their hands on the head of the recipient and "set him apart" to do the work of the Lord.

The following letter is recorded in the official journal under the date May 22, 1855, which also gives information about progress of the company and rules of the camp:

> *Tuesday:* President Alfred N. Billings appointed Joseph S. Rawlins wagon master for the journey, and called; and the appointment sanctioned by the company. Oliver B. Huntington was chosen clerk. The bugle sounded the call to prayer after the day's work was done when the president stated that he should expect everyone of the brethren to take turns in praying evening and morning; he wanted no one to refuse. A guard of four persons per night was established; it was not to be less. A good spirit and union predominated. One horse got away and went back, but the company rolled on sixteen miles southwest, and camped on the Sevier River. We lost one wagon tire and broke a wagon tongue. The best of feeling prevailed and a great degree of jocularity prevailed, but not so much as when laying at Manti.

PARTLY ORGANIZED for traveling, the company started from Manti on Monday, May 21. Historians are greatly indebted to those of this expedition who kept diaries, official and personal, which have given appreciable insight into the mission, its accomplishments, problems, and failure, the men themselves, and problems encountered in colonizing a wilderness among natives who were friendly one day and murderous the next.

A census of the expedition, for example, was taken and recorded by Huntington in the official journal under the date of their departure from Manti. Here again we are given some organizational procedures, an account of distance traveled, and reactions of the men.

> *Monday, May 21, 1855:* Traveled six miles that day and camped for night on Six Mile Creek. In evening bugle sounded for prayer, and Pres. Billings in addressing the brethren remarked that he expected every man to take his turn in praying evening and morning. A guard consisting of four men was established and it was decided that the night guard should never consist of less than four men. A good spirit and union prevailed in the camp. When a census and an inventory was taken of the camp, a day or two later, it was found that the company consisted of forty-one men, fifteen wagons, sixty-five oxen, sixteen cows, thirteen horses, two bulls, one calf, two pigs, four dogs, and twelve chickens. The company also carried fourteen thousand, six hundred fifty-six pounds of flour, thirty-two bushels of wheat, two and one-half bushels corn, thirty-three bushels potatoes, twenty-two bushels peas, four bushels oats, one whipsaw, twenty-two axes, six scythes, two iron bars, six trowels, seven hoes, eleven shovels, and five plows.

In his journal under the date of May 22, Alfred N. Billings[6] records, though not in as much detail as Huntington, other interesting information:

> *May 22, 1855:* Started at five o'clock in the morning. Traveled three miles before brecfast [*sic*]. Traveled two miles to Twelve Mile Creek South. Traveled twelve miles encamped one and one-half miles north of Willow Creek on the Sevier.

Under the date of Tuesday, May 29, we find an interesting entry in Huntington's official journal:

> Started early, and as usual the horsemen rode on ahead with spades and shovels to fix all bad places in the road, which was pretty good and as the day before, led through valley. Traveled northward fifteen miles to Mudd Creek, where we camped at one o'clock p.m. Being nearly east of Manti and not more than fifty or sixty miles away and being exceedingly anxious to hear from our brethren, friends, and families, the company decreed by vote to send two men back with letters to our families and to bring the news from the settlements. Lot Huntington and Stephen Moore were the two men chosen. The remainder of the day was spent by the company writing letters and fixing wagons.

Which road was referred to by Huntington? It is evident that they followed a trail previously known and used. The five wagons that had crossed this route the year before would not have cleared the way enough to leave a road. This was no doubt a reference to the Old Spanish Trail, as is indicated in his entry under the date of Thursday, May 31:

> Took the right Spanish trail and traveled over a good country for a road without water until two o'clock p.m., when we came to a large gulch where we found a little water standing in the rocks. By further search Levi Greg. Metcalf found two other pools down about a mile, from which we drew water to give all the stock a few quarts each. We got down about sunset, and at half past nine we started again and traveled over a good road ground until just daybreak when we came to other pools of standing water more convenient, where we watered all our stock giving them all they wanted, and we thanked God with all our hearts. Traveled during the day fifteen miles and during the night fifteen miles. Just as we were coming into camp, one wagon tongue broke down going down a hill; the tongue ran in the ground breaking an ox yoke. In a minute or two another wagon run [*sic*] against a

---

[6]Diary of Alfred N. Billings is in the possession of the Utah State Historical Society, Salt Lake City, Utah. The quotations from this diary are unedited, perhaps adding to its flavor.

50

cedar tree and broke a reach. Got our breakfasts while the cattle were feeding.

His personal journal also refers to the Old Spanish Trail under the same date:

> *May 31st:* Left the wagon trail and took the Old Spanish Trail, being led by some Indians from Huntington Creek who said we could save three days travel in going to Green River....

Billings in his journal makes the following entries, all are spelled as he wrote them:

> *June 1st:* Left camp one p.m. in the afternoon. Traveled five miles over Ridges and hollos down to Gunison Trail, down to Sandy cannion one mile over Ridge. Struck the trail again four miles to water. Small Stream, West Road. Good Feed and water.

And a little later:

> *June 2:* Started at nine a.m. in the morning. Traveled five miles down Dry cannion to the Bench, five miles to water. Smalle stream of water made by Springs. Water Brackish. Very warm, no grass. Road runs through Sandy region five miles to Green River Road, decending to the river. Encamped at eight p.m. at night on Gunisons old Camp Ground. Feed Good. Plenty of timber.

On Sunday, June 3, the missionaries rested and held a meeting with the Indians. Billings records in his diary:

> *June 3:* Sabath morning, lay on Green River. Found a place to cross one mile below camp. Half past two p.m. held a meeting. Several of the Nations were present. We had a talk with them, told them our business was to learn them the principle of the Gosple and to rais grain. They seamed to have the Spirit of the Lord upon them and to be well pleased with what we had told them. We had a first rate meeting. The Brethrin with a few exceptions spoke with the spirit of the Lord and seamed to bare the Spirit of their Mission.

This was in the spring of the year when floodwaters were often found in the rivers. But if the mission was to complete its work, it was necessary to cross rivers. Ferrying was the only solution. Since there was no ferryboat at the site of the Green River at this time, the record of the men themselves provides a much more colorful description of their experiences than one could devise. The most complete description seems to be that of Oliver Huntington in his official journal. His personal journal is a summary of the official journal, plus some personal comments. (Quoting freely from these journals seems to be indicated.) From the official journal:

> *Monday, June 4:* Moved our camp a mile down the river to a convenient place to ferry our wagons and loading over the river then some went to work at calking the boat which the president had brought along as a wagon box, while others herded cattle, and the remainder were busy about the usual duties of camp. At night we had the boat in complete trim and parts of three wagons and freight on the other side with the loss of only one wagon wheel which belonged to Brother Carl.

> *Tuesday, June 5:* The day commenced with hard work, carried out and ended the same. Allen Huntington proposed to raft the boxes and bows of the wagons and we did raft three, but with hard work, then three wagon beds with covers were tied and floated over. That was as difficult, so after running gears were taken [to] pieces and loaded over, a venture was made to put the beds [across] the boat and boat them over one by one, which proved the best and most safe and speedy plan. Two sets of hands for the boat ran it faithfully all day, and at night we only had two wagons left on the north side of the river. At one trial trip the river was crossed, the boat unloaded, rowed back and towed back to the landing in nine minutes; to cross over one wagon and its loading required three trips. During all our stay at this place the Indians manifested no desire to steal the least thing. We kept a couple of herdsmen with our cattle in the day time to keep them from straying and let them loose nights without guard.

> *Wednesday, June 6:* Lot Huntington and Stephen Moore returned and reported that they missed their way and were three days going to Manti. Grasshoppers were utterly destroying everything in all the valleys; fourteen Snake and Ute chiefs were in Salt Lake City waiting to see Brigham Young on his return from the southern settlements. The boys brought considerable of a mail, about seven papers and twenty letters. Towards evening we undertook to swim the cattle over but could get only eighteen head across. They would not swim, but ran into a huddle and would then swim round and round, in spite of clubs and whips they would run right over the men, shut their eyes and push for shore.

> *Thursday, June 7:* Had the same success in swimming cattle; could only get seventeen head over with faithful work over one half a day; we then took the remainder over with the boat towing two at a time. Many of them would not swim and floated across. Two swimming back after they were over. This work lasted till the eighth.

> *Friday, June 8:* About ten o'clock everything was over the river. We started from camp about two o'clock p.m., and traveled ten

miles, sandy road half the way, found bad salatarus water, but cattle would not drink any, two cottonwood trees near.

The journey from Manti had not been an easy one. There had been the usual problems of breaking a wheel, breaking a tongue, the straying of cattle, lack of good water at times, and the problem of fording. But these were not unexpected problems for people pioneering a wagon trail. The party reached the "jumping-off" place about 10:00 p.m. on June 10. Most traces of this pathway have been obliterated by time and the construction of modern highways. The Huntington journal gives a description of their experience:

> *Sunday, June 10, 1855:* Road extremely sandy; traveled eight miles; the day most excessively hot. Most of the teams were near giving out when they came to the canyon descent leading to Grand River. One of John McEwan's oxen gave out and was left near the head of the canyon, which, being of fast descent and extremely difficult, gave rest to the cattle. They reached the jumping-off place [Moab dugway] just at sunset, which is nearly three miles from the head of the canyon. The cattle had not had a drop of water or feed since morning, and labored hard in a heat that was nearly equal to a torrid zone. This canyon is narrow, crooked, and rough with rocks, the road following the bed of the canyon where it is either sand or rock. The jumping-off place is a perpendicular ledge twenty-five feet high, down which Wm. Huntington and Jackson Stewart, the year previous, let five wagons with their loads by ropes, taking their wagons to pieces. The knowledge of this induced President Billings to take a company of twelve horsemen in the morning and move rapidly into the canyon; all the way down these men fixed the road, and at the jump-off they worked a road over a point of the mountain covered with very large rocks; in half a day they completed a very passable road where in the morning it had seemed impossible to pass with wagons. By doubling teams up and all the men that could be spared to steady the wagons down we got all our wagons down safely about nine o'clock at night; three miles more took us to Grand river, the first water our stock got since morning. Brother Lot Huntington and Brother Metcalf had been there [before] and were our guides through. All our hearts sent up to God sincere thanks for our safe journey through. We got fifteen cattle over the river, the remainder would not swim.

According to Billings on Monday, June 11, the men got the boat in the river and fifteen head of cattle across. Huntington's account of June 12 gives some significant information:

> President Billings, with five others, namely E. Pettit, Oliver B. Huntington, G. Metcalf, Lot Huntington, and Wm. Holden,

crossed the river with horses to hunt a location. The remainder of
the company was left under the charge of Joseph Rawlins, getting
cattle over the river. Some Indians were about but appeared
friendly, although the day before an arrow was found sticking in
Brother Ivie's ox about an inch. This arrow was shot by a small
boy, whose father apologized and made the excuse that his son
could not shoot straight, and that it was an accident. He did not
want to shoot our cattle, he said, but wanted the Mormons to live
there in peace. The brethren made good progress in getting cattle
over, all but twenty head. President Billings, with his party, proceeded to the southeastern end of the valley, up Elk Mountain
creek [Mill Creek] abounding with the largest sage-wood any of
us had ever seen, which we took as an indication of good farming
land. In about ten miles we came to Pack Saddle Creek [Pack
Creek] which empties into the Elk, proceeded up this nearly south
to the head of the open valley, eight miles farther, and nearly
reached the high bench land at the foot of Elk Mountains [La Sal].
Here we found in safety the cache of three wagons and a plow
made by the party led by Wm. D. Huntington the fall previous.
After nooning, we started back, following down the creek. About
the center of the valley we came to the lands cultivated by the
Indians; these lands comprised about ten acres planted in corn,
melons, squashes and pumpkins. The land had first been cleared
of all brush, grass, etc., then a small hole was dug where the grain
was put in — no other working of the soil. All the superfluous loose
soil and rubbish was piled in ridges, forming dams, by which the
land was flooded in small quantities. All this was done by hand.
The seeds they got of the company out of the fall previous. Grass-
hoppers ate most of the first planting, but the Indians soon re-
planted it, and when visited by President Billings the whole
looked well — of a healthy dark green; it had recently been
watered, and the Indians had all gone hunting. The company
returned to Grand River and decided upon having the place of
location near the south side of the valley, and on the east side
of the river, near where it enters its perpendicular mountain-
walled banks. The brethren returned to camp about eleven o'clock.

They were completely moved across the river by June 15, as
recorded in the journal: "A little before sunset we were all in camp, and
the ground chosen for the building of a fort, as our resting place; there
were no accidents in crossing the river...."

Huntington, in his personal journal, gives an interesting account
of his impressions of the valley when these men entered it:

June 12th: I went with Brother Billings, Wm. Holden, Pettet, Lot
and Greg Metcalf across the river to hunt out a location, returned
on the thirteenth having pitched upon a grove near the bank of

the river a mile below our place of crossing, but we afterwards moved it to a nice spring creek on the opposite side of the valley. We had awful rain since I commenced writing this, the first we have had. I looked out of the wagon and saw wonderful mountain precipices all around from one to three hundred feet high. The mountains all around us are barren, soft and red sand rocks carved and molded into every shape and now all the molded water courses are streaming with the creeks and rivers rilling tumbling and pouring down the mountain sides. This is a great blessing and God send to us and our crops. The whole valley which is ten miles long N.W. and S.E. by two miles is all sand except about two miles square near the river which is good meadow land made by the Spring Creek we are on, settling on the valley. Very little timber in the country except sage wood, only one spot or passage way out of the valley to the S.E.

UPON ARRIVAL IN the valley, the men immediately started to work. They were divided into four "messes" or small companies in which they might farm together or each man work by himself. On June 17, President Billings chose as his two counselors Joseph S. Rawlins and William R. Holden, and Huntington was chosen as clerk. These appointments were unanimously supported by the members of the company. They then set about the business of building the fort, planting crops, and so forth, as is recorded in the Huntington official journal (and quoted briefly at the beginning of this chapter):

Monday, June 18: Brothers Clark A. Huntington, Levi G. Metcalf, and Moses Draper went with four horses and two yoke of cattle to the caches of wagons, tobacco, lead, etc., made the year before. They found the wagons, a little tobacco and lead, and ten spades, but all the other property amounting in value to three hundred dollars, the Indians had found and taken. The three brethren returned Wednesday, June twenty, and in the meantime all hands were busily engaged in grubbing brush, plowing land, building a dam and performing other camp duties; but the dam being in sandy land, it broke away on the night of the nineteenth and ruined the site, which obliged us to go a mile farther up the creek and take water from a beaver dam. All hands turned out on the twentieth and made a ditch three miles long to our farm.

Thursday, June 21: Considerable grain and potatoes were put in the ground, but quicksand in the main ditch made considerable trouble. The weather was hot, though every day brought a good breeze, and often a gale by the draft of the two canyons on the north and one on the south. The river had fallen rapidly. No Indians came about yet.

55

Saturday, June 30: Finished the corral on three sides a little after noon. Towards evening, St. John, the Elk Mountain Chief who had put in the corn we had seen, came in accompanied by four men and demanded great presents for the land, but after eating and smoking with the president, they seemed to soften down.

The summer was a busy one. By July the men had built a stockade corral of logs set three feet in the ground and six feet above. They had put in all their grain and had begun to harvest their alfalfa. On July 4, they began hauling stone for the fort which was laid out and staked and whose walls were 64 feet thick at the bottom and two feet thick at the top. There was a wide gate on the south and a narrow one on the west.

The weather was hot, but the men were kept busy building the fort and planting, cultivating, and watering their crops. They were visited by many Indians who came to trade. Some of the chiefs were friendly to the missionaries. Many religious meetings were held wherein a good spirit was manifest and at which some of the Indians spoke. A number were even baptized.

On one occasion Huntington records that the missionaries were full of "lightness" — laughing gayly — and were reproved by the Indians who said they were acting like fools, not men. The men determined to repent of their folly and reform in their actions.

Before the fort was completed, the Indians began to gather and watch. Some were pleased and others angry, but all were keen to trade. St. John, the chief, came on July 11 and told his people that the Mormons had come to do them good and they must remember this and, further, that there was not enough of the Indians to harm the whites if they wanted to do so. He asked his people to leave the Mormons alone and not to steal from them, for it was good to live together in peace.

On the evening of July 14, Arapine, brother of Chief Walker, arrived with a small package of letters and papers for the missionaries. He had obviously changed his attitude toward the Mormons because Huntington says, "The spirit of Mormonism was in him." The following day, Sunday, July 15, the record says:

> As soon as day light according to Indian custom of preaching, Arapine was out preaching to the Indians around us at the top of his voice. First he spoke the Utah language, and then in Navajo. At meeting p.m. he preached again. St. John and his brother both preached; meeting being given to the natives. The spirit of God ruled in power visibly. The work was beginning to take roots in their hearts.

But this friendship was not to prevail among all the Indians, for the mission was soon to come to an ill-fated conclusion. However, on July 22, some fifteen Indians were baptized, and all seemed well.

Building continued, and there are more observations on the surrounding area in the Huntington journal:

> *Monday, July 23:* President Billings, Brother Rawlins, McEwan and Metcalf went to Elk Mountain to hunt for timber. They returned the twenty-fourth and reported vast amounts of most excellent timber and easy access, the only difficulty was brush, when that was cut we could drive right to it with wagons; the timber was twenty-five miles distant.

> *Wednesday, July 25:* Commenced the houses in the fort. During the week haying was finished and Saturday night Ivie's mess had their house done.

> *Thursday, August 16:* Indians constantly coming from strange parts. Some came in from near Gouse [unknown] who had never seen bread and knew not what it was for. They said they were hunting friends and having heard of Mormons settling here, they had come to see us and wanted to be friends.

On Tuesday, August 21, Huntington and fourteen others of the men left to visit their homes in Salt Lake City. They were therefore absent during the closing months of the Elk Mountain Mission. The official journal was apparently reproduced by Huntington later from the Billings journal, for they are almost identical. During the Indian trouble, President Billings suffered a wound in his finger and John McEwan kept the Billings journal.

ANOTHER GROUP of six men left September 19 for a visit to or to remain at home in Salt Lake City. This was just before the time when trouble began to brew with some of the Indians. This trouble seemed imminent earlier in the month when President Billings recorded in his journal, under the date of September 5, "The chief's son came into camp and says the Navahos are hostile on account of one of their child's dying yesterday. Still we persued [sic] our journey, trusting in the Lord." No further mention of trouble is made in the journals until it is indicated on September 14 and 15 that the men began cutting their corn and hauling it in to keep the Indians from stealing it.

Both the official and the Billings journals report (September 20) that the Indians had dug up about a fourth of the potatoes, some turnips, and nearly all of the beets. Then it is indicated that most of the younger Indian men left for their hunt and only a few old men were left in the vicinity. But by September 23, serious trouble developed which resulted in the loss of several men and the abandonment of the Elk Mountain Mission. For a firsthand account, the Billings journal (McEwan as scribe) tells of the happenings:

> *Sunday, September 23:* We changed our herd ground this morning, feeling apprehensive of some mischief intended by the Indians. Early quite a number of them came across the river up into the fort. They were very saucy and impudent. On inquiring why we had turned our cattle in a different course some of the boys commenced loading their guns. Being discovered the Indians began to cool down a little. Shortly after this they left the fort, retired a short distance in front, consulting together. Soon three of them started for the field in the direction of the cattle. In a few minutes Brother James W. Hunt started with a lariat to get his horse. Charles, a son of Suit-sub-soc-its, or St. John, followed him on horseback; he kept telling Brother Hunt all the time to go on ahead of him, asking what he was afraid of. Brother Hunt kept turning his head occasionally towards him, as though being apprehensive of danger. They got nearly a mile from the fort, when Charles told Brother Hunt to look at the stock. He did so, raising himself on tip toe to look. That instant Charles shot him and then shouting to an Indian not far off to run and take two horses. The ball entered Brother Hunt's back ranging downwards about one and one-half inches from the backbone, left side and four inches from the small of his back.

The shooting occurred about 12:30 noon. Two of the missionaries, Ephraim Wight and Sheldon B. Cutler, were herding stock near by and heard the fracas. As the Indians fled, crossing the river to do so, Cutler jumped on a horse and raced to the fort to alert the others. Billings jumped on Cutler's horse behind Cutler and Peter Stubbs followed. Two others, John Clark and Richard W. Innes,[7] also followed "with water." Clinton Williams went after the stock on horseback. The account continues:

> ...The boys carried Brother Hunt in a blanket. Before they got within a fourth of a mile of the fort, the Indians recrossed the river and came charging toward the boys and stock, raising the warwhoop. Brothers Wm. W. Sterrett, Sheldon B. Cutler, and Clark A. Huntington acted as rear guard to the boys who were carrying Brother Hunt and fired upon the Indians, who had fired some eight or ten guns before our boys commenced shooting. President Billings was wounded by a ball passing through his

---

[7]Although this name is not in the original 41 men who comprised the group of missionaries, it does appear in the Billings journal (as recorded by McEwan).

forefinger of his right hand. The Balls whistled briskly all around. The brethren arrived safe inside; the horses and cattle inside of the corral, except what they had run off.

The Indians set fire to some haystacks at the north end of the corral, burning them to the ground. Some corn was also destroyed in the fire. About four or five men had to discontinue fighting and lend a hand in dousing the fire so that the cattle could be saved. Although the logs of the corral were badly burned, they held enough to keep the cattle from stampeding while the men fought on until "after dark." The Billings journal then relates:

> ...Seven of the Indians, Charles at their head, were seen to leave for the mountains. Soon the report of seven guns was heard. The day previous [Saturday] two of the boys, viz. Edward Edwards and Wm. Behunin, went hunting, expecting to return Sunday afternoon. Brother Clark A. Huntington talked to the Indians nearly all the time when they commenced mourning about their friends being killed. He did the same, telling them also that it was not good to fight, to shed blood, that we did not come to kill them but to do them good, etc. They answered him. Soon Captain Capsuin, a Tampi Ute, came down to the corner of the fort and corral where they talked to each other for some time. Then a few more Indians came. They said we had killed two or three of them and wounded as many and they would not be satisfied until they killed two more Mormons. They denied killing the two boys coming down from the mountains. Finally they said they wanted some bread and they would go away, talk the matter over and return in the morning and settle the difficulty. Then they left.

Billings tried to comfort his men during the night by reminding them of their mission and telling them to trust in God. He admonished them not to shoot foolishly "unless we were certain of doing execution." The Indian Charles had for several days before this encounter tried to trade a horse for the gun of Huntington. They had finally traded, but when Charles had shot Hunt, he took his horses, too. According to the journal, Charles "was the ring leader, seemingly, of this sad and melancholy affair. The other Indians engaged did not belong to any particular band nor chief. Some of them were Green River Utes and others White Eyes Utes, a strolling band of thieves and murderers."

Stubbs and McEwan "sat up and waited upon" Hunt throughout the night. Around three o'clock in the morning, Hunt's condition grew worse, and several of the men administered to him, laying their hands upon his head and praying for his salvation in the Mormon fashion: "We laid our hands upon him...blessed him and dedicated him to the Lord, asking God to take him if it was His will. No sooner had we taken

our hands from his head than he departed this life, strong in the faith."
Young Hunt was the son of Daniel B. Hunt who, at that time, was living
in American Fork, Utah.

On the following day, the Indians returned to the fort, telling the
missionaries that they were glad three of the Mormons had been killed.
They also acknowledged that they were responsible for the deaths of the
"two boys as they were coming down the mountain." The men gathered
for prayer to seek guidance whether they should stay at the Elk Mountain Mission:

> ...We all prayed and afterwards spoke our feelings and all agreed
> to leave it to Brother Billings to say, it being his place and preroga-
> tive as president of the Mission. We were all willing to stay and
> fight it out and die together or leave. He adjourned to talk with
> Clark A. Huntington who was engaged talking to the Indians,
> the other boys, viz. Clinton Williams, John Clark, Stephen B.
> Moore, Richard W. James, and Wm. H. Hamblin was taking care
> of the horses and guns, as they were all loaded and ready. Brother
> Billings soon returned and said that under the present existing
> circumstances he deemed it wisdom to leave for the present.

They had eaten no breakfast, but decided to leave forthwith, leaving
five horses and 24 "head of cattle with a calf, besides six head which we
gave to the Indians." On the north bank of the Grand River, they met
the brother of St. John (and uncle to Charles). Huntington related the
happenings at the fort, and the Indian "said it was too bad, but he was
only one against so many; however, we should leave our cattle, and he
would see that the boys were taken care of and buried." The Indian
and his sons started toward the fort, talking to the other Indians who
had taken part in the battle on their way. They succeeded in getting the
cattle and "sending them on. He then commenced driving the cattle out
of the corral, and the Indians began to shoot." The account continues:

> ...One Indian cocked his gun at him. It snapped, but he instantly
> shot an arrow into him in the small part of the neck above the
> breast bone. Another said he would follow the Mormons and kill
> one; no sooner was this said than he was caught by the hair of his
> head, pulled off his horse and hit severely on the back of his head
> and ear with his bow and left. The friendly Indians succeeded in
> driving away fifteen head of cattle and sent them after us. When
> we arrived at the Spring, some fifteen miles distant, we halted to
> bait our horses. In a few minutes, some Indians came along and
> delivered us eight cows, and they kept the other seven head them-
> selves, as they were wounded and bleeding, and after shooting
> three head down they brought us a little of the meat. The Indians
> engaged in this affair were baptized on the seventh of September.

60

...At moon rise we saddled up and traveled some twelve miles and camped for the remainder of the night; good feed; kept up a good guard.

On Tuesday, September 25, the little party of missionaries resumed their trek homeward. They went about 23 miles that day, camping for the night on the west side of the Green River. "Three of the brethren [James, Sterrett, and Huntington] were appointed to take the trail leading to Spanish Fork, thinking...they [might] meet some of the brethren on their way from the valley for the Elk Mountain Mission, and if so, they would inform them of what had transpired." They traveled without undue difficulty, leaving notices posted along the way, reaching Manti on Sunday, September 30, 1885.

Thus ended the first attempt at colonization in Moab, and it was to be two decades before settlers of any permanent nature were to venture into the valley. The fort built by the members of the mission has been destroyed — nothing but a pile of rocks is left to mark this first epoch in the colonization of the valley. A marker has been placed near the site of the fort in the lower part of the valley. Even the landmark of the old irrigation ditch which the men took out of Mill Creek and which, because they were unable to turn off the water, became through the years an arroyo meandering through the town has now been drained and covered until the present generation does not recognize it as a landmark. For many years this arroyo bore silent evidence of an early period in the valley's history, but this, too, has given way to progress. Even the folktales are rapidly fading into a dim past. But such is the progress of humankind.

Chapter 4

Early Pioneers during the 1870s

Two decades were to pass after the failure of the Elk Mountain Mission before any significant numbers of people were to begin finding their way into Grand (or Spanish) Valley. During the years from 1867 to 1876, many prospectors from Nevada and other western regions doubtless passed through southeastern Utah on their way to the rich strikes of silver and gold that were made in the boom camps of Rico, Silverton, and Telluride (Colorado), and to other lesser known strikes in western Colorado.

The Old Spanish Trail would be the logical route for these prospectors to travel. This route would take them across the Green River near where the town of Green River, Utah, now stands, thence in a southeasterly direction to Moab where there would be a good ford across the Grand (Colorado) River. From there they would move in a southeasterly direction to Coyote (the town of La Sal) and thence southeasterly again through Lisbon Valley and up the old Three-Step Hill. Still following in a southeasterly direction, they would travel to Piute Spring (now Monticello, Utah), Cross Canyon, and the Big Bend of the Dolores River. There they would leave the Old Spanish Trail (that still kept in a southeasterly direction) and turn easterly up the Dolores River to Rico and other newly found mining camps, where they might prospect or work in the mines for wages.

This area was explored, mapped, and surveyed during a 4.5-year period, 1866 to 1871, by F. V. Hayden's surveying party. Knowledge of the country through the surveying party was made available to the

63

people of the 1870s. This, in addition to the prospectors and miners who returned to Nevada, passing through the settlements of Mt. Pleasant, Salina, Spanish Fork (Utah), and others, circulated information about the "wonderful" country in southeastern Utah, where the land was a wave of grass that was belly high to a horse, with numerous streams and springs, where game of all kinds was plentiful, the climate good, and summer and winter range excellent.

The only danger was from Ute and Piute Indians who numbered several thousand and who claimed a territory in western Colorado and eastern Utah as large as the state of Ohio. These Indians frequently stole horses from the white settlers and at times went on the warpath. But the advantages tended to override the dangers.

Returning members of the Elk Mountain Mission of 1855, many of whom were from the vicinity of Salina, Manti, Spanish Fork, and the areas along the Old Spanish Trail, no doubt had related stories of the fertile soil and rich grazing lands.

Although there is no written record to bear out these assumptions, it is interesting to note that most of the early cattlemen who went into the area originated from the settlements named above. W. L. Taylor (son of Crispen who is discussed subsequently) reported that his father had talked with James and John Ivie who had been members of the Elk Mountain Mission. Stories he told coincide with the events of the diaries. This may well have been one source of information about grazing possibilities.

Exactly who was the first white person in the valley after the abandonment of the Elk Mountain Mission is not definitely known. There seems to be some question as to whether it was Crispen Taylor or two Green brothers (George and Silas). Either before or shortly after the arrival of the Greens, Crispen Taylor made a trip into the valley.[1] This was probably during 1874. Taylor's son said that Crispen got his information about the country from the Green brothers, although he had also talked to James and John Ivie of the Elk Mountain Mission. The Taylors were from Little Salt Creek, Juab County, and knew the Green brothers because they had ridden together.

Evidently Taylor was alone, just looking for new grazing land. According to his obituary[2] in 1908, Crispen, in 1875, together with two of his nephews, brought a herd of cattle into what is now Moab Valley. Shortly after this the Ute Indians drove them from the valley. This would indicate that he preceded the Green brothers into the valley, as

---

[1]Mr. Taylor's son, W. L., stated that his father was here in 1874, to the best of his belief. This was, he stated, three years before the Green brothers were killed.

[2]*Grand Valley Times,* June 19, 1908.

he would doubtless have come in looking for grazing land before he brought in his cattle.

It had been generally supposed by many that the two Green brothers, George and Silas (from Chicken Creek, now Levan, Juab County), who had brought a herd of cattle, were the first. The exact time of their arrival in the valley is not known for sure, but it must have been (in light of later events) about 1874 or 1875.[3] According to reports, they must have driven about four hundred head of cattle with them, which they put to range in the Grand Valley. The two brothers lived in the southern part of the valley near the Old Mormon Fort (built by members of the Elk Mountain Mission in 1855). It is generally supposed that they were both killed, probably in the winter of 1876–77.

The last time either of the Greens was seen alive had been during the winter of 1876–77 when some of the Taylors, with cattlemen Mike Molen and Brown (first name unknown), had organized a cattle drive and had set out for winter range near the settlement of Green River with about a thousand head of cattle. With Crispen Taylor in charge of the drive, they had gone as far as Cottonwood, but it was bitterly cold and the cattle were freezing. Molen decided to return home with his cattle, and after some trouble cut his cattle from the herd. It was on this trip that Silas Green traveled with the group for three days to show them the trail. He had apparently been to the settlements for supplies. He left the company to go into Grand Valley (Moab) to meet his brother around Christmas time. He apparently could not find his brother and must have set out to look for him when he was killed. W. L. Taylor[4] stated that his father Crispen had told him there were no other cattlemen or settlers in the valley when the Green brothers were here.

During the summer of 1877 a prospecting party, of which Lester Taylor, Nief Spafford, Hank McBride, and Mart Taylor were members, went into the valley in search of gold. They found the remains of Silas[5] on Pack Creek (now called Poverty Flat) in the upper part of the valley. They said that he apparently had been dragged by the heels into a wash, for his shirt was rolled up over his head. Since no trace of George was found, many supposed that he indeed must have drowned. The only explanation for this was given in an interview by J. T. Loveridge who stated that he had been told the last time George was seen he was on

---

[3]In a letter to the author, dated May 16, 1934, Henry Hinckley of Monticello, Utah, says: "The Green boys took the Glen Clove milk cows the winter of 1877–78 into Moab Valley to herd for the winter, about seventy head or such a matter. I'm not sure."

[4]Taylor, *op. cit.*

[5]W. L. Taylor stated that Hank McBride (of Fillmore, Utah) was the member of the party who found the body of Silas.

a cliff above the river (Grand, now Colorado). But several of those interviewed repeated the story of the possible drowning of George.

Nothing piques the curiosity of people like a mystery. And the disappearance of the Green brothers, the discovery of one body with death attributed to the Indians and no evidence found as to the other brother, resulted in considerable speculation and wonderment. W. L. Taylor and others indicated that a search party was sent in when the Green brothers did not return to the settlements; some early settlers indicated that the cattle were killed or driven off by the Indians, although some livestock was found, which only added to the mystery. If one is familiar with early frontier people, one is aware that frequently those who do know of certain events are unwilling to talk about them and those who do not know are willing to talk but cannot produce evidence and are unwilling to be quoted. However, this event has led to much interest in and speculation about the Green brothers, not only their death (or disappearance), but their origin, why no family sought for them, and many other questions. It was not until 1973 that the author learned about the origin of these brothers and perhaps their impact upon other settlers and participants in the history of this region. According to George Bott[6] and G. R. Fish, George and Silas Green were related to the McCleskey family of Georgia. Mary Ann McCleskey, wife of John Wesley Robinson and mother of William Green Robinson (cattleman at La Sal and Paradox, Colorado), was the daughter of Benjamin Green McCleskey and Huldah Boyd of Georgia.

According to the McCleskey and Robinson families, George Green made a trip to Georgia (from the West) and persuaded his niece's husband, John Wesley Robinson, to return to Colorado with him. John Wesley Robinson had been a teamster and wagoner for the Confederate cause. While Robinson was away, units of the Union Army, operating through the Gainesville (Georgia) area, had foraged for and eaten nearly everything, and their opportunity, as they saw it, lay west. Probably the visit of George Green further indicated this. Stories, unverified but persistent in the family, indicate that John W., and possibly other relatives, did go west to Colorado as teamsters with exploration parties. Whatever the facts of that situation, it is known that some of the family did go to the Rocky Mountains. On page 462 of book I, Hall County deeds, J. E. O'dell, father of Martha N., George W. McCleskey's wife, deeded a piece of property to his daughter with this stipulation:

> ...that if George W. McCleskey, the husband of said Martha N. McCleskey, should never return from the Rocky Mountains where

---

[6]Garnett Robinson Fish, in a personal interview by the author; and George F. Bott, "McCleskey-Robinson Descendants," 1968 manuscript in the possession of G. R. Fish.

he is now absent on an adventure for gold...[and] should he return and refuse to accept the land and to live on it as a home for his family, then, the same to revert to said J. E. O'dell and the decision to be made within twelve months from his return from the Rocky Mountains, but his decision to not control the said Martha if she desires to accept.

John Wesley Robinson did return to Georgia and after the Civil War salvaged everything he could, took the family and migrated to Colorado in 1869. This would indicate that the Robinsons had moved to Colorado prior to the death of their Uncle Silas. No further mention is made of George. Thus his disappearance must have gone unnoted by his family in Colorado. Some members of the Robinson family settled at Pueblo (on Greenhorn Mountain) until 1888.

The McCleskey and Robinson family legend and records would seem to indicate that the Green brothers were instrumental in the west-ward migration of part of their family. But communication and travel may have been responsible for lack of further contact. The Robinsons eventually settled in Gardner, Colorado. Their eldest son was William Green Robinson (Figure 4.1) who later became a partner in the cattle

COURTESY GARNETT ROBINSON FISH

Figure 4.1. Home and Family of William Green Robinson, Paradox, Colorado (La Sal Mountains; mother, Mary Jane Ray Robinson, in doorway)

67

business with "Spud" Hudson in the Blue and La Sal mountain areas. As indicated in a later chapter, William Green Robinson was a member of the posse in the Pinhook massacre of 1881.

Of further interest is the fact that William Green Robinson married Mary Jane Ray, the second child of Thomas and Elizabeth Lean Maxwell Ray, first settlers at Paradox, Colorado, and La Sal, Utah. William Green Robinson's son, Walter Lee Robinson, was born at La Sal, Utah, in 1884.

Other cattlemen and adventurers were beginning to find their way into the Moab Valley and vicinity. George Winters, of Texas, was through the valley before the Green brothers were killed. He met them when he went through the valley.

The Taylors did not take their cattle into Moab the year they took them to Green River, but kept them at Green River that winter and took them into Moab during the winter of 1880–81.

Following the death of the Green brothers in 1877, a mulatto, William Granstaff (called "Nigger Bill" by the settlers), and a French-Canadian trapper (Frenchie), whose name is not definitely known,[7] went to the valley. These two were together and had journeyed with one burro to prospect, taking possession of the Old Mormon Fort. Here they lived and raised a garden of corn, melons, squash, and the like. They nearly starved when they first arrived, but because they got there shortly after the death of the Green brothers, the two prospectors were able to find one of the Green cows, thus avoiding starvation. They lived separately — each in half of the fort — and each laid claim to a part of the valley.

In the fall of 1877 the Rays, Maxwells, and McCartys arrived in Moab Valley. They crossed the river on October 11, 1877, and lived at the fort until they left for La Sal on New Year's Day, 1878. There were five wagons in their company. They brought in some horses and cattle (largely milk stock). They noted the extremely high sagebrush in the valley and settled near the place where the Elk Mountain Mission men had cleared the land for farming, for in these places the brush was short and stubby. Cornelius Maxwell had evidently passed through the region about 1873 on his way to Mancos, Colorado, and must have seen the possibilities of the country at that time.

In the spring of 1878 A. G. Wilson (former member of the Mormon Battalion) and his son Alfred arrived in the valley looking over the country. While there they made a trade with the Frenchman for his land, but when they returned later in the year the Frenchman had traded it to Walter Moore and had gone.

---

[7] J. H. Shafer remembered the name as "Lurkin," but Fred Powell, another early settler, gave it as "Felippe Duran."

In the fall of 1878 Alfred and Ervin Wilson took cattle into the valley. There were four men in their party — the two Wilsons, George Winters, and another man.[8]

John H. Shafer, C. M. Van Buren, and a man named Buchanan arrived in the valley in the fall of 1878, according to Shafer. They brought cattle with them. Shafer, a resident of Grass Valley, had heard the Maxwells and McCartys tell of the rich grazing lands in Grand Valley. Upon his arrival he stopped temporarily at the fort and told of how, while he was staying at the fort, the Frenchman tried to kill the mulatto, whose life was saved when Shafer knocked the gun away. The Frenchman later traded his land to Walt Moore and went down river trapping. He apparently disliked company, and the promised population growth made him uncomfortable. Nothing more was heard of him.

Shafer and Van Buren settled as ranchers in the upper valley. They built a cabin on Pack Creek about eight miles above the present site of Moab. Shafer temporarily stayed with Stephen Aldridge who was living on Mill Creek. Aldridge had arrived in the valley the previous winter (early 1878), but did not remain long in the valley. Shafer also returned to the settlements and remained for several years before returning to Grand Valley. Shafer reported that when he arrived in the valley and settled in the upper valley, he saw signs of Indian farming on Pack Creek.

Fred Powell also claimed to have come into the valley in the fall of 1878 for the purpose of farming. He is reported to have accompanied Van Buren, who had probably been to the settlements for supplies. Powell established himself on a 160-acre tract of land south of what is now the town of Moab, between Mill and Pack creeks. He gave the following account of conditions as his party found them when they first entered the valley: The party stopped at the fort where they found the mulatto and Frenchman living. The two had a small garden and raised a few vegetables. The newcomers were invited to sit down to lunch, but found that the store of food held by the two hosts was indeed small. Having brought flour with them, the visitors took out a sack and Powell soon had a big stack of flapjacks on the crude table.

The mulatto and his companion "fell to" and eagerly sampled them, telling the newcomers they had been without flour of any kind for some time. Powell saw the point and kept busy mixing batter and frying the flapjacks. It seemed strange to him, however, to see a pile of squash near the table receiving no attention whatsoever from the two hosts, while the travelers were hungry for fresh garden food.

---

[8]Ervin Wilson could not recall the name of the fourth member of his company when interviewed in 1932.

Inquiring why the settlers did not vary their meals by eating the vegetable, Powell was told: "Good Lord, man, my partner and I have lived on the doubly condemned things all summer. We waited for some-one to come along with flour and were ready to trade the entire garden for a small sack of it; we are done with squash for all time." Since the newcomers had been without vegetables for as long as the others had been without flour, a trade was made which satisfied both parties. Powell returned to the settlements but went back to the valley in the spring with his father and his sister Louise.

Walter Moore arrived in the valley in December of 1878. He bought the Frenchman's claim and spent the remainder of the winter in the fort.

In March 1879, A. G. Wilson and his family and George Fred Powell and his father and sister Louise arrived in the valley as perma-nent settlers. They came from Castle Valley, lured by free government land. They had some difficulty in getting their wagons into the valley. At the first dugway it was necessary to let the wagons down with ropes.

The Powells settled on the land that Fred had homesteaded on his first trip the previous year. The Wilsons staked out land in the south-east part of the valley. There were no houses in the lower valley at that time. They found the ditch made by the Mormon missionaries partially washed away.

In March 1879 Jeremiah Hatch and his family arrived in the valley. With him came Lorenzo Hatch and his family. A little later William A. Peirce brought his family to the valley. The settlers had come from the San Juan country.

Others who added to the growing settlement in 1879 were Carl J. Boren (Bo-reen') and Tom Farrer; Joseph Burkholder arrived in May of that year. He came into the country as a prospector and later took up a ranch on the mesa above Moab.

Burkholder reported that when ne came into the valley there were very few people living there, and the crops were a few watermelons and squash. Burkholder had come to Utah from Montana via the stage. Originally from Pennsylvania, he had served with the Union forces in the Civil War, specifically with General Grant at Vicksburg and Chat-tanoogah and in other battles. He had served with the Vigilantes in Montana and thus was well prepared for frontier life. He reported that the Indians at Moab were generally friendly, and if a white man made friends with them, they would do anything for him. They lived largely on what they could hunt and get the whites to give them. This is verified by other early settlers, including Frank Silvey and Jane Warner Peterson.

Others no doubt went to the Moab Valley during the 1870s, but their names and the dates of their arrival have not been documented.

Some who arrived early but to whom a definite date of arrival cannot be assigned include Al Geyser, Jim O'Fallon, and Judge L. B. Bartlett. Early settlers of La Sal will be discussed in chapter 5.

The settlers in the valley had taken up claims in various parts of the valley. In the spring of 1879, they built two new ditches, one on the south side and the other on the north side of Mill Creek, both ditches tapping the creek. The water was used for irrigating crops. Considerable corn and a little wheat (which was of excellent quality) was raised in 1879.

At one time during that year, settlers petitioned the Post Office Department in Washington, D.C., for a local post office. The petition was granted with the result that the Plainfield Post Office was established in the upper valley. J. H. Shafer and Joseph Burkholder both told the author that the first postmaster was C. M. Van Buren who lived in the upper valley. However, the Daughters of Utah Pioneers' book, *Saga of San Juan*,[9] cites the postal archives in our national capital as stating: "A post office was established November 26, 1879, in Plainfield, Piute County [later San Juan County], with Cornelius Maxwell postmaster." Maxwell was a resident of La Sal, some distance from Plainfield.

The post office was to accommodate the settlers in the lower as well as the upper valley, but it soon was moved to the lower valley where the majority of the inhabitants resided. Afterward, the upper valley became known as Bueno or Spanish Valley (now Poverty Flat). William A. Peirce was the first postmaster at Moab.

Thus ended the period of the 1870s, and the story of Moab and La Sal can begin.

---

[9]Daughters of Utah Pioneers, *Saga of San Juan* (Salt Lake City: San Juan County Daughters of Utah Pioneers, 1957).

Chapter 5

Settlement of La Sal and Coyote

Legend tells us that one of Escalante's men awoke one August morning, looked upon the mountain crests whitened by snow or hail, and exclaimed, "La sal! La sal!" because they looked like mounds of salt. But there is no historical support for this story.

Who did apply the name for this mountain range we do not know. But we do know that the cartographers of the Dominguez-Escalante expedition of 1776 used the name, along with the names Sierra Abajo and Datil Mountain (Monument Valley) as though they were in common usage. In his diary, Father Escalante described the place where the San Miguel and Dolores rivers meet near Paradox Valley: "...near here is the small range which they call Sierra de la Sal because close to it there are salt flats, where, according to what we were told, the Yutas who lived hereabouts get their salt."[1]

In 1775, Fray Francisco Atanasio Dominguez was a recent comer to New Mexico, where he had been made superior of the Franciscan missions. Fray Silvestre Velez de Escalante had arrived earlier and was at this time stationed with the Zuñi Indians. Early in 1775 Dominguez had been sent by his superiors in New Mexico to inspect the Franciscan Custodia or subprovince of New Mexico.[2] He was to give a detailed report of the missions there and to correct any abuses he might find. But to us, his more important charge was to discover a route between the

---

[1]Herbert E. Bolton, *Pageant in the Wilderness* (Salt Lake City: Utah State Historical Society, 1950), p. 36.

[2]*Ibid.*, p. 6.

old province of New Mexico and the recently founded colony in California. In connection with this latter assignment, he was to contact Father Escalante and learn whether Father Garces, in the course of his lone horseback ride from California to Oraibe, had made contact with Escalante.

Dominguez summoned Escalante from Zuñi to Santa Fe to plan an expedition to explore a route from New Mexico to Monterey in California, an expedition which materialized in 1776 under the leadership of the two men. One of the guides for the expedition was Andres Muñiz who may have passed the names on. Muñiz had been a member of an earlier expedition in which New Mexican traders were sent north into the area that is now Colorado, exchanging with the Indians Spanish goods for pelts. One such expedition was that made in 1765 by Juan Maria de Rivera. Although Rivera's report of the trek has not yet been discovered, its contents are known through references made by later travelers over the trail. It is possible that, much earlier, one such expedition may have reached the Colorado River near what is now Moab.[3]

> *September 13* (1776): This Rio de San Buenaventura is the largest river we have crossed and is the same one which Fray Alonso de Posada, who in the past century was custodian of this Custodia of New Mexico, says in a report, divides the Yuta nation from the Cumanche, according to the data which he gives and according to the distance which he places it from Santa Fe.

This suggests that white men may have traversed the country at a very early date.

During the next century various geographic and geologic expeditions passed through or toured the region. Some of those who led expeditions or parties were John C. Fremont, 1842–44; John W. Gunnison, 1853; Captain J. N. Macomb, 1855; J. S. Newberry, 1859; W. H. Jackson, 1878; W. H. Holmes, 1875. These included government surveys, railroad surveys, and the like. Prior to these, of course, Spanish traders tramped over the Old Spanish Trail, as discussed in a previous chapter. Side trips that may have been taken one can only surmise. How far into the San Juan region they may have gone seeking Indian slaves, or how much prospecting and trapping was done on the La Sal Mountains and in northwestern San Juan near the Green River, we have no idea. But until La Sal was settled, no white people called what is now San Juan County their home.

Indian hostilities frequently interrupted government surveys between 1871–77. Prospectors, trappers, and government explorers from

---

[3]*Ibid.*, p. 169.

1840 to 1870 found the Utes and Piutes well established and often a hindrance to work.

Immediately before settlement by the whites, the Navajo visits north of the San Juan River seem to have been warlike raids. Tradition records many raids back and forth across the river. Another evidence of the hostile relations which existed among the various tribes was the Piute slaves among the Navajos and the Navajo slaves among the Piutes and Utes.

During this early period, and until the period following the American Civil War when the Navajos were broken in spirit and placed on their vast reservation deserts, they were the bedouins of the West. They roved a wide territory in northwestern New Mexico, northeastern Arizona, and southeastern Utah, taking a huge toll of hoof and humans to replenish their home establishment with stock or slaves which they might sell for ransom. While under the rule of the Spanish, the Navajos carried on a desultory warfare with the whites who tried to enter their territory, and continued for nearly twenty years after Mexico had ceded the territory to the United States.

One of the missions of those settlers who came through the famous "Hole-in-the-Rock" crossing of the Colorado into the San Juan region was to befriend and serve as a buffer against these nomadic Navajo Indians.

As was true of permanent settlers in the vicinity of the Blue (Abajo) Mountains, it was also true of La Sal — that by the time permanent settlers reached the area, the cattlemen had preceded them, and the settlement was rather sporadic and transient.

La Sal today is an unincorporated small ranching, farming, and mining outpost community in the northeast corner of San Juan County. The ranch headquarters (built in 1896) and store are still much the center of activity.

In the history of the first settlement of La Sal (now called Old La Sal), it is important that La Sal proper not be confused with the present La Sal Post Office, which was originally known as Coyote by the Rays, Maxwells, Webbs, Goshorns, and others who first lived there.

The first settlers of La Sal were Mr. and Mrs. Thomas R. Ray and their family of eight children (Figure 5.1). The pioneer Rays were from Tennessee. A part of the post–Civil War period of westward migration, they, together with the Cornelius Maxwells, had crossed the Plains and, like hundreds of other western pioneer cattlemen, began looking for a "cow heaven" where cattle could range the year round without attention. They stopped en route in Missouri, Denver (which was then just a saloon on Cherry Creek), and northern Idaho. They went on to Chico, California, in the early 1870s. After a residence there of several years,

75

they moved to Mt. Pleasant, Utah. Southern Utah at that time seemed to fulfill the requirements for cattle ranching — plenty of good feed on the range and in the mountains, together with mild winters.

Cornelius Maxwell had (as stated previously) evidently passed through the La Sal area in 1873 on his way to Mancos, Colorado, and thus had knowledge of the excellence of grazing opportunities. The Rays, McCartys, and Maxwells were associated by intermarriage, thus it is not surprising that they all settled in the La Sal region. Furthermore, the three families remained together in Mt. Pleasant.

EARLY IN THE SPRING of 1877 the Ray family left Mt. Pleasant and headed for the new country — La Sal. Thomas Ray had a good team and wagon and about sixty head of fine Durham milk (milch) stock as the family embarked on their journey to their new home. They proceeded without serious difficulty to the head of Moab Canyon (the dugway). Here they experienced the arduous task of getting their wagon down the 25-foot perpendicular cliff (jumping-off place). They also had difficulty in crossing the river, but did manage to reach the opposite side of the Grand (Colorado) River in safety, where they camped near the Old Mormon Fort on October 11, 1877. They remained there until New Year's Day.

Figure 5.1. The Tom Rays, First Settlers of La Sal

The Rays found the Frenchman and the mulatto living at the fort — the only settlers in the valley at that time. The mulatto told Ray that he had forty head of "horned stock" (cattle) running near the river, cattle he had brought into the valley that year from "the settlement." He told the Rays that he and the Frenchman had been in Moab Valley only a few months and that they were afraid of Indians, but would continue to stay and take a chance.

Because Ray didn't like Moab Valley as grass country, he and his family struck out over an old Indian trail by way of Cane Springs and Coyote to the east side of the La Sal Mountains. Here they found a wave of grass, and plenty of water for irrigation of farmlands. They settled on a site about six miles beyond Coyote and built the first cabins in that district on a small stream they named "Deer Creek," about a mile southwest of where the main settlement of La Sal was established a year later. These cabins were built in November, December, and January 1877-78.

About two months after the Rays crossed the Colorado (Grand) River, the Maxwells, McCartys, Niels Olson, the Taylors (Lester, Arthur A., Crispen, and "Buddy"), and John H. Shafer came. The Maxwells, McCartys, and Niels Olson went on to La Sal, settling on the south side on a small stream which they called "Coyote Creek."

This party consisted of Mr. and Mrs. Cornelius Maxwell (parents of Mrs. Tom Ray), a son (Philander Maxwell), Niels Olson, and Tom Maxwell. With the McCartys were Dr. William McCarty and several members of his family, some of whom were to become known throughout the nation in an adverse way (chapter 10).

These families had come from Tennessee during the post-Civil War period, as had the Rays. Old Dr. McCarty had been a surgeon in the Confederate Army. With his family of three sons and four daughters, he emigrated to Montana shortly after the Civil War. There, in that new territory, his services as a surgeon were not too much in demand. Seeking a livelihood, he had gone into the business of buying and selling horses and cattle. With his sons he had made annual journeys south into Utah where cattle could be purchased for reasonable prices from the Mormon ranchers. These same cattle could then be sold for good prices in Montana. The northern range, excellent in summer, was swept by blizzards from the Canadian Rockies during the winters. Therefore, the McCarty family had moved south to settle in Grass Valley, Utah.

After an incident with Navajo raiders in which Tom and Billy McCarty are reported to have killed several of the raiders, they left Grass Valley and went to Nevada. After about two years the entire family was reunited at Mt. Pleasant, Utah, where they met Thomas Ray and his family, former acquaintances from Tennessee, who had just arrived in Utah after a few years at Chico, California. In party with the Ray and

Maxwell families, they set out for the La Sal Mountains seeking grazing grounds. The mountain uplands furnished a perfect cattle range, and they had the entire valley to themselves. A little later Billy McCarty and his family (wife Lettie was a daughter of Cornelius Maxwell) joined the others at La Sal. Other members of the McCarty family who lived there were Lew and Eck, sons of Tom (one of the outlaw sons of Dr. McCarty), and Fred and Pearl, sons of young Billy. Eck later married Fannie Anderson of Moab. There is no evidence that Tom and George, sons of the doctor, were in the Moab or La Sal area except during periods when they were on hideout from the law.

The Maxwells, McCartys, and Niels Olson settled on Coyote Creek, which is about one mile northwest of what is now called the La Sal Post Office. Here they built substantial cabins — three in number, about 75 yards apart — for protection from the Indians. Philander Maxwell and Billy McCarty at that time had about two thousand head of cattle. This was the first large herd of cattle to range in San Juan County. Niels Olson also settled at La Sal.

This pioneering expedition preceded by two years the celebrated "Hole-in-the-Rock" expedition to Bluff on the San Juan River.

Lester, Buddy, and Arthur Taylor and John H. Shafer took up homesteads in Moab Valley, but since they had a considerable number of cattle (about three thousand head), they needed a summer range. On one exploring expedition, they found a vast range on the northeast side of the La Sal Mountains. About a year after the settlement of La Sal, the Taylors and Shafer drove their cattle to the vicinity of what is now known as Taylor Flats. Here they built a cabin and corrals. About a year later they built a corral near the head of Hop Creek on the east side of the La Sals.

KIRK PUCKETT CAME to the Taylor district in 1880. He was a prospector and owned a small herd of fine Oregon horses. He explored the Sinbad Valley and lived there for some years before leaving the country. Kirk's Basin was named for him. Sally's Hollow was named for Sally Culbertson (a man) who settled there about 1886, but who did not remain long.

Frank Silvey[4] says that one of the first wagon roads across San Juan County was made soon after the arrival of the La Sal pioneers. He says that Niels Olson hired out to drive an ox team for Andy Menefee in an effort to cross the country to Mancos, Colorado. Menefee had friends there and was homesteading. With three ox teams and wagons,

---

[4]This book relies heavily on Silvey's notes for the history of La Sal; also on interviews with Neal Ray, eldest son of Thomas Ray, early settler.

in company with two other drivers, these men crossed the Colorado and pushed on to Coyote where the Maxwells had just arrived. Here, as the Indians would say, "wagon road came back" as only the Rays had made tracks to La Sal, six miles away, and that was east. Olson and Menefee knew that they must go southeast a distance of about a hundred miles before they could reach Mancos. No one knew the country at that time, but after exploring ahead a few miles they found an old Indian trail which was headed in the right direction.

What they would find was uncertain. Were the mountains passable? Was there water for stock? Were the Indians friendly or hostile? Certainly these questions must have been in their minds, but if fear of disappointment had prevailed among pioneers, the West would today be unsettled. With stout hearts, stout oxen, and stouter wagons, these men, as countless others, said "Mancos or bust!" And they struck out across the country, mashing down sagebrush and in places cutting trees so that the wagons could go through. Little difficulty was experienced until they reached the lower end of Lisbon Valley. Here they realized that they must leave the valley and gain the top of a rise of about fifteen hundred feet. Finding some fair water in rock tanks near the foot of the hill, they camped and explored ahead on foot.

The terrain was rough, the underbrush heavy. The obstacles were conquered by maneuvering the wagons up a series of three "jump-offs"; thus the road became known as the Three-Step Hill. They continued on to the Dolores River near what is today called the Big Bend of the Dolores. At this place they found a few wagon tracks leading southeasterly, which they followed to Mancos.

Niels Olson returned to Coyote and La Sal over the new road they had blazed, which, according to present information, was the first wagon road to cross present San Juan County.

Although virgin grazing land had lured the Rays, Maxwells, and McCartys to La Sal, when it came to procuring stable supplies which even a reasonably self-sufficient farm and ranch would require, the unsettled country imposed a heavy toll. For example, during the first two years of the settlement, 1878–79, the Rays hauled supplies once a year from Salina, two hundred miles away. In 1880 La Sal pioneers began getting their supplies from Durango, Colorado. At this time the Rays were milking from 35 to 45 head of cows and making butter. The butter, carefully prepared, was packed and salted down in whiskey barrels and found a lucrative market in Durango, a thriving mining town some 135 miles from La Sal. Because it was a scarce item in the mining community, it brought fifty cents a pound. Vegetables and grain also netted good prices. On a two-week trip the produce was hauled from La Sal to Durango by way of the Three-Step Hill, and the return load contained supplies to last for eight months to a year — stable supplies which could not be produced by the ranchers.

An item about La Sal appears in the *Dolores News* of Rico, Colorado, on Saturday, November 22, 1879.[5] There is an article referring to reports of mines discovered on the Sierra La Sals and the Blue Mountains. "There is [*sic*] no settlements between Rico and Sierra La Sal. At the latter place there is a town, with a post office, and four families." From Sierra La Sal to Salt Lake City the distance is four hundred miles. The altitude of Sierra La Sal is six thousand feet. The mountain contains mineral. No salt is to be found. The country along the route traveled is rather fertile. There is an abundance of grass, but water is scarce. As a stock-raising region, the area around La Sal cannot be excelled. All kinds of vegetables are produced in the greatest abundance. The few inhabitants are located near the town and devote all their time and attention to raising stock.

"At Sierra La Sals, the party [from Rico] found an Eastern Company working a grey copper and galena lode, quite extensively, at the same time making preparations for erecting machinery and the necessary building."

The Solid Muldoon, published weekly at Ouray, Colorado, in 1881 tells us more about La Sal in early times[6]:

> Southeast Utah is a very fine grazing country, and there are many large herds of cattle being pastured there at present. The largest herd, about 6,000 head, is owned by Mr. Hudson. These cattle range in the Blue Mountains....The La Sal Mountains, 35 miles north, has [*sic*] been prospected a little and some very large bodies of low grade ore has been found which will undoubtedly be worked with profit as soon as machinery can be taken in....Grand Valley is about 20 miles long by one and a half wide and is being settled rapidly by Mormons. The post office is called Moab, and is in Emory [*sic*] County. The farmers raise very fine crops of wheat and corn. The soil is a light sandy loam.... La Sal mountains, about 20 miles east affords pasture for large herds of cattle and horses in summer....Mr. William McCarty, is on Kiota [*sic*] Creek at the south side of these mountains. He also has a fine winter stock range at Kane Springs....Ranching is carried on very profitably around La Sal. Thomas Ray, the postmaster, has a very fine ranch and raised about 3,000 pounds of oats, 2,000 pounds of wheat and about 500 bushel of potatoes last year from twenty acres....Ranchers have been timid about putting in large crops on account of being close to the reservation,

---

[5]*Dolores News*, Rico, Colorado, Saturday, November 22, 1879, vol. 1, no. 11, p. 1.

[6]"Among the Mormons," *The Solid Muldoon*, July 8, 1881, vol. III, no. 27.

and as they have been considerably troubled by the Utes every summer.

Although this article refers largely to La Sal, it also confirms the establishment of a settlement which had been named at Moab.

The next group of settlers came to La Sal early in 1879, and later from what were called "the settlements" — Salina, Mt. Pleasant, Manti, Spanish Fork, Grass Valley, Rabbit Valley, and Colorado. They came for the purpose of homesteading, prospecting, or finding a new start. Among these were the Webbs, Tom Goshorn, Bill Hamilton, King "Cam" Young, and William Green Robinson. J. W. Webb was interested in placer mining. Frank Silvey says that the Webbs, Young, and Hamilton built their cabins of pine logs a mile northeast of the Ray Ranch, about the middle of La Sal Flats. Because of possible Indian outbreaks, the cabins were built sixty yards apart, in a triangle. The Young cabin was much larger than the others — a two-story affair, with loopholes all round the upper story for riflemen (in case of Indian trouble). The settlers of La Sal proper, according to Silvey, had no killings or serious trouble with the Indians at any time. He says that most of the settlers remained at their homesteads during the outbreak in 1881.

In the spring of 1879 a mail route was established through La Sal, and Mrs. Tom Ray was appointed postmistress. This route, beginning at Salina, Utah, thence to Green River, Moab, La Sal, Paradox, Naturita, and Placerville, ended in Ouray, Colorado, a distance of some 350 miles, or a round trip of seven hundred miles. The first mail carrier, says Silvey, was a man by the name of Howard, who carried the mail for several months. Tom Brewster then became the regular carrier for about two years.

This mail route was perhaps one of the strangest in the United States, and certainly one of the most dangerous. It had no regular schedule, but somewhat of a "go as you please" timing. Sometimes it took a month for the mail to go through, sometimes six weeks to make the round trip. The mail carrier had a saddle and a pack horse loaded with a light bed, some flour, bacon, coffee, and a canteen of water. He camped whenever the horses began to show evidence of tiring. As there was no change of horses along the way, extreme care had to be taken of the horses.

During high-water periods, it was necessary to ford the Price River. It was also necessary to swim the Green and Grand (Colorado) rivers as well as the Dolores and San Miguel, all of which were dangerous in high water. During the winter months the La Sal Divide often gave trouble, and a constant lookout for hostile Indians had to be maintained. Over this entire route, there were perhaps less than one hundred people to serve between Salina (Utah) and Ouray (Colorado).

Small leather mail sacks served for all mail along the route, for few people wrote letters then and few took even one small newspaper. But it is said that thousands of dollars in currency were sent over this route by registered mail, and that the bags of money reached their destination safely.

Sometimes heavy winter storms delayed mail service, thus a mail carrier had to become an expert on snowshoes. During the big snows of February and March 1885, the snow at La Sal reached a depth of five feet on the level and ten to twelve feet in drifts. All travel was stopped except with snowshoes, but there were few who were adept at this kind of travel. Before the February storms, the mail was coming through from Paradox three times a week. Afterward it was two weeks before the carrier, Calan (first name unknown) of Naturita, a novice at snow-shoeing, arrived at La Sal, completely exhausted, with snowshoes gone. Until the mail could be carried again on horseback, Jack Silvey, an experienced snowshoer, took Calan's place.

The mail route was the first and only one to be established in southeastern Utah and a considerable portion of western Colorado, and meant much in the settlement of the area.

The post office was officially moved from La Sal to new head-quarters at the ranch, August 6, 1901. At that time the settlement was called "Coyote," so called by the Rays because of the numerous coyotes in the area. The Post Office Department retained the name of La Sal, and the new ranch and townsite gradually took this name also.

Many whites saw southeastern Utah for the first time as a result of Indian depredations. As members of posses pursuing renegade Indians, they came into the La Sal Mountains for the first time and were enthusi-astic over its possibilities. Among these was Jack Silvey, who after re-turning to Leadville, Colorado, from pursuing the Indians who had slain two Colorado men (originally thought to be three), he had encoun-tered the battle between part of the whites and the Indians at Pinhook in the La Sal Mountains. Silvey had lived in Leadville (then known as Ore City) since 1873. Greatly impressed with the La Sal Mountains, he wrote to his parents at Warrensberg, Missouri, urging them to sell out there and come out to La Sal. This the Silveys did the following spring, and arrived in La Sal in June 1882.

John Silvey left Warrensberg in April to join his sons, Jack, Will, and Charles, in Leadville. The Silveys were of pioneer stock, originating in Zanesville, Ohio. The grandfather had come from Ireland in 1776, settling in Ohio. The family moved from Ohio to Missouri, to Iowa, back to Missouri, and thence to La Sal.

Leaving Leadville about April 10 in company with son Jack, Silvey was joined at Saguach by William Silvey and Frank Hulburt, and the little party of men began their long trip with team and wagon to the La Sals. Gunnison City, Colorado, was the first small town they found on their route (Montrose and Grand Junction weren't impressive).

Reaching at last the head of Moab Canyon about June 1, they experienced difficulty in getting down the "dugway" but finally reached the river, which was high. The only means of crossing the river was by a large one-man rowboat. Taking their wagon apart, they made two trips across with the "running gears" of the wagon. Then the wagon box, horses, and passengers had to be rowed and lead across. In order to gain room for the oarsman to handle his oars, they placed the wagon box crosswise of the boat, and the horses were tied on behind. One of the horses refused to swim and nearly drowned, but the men finally got him to land.

At Moab they found twenty settlers (April 1882) and a post office, but no store. Going to La Sal they found the Ray family settled on Deer Creek with good cabins, stables, and corrals, with a fine crop of oats, potatoes, and a garden.

Writing to his wife in Missouri, John Silvey said, "I will meet you and Frank at Durango August first." Mrs. Silvey and Frank arrived on that date, but the father and brother were three days late. It had taken them longer on the trip (La Sal to Durango) than they had estimated, and the trip by rail had been faster than anticipated.

Durango at that time was a town of about three thousand inhabitants. A railroad had just been completed to Silverton, and it was a supply point for northern New Mexico, with a great cattle country to the south and west. Indeed it was a "boom town."

After the arrival of the male members of the family, the wagons were loaded and the return trip begun. As their destination became known along the way, they were asked if they did not know that the Indians were "bad" out in the La Sals and that it was dangerous for them to go. But the men replied that they were well armed and were going to take a chance.

One midnight as they were camping, young Frank (about fifteen years old) was awakened suddenly by a series of what seemed unearthly yells and yip-yipping. Jumping up in bed with gun in hand he shouted, "Indians!" But his brother Will laughingly explained that it was only a coyote.

Coming to Three-Step Hill, the men cut two fair-sized cedar trees which they fastened with log chains to trail behind the wagon. Using these as rough locks, poked through the spokes of the rear wheels, they tried to move down the steep slope. But they were delayed when all of this weight and caution were not enough. Using more logs and rough-locking the wheels, they finally managed to reach the level floor of the valley.

When they arrived at Coyote, they were welcomed with kindness by the Maxwells who insisted that they remain overnight. The next day, after traveling over a low divide, they reached the Rays on Deer Creek, a distance of six miles from Coyote. The Rays also greeted the travelers with hands of fellowship. The Rays ran the post office — the family at that time consisted of five boys and three girls, all except one were of school age. They also met Niels Olson. All had been uneasy about the Silveys, for they were three days behind schedule.

Olson asked them how many homesteads they wanted. When he was told "two or three," he replied that he had a good ranch of his own and was in charge of two more that had three good cabins on them, which he would sell at a reasonable price. After looking the ranches over, the Silveys purchased them. Obtaining some potatoes from Tom Ray, they planted a fair-sized patch at once.

Soon after their arrival, they began rebuilding and repairing the cabins. Needed lumber could only be obtained by "whipsawing" it out by hand. Tommy Goshorn owned the only whipsaw in the district (he had taught Olson to use it, who in turn taught Ray). They now taught John Silvey and his sons Will and Frank. This was a slow way to get lumber and required hard work. Two men could produce from two hundred to three hundred feet of lumber per day on an average. In time they secured enough lumber for a floor, a roof, and so forth.

Shortly after the arrival of the Silveys, their daughter, Mrs. Clara Fletcher Savage, moved to La Sal from Missouri with her eighteen-month-old son, Ralph Fletcher. From hides acquired by trading with the Indians, Mrs. Savage fashioned buckskin gloves which became prized possessions of many early La Sal and Moab residents.

A number of prospectors came to La Sal from the mining camps of western Colorado; therefore, at that time there was a larger population in northern than in southern San Juan County. Before 1878–79 all settlers ran the risk of being attacked by Indians who still claimed this district as their own, for the county was not politically organized until April 1880.

THE FIRST SETTLERS in Paradox Valley were the Talberts who settled at a fine large spring in the northwest prong of the valley. Tommy Goshorn, who had for a time stopped with the Webb family at La Sal, explored the head of Paradox Valley in the summer of 1880. Here he found a number of springs (thirteen, according to Silvey) on a tract of land of about a hundred acres, which he planned to settle as a homestead.

In the spring of 1880 Goshorn left La Sal for Paradox. He took his team down Paradox Hill, which he had been told was impassable. But by rough locking the wheels of his wagon as the Silveys had done, he and his oxen made it to the bottom without encountering disaster.

A few months after the Indian battle of June 1881 (detailed in chapter 9), Alonzo Hatch established the first settlement near an unnamed spring and meadows in the northwest end of Dry Valley, where he lived for about a year before he abandoned the site and moved for a time to Moab. Hatch Ranch, Hatch Rock, and Hatch Wash are named for him. A few miles to the southeast (in Dry Valley) in the early days, this wash was known as Hudson Wash, named for "Spud" Hudson, an early-day cattleman. Where the wash enters the mesa above, it is named East Canyon. Continuing in a southeasterly direction, this wash starts near Piute Knolls. About eight miles below Hatch Ranch, Cane Springs Wash, with a total length of about ten miles, runs into Hatch Wash, thence down to the Colorado River about twelve miles, where it is also called Cane Springs Wash. Since Hatch (or Hudson) Wash has a total length (including East Canyon) of 75 miles and Cane Springs Wash has only about ten miles where it intersects Hatch Wash, some think it should have been called Hatch Wash at its mouth on the Colorado River.

Early in 1882 an old prospector called "Doby" Brown settled at an unnamed spring about five miles northwest of the Maxwells and McCartys, who lived at what was at that time called Coyote. After a few months' residence there, Brown abandoned this location for one near the head of Castle Creek at about the place where Castleton Post Office stood in Little Castle Valley. There he resided for a number of years. The abandoned place he had left west of Coyote was named for him — "Brown's Hole." Indian Creek was not settled until 1884.

A number of settlers and prospectors, fearing an Indian uprising during the fall and winter of 1881–82, congregated at La Sal. About twenty men stayed throughout the winter, and the majority of these lived in a two-story building that doubled as a fort. No Indians appeared during this time; therefore, with an early spring, the settlers and prospectors were able to leave La Sal, some going to Paradox and others to prospect in the nearby mountains. The Tom Ray family and Niels Olson remained.

In his memoirs, Matt Warner (Willard Christiansen — discrepancy explained later) says that he started a horse ranch in the La Sals, but the date is confusing.[7] In one statement he suggests that it was 1881 or '82, but in another he indicates that it was 1888 or '89. Warner says[8]:

> ...I took with me Johnny Nicholson, Niels Olson, my foreman, and George Brown. We didn't stop or slow down in our movements till we was clear down in the pass of the La Sal Mountains. ...I guess I picked about the most out-of-the-way place in the United States to hide from the law. The La Sal Mountains was in the biggest Indian country and unsettled wilderness then in the United States. To the south was the country of the Five Indian Nations. Some distance to the northwest was Robbers Roost. The mountain range was like a great green and blue island in the middle of the fiercest red, white, yellow, pink, orange, and brown rock-and-sand desert you ever saw. We camped in as purty a grass and timber country as ever lay outdoors with regular forests and sometimes a lake and meadows covered with grass, flowers, and wild strawberries, and we looked right down on all sides into a wild, broken, painted, burning desert that was like an ocean of rock waves beating against the base of our mountain. The nearest whites was at Moab, thirty miles northwest of our camp. We didn't see anybody but the Indians except when we went to Moab for provisions and the Indians wasn't any too friendly when we happened to meet 'em....These same Indians was a treacherous lot and had killed whites less than a year before that.

His account of how he and Tom McCarty raced his mare Betty throughout Colorado, his meeting with Butch Cassidy and the ensuing Telluride bank robbery indicate the time was shortly prior to that event, which was 1889.

There are many inconsistencies in Warner's story. However, inconsistency is not uncommon in his recollections. He says further that as he, Tom McCarty, and Butch Cassidy were fleeing from the Telluride bank robbery, he stopped at his horse camp or ranch in the La Sals and gave his entire horse herd and ranch outfit to Niels Olson, George Brown, and Johnny Nicholson.

A more accurate account of Warner's location at La Sal is probably given by Pearl Baker,[9] who says:

> Shortly after this, the McCartys moved from central Utah to the La Sal Mountains....They sent for Lew [Tom's son] to

---

[7]The quoted materials which follow would indicate that the date was less than a year after the Pinhook massacre which took place in 1881.

[8]Murray E. King, *Bandit Riders* (New York: Bonanza Books, no date), pp. 102–03, 124–27.

[9]Pearl Baker, *The Wild Bunch at Robbers Roost* (Los Angeles: Westernlore Press, 1965), pp. 69–70.

come home [he had been with Matt and Tom], and knowing Matt had a string of good horses, painted the advantages of that country for a horse ranch in glowing colors. Matt took his horses to their ranch, and went on down into New Mexico, just looking around. ...(Brackets in the original.)

Whichever year Warner had his horses in the La Sals, we know that before the robbery of the Telluride bank, he and Tom McCarty spent the summer racing Matt's mare (Betty) all over the western slopes of the Rockies. Kelly[10] mentions Warner's bringing his horses to La Sal. All that can be gleaned from these various accounts is that Matt Warner spent some time in the La Sals with his horses, at least some of them.

THE THOMAS RAYS had a large family for whom they wished to secure at least the rudiments of an education. One of Ray's most significant contributions to La Sal was his work in establishing schools in the little town (details of this are in chapter 16). The school which he was instrumental in starting was the second one in San Juan County.

During the summer of 1885 Charles H. Ogden and Jim Blood, representing the Pittsburgh Cattle Company, bought the cattle and ranch interests of the three Maxwells (Philander, Tom, and Cornelius) and of Billy McCarty, Green Robinson, the Rays, and Niels Olson. Dr. McCarty and his son George had previously moved to Haines, near Baker (Oregon), leaving the ranch to his sons Bill and Tom.

After selling their interests at La Sal in 1885, the Rays moved to Paradox. Because Mrs. Ray, who had been postmistress, was leaving, John Silvey was appointed postmaster to fill the vacancy. The Maxwells and McCartys moved to Oregon and resided there for a number of years, after which some of them returned to Moab.

In the fall of 1887 the Silveys traded their ranches at La Sal to the Pittsburgh Cattle Company and moved to a place near Paradox in what became known as Silvey's Pocket. They later moved their cattle to Hatch Ranch. In this vicinity is "Looking Glass Rock" which was named by John Silvey in 1889.

From this date on, the history of La Sal is largely interwoven with the history of the large cattle company, which, although it has traded ownership several times, has remained the dominant factor in the community. (The history of the cattle industry is given in chapter 11.)

An extended drought, low cattle prices, and rustlers were probably the main forces in transforming an exclusive cattle land into an important sheep country. The Taylors brought the first sheep into the La Sal

---

[10]Charles Kelly, *The Outlaw Trail* (New York: Devin-Adair, 1959), p. 25.

Mountains in August 1895. More herds of sheep followed, and within a few years sheep outnumbered cattle many times over.

A NEW ERA in the history of La Sal began about 1909 when George W. McConkie and Walter D. Hammond from Moab claimed homesteads at La Sal with a view to developing dry farms and building wholesome rural homes for their young families. By 1915 a number of others had joined with them, and the venture looked so promising by 1916 that the farmers appointed an organization for marking out and administering a townsite. During the next few years about ten residences, a church, and a school were built. People, largely from Emery and Sanpete counties and from Moab, continued to come for a year or two after 1915, but when they had experienced a few years of poor crop yields, they realized that the small amount of available water could not profitably support a sizable settlement, and most of the dry farmers moved away. A small number of farms near La Sal are currently operated by the progeny or relatives of the 1910–20 settlers.

The religious activity of La Sal has been as varied as its inhabitants and history. The first organized church unit was an LDS branch, August 2, 1915. Then in October 1917 it was made an independent ward, with Walter D. Hammond as bishop. It was later disorganized as a ward and made a branch dependent upon the Moab Ward in November 1924, and since that time has been made an independent branch and a branch dependent of one of the Monticello wards several times. Other religious groups are served by missionary work.

Because La Sal has few aspects of a town, it has not been greatly affected by various mining efforts near by until the advent of uranium mining (chapter 13). This latter activity has had considerable influence upon the settlement, and with reactivated interest, may have even greater influence.

Ranching and farming were the purpose of La Sal's first settlement and are the main purpose for La Sal today. Agriculture is almost certain to retain its prominence in the economy of La Sal in the future. The older settlement was abandoned in the early 1930s because of frequent floods. Only a few buildings remain there.

Chapter 6

Finding a Name
for the Community

During the early settlement of the Utah Territory, Moab was known variously as Grand Valley, Spanish Valley, and Mormon Fort. These names were even on several maps of that period. Moab was first placed on the map with its present name when a regular mail route was established between Salina (Utah) and Ouray (Colorado). This route was established in March 1879, but according to George F. Powell, Joseph Burkholder, and Frank M. Shafer, the post office at Moab was established in March 1880. (In a newspaper clipping recently found among the author's notes for the first edition, there is substantiation of this date. The article states that Shafer wrote to the postal department for an abstract of the official records and was notified that the Moab Post Office was established on March 23, 1880, with William A. Peirce as postmaster. At that time Moab was in Emery County. Between the years 1880 and 1890, the post office is shown to have been in both San Juan and Emery counties. Not until June 19, 1890, was Moab listed as being in Grand County. Shafer was twice postmaster — February 20, 1892, to May 1898; and again January 23, 1917, for many years.)[1] William Peirce figures prominently throughout this chapter in the naming of the town.

---

[1]Moab *Times-Independent* (date unknown, but would be about 1934 or 1935).

The Far Country: Moab and La Sal

Origin of the name for this Utah town is unclear, yet there is consensus among those who were interviewed for this book (first edition as well as this edition) that a "committee" was selected by the townspeople to give the tiny community a name. When the petition for a local post office was submitted to the federal authorities, the settlement clearly needed a name in order to be eligible for a post office. According to Fred Powell (George F.),[2] the people of the settlement held a social gathering where the committee of six men — Powell, A. G. Wilson, Peirce and his brother James, and Jeremiah and Lorenzo Hatch — was appointed to choose a name.[3] Powell insisted in 1924 that the name was first proposed by William Peirce (who was a student of the Bible) and that it had religious significance. However, though queried carefully, he stated that he did not know the religious reference intended by Peirce. A second theory, advanced by some later settlers, is that the name was taken from the Ute word "moapa" meaning "mosquito." Let us explore these two possibilities.

First, for the purpose of historical background, the author digresses long enough to restate what she stated in the first printing of this book (as serialized and copyrighted in the Moab *Times-Independent*, 1937) wherein she said: "Others of the earliest settlers concur in this idea — all agreeing that the name had a religious significance and was taken from the Bible. The people of Bethlehem referred to the ancient biblical Moab as 'The Far Country.' It was a land of flat-topped mountains. The similarity is evident." Others who read the 1937 edition may have mistakenly supposed that the above passage is irrefutable evidence that Moab, Utah, was indeed named for the biblical Moab and means "the far country." This is unfortunate, for the words were clearly written as a conjecture, not as fact. The author hastens to explain this position: After a lifetime of research and study about Moab (Utah), she has been unable to locate any written record, nor has she been able to get anyone interviewed by her to substantiate the story, that Moab is a New World replica or facsimile of that ancient Moab.

To be sure, Powell, in the two interviews (the second was shortly before his death), again reiterated what he had said in 1924; namely, that William Peirce had suggested the name and that it had "religious significance." This is substantiated by other interviews with June Peirce (a son of William A.); Ervin, Joe, and William Wilson (sons of A. G. Wilson); Tom Trout (a later arrival who stated that he was given this

---

[2]Interviewed for the first edition in 1924. He reiterated his first statements in an interview in the 1930s.

[3]The committee members' names have appeared in no written accounts (prior to this), but have been verified by Powell, the sons of A. G. Wilson, and William Peirce. A composite identification was achieved.

90

information by Bishop Randolph Stewart who arrived in 1881); and many others. No one could identify the significance of the meaning other than to state that "Billy Peirce was a student of the Bible." With the verification stated, the author has accepted Powell's statement as true since he was a surviving member of the committee chosen to name the town. She believes this theory may be accepted as authentic.

There are several possibilities to which a Bible student might refer in proposing the name of Moab. For example, it might be related to statements made in the Old Testament by the Prophet Jeremiah, or it might refer to the "Land of Moab," a place of refuge for Moab (son of Lot and nephew of Abraham) and his followers. But when Fred Powell was pressed for a reason in the 1930s interview he suggested that, although he did not know, it might have been suggested because of the similarity the people of Utah's Moab saw between themselves and the long hard travel of the pilgrims in biblical times to the Land of Moab. This latter possibility was presented by this author in a paper written at Brigham Young University April 1931. This deduction was later changed by her because of further studies about biblical history of the "Land of Moab."

King Hussein of Jordan[4] tells us that "the Dome of the Rock," in what was the Arab-occupied part of Jerusalem, was known as the "far distant place" when the Prophet Mohammed made his spiritual journey to heaven.

Biblical Moab occupied a lofty tableland to the east of the Dead Sea. It was bounded on the east by the Arabian Desert, on the south by the Land of Edom, and on the west by the Dead Sea and Jordan Valley. Its northern boundary fluctuated at different periods between the Arnon River and an indistinct line some distance north of Heshbon.[5]

The tablelands were elevated some three thousand feet above the level of the Mediterranean Sea and some 4,300 feet above the Dead Sea. The northern portion consisted of broad stretches of rolling country, the reddish soil of which was and is fertile, while in the southern portion more hills were to be found, the deep wrinkles in the topography interfering with agriculture.

Marden describes the narrow passage through the rock bastion that hides Petra[6]:

> ...The trail continued past that magnificent sight, past...cliff faces in colors that seemed to have melted and run together in

---

[4]H. M. Hussein, King of Jordan, "Holy Land, My Country," *National Geographic* (December 1964), vol. 126, no. 6, pp. 787–88.

[5]James Hastings, D.D., *et al.* (eds.), *Dictionary of the Bible* (New York: Charles Scribners' Sons, 1943), p. 626.

[6]Luis Marden, *The Other Side of Jordan*, as cited in *ibid.*, p. 795.

pendulous fingers. In crevices of the red rock little lizards flirted, their color a dusty gray flecked with rose-red, exactly mimicking the sandstone to which they clung with padded feet.

Most of the country is gently rolling plateau, averaging some three thousand feet in elevation and gradually rising and narrowing from north to south. According to Pfeiffer[7]:

> ...Here and there steep-sided valleys cleave the western portion of the tableland in their plunge to the Dead Sea shore. Of these the most spectacular is the gorge of the Arnon which, at its maximum, reaches one-third of a mile in depth, and is as much as three miles wide at the rim.

Throughout much of their history the Moabites and Israelites, although they were related, did not meet harmoniously. As the Israelites settled in the Land of Canaan, some of the tribes traded with the Moabites, and during the reign of David and Solomon, Moab was brought largely under the control of Israel.

These biblical citations are given here to justify the author's inference in the first edition of why the town of Moab, Utah, was given the name it now bears. In the summer of 1972, the author stood on the shores of the Dead Sea and looked across it to the Land of Moab and felt that she had been correct in her association of the name and its meaning. However, this is a *purely subjective* interpretation. The ancient Land of Moab (now Jordan) is indeed similar in geography to Utah's Moab. The rugged, colorful sandstone formations remind one of the country surrounding Moab in southeastern Utah. And when one looks across the Dead Sea, one is struck by the similarity — the flat-topped mountains (or mesas), the terrain, the sandstone formations — and it is beautiful to behold!

A LATER POSTMASTER at Moab (Utah), Henry G. Crouse, tried unsuccessfully to change the name of Moab to Uvadalia. This was about 1885. William A. Peirce not only had much to do with the naming of Moab and serving as its first postmaster, but he was the first LDS ward clerk, and the father of the first white child born in Moab; namely, Hugh Peirce, born December 4, 1879. The author has examined the brown paper record which Mr. Peirce made and kept, in which he recorded the account of Hugh's birth among other vital statistics.

---

[7]Charles F. Pfeiffer (ed.), *The Biblical World: A Dictionary of Biblical Archaeology* (Grand Rapids, Michigan: Baker Book House, 1966).

In 1880, O. W. Warner, Thomas Pritchett (first justice of the peace), Henry Penney, and others came into the valley. In November 1880, Amasa, Thomas, Louis, and Libbie Larsen (she became Mrs. Lemon) came into the valley. Also that same year came N. E. Wilson and family, L. L. Crapo and family, Chris Boren, and the Gibson family. During that winter the following lived at the fort: the mulatto, Mr. and Mrs. Billy Belan, Tom Pritchett, and the Larsens.

In July 1880 J. T. Loveridge went through Moab Valley driving cattle. He and his partner went round the side of the valley, and he did not know there was a settlement until his return, when, stopping at Coyote, he happened to be there at the time Joe Wilson was shot by Indians and Ervin escaped and made his way to Coyote in the latter part of August 1880.

Erastus Snow of the General Authorities of the LDS church was visiting in Moab at this time and appointed A. G. Wilson as presiding elder over an ecclesiastical branch of the church at Moab.

In January 1881 Bill Gibson and his family came into the valley and took up their abode in the fort — the Larsens having moved out. John Teuscher also came in about the same time.

During the winter of 1880–81 the Taylors (Lester, "Buddy," Crispen, and Charles) wintered their cattle in the valley. Lester returned to the settlements, but the others remained with the cattle. The winter was mild, and they camped down near the fort. Some time during that winter or spring — probably in the spring of 1881 — Charles Taylor and Luanne Gibson were married by justice of the peace Tom Pritchett. According to all available information, this was the first marriage ceremony performed in the valley. There has been some question raised concerning this, but it seems evident that this was the first by date. Libbie Larsen reported that the wedding took place soon after her arrival, probably about February 1881. Hyrum Taylor stated that the couple were married when he first came to the valley in the spring of 1881. Lydia Ann Taylor (Mrs. Lester) also gives this account, as do many other settlers who were here during or shortly after that occasion. Probably the second marriage was that of Louise Powell and Walter Moore, September 4, 1881.

At the Sanpete Stake conference in October 1875, it was determined to open up the country to the east of Sanpete County, and Orange Seely was designated to pioneer the way and open up church colonies. He had been appointed bishop of a vast scope of country extending from Sanpete over into what is now Grand County, but at that time was a part of Emery County. He did found an ecclesiastical settlement in the Moab Valley, but it was not until 1881 that this was accomplished. Randolph Hockaway Stewart was called to be bishop of this new ward.

93

Bishop Stewart was called from Bear Lake (in northern Utah) where he had been bishop for some twenty years. He and his families started out on the journey, but stopped at Huntington and built three log houses where they remained for one winter. They came to Moab in the spring of 1881. With him on his first trip to Moab was his wife Sarah Ann and her family, and his brother-in-law, Alma Lutz, and his family. About June his two other wives and families joined him and the others in Moab.

Those who came in first brought two or three wagons, one of which was lost in fording the river. The boys who were driving did not know the ford and the water was high. All those crossing managed to reach safety, but the loss of the wagon and team was costly. After they reached the valley, they camped in tents and sheds for some time, for they could not build houses immediately to accommodate all of the newcomers.

At a meeting held February 15, 1881, at the house of Alfred G. Wilson at Moab, attended by Christen G. Larsen (president of Emery Stake), Orange Seelcy, Randolph H. Stewart, and other visitors, the Saints in Moab were organized as a ward with Randolph Hockaway Stewart as bishop, Alfred Wilson first counselor, and Orlando W. Warner second counselor.[8] The new ward became a part of Emery Stake.

Bishop Stewart homesteaded land all along the hillside and lower valley. His daughter, Annie (later Shafer), was seven years of age when they arrived in Moab. She reported that the mulatto and "a Dutchman" (Dutch Charlie) were there when they arrived at the fort. Her brother Calvin worked for Dutch Charlie, who had the only store when they arrived. Cal worked for him for ten cents a day. One day the Dutchman told the boy he would not need to come back anymore. The Dutchman must have had premonition of trouble, for he was killed that night.

Bishop Stewart was the originator of the Stewart peach which he raised in Moab. A man named Richardson, who lived up the river, called it the "Stewart" peach. His wife was an artist and painted it, sending it to a nursery which advertised it.

The Stewarts had their own mill and ground their own corn and wheat, although they could not make flour — only bran and corn meal. They raised good cotton, but because they could not get a cotton gin, they had to pick it by hand. Sarah Stewart made yarn of the cotton. She made their first hats from wheat straw. Heads of the wheat were cut off, the straw soaked in water until it was ready to braid, then dyed and braided, and shaped over a bucket. Fashion must be observed!

---

[8]*Deseret News*, Salt Lake City, vol. 30, no. 94.

Starch was made by grating potatoes and mixing them with water. The starch settled in the bottom of the container. Lye was made from cottonwood ashes soaked in water. This lye made soft soap, satisfactory for cleaning.

Sugar cane was raised for molasses. The cane had to be stripped and the top cut off. It was then hauled to a mill and ground.

On April 7, 1881, Bishop Stewart and William A. Peirce wrote an optimistic report for the *Deseret News* in which they estimated the valley would sustain about a hundred families when all areas were under cultivation[9]:

> The land in this valley is all taken in quarter sections, and there are about sixteen families here, and it is concluded that this valley will sustain one hundred families when it is all put in cultivation. It is a distance of twenty to twenty-five miles to wood and timber. There are three thousand acres of good land here, which we are satisfied is well adapted to crops of almost every kind. There is a good chance open for a man to put a grist and sawmill here, and we also need a good blacksmith and shoemaker, who would find plenty of employment and ready pay. Our climate has proven very healthy so far. The Grand River abounds in fish of various kinds, some of them to the tune of thirty to forty pounds weight, and there is an abundance of deer in the mountains near at hand. The best time to view the country is in the months of June or July....We are putting in crops and the trees are putting on the robes of green. The health of the people is generally good.

Orlando W. Warner, formerly of Deseret, Millard County, visited the valley in 1880, but before the season was over returned to Millard County where he remained during the winter of 1880–81. He then brought his family to Moab in July 1881, and set out a large number of fruit trees which became the nucleus of the fruit industry which was to develop in the valley. Warner also built a grist- and sawmill costing about $2,200, which stood as late as 1884. For the gristmill he used a fine pair of French burrs which were imported from Ohio; for the sawmill (a plantation mill), a circular saw was imported.

---

[9]*Ibid.*, vol. 30, no. 211.

Chapter 7

A Period of Expanding Settlements

When in the fall of 1881 the Taylor families arrived in the Moab area, they had been traveling for a month from Little Salt Creek in Juab County. The party was headed by Norman Taylor and his two wives Laurana and Lydia (who were sisters) and their children. The nine children by the first wife were Lester, Loren Sylvester ("Buddy"), Arthur A., Polly, Rufus, Augusta, Adelaide, Helen, and Andrew A. Lydia's seven children were Ernest, Edwin, Charles, Hyrum, Elmer, Alfonso, and Lydia. However, they were not all "children," for three of the male offspring also had wives: Lester was accompanied by his wife Lydia Ann (Colvin) and her five children; Buddy brought his wife Rhoda and two children; and Arthur A. was accompanied by his wife Sena (Jensen), a bride of one day when the party had started out from Juab County. Also in the group was John H. Shafer, a friend of the Taylors, who had previously been in the valley, and his bride of one day, Mary (Forbusch), a younger sister of Laurana and Lydia Taylor. The entourage traveled in fourteen wagons, driving "some" stock before them.

The travelers experienced little trouble on their trip, except for slight delays caused by the loss of some horses or a breakdown of one of the wagons. On these occasions, only five or so miles could be realized in a day. At night the fourteen wagons were formed into a circle and tents were pitched in its enclosure.

The day before the party reached the Grand (Colorado) River, two men (who were strangers to the Taylor party) had drowned while trying to ford the river. The Taylor party could see the bodies of the

97

men on the opposite shore, which made them feel disheartened. Most of the group waited until morning to cross the river into the valley.

Lester Taylor and his family stopped with Judge Bartlett, and the other families stayed temporarily at the fort which some people named Gibson were occupying at that time.

DONATIONS BY CITIZENS made possible the building of a meeting house and a schoolhouse on the southeast corner of the courthouse block during 1881–82. The building was made of logs (24 by 30 feet) and was used for all public gatherings until 1888–89, when a second meeting house was erected to replace the first, which had burned down. Figure 7.1 shows an early schoolbuilding in Moab, typical of those log structures that dotted the West during pioneer times.

Laurana Taylor was the first schoolteacher in the valley. (This was before the first formal school district was organized in 1883.) A brief history of education in Grand County is given in the *Grand Valley Times*[1]:

> When Moab was yet in swaddling clothes; when the valley comprised a portion of Emery County, and its population was much more meager than it is today; school district number one, in which the Moab schools are situated, was established. This was years ago. To be exact, the date was August 8, 1883.... The first board was composed of O. W. Warner, chairman; W. H. Allred, treasurer; and Hyrum M. Taylor, clerk. The schoolbuilding under their management was by no means an imposing structure. It was built of unhewn logs, and a mud roof protected the students from sun and rain. Rough benches took the place of desks....J. Alma Holdaway was the first teacher. He received thirty dollars a month for his service and his contract included a provision allowing him to "board" round among the patrons of the school. Miss Augusta Taylor succeeded Mr. Holdaway as instructor. She taught ten weeks and received seventy-five dollars for her work.

Other early teachers serving for short periods of time were George W. McConkie, Hyrum Allen, and Helen Berkley. After 1885 regular teachers were employed for longer terms, though school terms were quite seasonal. Figure 7.2 shows another early schoolhouse in Moab.

Upon completion of the first public house there was a celebration in Moab, an event which ended rather noisily and sadly, according to accounts. The building was made of whipsawed lumber, and all hands worked hard to complete it so that they might have a community dance. Hyrum Taylor was manager of the dance and it was arranged to alter-

---

[1]"Something about Moab's Public Schools," *Grand Valley Times*, April 29, 1910.

COURTESY MOAB MUSEUM

Figure 7.1. An Early Log Schoolbuilding in Moab

COURTESY MOAB MUSEUM

Figure 7.2. Another Early Schoolhouse in Moab

nate dances by numbers that everyone might have an equal chance and no one be favored.

Bill Gibson had had his turn but decided to dance again. When told he could not do so for this would deprive someone else of his turn, he became angry. There had been some ill feeling between the Taylors and Gibsons, thus the scene was ripe for trouble. Probably many of the patrons of the dance had imbibed rather freely in spirits, and thus many were easily angered. Gibson left the hall and in his anger seized a yoke (oxen type), evidently intending to vent his wrath on the first Taylor who approached. However, the first person to step up on the doorstep was Calvin Stewart, who was struck with a severe blow on the head, which fortunately was not fatal. Within a few minutes about ten men were fighting and none knew why or what it was all about. Thus the first dance held in Moab ended in a riot.

THE LINE OF the Denver and Rio Grande Railroad from Denver to Salt Lake City was begun shortly after the arrival of the Taylor party. During the ensuing winter, some of the people of Moab worked on its construction near Thompson Springs. The first passenger train went through Thompson to Salt Lake City in April 1883. This was of pronounced significance to the growing community, boding enormous economic benefits to follow. And because the railroad was only 35 miles from Moab, the freighting distances were greatly shortened and the danger from storms lessened.

The advent of the railroad greatly improved conditions in the valley because it simplified transportation. Heretofore it had been necessary to go to Salina and Richfield for supplies, all freighting being done with wagons, which made travel very slow. Freighters made their trips in the fall, bringing in supplies for the winter. Often storms delayed them, or even made it impossible to return before spring. Louise Grimm gives this account of her first winter in the valley: Her brother, Fred Powell, had gone to the settlements for supplies. The storms came up and he could not get back and had to stay all winter. It was a hard winter in the valley and Mrs. Grimm and her father didn't have many supplies on hand. Because they had raised a crop of vegetables, they were spared starvation. And since they had only one sack of flour on hand, it was necessary for them to grind corn and wheat in a coffee mill for their bread that winter. During the winter the Indians were hungry — there were heavy storms and snow. Many times they offered to pay a dollar for a loaf of bread, but she had no bread to give them.

When other families began to come into the valley at this time, a thriving settlement was soon established. In 1883 a party consisting of the Johnson, Newell, Somerville, and McConkie families passed through Moab from Mona, Juab County, on their way to the San Juan area to settle. They went as far as the region on the Animus River in New Mexico, where they had intended to stay, but hadn't found favorable conditions existing there (the Stockton war was in progress). Since some of the party had been impressed with the Moab Valley, they decided to return, which they did in August 1884. The party included the families of George W. McConkie; J. H. Johnson; Orris Newell; and George W. Johnson, Jr.; as well as Mrs. George W. Johnson, Sr.; D. A. Johnson; Minnie Johnson; and Andrew Somerville.

The McConkie, Newell, Somerville, and J. H. Johnson families settled in the upper valley, known as Bueno or Spanish Valley, now Poverty Flat. A number of families were living there at that time, and in the spring of 1885 an ecclesiastical branch of the LDS church was organized with George W. McConkie as president. A Sunday School, Primary, and Relief Society[2] were organized at quarterly conference, September 1886. Both school and church meetings were held in the McConkie home. Eight families were reported living there. Meetings ceased about 1890 when most of the families moved away.

SHORTLY AFTER the arrival of the Taylors in the valley a ferryboat was built, first built and operated by Norman Taylor. There seems to be some disagreement as to the exact date that this ferry was built, but it was in operation at least before 1885 for in the journal of F. A. Hammond,[3] president of the San Juan LDS Stake, dated Monday, July 20, 1885, the following notation is made:

> *7:00 a.m.:* Hitched up and drove four miles to the ferry on Grand River. Kept by Norman Taylor. Paid four dollars for crossing five horses and one wagon. The river is some seven hundred fifty feet wide. Stream not very rapid. High bluffs each side. The valley here at the mouth is some four miles wide. Good deal of meadowland. Directly opposite is a dry wash we follow up on our way to Green River.

The first boat built — a year or two after the Taylors arrived in the valley — was extremely small, only 28 feet long. In order to cross the river the men were required to dismantle their wagons so that these

---

[2]These auxiliary organizations provide for the teaching of religious classes for all members not only on Sunday but throughout the week. "Primary" is for young children and is usually held on a weekday afternoon. "Relief Society" is the women's organization, also held on a weekday.

[3]This journal, examined by the author, is in the possession of members of the family.

Figure 7.3. Ferry at Moab, Taken at High Water

could be transported in small pieces. A man named John Gordon came to Moab to show Norman Taylor how to build a larger ferryboat. They built it sixty feet long and eighteen feet wide (probably completed in 1884). It was operated for some time by Taylor.

There were several mishaps with this ferryboat, but, on the whole, it proved to be successful. At one time Taylor was thrown from its deck and, being unable to swim, was rescued by his assistant just before he was submerged by the muddy waters of the Colorado. At another time (during the troubles with Indians farther south), the boat was too heavily laden so the captain (not Taylor) cut the cable. He was thrown from the boat and drowned and some supplies were lost. And several times a cable was broken, permitting the boat to drift downstream where it came to rest upon a sandbar. Figure 7.3 is a ferry that is typical of the kind in use at that time; however, this one landed downstream in the willows.

The boat was later leased and operated by different parties. In 1897 officials of Grand County purchased the ferry, after which the fare was reduced from $2.50 to fifty cents a wagon.

Old-timers recalled that posted on the ferry was the following sign: "We accommodate to accumulate. In God we trust; all others, spot cash."

The settlement grew continuously with frequent newcomers. Among these were the Holyoaks, C. C. Wilcox, Herbert Day, a Mr. Robinson, Empeys, Buchanan, McBrides, Olas "White Horse" Johnson, the Lances, Murphys, and others. Felix Murphy had been a member of the Mormon Battalion.

Moab's first real store was managed by Hyrum Taylor in 1882. John Teuscher had had a few goods in a tent prior to this time, and Dutch Charlie had made available some supplies, but A. G. Wilson and Hyrum and Norman Taylor brought a variety of merchandise into the valley in September 1882 and opened a store which Hyrum managed. He later bought all of the stock and operated the store by himself.

Chapter 8

Indian Episodes
on the Frontier

Relations between the whites and the Indians in the Moab–La Sal area were generally fairly good after the pioneers were permanently settled in the region. Occasional disputes were raised and sometimes real trouble threatened, but it was more often avoided than sanctioned. However, there were some episodes that must be documented, for they were more than disputes or outbursts (chapter 9); but there were also those which tempered the harshness of frontier life with a bit of drollery. To understand these, we must go back to 1877–78.

After many years of working with the Indians through Chief Ouray (of the Uncompahgre or White River Utes) and Chief Ignacio (of the southern Utes), the whites were able to sign a peace treaty whereby all of the vast territory on the western slope of the Colorado was to be "ceded" to the whites. In return, the Uncompahgre Utes were to receive a certain amount of land situated in eastern Utah, now known as the Uintah–Ute Indian Reservation. The southern Utes agreed to a reservation fifteen miles wide and eighty miles long in southwestern Colorado, bordering on New Mexico. They were also to get their rations from the U.S. government...and some money.

The majority of the Indians was satisfied with this arrangement, but some were not. More especially, the younger Indians were unhappy about the treaties, for they liked to roam freely over the country that had always been theirs. Thus a number rebelled and would not accept rations from the government; nor would they stay long on the reservation.

After the western territory was opened to settlement and was homesteaded by whites, large numbers of settlers came into the Gunnison region, then to Montrose, Grand Junction, and other areas. Rich silver and gold mines were found at Lake City, Ouray, Telluride, Silverton, and Rico, Colorado. Soon afterward, the town of Durango "boomed," bringing in many thousands of miners, prospectors, and ranchers.

Because the San Juan County area was sparsely settled at that time, it looked like a "happy hunting ground" for the dissatisfied Indians who resented being restricted to a reservation. Both northern and southern Utes, with a few Navajos and what were called Piutes or "renegades," were included in this group.

Early in the 1880s a number of small bands of these Piutes invaded northern San Juan County. They bitterly resented being forced to live on the reservations and were spoiling for a fight. Joseph Burkholder suggests that all of the trouble with Indians in the Moab–La Sal area was caused by these renegade Indians and *not* by the reservation Indians. The renegades, determined not to be confined, had camped on South Montezuma near the head of Pack Creek and Dodge Springs. They doubtless felt like going "on the warpath" and getting some fresh horses. (The band of Piutes at La Sal almost constantly ran horse races among themselves. They had made a race track near La Sal and would rope yearling calves and drag them up and down the track, making trails about twenty feet apart, to make the tracks smooth, but it only succeeded in angering the settlers.)

These Indians were always begging "biscuits" from the pioneer women. Neal Ray said that he felt the reason the Indians didn't molest the Ray family was that Mrs. Ray was always kind to them. When they were ill, she cared for them; and when they begged for biscuits, she fed them. They often left items of their personal belongings with her as they traveled through the area, picking them up on their way back. But kindness to these Indians was no guarantee of peaceful relations, for Mrs. Wilson of Moab also fed them, cared for their sick, and was exceedingly kind to them; yet she lost two sons killed by these Indians. Another son was wounded and marked for life, and a fourth barely escaped with his life.

After a hard winter in which supplies were low and the Indians had begged innumerable meals from his family, Tom Ray told them that his "papooses" would soon be out of biscuits and that the Rays must go to Durango (a distance of 135 miles) to get flour. He said that he couldn't and wouldn't give them any more biscuits.

The Indians demanded, "Your squaw cookum!"

Whereupon Ray, picking up his Winchester, told them, "You go! Vamoose, pronto!"

The Indians hastily left for their own camp, but the next day the old Indian, "Wash," rode to Coyote (La Sal) and, finding no one at home but the elder Maxwell couple, grew bold. "Your squaw cookum biscuit for me!" he said.

"Damn you! Get out!" Maxwell replied. Wash was sitting on his pony near the small gate that led to the Maxwell cabin. Raising his "quirt" he struck Maxwell over the head and shoulders. Maxwell made a rush to the cabin for his gun and, poking it through the open window, tried to draw a bead on Wash. By this time Wash was some fifty yards away and had gained the timber, dodging among the trees. It was difficult to get a good shot, but finally Maxwell had him in his sights and started to press the trigger. At that moment, Mrs. Maxwell saved the settlers from a possible massacre (the whites were outnumbered ten to one and most of them had but a few rounds of ammunition) by deflecting the shot.

THE YEAR 1880 seems to have been rather eventful in Indian-white relations. Shortly after the Indians had been so unruly in La Sal, Philander Maxwell made a visit to Moab on horseback.[1] After visiting a couple of days, he left Moab on August 26 at an early hour and arrived at the head of Pack Creek near the old Indian trail that starts up the hill to Coyote and La Sal. Three Indian squaws suddenly appeared from the bushes and waved for him to stop. They jabbered in an excited way to him, but he could not understand what they were saying. Finally, one squaw rushed over and broke off a large switch from a willow tree and, hastily giving it to him, said, "Vamoose! Go! Indian heap *mad*!" At last he partially understood, and keeping a sharp lookout for Indians, hastened on his way, arriving home at Coyote without event.

But a few hours later Ervin and Joe Wilson, coming up the trail riding double and bareback on one of their work mares, were not so fortunate. They were looking for some horses that had strayed a few days previously, and were taking the stock to the mountains. Seeing no Indians and not anticipating danger, they started up the trail that leads to the mesa and Coyote. Earlier in the day, two of the Maxwells had taken some of their horses from the Indians, which apparently had angered the Indians and accounted for the warning of the squaws to Philander Maxwell.

Whether the Indians mistook the Wilson boys for the other whites or whether they were just out for revenge on any white is not known. From ambush they fired upon the Wilson boys and the horse was shot out from under them. As the shots were fired and the horse struck, Joe evidently threw his foot up to dismount; his left foot caught a bullet.

---

[1]Frank Silvey papers; Addie Taylor Maxwell (Mrs. Philander), interview, 1934.

Ervin Wilson told the author that this shooting took place on Pack Creek, around the Baty place, almost on top of the hill on the righthand side of the road. The boys were on a little ridge near the top. Young Ervin escaped and made his way on foot toward Coyote. He had never been to Coyote before, but knew the general direction in which it was located, and with his dog started for the settlement.

Joe crawled through the heavy brush for some distance, keeping hidden from the Indians for a time. But his progress was slow, and the loss of blood and pain in his foot were great.

The Indians easily followed the trail of blood. An Indian, from a distance of only a few feet, fired at Joe's head. The bullet cut off the center of his nose and shot away his left eye. "Bueno. No vamoose no more!" said the Indian, leaving the boy for dead.

Joe lay there all night and until late the next morning when two Indian squaws (a friendly band of Indians under the leadership of Little Chief was camped near by) caught his work horse, put Joe on it, and started home with him, accompanying him to the head of the valley. There has been much conjecture and many stories exist about how Joe reached home, but one must rely on Ervin's statement that "No one knows much about it. He never did say how far the Indians brought him"; a contemporary account which appeared in the *Deseret News* on September 2, 1880, submitted by W. A. Peirce[2]; and an account by Francis M. Lyman[3] dated August 28, 1880. Lyman was visiting at Moab in company with Erastus Snow of the LDS church.

The account in the *Deseret News* is valuable for its contemporary reporting of the event:

> We have just had a visit from Elder Erastus Snow and party who were en route to the San Juan country, and while the party [was] here one of Brother A. G. Wilson's boys, age about fourteen, came in from the La Sal Mountains, about fifteen miles distance, severely wounded by Piute Indians. This boy, with an elder brother, had started on the morning of the twenty-sixth to take some cows from the valley up into the mountains, where they came upon the Indians and a number fired upon them — about eight or ten as near as they could tell. The younger boy was wounded in the left foot, also in the nose and left eye, the ball entering the lower corner of the left eye and carrying away the entire bridge of the nose and coming out the lower corner of the right eye, and his horse was shot down while he was on his back. The older boy escaped unhurt by running and hiding until he

---

[2]*Deseret News*, Salt Lake City, September 2, 1880.

[3]Account in history of Moab Ward, LDS Church Historian's Office, Salt Lake City.

reached a place of safety. The wounded boy, after being shot in the foot and his horse shot from under him, crept off quite a distance, three miles, into some timber where the Indians followed him and four or five of them surrounded him and gave him the shot in the nose as I have described above, and left him for dead. So after lying in this condition all night he was tracked up the next morning by some friendly Indians, who brought to him water and dressed his wounds and put him on to a horse and brought him into the valley arriving about a half hour after Brother Snow and party drove in. These Indians who did the shooting were a small renegade band who will not be subject to rule nor stay on the reservation. They happened to be camped near the camp of friendly Indians when they made the outbreak, some of the more friendly Indians being away at the time after deer in the mountains, but heard the shooting and when they came in at night the squaws told what had happened and they traced the boy as I have said. This renegade band, as soon as they had done their bloody work, took to the mountains and bid defiance to all pursuit. There was a party of citizens went and had an interview with the friendly Indians who told that the other Indians had fled into the mountains and it would be of no use to follow them.

Francis M. Lyman's account is also valuable as a contemporary report and indicates some of the emotion felt at the event. He reports the story much as Peirce does, adding that they saw Joe when he returned, and Joe reported that he was shot as he was throwing up his leg to get off the horse. He reported further:

> Seven men were equipped and sent to the murderous scene to recover the supposed corpse of the older brother, viz: Brothers Wilson, John Gillespie, Mr. L. B. Bartlett, James Peirce, Joseph Meeks, and a miner, on horseback and Orlando W. Warner with his team with box full of hay and blankets to bring the corpse upon and at six p.m. they started.
>
> At six next morning, all very agreeably surprised to see Ervin, the lost, come riding home, safe and sound on a borrowed horse, followed by his faithful dog. He had not seen nor heard of the searching party. He had fled to Coyote Creek, forty miles from Moab, where he traveled after sundown and before sunrise. Stopped at Maxwell's ranch, on Coyote Creek, till nearly sundown, when he borrowed horse, saddle and gun, and made way home, traveling all night. Got breakfast, took fresh horse and went in search of searching party. Excitement subsided in valleys.

An Indian followed Ervin all the way to Coyote and had nearly caught up with him when Ervin reached safety. Neal Ray and Philander

Maxwell were riding and saw Ervin come in, followed closely by the Indian who left after exchanging a few shots with them.

Mrs. Grimm (Louise Powell) said that she was probably the first white person to see Joe after he was shot. He stopped at her camp as he came into town. She told how Mrs. Wilson prepared her own salve with which to treat Joe's wounds. Gathering prickly pears, she roasted them, scraped out the inside, mixed it with tallow and soft pine gum. This made a salve with which to doctor the wounds. Simple though it may sound, it proved effective, as is evidenced by the fact that Joe Wilson lived many years, dying of natural causes.

THE TERRITORY now in western Colorado and eastern Utah was held by the Indians of the southern Ute, Uncompahgre Ute, and Piute until 1878. Then the discovery of gold and silver in the 1870s at Leadville, Aspen, Ouray, Telluride, Silverton, and Rico resulted in an influx of prospectors from all over the world. Their ranks swelled those of the grazing cattlemen, and both groups contributed to a final settlement. Among those who joined the settlement were members of the Robinson clan from Georgia, who participated in this colorful chapter of western history.

William Green Robinson[4] is known to have participated in one fracas, the "Pinhook Indian Battle of Southeast Utah" (described in detail in chapter 9). He is thought to have participated with others of his cattlemen brothers in another encounter which nearly cost their lives, a story which is known in every branch of the Robinson clan. As the story goes, the men were riding for cattle in southeastern Utah when unknown and hostile tribesmen came into the area to incite a general war. These were probably the renegades which are referred to frequently in this and the succeeding chapters.

The cattlemen decided to stay and save as much stock as possible. Two of the men, either Green or a man by the name of Mont and one unknown cattleman, were cornered in a canyon while making camp and preparing to roast a calf. It was evening, but the Indians fired on them, a shot cutting the bandana off Robinson's head. The bandana was worn over an infected eye. The cattlemen broke camp and rode into an aspen grove, working their way to the head of the canyon. Here, they separated a short distance, shouted and shot their pistols, and prepared to run for freedom. The Indians descended on the camp from the opposite direction, probably believing another party had killed their quarry. Since it was barely dark, the cattlemen rode out past the war party, which was now interested in the roasting calf.

------

[4]Bott, *op. cit.*, p. 8.

The cattlemen did not pause for several days' ride to Colorado. Estella Robinson (sister of William Green Robinson) confirmed this story in 1948, stating: "I remember that; I can still see them ride up to the gate. Their horses were about dead and they were worn out, but alive."

The impact of the Pinhook battle of 1881 had repercussions in Moab which might be rather unexpected. It was at this time that "Nigger Bill" decided to leave. He was charged with selling whiskey to the Indians, and, knowing the seriousness of this offense, he feared drastic action on the part of the settlers; therefore, he saddled his horse and left the country. No one knew where he went, and nothing was heard of him for some time. In 1884, Arthur A. Taylor saw him in Salida, Colorado, where he ran a bootblack stand. Taylor talked to Bill, and was told that when Bill left, he went up Cane Springs and was forced to shoot his horse when the animal broke its leg. He walked from there to Salida. He told Taylor he left because he was afraid the people would kill him for selling whiskey to the Indians. Before he left, he told Mr. Gibson — to whom he had rented his land — "The men are gathering up guns to go on the mountain to hunt Indians, but I think I'm the Indian they are after."

His name is preserved in the annals of the region through the canyon which bears his name. This is "Nigger Bill Canyon" where he grazed his cattle while a resident of Moab.

FRANK SILVEY also tells of his first experiences with Indians after they settled at La Sal. He says that about two weeks after their arrival at La Sal, the men left early one morning to whipsaw lumber about a mile from their cabin. He was left alone with his mother. About 10:00 a.m. he heard (what to him) was a weird shout. He stepped to the door and went part way round the cabin, where he saw on a small ridge a lone Indian at perhaps a distance of some two hundred yards. Seeing the young boy, the Indian shouted again and waved his hand with a "quirt" extended in a circle. Frank did not know the meaning of this so returned to the cabin where he told his mother, "I see an Indian and I don't know what he wants but I will try to find out."

He reached up and took his Marlin repeater from its place on the wall, setting it near the door, for he wanted to be prepared for whatever might happen. His mother didn't seem frightened and said nothing. The young boy again went round the cabin where he saw that the lone Indian had advanced a considerable distance with his gun across his saddle bow. Near the cabin door he stopped his pony and again waved his "quirt" and pointed toward the mountain. "Utes wickiup corral white men 'wano.'"

111

They could not understand him but motioned him to get down, which he did, tying his pony with a long buckskin lariat. Mr. Silvey, John, and Neils Olson came for their dinner. Since Olson could understand a little Indian talk, he told the Silveys that the Indian wickiup was near the Taylor corral at the head of Hop Creek and that the Indians wanted to be friendly for the time being. After a filling dinner, the Ute rode off singing a humdrum Indian song and lazily whipping his pony over the shoulders.

The next time, eight Indians came; among them was "Bridger Jack" and "Cowboy" (at that time perhaps about eighteen years old). Mrs. Silvey cooked and fed them all, as was her policy. The Mormons at Bluff City had done this, treating the Indians as well as they could afford to do under the circumstances. It seemed effective in most cases. But the white families also had to protect themselves, for they had to haul their supplies, as in case of the Silveys, 135 miles and they had but little money. Two days later, six Indians came and were again fed. Mrs. Silvey always had blancmange for dinner with sugar and cream. The Indians were very fond of it.

Because Bridger Jack could understand and talk English rather well, the Silveys told him they could not feed so many any more and must protect their little supply of food. The Indians all seemed to understand, and the Silveys were no longer bothered by feeding them in large groups.

"Cowboy" came down from the Indian camp in the mountains many times alone and, when food was set before him, would eat it quite as mannerly as any white. Bridger Jack came quite often. He would trade buckskin for potatoes or money, and would sometimes bring a piece of venison. He said the Utes numbered about three hundred and were chiefly after buckskin, and that as a rule he had his wickiup alone and did not hunt with them much. After killing many deer (it was estimated they killed three thousand), chiefly for their hides, in about a month's time, the majority of the Indians left for their reservation near Ignacio.[5]

Some of the problems with and attitudes toward the Indians as late as 1894 are indicated in a petition filed with the Grand County Court as follows:

Moab C. H. Grand County, Utah, Dec. 4, 1894.

To the Honorable the County Court of Grand Co., Utah.

We the undersigned citizens of Grand County and vicinity of the Little Grand Valley respectfully represent that our lives

---

[5]Silvey, *op. cit.*

and property are jeopardized by the threatening and reckless disposition of the Southern Utes and Navajoes and a few Uintas, now in this region. We respectfully submit this statement of facts and urge a consideration and action at once by your Honorable Body.

The Indians number about four or five hundred and are all well armed and are off of their reservation about 150 miles from their agency. They claim all this region including the Little Grand Valley and the La Sal Mountains as their hunting and grazing country; and, are now killing the cattle of the whites and that they intend to remain and continue to do so; notwithstanding the protestations of the stock owners and tax payers, all law abiding citizens of the two counties, Grand and San Juan.

Owing to the present state of affairs we deem the situation critical and urge some immediate action upon your part to prevent bloodshed and give protection to all citizens and property in this region.

We have personally interviewed the Indians in their camps, and in the conversation with each and all of them they claim all this country and intend to remain and commit depredations, killing cattle, etc. Some of them saying they will come over into the Little Grand Valley and take possession and that the whites will all have to leave the valley and go across the Grand River.

We also gleaned from them that more Indians, cattle and sheep owned by them are coming into this country and are now on the road.

We therefore as law abiding citizens and bona fide citizens ask for protection and as well inform your Honorable Body of the urgent necessity for some lawful and precautionary action to prevent trouble as well to secure the necessary arms and ammunition from the proper source, Etc. Etc.

(Signed) John Silvey, Hiel Savage, H. C. Goodman, R. L. Kirk, Frank Silvey, Albert Holman.

I do certify that I am well acquainted with the signers of this article and believe that it is necessary to be prepared to defend [a word here illegible] at once.

M. H. Darrow
Sheriff of Grand County

The problem was evidently solved peaceably, for there is no further indication of trouble.

While major Indian troubles tended to quiet down, there were problems with some renegade Indians in San Juan County for many years. In fact a pitched battle occurred between a band of renegade Indians, and a posse under U.S. Marshal Aquilla Nebeker was called as late as February 1915.[6] The Indians were protecting Tse-Ne-Gat, an Indian who was wanted for murder in Colorado. Marshal Nebeker had gone to Bluff to recruit a posse. Old Poke and Old Posey were the leaders of the Indian band.

The following week the paper reported that Hugh L. Scott, chief of staff of the United States Army, famous as an Indian fighter and mediator, was on his way to Bluff from Washington to deal with the renegade Indians under Old Poke and Old Posey, who were defying a posse of citizens under Marshal Nebeker. General Scott was expected to come by way of Moab. Another item that week reported that four Indians, members of the renegade band in San Juan County, had been captured by a posse and taken to Salt Lake City by Sheriff J. T. Pehrson and M. A. Barton of Monticello. The Moab *Times-Independent* of March 26, 1915, reported that General Scott was successful in his mission. He persuaded the Indians to surrender peacefully and give up Tse-Ne-Gat. General Scott and party, accompanied by Poke and his son, Tse-Ne-Gat, and Posey and his son, Posey's Boy, reached Moab Monday night, remaining until 1:00 p.m. the following day. General Scott was paid the highest praise throughout the nation for his peaceful capture of the Indians who were being taken to Salt Lake to stand trial.

There were occasional spurious outbreaks, but the most damaging of the Indian depredations came to an end, and there were no further outbreaks in the Moab–La Sal areas after this time.

During the long period of settlement, there were many friendships and associations with the Indians and the settlers. One of the annual events vivid within the minds of old-timers and until the 1920s was the trading trek of the Indians from one reservation to another. Many of these regular traders became friends of local people, but of course there were also some unpleasant incidents. Within the author's memory is the awesome length of the caravan, in single file, as they rode through Moab to and from their reservations.

[6]Moab *Times-Independent*, February 21, 1935, reporting files "Twenty Years Ago This Week."

Chapter 9

The Pinhook Draw Massacre of 1881

By the beginning of the 1880s many tragic problems engendered by the confrontation between the Indians and the whites had been more or less satisfactorily resolved. Later generations have commented upon the plight of the Indian, and we have most assuredly not arrived at an end of recrimination and self-castigation. An author has small latitude in a work of this nature to deal with the broader philosophical problems; however, one is not reluctant to conclude that the so-called Pinhook "massacre," occurring as it did in the region with which this book is concerned, affords a singular opportunity to examine a microcosm of certain facets of human nature which (prior to 1881) doubtless precipitated bloodshed.

By 1881 Indian problems in Utah and surrounding states had largely been settled. Before the end of the Civil War, Kit Carson had placed the militant Navajos on the bleak Bosque Redondo Reservation where they were endeavoring to exist. Under the threat of family break-ups, this family-oriented group had become peaceful. The Utes and Piutes were also settled on reservations. However, there were still some renegade groups who refused to conform and who caused problems in numerous areas for some years thereafter. The Apaches in Arizona were rather well contained in the 1870s. But it was in June 1881 that the last serious trouble with the Indians in the Moab–La Sal area occurred in which a number of fatalities resulted. In this "massacre" thirteen white men were killed and several wounded, and an unknown number of Indians (at least eleven) were killed and many wounded.

In relating the events of this chapter, the author draws heavily upon interviews and journals of those who were either in attendance during the battle or chronicled it from those who gave eyewitness accounts. Among the most pertinent were the accounts by Frank Silvey and Joseph Burkholder (who was on the scene shortly after the fateful battle). Silvey's large amount of material was researched, for he had interviewed two survivors of the Pinhook battle: John Brown of Moab, member of the Blue Mountain posse, and Jordan Bean, who in 1940 resided in Bridger, Montana, the only surviving member of the posse at that time. (Charles Peterson of the Western Historical Association permitted the use of the A. M. Rogers account from the microfilm "Echo." The Colorado State Historical Society and the Denver City Library allowed the use of their microfilms of Rico's *Dolores News* and Ouray's *The Solid Muldoon*, which gave contemporary information and local atmosphere.) Dan Winbourn supplied the information about the story which A. M. Rogers, who had lived for many years with the Winbourn family, had told him. Wayne R. McConkie, professor of geology at Dixie College in St. George, Utah, prepared the map of the area. He, together with the author, has researched this battle carefully and has gone over the area many times and talked with old-timers about the stories of the battle.

Piecing together the chronology of events has been a tedious and often frustrating process; many gaps and inconsistencies exist. Numerous myths and some tradition result in opposing accounts and credits. To avert redundancy, the author has combined the stories, pointing out supporting accounts and conflicting stories and inconsistencies. Some contemporary accounts from primary sources are then given. Research has led to some conclusions and theses which are presented. One startling fact was observed: Even in regional history and contemporary accounts of events at the time of their occurrence, there *is* a microcosm of attitudes and actions which relate to the history of national, international, and cultural groups and civilizations.

COMBINING VARIOUS ACCOUNTS leads to the conclusion that the trouble in 1881 rested with a group of renegade Indians — a mixed group of Utes, Navajos, and Piutes. Hostilities originated near Cross Canyons in Colorado. Perhaps the agitation and conflict were the result of a buildup of previous events. But the specific event which triggered the action in 1881 began with Dick May, who lived at Big Bend, now Dolores, Colorado. He had a small herd of horses near Cross Canyons.

But let us return for a moment to 1880, when Joseph Burkholder and his partner Malloy, with Isadore Wilson, went to the mountain in the early part of May 1880 and camped at what is now the Gardner place on the mesa. The Wilson boys had a corral near a place where Burkholder and his friends camped overnight. They hobbled their horses

116

when they arrived, and the following morning set out to find the horses. When they returned to camp, they found a small Indian boy, a lad whom Burkholder had previously befriended. The boy told the three men that there was a large band of Indians camped on the north slope of Bald Mesa. He said, "Heap tall man. Heap mad."

This was apparently the group of renegades who had killed the Indian agent, Meeker, in Colorado.[1] The other Indians had driven the renegades off the reservation, and the renegades had gone down to the La Sals. The three men packed to leave, taking the boy with them. They rode to the Indian camp where the Indians held a pow-wow. The boy came to Burkholder and said, "You pike away, pike away!" (meaning, "leave in a hurry"). Burkholder told him they wanted to go to their cabin for tools and food. He said that they would camp one night and then go away. The boy returned to the Indians and talked to them. The Indians agreed that the three white men could remain "one sleep" and then must go. But about 25 or thirty Indians left one by one until only about four or five remained. At about 4:00 or 5:00 p.m., the Indians made a fire and cooked food. After eating, the other Indians left.

The following day the three men returned to Moab. They had a small wagon in which they then went from Moab to Rico, Colorado. About two weeks after the three had left for Rico, the same band of Indians moved to Pack Creek. (They seem to be the group who shot Joe Wilson.) Then they moved over to the Blue Mountains but returned the next year following some trouble they'd had in the Dolores country.

This band camped near Dodge Springs in 1881. It is thought that they were about forty in number (besides squaws, babies and children, and old men who were to look after the extra ponies and goats). They left the main body of Utes and Piutes and struck out on a foraging trip to the Big Bend of the Dolores River and to Mancos, Colorado. Here they gathered up some of the settlers' horses and started for their camp near the Blue Mountains. Near the Big Bend of the Dolores, they killed Dick May. Conflicting accounts give the date of the killing as May 1 or May 10, 1881.

Although one account indicates that Dick May and his brother Billy saw the Indians with what they presumed to be some of their horses, and that Dick May was shot by the Indians while he tried to cut out the May horses, the consensus indicates another method by which he was killed. The first reconstruction has it that Billy heard a shot and saw his brother fall from his horse, but since Billy was unarmed he fled hastily, driving all but two of the horses. He then galloped home

---

[1] This will later be referred to in the *Dolores News* account.

and told a neighbor about the death of his brother and the two of them circulated news of the tragedy.

In other versions, there seems to be agreement that the trouble began at Burnt Cabin Springs about a week before the Pinhook battle. There is also considerable agreement in the events leading up to and following the killing of Dick May and John Thurman. Frank Silvey, in his account (others are in close agreement), indicates that Dick May and John Thurman were partners and met their deaths on Cedar Point at the hands of the Indians while trying to cut out their horses which the Utes had stolen. Silvey, in another account, states that Thurman was foreman of the J. H. Alderson ranch, since called the Burnt Cabins, and that he was riding with May and a man by the name of Bryon (or Byron) Smith when an Indian felled May as they were rounding up horses which had been sold to Thurman. First reports have it that Smith had been killed, too, although searchers did not find his body.

News of what had happened spread when the bodies of May and Thurman were found. Mancos people were notified, as were the people of Rico and Disappointment Valley. A number of Dolores and Mancos settlers had missed horses which they felt certain the Indians had taken. But the country was isolated and population so sparse that it was slow work to gather enough men to cope with a large number of Indians, to follow them and avenge the killing of Dick May, as well as repossess the stolen horses. It took at least two days to gather the posse. A rather full account is given by Frank Silvey[2] and by Joseph Burkholder in a personal interview with the author. In any case, the Indians knew the country well and would be certain to have the best of any fight. The country into which the whites were pursuing the Indians was unknown to many of the posse.

Captain W. H. Dawson of Disappointment Valley was leader of the company with Billy May as his aide. About sixty men responded to the call to follow the Indians. The group divided, Billy May acting as captain of the Durango, Mancos, Rico, and Dolores River boys; Dawson was to lead the others. Dawson and his men left a little ahead of the others and began following the Indian trail leading northwest toward the Blue and La Sal mountains. Dawson and his group were the only men who participated in the battle which followed. May and his men were looking for a trail off the rim of the Little Castle Valley to find a route to head off the Indians, and arrived too late to help Dawson and his men.

---

[2]"The Pinhook Indian Battle. Jordan Bean Sole Survivor of Battle on Northwest Side of La Sal Mountains, Found Living at Bridger Montana," Moab *Times-Independent*, September 5, 1940; and "Last Survivor Recounts Pinhook Indian Fight," Moab *Times-Independent*, September 6, 1940.

Near Cahone the posse found the body of Dave Willis, a pioneer rancher of Mancos who had been out hunting horses. From the evidence, the Indians had killed him. The posse buried the body near by. Going to Piute Springs (Monticello), they found the body of an unknown prospector who had been killed in a small cabin near the spring. The body was buried about 150 yards east of the spring.

When the Indians arrived at the Vega, they needed fresh horses and so they stole some from Spud Hudson and others, then went on to their camp at Dodge Springs. They evidently were aware that the men in the posse would soon be on their trail, for they broke camp immediately, taking all the stock with them. They steered toward the south and west of the Blue Mountains, to that country uncharted by whites and so well known to the Utes and Piutes.

As a result of disappearing horses, a posse of Blue Mountain men, headed by Spud Hudson, began to follow the renegade Utes before Captain Dawson crossed the Colorado state line. According to Frank Silvey, and supported by the William Green Robinson family records, the Utah party consisted of John B. Brown, Dudley Reece, Green Robinson, a Mr. Peters, Hudson, and others whose names aren't known. There were only about a dozen in the posse. They trailed the horses to Dodge Springs and found the Indian camp deserted, but they saw tracks leading westward. Knowing the Indians had a force of forty or fifty, the members of the posse felt it unwise to follow the Indians. They therefore returned to the Double Cabins and scoured the country for reinforcements. In a couple of days they had about 25 men, chiefly cowboys, with a few prospectors, ranchers, and ranch hands.

Following the Piute trail which led westward, the Blue Mountain posse reached the south side of the Blue Mountains where the trail suddenly turned north toward Indian Creek, thence up Hart Draw Canyon (north and west of Indian Creek) to Hatch Ranch (not named at that time). The Piutes had their goats with them, making their progress slow, and the cowboys gained steadily. Despite this, they were still about four days behind the Indians; thus it would be a long chase unless the Indians made a stand to fight along this route. Many old-timers familiar with this route have wondered why the Indians did not make a stand and fight, for there were many places along the route where it would have been easy to set a trap for the pursuers and wipe them out. One may only conjecture that the Indians either did not believe the whites would follow them beyond the rimrocks of the west side of the Blue Mountains, or that the posse would overtake them and be led into an ambush.

Although Indian signs soon became fresher and the cowboys found a played-out Indian pony and a couple of goats, leading them to believe they might soon overtake the Indians, the cowboys were by then out of food but still determined to follow the band of desperate Indians who had left a trail of blood from the Dolores River to the Blue Mountains. The trail indicated that they had turned back to the La Sal Mountains.

Meanwhile the posses under Dawson and May were also pursuing the Indians, the latter a day behind the former.

In an effort to intercept the Indians, the Dawson posse cut across the country by way of Three-Step Hill into Lisbon Valley, up the valley to Big Indian, and on the head of Pack Creek. (See Figure 9.1 for points of interest as the story of the battle unfolds. Circled numbers on the map will be explained as the action occurs and reference points are needed. Positions of events must be estimated, since existing roads and trails may not always follow the Indian and early trails. The route is shown from La Sal through La Sal Pass because some of the rescue parties, discussed subsequently, seem to have followed this route. Ervin Wilson also went from near Pack Creek site to Coyote, across Upper Cane Springs, west of South Mountain. It would seem that the Indians came by way of Indian Creek and Hart Draw to lead any pursuit into a trap. It would have been possible for them to wipe out an army of men in Hart Draw at the Wind Whistle Trail which came out of Hart Draw onto the Hatch Point country. Thus it would appear that the pursuit was farther behind than the Indians anticipated.)

The numbering of events and locations begins at Mule Shoe (1)[3] where events enter the map area. Mule Shoe is the location where the Indians and whites left the route they had been taking and watered their stock and themselves before beginning the climb into the mountain. Both camps were within a mile of each other. Dawson's posse, following the trail of the Indians, came out of Hatch Point country and camped at Mule Shoe. May's posse followed this same trail a day later.

At the Pack Creek site (2), the horse and goat tracks appeared to be fresher, and leg-weary Indian ponies were seen at regular intervals. The Indians were greatly hampered by their tiring ponies and a rather large herd of goats. Dawson's posse managed to capture some Indian squaws and some horses.

A stand was made at Squaw Springs (3) and an Indian squaw was killed. There is some fuzziness in accounts, but it appeared that the Indians moved to the little flat on Mill Creek where Shafer Creek comes in. Shafer Creek lies under Boren Mesa (4). There is a bench area which flattens out and makes a good camping ground. Evidently the Indians were surprised here, for this is the location about which Burkholder tells of the goats that were left behind by the Indians. There is

---

[3]Refer to the figure and its legend, pp. 122–23.

also an account of the Indians having been pushed out of a camp in this location. The Indians could have used the good cover of trees along Shafer Creek, through the saddle into Mason Draw and down to Pinhook where the posse was caught in the crossfire of the first day's battle. The distance given fits better than the route around by the Wilson camp (10) at Gardner Spring. The Indians would have been more exposed to observation and attack on this lower route. Further, the Colorado men would not have recognized this as a possible flanking move to be covered in their retreat on the second day. It was in the brief exposure on Wilcox Flat (9) that the posse killed at least seven Indians, from the Bald Mesa (8) overlook.

Prior to this encounter, Billy May and his men from Dolores and Rico, numbering about sixty, overtook Captain Dawson and his men near the head of Mill Creek, but for some unknown reason May's posse did not join that of Dawson. Instead they trailed along a short distance behind. Many were surprised, for it had been May's brother who was killed and he was expected to take the lead with his men. Dawson and his son and party, however, decided to go on at any cost to accomplish what they had set out to do, which was to seek revenge for the killing of three white men, and to recover the stolen horses.

The Indian trail was so fresh that Dawson decided to detail four men to scout ahead some distance to protect the main body of men. This was done across Wilson Mesa and for some distance down a hill heading to a prong of Little Castle Valley.

The scouting party of four men, after nearly reaching the bottom of the long hill leading to the valley, saw an arroyo or gulch about half a mile ahead of them. Just beyond was a low hill covered with a growth of scrub oak and large and small boulders. Looking at this point intently for a few minutes, they saw, or imagined they saw, a red blanket flit for an instant then disappear behind a rock. They also positively saw an Indian pony moving about among the brush. Although they were not certain that the Indians were setting up an ambush, they thought it good wisdom to report at once to Captain Dawson.

After brief consultation with his men, Dawson decided to send a part of his small force ahead a short distance on the trail to investigate, with instructions to fall back to the main body if they were fired upon. He called for fifteen volunteers to carry out the dangerous task, and twenty men promptly stepped forward. Captain Dawson chose fifteen, telling them to be careful and to remember that if they were fired upon, the others would be close behind. They were instructed under such conditions to return to the main group as quickly as possible, or to seek the nearest shelter of rocks and brush.

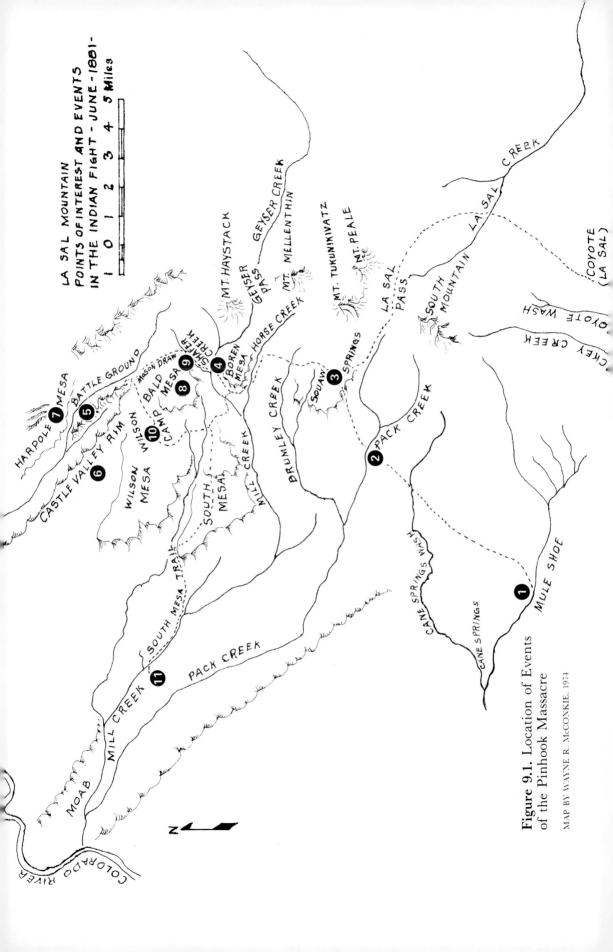

LA SAL MOUNTAIN
POINTS OF INTEREST AND EVENTS
IN THE INDIAN FIGHT - JUNE - 1881-

1 0 1 2 3 4 5 Miles

Figure 9.1. Location of Events of the Pinhook Massacre

MAP BY WAYNE R. McCONKIE. 1974

Legend for Figure 9.1:

1 Mule Shoe, where the Indians and whites left the route and watered before starting the climb into the mountain, and both camps were within a mile of each other.

2 The Pack Creek site where squaws and horses were taken.

3 Where the stand was made at Squaw Springs and the Indian squaw was killed. Though accounts are contradictory, it seems the Indians moved to the little flat on Mill Creek where Shafer Creek enters it. Here Burkholder tells of the goats, and here the Indians told of being pushed out of camp. They could have used the tree cover along Shafer, through the saddle to Mason Draw and down to Pinhook. Distance given fits the time element better than the route via the Wilson camp at Gardner Spring, the Indians being more exposed to observation and attack on this lower route. Also, the Coloradans wouldn't have recognized this as a possible flanking move to be covered in their retreat on the second day. In the brief exposure on Wilcox Flat, they killed at least seven Indians, from the Bald Mesa overlook.

4 Boren (Bo-reen') Mesa above Shafer Creek. Near mouth of creek is a bench area that flattens out, making a good campground. Indians had apparently camped there and were surprised by posse who pushed Indians out of their camp. The posse killed at least seven Indians from the Bald Mesa overlook.

5 Location where most of the whites were killed. The Indians were on Porcupine Ridge and in oak brush and on Castle Creek (Pinhook Draw), under Harpole Mesa.

6 Where May was supposed to be trying to get over the Castle Valley Rim, a move that will always be difficult to explain.

7 On second day of battle, the posse found itself trapped between Indians on Porcupine Ridge and those in oak brush and Castle Creek or Pinhook Draw under Harpole Mesa. (Site of present monument.)

8 Small grove of aspen on Bald Mesa where the whites made their stand after retreating from the battleground. Silvey and others hold that Indians shooting from Harpole Mesa were trying to divert attention from nearby Indians under Harpole Mesa. These were giving the posse trouble until it was realized that the Indians were in the aspen and the whites eliminated this group. Distance from Harpole to area where the men were killed was too far away to shoot effectively.

9 Wilcox Flat area where seven dead Indians were found. Events of the second day must have been discouraging to the Indians or they'd not have given up their stolen horses as easily as they did.

10 Location of the Wilson camp where Burkholder found the strange gun. The Wilson boys could have been working their cattle here or from a camp in Castle Valley. In any event, they must have wandered unaware into the Indian position.

11 Site where Boren saw the Indians by his ranch. One part of the Moab group followed them over the South Mesa.

Slowly and carefully the fifteen men advanced to within about forty yards of the gulch. This was the area which became known as "the battleground" (5). Suddenly the Indians, who had been concealed in the rocks and brush on the hillside, poured a murderous volley of shots into the advance guard. Four men fell dead instantly. Immediately the others looked for a place of shelter. Realizing that they must cross about 150 yards of open ground to reach their comrades following behind them, and seeing the gulch only a few yards ahead, they made a dash ahead and reached the gulch in safety. But here they learned that they had made a serious mistake, for the Indians crawled through the brush and rocks above them and poured in an effective crossfire upon them. They could not return the fire to advantage because they were unable to see the Indians except for a fleeting glance of a hand or gun. This trap, in which they obviously found themselves, was between Indians on Porcupine Ridge and those in the oak brush and Castle Creek or Pinhook Draw under Harpole Mesa (7).

After about an hour of fighting, six more of Dawson's men were killed in this trap. The remaining five crawled to a cave or a hole in the gulch where the Indians could not see them. This was the second day of the battle and the Indians had evidently gone up Mason Draw (9) to Bald Mesa (8). The Indians must have been hidden all through the brush and on top of the mesa. The brush was short and choppy (near the site of the present monument) and provided excellent cover for the Indians.

By now Dawson's main body of men had come to within about two hundred yards of the gulch. They had seen the four men fall from the bullets of the Indians and the remainder run for the shelter of the gulch, but they were powerless to help, for the Indians were sending a rain of bullets, compelling them to hastily seek scanty shelter among the small boulders and scrub oak. Here the patter of bullets was virtually incessant. Jim Hall of Rico was wounded in the leg at the beginning of the battle and suffered much pain and loss of blood. Jordan Bean had received a serious head wound in the first volley and lay senseless in the sun. There was no water available, and the sun beat down with merciless intensity.

The Indians seemed to have ample ammunition and were better armed than the posse, nearly all of them having .44 Winchesters. The posse had a hodgepodge of old buffalo guns, Sharpes rifles, and a few Winchesters, old-fashioned black powder guns with short range; thus the slow velocity of the bullets precluded accuracy in distance shooting. Because the Indians were concealed a greater part of the time, damaging shots were difficult.

One Indian, thought to be a chief, exposed himself almost derisively by climbing onto a huge boulder. The members of the posse could hear his voice, no doubt shouting instructions to the other Indians about how to go about getting a shot without taking chances themselves. Many of the posse fired at this man, but the slow-moving bullets fell short and he escaped unharmed.

At this stage of the battle, the whites heard several shots in quick succession a short distance down the valley. The next day the bodies of two men, apparently unarmed, were found riddled by bullets. After a time they were identified as the Wilson brothers, Alfred and Isadore, of Moab, who had camped on Castle Creek (10) and had come to investigate the shooting. They could have been working their cattle from here or from a camp in Castle Valley. In any event they must have wandered unaware into the Indian position and thus became casualties of the battle. It was at this camp that Burkholder later found a strange gun.

Captain Dawson and his men wondered why Billy May and his sixty men did not come to their aid, knowing that with a small force of men they could not hope to make a flanking movement on the Indians to try a rescue of the boys in the gulch. Number 6 on the map indicates the area where May was supposed to be trying to get over the Castle Valley Rim, according to his statement. This is a move that will always be difficult to explain. Dawson, not knowing that the greater number of his men in the gulch had already been killed, and wanting to help them at any cost, knew something must be done. So far it had been every man for himself, hunting the best place possible for shelter against the bullets of the Indians. Dawson and his men decided to send a volunteer runner to make a dash for the gulch. His task would be to persuade those hiding there to make a run for the main body of men to escape the lethal trap.

Pat McKinney, a fast footman, volunteered to perform this dangerous mission. Stripping to his underwear and socks, hatless, he crept forward through the brush and boulders as far as possible, then stood suddenly erect and made a dash for the gulch where the remainder of the advance guard was crouched.[4] The Indians saw him at once as he streaked across the open space, and a hail of bullets cut the dust round him. Fortunately, he managed to reach his destination unhurt. When he learned that eight of the fifteen had been killed and three wounded, he thought it best they all remain where they were until

---

[4]The author visited the battleground area with Wayne R. McConkie, who has spent many years walking over the terrain of this vicinity, and both agree that one cannot buy the story that someone ran any distance in his socks. Cowboy boots were hard to walk in, to say nothing of running, but it would appear that *no one* ever ran unshod on *those* rocks. It would be a painful experience to walk carefully in that situation, for one's bare feet would be torn to shreds.

darkness of night would allow their escape. This they did, and quietly escaped under cover of darkness.

Meanwhile, Captain Dawson had sent one of his riders, mounted on the swiftest horse they had, to Rico for reinforcements.[5] He recognized that even May's men, when they should arrive, might not be sufficient to cope with the Indians. He and his men waited anxiously for some sign of Pat McKinney and the trapped men, but saw nothing. The Indians kept up a fire on the whites at intervals, hoping to get in a killing shot, since the whites had little cover.

At twilight a cloud of dust up the trail announced the arrival of Billy May and his men. May explained that they had not arrived sooner because they had thought they could find another trail off the mesa and cut ahead of the Indians, thus surprising them. After riding many miles along the rim of Little Castle Valley (6), they found no trail off the rim, and were forced to turn back. One can imagine the anger and disappointment of the men who had seen their comrades slain and had themselves been in grave danger, knowing that the added force might have enabled them to rout the Indians.

Darkness fell, and in a short time Pat McKinney and the remainder of the advance guard joined the main body of men. Since all must have water and something to eat, they carefully gathered up the wounded, retiring two miles southeast to a large spring where they spent the night. At daybreak, they were all in the saddle, with the exception of two men who were left to care for the wounded.

The Hudson group reached the battleground a day too late, as did seventy men who came from Rico in response to the courier who had been sent for reinforcements. By the time they reached the site, the Indians had taken their best horses and vanished. The Indians left two of their dead on the battlefield, but the trail showed a number had been wounded.

Bean, in his account to Frank Silvey, stated[6]:

> One man has never been given credit in any article I ever saw (except by myself), and I want him and the other eighteen boys he brought with him recognized, as they should be. The first day of the fight, June 15, 1881, a Mormon by the name of Walt Moore of Moab, a big man in body, heart, and principle, heard the shooting and gathered up eighteen men, and came to us or no man would have come to be there. They came up with Moore. The Mormons were herding cattle on the side of the La Sal Mountains. No one knew the Wilson boys were there until their bodies were found.

---

[5]This is verified in the later citation from the *Dolores News.*
[6]Moab *Times-Independent*, September 26, 1940.

Bean's account, however, does not exactly coincide with others' remembrance of the battle, for other evidence indicates that the Wilson boys were killed prior to, or early in the period of, the battle.

Joseph Burkholder adds another segment of the story, which is supported by Frank Silvey[7] who relates that Burkholder, Walt Moore, and about fifteen others from Moab were camped at the east side of Wilson Mesa at about dark on the day of the battle. They learned what had happened and gave every possible aid to the wounded; doubtless had they known the Indians were about to massacre the whites, they would have volunteered to aid the Coloradans. Knowing the territory as they did, they would have warned the men under Dawson not to be led into the trap under Bald Mesa (8).

Burkholder, after referring to the killing of Dick May and "Sherman" (i.e., Thurman) by the Indians, in which he said the Indians took about $2,000 which Thurman had paid May for horses, said that the Indians came over to the La Sal Mountains and camped overnight. He told of the posse from Colorado who came down to the Blue Mountains after the Indians. What follows now, until otherwise indicated, is Burkholder's story as related in an interview.

Al Geyser was on the La Sal Mountains with a herd of cattle. He came down to Moab to Burkholder's camp that night and told him of the trouble with the Indians and said that the Colorado party was to come to Pack Creek that night. The Indians had moved farther into the mountains. Geyser wanted help to get the Indians out, and nine men agreed to go with them. Moab at the time was yet a small community. Doubtless they were aware that given the element of surprise and disposition, the Indians could have wiped out the settlement of Moab. Therefore these men went round from one camp to another collecting men, guns, and ammunition. Thus they were rather late in getting started. Boren came down from his ranch and said he had seen two Indians north of his place (11), which was five miles east of town, toward Mill Creek. Thus the posse from Moab thought it best to investigate this before leaving. The party divided, some going up Mill Creek and some through the hills. Only two of the Indians were found, and they had gone up the trail to the South Mesa. This was the first the white party knew of this trail.

THE COLORADO PARTY took the Squaw Springs trail, encountering the Indians at Horse Creek Fork. There was a running fight from the fork down to Castle Valley. Burkholder and the others did not arrive until late. When they got to the point where Shafer Creek runs into Mill

---

[7]Frank Silvey notes, Utah State Historical Society, Salt Lake City.

Creek, they camped overnight. It was just sundown when they arrived. They could see smoke and a camp where Shafer Creek empties into Mill Creek, but they disagreed as to whether it was whites or Indians. One man had field glasses and he looked down toward the camp. But the camp was in a hole, so he saw little. After dark, two of the party went down the creek to make sure it was Indians. When they crossed the creek they ran into a herd of goats and decided it must be the Indians since the Colorado party would not be apt to have these animals. It was later discovered that the Indians had left the goats when they had been attacked.

Burkholder knew the Wilson boys (Alfred and Isadore) camped at their corral and wanted to go there for something to eat. The party went down to the Wilson camp (10) but found no one there. They did find an old musket (the muzzle-loading type). They were mystified because they knew it did not belong to the Wilson boys who had been driving their cattle away from poisonous weeds when they were attacked by Indians.

Just as Burkholder's party was leaving the camp, they looked back and saw a party leaving the camp on the other side of the creek. Burkholder proposed waiting. It turned out to be a party of white men — the Colorado party — who related the previous day's events, saying that during the battle, eight [ten (author)] of their party had been killed and two [three] wounded (in addition to the two Wilson boys who had been killed). The two parties went to the Wilson camp for breakfast, then scattered, looking for the dead and wounded men.

The first body to be found was opposite the point where the old trail goes up and over Harpole Mesa (7). They were out in the flat about 150 to two hundred yards. The men dismounted and collected round the body when Indians opened fire on them. One horse was killed, but none of the party was hit, the bullets going over their heads. It turned out that the Indians had taken the guns of the men they had killed and, since these guns were bigger and heavier than those they (the Indians) were accustomed to using, they had difficulty in hitting their targets. The Indians were evidently shooting from the top of Harpole Mesa. Silvey and others hold that the Indians shooting from Harpole Mesa were trying to divert attention from nearby Indians under the mesa. These were giving the posse a lot of trouble until the posse caught on and eliminated this group of Indians. The distance from Harpole to the area where the men were killed was a long way to be doing any effective shooting.

The posse climbed upon their horses and retreated from the line of fire at the battleground. The Indians followed, and the whites attained a bluff opposite Pinhook Draw on Bald Mesa (8), where there was a small grove of aspen. When they got there, an old squaw who had been left behind or had dropped out of the band came through the brush. The Colorado men shot and killed her. This, said Burkholder, was the only spot on the record of the posse.

The white men held a council. The Colorado party said they had two wounded men in camp and were anxious to return to get these men out. They started back, getting only as far as just above the ditch where it winds across Bald Mesa. Suddenly there were Indians all around them. These must have been the Indians below Harpole Mesa which their brothers sought to protect in their shooting from the Mesa. The posse, which had taken refuge in the clump of aspens, stood the Indians off for a couple of hours. Then the party divided and six or eight men ventured from the aspen grove to look over a ridge where they could see down upon the flat. There was considerable shooting again, but after another couple of hours the Indians left. It was learned that they had gone through Fisher Valley to Dolores and back to the reservation. After the battle was over, a government party came in and found seven dead Indians at Wilcox Flat (9). The events of the second day must have been discouraging to the Indians or they would not have given up their stolen horses as easily as they did.

A contemporary account is given by A. M. Rogers in an article titled "A True Narrative of an Indian Fight" wherein he says[8]:

> In the summer of 1880, two stockmen, Joshua Alderson and John Thurman, brought a band of 1,500 head of horses from Oregon and Nevada, and located on the public domain in the vicinity of Ute Springs, on the border of Utah and Colorado [western border of Colorado on the Ute Indian Reservation]. They built a cabin on the Ute side of the line. They were unmolested during the winter.

> *May 1881:* Dick May and Barnes Smith visited Thurman to buy saddle horses. He carried about $1,200 on his person.... About three or four days after May's departure from home, a Navajo, called Little Captain, rode in to May's ranch, at Dolores, and informed May's brothers, George and Billy, that Dick and Thurman had been killed by Indians. A crowd was hastily called to go to the scene of the murder. May was found lying across the threshold of the cabin with two bullet holes in his body; a double-barreled shot gun, with two empty shells, lying across his lower limbs. The cabin was burnt. Thurman's body was found about

[8]"Echo," *op. cit.*, April 1912, pp. 38–48. According to the account in the *Dolores News*, Rogers was not a member of the original posse caught in the massacre, but his name is listed among those who made up the followup posse. Dan Winbourn, with whom Rogers resided many years, confirmed that Rogers was not in the original posse.

a half mile from the cabin, pierced with several bullets. There was no evidence of Smith.

Rogers felt a responsibility to clarify the stories as to what had happened to Smith as he stated:

> About four years later Smith was seen and recognized by two reliable men, who knew him well, in a penitentiary at Santa Fe — for stage robbery. He told of hair breadth escape from suffering, but his story was mixed. Probably the Indian side of the story is more reliable.

Then follows a somewhat dramatic and detailed account of events as they occurred. The account resembles in many details those given previously, but from the pen of one who was very close to the story from the beginning, it adds color. The following quotation begins with formation of the posse and their progress:

> ...Volunteers from Dolores and Mancos and Rico (65) started in pursuit of the Indians. The trail was easily followed as they [Indians] had stolen several hundred horses of Thurman and partner. The trail led across the country to the south end of the Blue Mountains, now part of La Sal Forest, via Verdure, across Johnson Creek, up that stream and across the mountains into the head of the Cottonwood and down to Indian Creek, where they joined a large party of Utes, mostly Uncompahgres, but a few southern Utes among them. They had been wintering a large herd of goats and ponies in Indian Creek Valley....This party, some 180 bucks, squaws and a few papooses, broke camp and drifted northward, taking their ponies, goats and stolen horses with them. At Hatch Wash [then Hudson's range], six pursuers got beef and four left, but Green Robinson and John Brown [who married Thomas Ray's daughter Fannie] of Moab, procured a supply of meat and hastened back. They were misdirected by Ron Hatch, took a cut-off and entirely missed the party.

Thus Rogers indicates that the party divided but that the main division of the posse followed the Indian trail as indicated in earlier versions.

> The main party, now 59, followed the Indians on, and at Mule Shoe Bend found the Indians had been down to Cane Springs for water and had doubled back on the trail and were camped on the mesa within about one mile ahead of them. Volunteers went down to Cane Springs and watered the stock, filled the canteens and returned to the foot of the hill, where the Indians were camped on top....That night, June 12, 1881, was clear and beautiful but there was a total eclipse of the moon. Two whites reconnoitered the Indian camp and demanded surrender of the

130

murderers, counting on the superstition of the Indians to cause them to give up. A majority opposed the idea, urging cause for fight.

Rogers then presents a dramatic and moving account of how Dawson issued the clarion call to arms and the response of his men to their sense of duty and revenge.

> Next morning, June 13, Capt. Billy Dawson gave the command, "Boys, strike for your country and your homes." Twenty-two whites mounted. The command, now 37, followed the retreating cavalcade of Indians across the mesa to the place where the Upper Ranch on Pack Creek is now located ["Old Barbor Ranch"]. The Indians bivouacked among the fire killed piñons and cedars...hunters camped on the hill to southward a short mile away. Scouts reconnoitered and located the horse and goat herds guarded by squaws. That night there was a bright comet in the northern sky. The scouts again counseled demanding the guilty Indians, stolen horses, and heavy tribute — but the fighters rejected....About the time the morning star appeared above the majestic peak, the whites descended on the squaws and captured nine and took about 1,800 head of horses, some domestic and some Ute....Captain Billy Dawson injudiciously selected an unlucky thirteen to guard the captured stock and squaws. The Indian squaws tricked the guards, stampeded the horses and struck out for the scrub timber. The discomfitted heroes saddled and wound their way to Moab, some eighteen miles away. The fleeing Indians struck out via Squaw Springs trail. Twenty-four men started in pursuit. At Squaw Springs a few made a stand and fired several shots, but one Indian was killed....The Indians fled, the whites followed until the party reached a dell where the foe was forced to make a stand owing to the riding stock being unable to go further. The whites stopped. Then the real Indian fighting began. It was like corn popping at the head of Little Castle Valley on the west side of the Sierra La Sals.

Although Rogers writes descriptively of the country and in detail about actions not described otherwise, one has a feeling that he is looking on as an observer.

> ...Dave Willis was the first man to fall. Jordan Bean was hit in the head, but ultimately recovered. Harg Eskridge got a bullet in his ankle, Jim Hall in the calf of his leg. Capt. Billy Dawson, Tim Jenkins, Dick Baumgartner, Tom Click, Hiram Melvin, Jimmy Heaton, Hard Tartar, Wiley Tartar, Jack Galloway, and Rogers found themselves close herded in a shallow arroyo where the Indians were too numerous and hostile for comfort or safety. Dawson, Jenkins, and Baumgartner had their horses with them

131

and succeeded in making an honorable retreat. Others all dismounted and the Indians had killed or captured the stock.

Rogers says that he tried to sneak out and managed to do so under fire. The other men followed the arroyo about a half mile into a cul-de-sac from which they could not escape and where they sold their lives as dearly as possible. He says that he hid in some scrub oak where he was taunted by the Indians to come out and fight. He finally did so and killed an Indian, taking a money belt with $16 in it.

According to his account, about 3:00 p.m., the firing ceased. At about 5:00 p.m. he ventured out to seek water, but saw Utes near. All that night, next day, and until the afternoon of June 16, he lay squeezed in between two large boulders. Indians were still hiding all around.

Sometime after noon of the third day, his comrades returned from Moab and found the dead bodies. They found Jordan Bean wounded and Marion Cook hiding. Also missing was George Taylor. His remains were later found and buried.

Rogers further reported that the posse captured about sixteen hundred head of horses. Four companies of the Ninth U.S. Cavalry came and followed the Indians back to their reservation, and the Rico volunteers returned home.

He expresses himself as feeling the campaign was "senseless, foolhardy, and reckless." They were told by the Indians that they felt remorse because later the Great Spirit had darkened the moon and burned up a star and they therefore had no more heart to fight, but hot blood demanded a fight. Rogers talked with an Indian who told him that Smith had told the Indians that the white men were going to take the reservation away and the only way to prevent this was to kill the white men. The Indian said that Smith took the money and four horses and went south.

Rogers' account sounds authentic, yet there is the controversial listing of his name as among the followup posse, and his statement to Dan Winbourn that he had not participated in the original posse fight but stated he was wounded. As a journalist and a member of the group who found the battleground and went over it and heard accounts by those who had participated, he possibly felt that it was significant to preserve the account and thus joined fact with fiction to point out his feelings about the foolhardiness of the campaign.

WILSON ROCKWELL, in his "Monument Creek Killings,"[9] gives a version of the events which contains a few variations from the others given. He

[9]Wilson Rockwell, *The Utes: A Forgotten People* (Denver: Sage Books, 1956), pp. 220–24.

states that in the spring of 1881, John Thurman was pasturing a large herd of horses on a ranch which he and Dave Willis owned near Monument Creek, a half-mile east of the Utah border in present Montezuma County. One day he (Thurman) discovered several Indians trying to catch some saddle horses and gave them a beating. The Utes left in a very angry mood. Willis was on his way to Chama, New Mexico, at the end of the railroad, to get his family who had been visiting in the east at the time of this encounter.

Dick May, who had a ranch near the present town of McPhee, started for Thurman's to buy some unbroken horses at about $50 per head. He had between $600 and $1,000 in bills on his person. He was accompanied by a visitor, not well known in the region, Bryon Smith. At about 11:00 a.m., May and Smith met Erastus Thomas, Henry Goodman, the Quick brothers, and some other cowboys who were gathering cattle near the head of Yellow Jacket Canyon. Goodman told May and Smith that they had passed some Utes who were angry about something. They advised May and Smith to turn back, but the men insisted they would go on.

Pat and Mike O'Donnel had a camp at Willow Springs near Thurman's cabin, and on the following morning, May 1 (some accounts say May 10), 1881, one of the employees, sent to borrow some baking powder, saw a grisly sight: The cabin was burned to the ground, and there were two dead horses lying in front of the ruins. The body of Dick May, burned nearly beyond recognition, was found among the ashes. Some fifteen hundred to two thousand pounds of oats, left stored in the cabin for winter horse feed, had fallen over the dead man's body during the fire, preventing it from being cremated. There was a pocketbook on him, but the bills had been either destroyed or stolen. Some silver money remained.

May had apparently been killed immediately after breakfast. A number of empty cartridges showed that a fight had taken place. Two horses had been killed. Neither Smith nor Thurman was in sight.

Soon a group of men was on its way to Big Bend (now Dolores) to report the killing. According to Rockwell, on May 3 a group from Big Bend and Mancos rode up to Thurman's burned cabin to investigate the tragedy. This indicates that Rockwell accepts the May 1 date, and the lapse in time would be the result of travel and gathering up a group of men to investigate.

Thurman's body was found on the fourth day three-quarters of a mile from the cabin. He had evidently set out to catch a horse when he had been killed because he was found with a plaited hackamore. Smith's body was never discovered. Some Indians later reported that he ran down into a deep canyon and was believed to have been shot.

When Dave Willis returned, he organized a posse from Big Bend and Mancos to follow the Utes. Bill Dawson, sheriff of Dolores County, and his posse from Rico joined Willis' posse and the group set out on the trail of the Indians. They followed the Utes to the south side of the Blue Mountains and onto the foothills of the La Sals. There they lost the trail. They scattered, but were able to pick it up farther on. It led to the north side of the La Sals where they overtook the Utes in a large, sandy, sagebrush wash.

When the shooting began, Davis Willis was shot off his horse early in the fight. Sheriff Dawson of Rico then took charge of both posses. About ten of his men jumped from their horses and crouched down in a sandy arroyo to escape flying bullets. Dawson, realizing that they were in a trap, sent Tim Jenkins, an old Indian fighter, to order them out. He weighed only 110 pounds, but was well versed in the ways of Indian warfare.

The men scattered in the arroyo a hundred yards or so, and Tim rode up and down the gulch while the Utes shot at him from the rocks on the rim. He explained to the cornered men that they were perfect targets and urged them to get out and join the rest of the posse before the Indians started to pick them off. However, they were paralyzed with fear, and no one dared to make a run for it.[10]

Finally, in order to save his own life, Jenkins left the doomed men to their fate. All were killed in the arroyo. In the battle Jordan Bean was shot in the head but not killed. He hid in oakbrush that night, and could hear the Utes beating the brush looking for him. He recovered sufficiently the next day to be taken home.

ONE FINAL VERSION of the events comes from a primary source which sets the tone and gives a feeling of the atmosphere of the time when these events took place, and also provides some background for possible causes or reasons that this tragic event occurred. The *Dolores News*, first published in 1879 in Rico, Colorado, gives an incisive account of the happenings surrounding the Pinhook "massacre." The quotations from this publication, cited in the following paragraphs, relate the events leading up to, during, and following the massacre. One fact stands out, supporting Al Rogers' position that the battle was the result of foolhardiness and man's insistence upon blood revenge. This thesis is also supported by editor David Day of *The Solid Muldoon*, the Ouray, Colorado, weekly newspaper of this period.

Beginning with the first issue, it is evident that the editor (and subsequently other editors) of the weekly *Dolores News* harbored a dislike

---

[10]This agrees with the account in the *Dolores News*.

for the Utes. For years, the newspaper carried either an editorial or a story (sometimes both) pointing out the "problems" with the Ute Indians, emphasizing unpleasant incidents and often overstating facts in an effort to gain advocacy for its position that the only solution was to drive all Indians from the state.

For example,[11] on October 14, 1879, there is a first-page report of an uprising of Utes (the Uncompahgre) and a warning by the governor for the people to be alert. The second page has an article, "White River Utes on Warpath," which tells of the massacre of Indian agent Meeker, his wife, their two daughters, and all of his assistants at the agency. Colonel Thornberg and thirteen soldiers were killed and thirty wounded; Los Piños and Uncompahgre Utes for three weeks had been setting fire to the country to the south and west.

On October 24, the *News* suggests in an editorial that "Indian chief Jack, who murdered the agent Father Meeker, should be hung or shot on sight, the ungrateful wretch." And on November 8, under the headline, "Soldiers in Juan," it says:

> The way to keep the horses in the stable safe from thieves is to keep the door locked. The way to keep the Indians from murdering white people is to remove them from off the reservations and out of Colorado, but, if they must stay in the state, surround them by a cordon of military with guns in their hands, and whenever they commit outrage let these guns do their duty.

What would be looked upon today as irresponsible journalism was accepted in pioneer days; moreover, it was encouraged! On the second page of the May 8, 1880, edition appears an item under the heading "Removal of Utes from Colorado" which is highly biased, listing all of the murders committed by Indians but with no mention of crimes against them committed by the whites.

Later issues[12] report that "it has been announced that Victorio has been killed and most of his band has been sent to the happy hunting ground. May the Utes follow the path of the Apaches." And in the following edition there are two articles berating A. B. Meacham, Indian agent who favored the Indians. The Utes were called liars and robbers.

Because of this constant harangue, feelings were intense against the Utes. When a serious incident occurred, the people were keyed for action. Thus is recorded the reports of the Dick May killing and the events that followed, as they appear in the newspaper[13]:

---

[11]*Dolores News*, October 14, 1879, vol. 1, no. 7.

[12]*Ibid.*, October 30 and December 11, 1880, vol. 2.

[13]*Ibid.*, May 28, 1881, p. 2; June 4, 1881, p. 3.

Billy May came in today and is trying to raise some men from the Mancos and other points, to go into the Blue Mountain country. He says that some men started to gather the cattle and were fired on by the Indians, who have congregated there; and were compelled to return. The Utes are driving off all the horses belonging to Hudson and other stockmen. The men who were in there counted over sixty of Thurman's and many of Dick May's horses, taken at the time of their owners' murders, were mainly in the hands of the Indians, who have many hundreds belonging to various others. If 75 men can be raised, Mr. May thinks the Utes will not make a fight except such as might be made from the brush. He says the Indians do not seem to feel at all alarmed, but do all their deviltry in open fearlessness. The settlers won't stand for it. We believe plenty of men can be raised here.

War on Mancos was predicted, and the following week, June 11, an article appeared under the subtitle "Indian Intelligence":

In our last issue we stated that Billy May was here and would try to raise a force of men to assist him and other settlers in securing their stock. The Indians have about five hundred head of horses which they have stolen from Alderson, Hudson, May, Johnston, Thurman, and others. The round-up party which was fired on near the Blue Mountains caught the Indians in the act of driving off Hudson's herd (about one hundred head). On Tuesday and Wednesday many of our boys started out for Big Bend to join with men from the Mancos, La Plata, and San Juan rivers and it is supposed that the concentrated forces from all sources will aggregate at least seventy-five men. The party from Rico numbered thirty-one and they are all stayers. They intended to start from Big Bend Thursday noon for Blue Mountains and vicinity and will rescue the property of the cattlemen at any cost. It is said by those who are personally acquainted with nearly all the men who are in the outfit that it is the best lot of men who ever started out for a purpose of this kind, having been on the frontier for many years and having had brushes with Indians before. We fear that the Indians will make a desperate fight for the stolen property, and while it is certain that the cowmen will get away with their baggage in the end, still that would be no recompense for the loss of but a single life from the ranks of the Rico boys. The party leaving Big Bend will be well mounted, provisioned, and armed with rifles and revolvers. They will be gone about three weeks in all probability. In the meantime, many companies of soldiers are being forwarded to the Indian country.

Two weeks later the *News* once again stirred emotions with the following account headlined in large letters: "War! with the Indians — Rico's

Boys Who Went to Recover the Property of Unprotected Settlers Have Met a Sad Fate," and datelined "Rico sends forth another bold little army — by special courier June 23, 2:00 p.m." (special editions appeared during this week)[14]:

> A special courier arrived here from the Grand River country last night and furnishes the facts embraced in the following: War has begun with the Indians in Grand River country, at last. The Rico party, who started out the first instant, were attacked on the morning of the 17th, in Grand Valley, about 140 miles distant from Rico.
>
> An attack was anticipated by both the whites and the Indians. The captain commanding our forces gave orders not to fire until after the Indians had discharged a volley, which command was obeyed. The Rico party was moving camp, as were the Indians also, and thus encounter was precipitated, resulting in the killing of our boys.
>
> When the fight began the whites, numbering 18, were in the advance, the Indians, some 40 or more in number, commenced fighting and then retreated, with an occasional volley into our forces who were in rapid pursuit. The Indians finally reached a rocky bluff, and used the massive rocks as breastworks, which gave to them a very great advantage over our boys. In fact was more than half of the battle for the victory of the Indians.
>
> The band is the same who has been committing the various murders and depredations in the vicinity of Big Bend, where May, Smith, and Thurman met their sad fate. Some of the stolen stock, together with arms and articles of clothing which belonged to the murdered men, were found upon the ground near where the Indians first opened fire and retreated from.
>
> The eighteen brave boys of Rico fought nobly, and compelled the copper-colored hell-hounds to leave behind them one hundred head of horses and a large number of sheep and goats. During the battle of two days, a white man and Mexican were seen with the Indians, apparently commanding different squads of Indians. On the second day the Mexican rode to the summit of a knoll, patted his Winchester and six-shooters and cried aloud, "Shoot you cowardly s--s of b-----s," and the boys fired but failed to get him.
>
> The eighteen were equally nerved, and the only difference between the front and rear was the difference in horse speed. On the first day, J. H. Eskridge, James Hall, and Dave Willis were almost surrounded by Indians, and instead of retreating, these three of the world's bravest men stepped in and fought hand to hand with more than ten times their number, killing several

---

[14]*Ibid.*, June 25, 1881, p. 1.

Indians. Here Willis was riddled with bullets; Eskridge, whom it is supposed the Indians believed to be captain (as he had a large, gaudy chihuahua hat), had the hat riddled with bullets so that it cannot be worn, and his hair was nearly all cut off with scalp wounds and grazing bullets. Hall was wounded in one knee, one shoulder, and the ribs of one side were seriously injured. Here the Indians retreated, and soon afterwards fired upon the boys again, wounding Eskridge in the ankle so seriously that amputation will be necessary if he lives until that aid can be rendered. He laughs most all of the time with his suffering, and when forebearance of pain ceases to be a virtue, he shrieks as loud as his lungs will permit and at last account wanted to fight. Hall bears his suffering bravely too. Both are unfit for battle. Eight of the eighteen were missing on the evening of the first day. Jordan Bean of the missing ones, alone, was found on the second day, shot through the head, but conscious and able to talk, saying that he did not know that one of the remaining seven was dead, but felt positive that they were *all* dead. The names of these are: Jack Galloway, H. H. Melvin, Tom Click, T. C. Taylor, the two Tartar brothers, and a young man unknown.

Some hopes were held that they have gone safely to the Old Mormon Fort in Grand Valley.

When D. G. Taylor started for Rico, the Indians had received reinforcements, and doubtless there are several hundred warriers at the field of the late battle ere this time.

The determined one hundred men who leave Rico today, will rescue the survivors of the first party and avenge the death of the departed or fall where they fell.

Mr. William May, who has the death of a brother to avenge, seems to have become displeased, and left the main party. It is not known by the courier where he is with his squad.

In a later account, the *News* datelines this story with "By Courier, June 24, 9:00 a.m.":

J. H. Lester, just in from the seat of trouble, says he is certain that the white party reached the old fort in Grand Valley, that he saw the same band of Indians on last Friday, that our first informant was wrong as to the day of the battle, that they fought on Wednesday and Thursday, and not on Friday and Saturday, that he well knows that several of the Indians were killed and wounded.

The July 2, 1881, edition carried the following on the second page, titled "Last Version of the Grand Valley Indian Battle":

The first day's fight began on a small creek, near Mill Creek, the Indians firing and retreating for a distance of seven miles, into Little Castle Valley, which is about eight hundred yards wide, walled in with steep bluffs on both sides. The Indians took shelter or protection in the rocks at noon, from where they kept up a continual firing for about an hour and a half, when they divided their forces, sending mounted, to the valley, sixteen Indians armed with Winchester rifles. Capt. W. H. Dawson had with him in his engagement, eighteen men, whom he says were brave without an exception. The party of eight which were killed, together with the Wilson brothers, were in the rear and were first seen by the Indians who were mounted and sent into the valley. Dawson with the remainder of the party, was further up the valley and nearer the Indians who were firing from the rocks. The killed, it is supposed, fought for about seven hours where they were killed. They had been engaged in the running fight from 10:00 a.m. and fought till sunset; several had been wounded before being killed; Jack Galloway had one hand neatly bound and tied with a handkerchief, when found.

On the next day a detachment was sent out in search of the killed and wounded, coming in conflict with the Indians again. Here the Indians would have prevented their finding the lost, and the party wisely retreated a distance of four miles, hotly pursued by the Indians, where the white party having a little advantage, killed several Indians.

It is estimated from all seen and known that eighteen Indians were killed. The white party fought in every conceivable manner, the Indians having a great advantage the first day. The mounted warriors would charge and a number of the footmen would sneak up nearer the whites and fire. The dead bodies were found on the fourth day (Sunday) and were so decomposed that it was almost impossible to bury them at all, but they were buried about where they fell. Five were buried in one grave and three in another.

To say that our friends were faultless, who have gone from us, would be untrue, for they were men. Who has not a fault? They were our friends and comrades. Mothers, sisters, fathers, and brothers, and bereaved wives and children, will weep for those who are no more. They are gone, and who will measure the time of their leave? They loved and were loved. The tender chords have been severed and cannot be forgotten, and when the news breaks the silence of their absence at home, reader, do you think tenderly, or do you realize that they are gone? The dear ones at home hoped that they might sometime return, but alas! they are now gone forever.

A printed account of the Indians' sorrow was of course never made. But by this time feelings were running high. The above article was followed with brief obituaries of the men who had been killed, and at the end an ode to them. Though probably not calculated to incite, it nevertheless would arouse the populace:

> Goodbye, brave boys, may your sleep be sweet,
>> Though the sickle of fate seems cruel,
> 'Tis truly the brave whose names are meet,
>> For gems in memories' jewels.
>
> Though the hearts of your friends are rent and riven,
>> Their grief is not mingled with shame —
> In the rightful cause each life was given,
>> In the line of the fearless each filed his name.
>
> With the lives of such, the way is paved,
>> The progression's ponderous wheel,
> For eyes unborn shall be engraved
>> The gratitude we feel.
>
> Each name shall be enwreathed with flowers
>> Such as may chance to grow,
> With the field in wakeful hours,
>> Where thoughts in leisure flow.

On the following Tuesday, the *News* printed an "extra," stating that "Henry W. Heaton, just in from the Big Bend, gives the following as obtained from a reliable source." No one knows the editor's reason for issuing an "extra," but most likely it was for this article:

Heaton started from Big Bend on the 27th, at noon, to meet an anxious father at Rico.... Willis Rogers had just arrived a few hours previous to Heaton's leaving Big Bend. Rogers had gone with Mr. Bean who was going out to bring in the wounded, when they met the survivors of the first Rico party, who told Rogers they had buried the two Tartar brothers of Rico; the two Wilson brothers, ranchmen on the Mancos; H[iram]. H. Melvin, of Rico, lately of the Big Bend; John Galloway, of Rico; Tom Click, of the Dolores; Dave Willis, Mancos; and James A. Heaton, brother of Mr. Heaton who brings the news; making nine buried. Dave Willis was killed from the Eskridge-Hall party, of which W. H. Dawson was captain. The eight who were reported missing were the Tartar brothers, Galloway, Click, Melvin, Heaton, Bean, and [T. C.] Taylor. The Wilson brothers who heard the shooting from their cabin, went to the aid of the party and were killed, together with all, except Jordan Bean and T. C. Taylor. Jordan Bean escaped with a scalp wound, and as stated above, Taylor is still missing, his fate unknown.... The remainder of the Rico party are expected to reach Big Bend tonight, on their return.... It is stated that the eight unfortunate brave men were found lying close together, that a thirty-foot rope would have reached across the spot where they were found.

The Colorado residents now knew that the men who had set out to do battle with the renegade Indians had at least succeeded in engaging in a bloody fight, but returns were still coming in, and on July 9 the *Dolores News* carried the following:

> The last of the outfit who left Rico on the 22nd... to go to the seat of the trouble with the Indians, returned yesterday, and some of the Rico men are now in the Indian country.... When Taylor arrived at Rico on the afternoon of the 21st of June, bringing the intelligence that an attack had been made by the Indians on Little Castle Valley and that some of the Rico boys had been wounded, and several others. were missing, no time was lost in sending reinforcements to them. Taylor's account had left the impression that the survivors were trying to reach Grand Valley with the wounded and that it was the purpose of the Indians to cut them off from escape.... [T]here were about forty men, well armed and mounted, who turned their horses' heads to the west, and started for the scene of the disastrous battle. All of that party realized what a forlorn hope was theirs... but... while there was the semblance of a chance that they could render help [to those who had been in the battle], they were not men to hesitate. Some of the party reached [the] Big Bend of the Dolores that night and early in the morning were overtaken by a portion of the remainder, and feeling that no longer delay could be sustained, they started out. On reaching Cross Canyons the necessity of organization became apparent, and drawing up into a line at the springs, Worden Grigsby was unanimously chosen as captain. At Piute Springs the names of the outfit were enrolled and showed up twenty-six strong, being in name as follows: L. Alderman, Al Bradley, John Carey, John Clark, Thomas Carroll, Pat Cain, W. M. Eccles, Dyson Eskridge, S. C. Grant, Worden Grigsby, Gus Hefferman, William Huntley, Yours Truly [the editor, probably Charles A. Jones], W. H. Lilley, Mike Murphy, D. McIntyre, S. W. McCormack, Sam McCreary, H. Phillipi, J. Phillipi, George Perkins, A. M. Rogers, John Silvey, Frank Summers, "Kid" Thomas, D. G. Taylor.
>
> At this point Messrs Carroll and McIntyre were compelled to return, their horses becoming lame and footsore. The remaining

twenty-four reached Coyote [140 miles from Rico] in two days and
a half, arriving there at 11:00 o'clock at night. It was the intention
to keep right on to Grand Valley that night unless some news was
heard. Here we found Bob Brown and a Mr. Alderson, who had
both been in the fight, and there for the first time the news of the
extent of the massacre was ascertained. Brown told us in a straight-
forward way all the particulars of the fight, and informed us that
the wounded men and their surviving comrades had left the Piute
Springs that day by another route, and that we had barely missed
them. He stated that nine men were numbered among the dead
and one man was still missing. . . . [T]he next day was spent at
Coyote and that evening several of the boys left for home.

Leaving Coyote [a city of one main building, a corral, and
a few outbuildings, inhabited by two men], the road to La Sal was
taken, and from there a fragment of the original forty men left for
the battlefield, thinking that if the victorious Indians were still
in the field, and not too heavily reinforced, to avenge the mas-
sacred boys in a measure, or else leave more blood to mingle with
theirs. Nineteen were in the party which, under the guidance of
George McCarty, left La Sal for the battleground.

The party traveled through a pass in the La Sal Mountains and discovered a trail near Mill Creek where they crossed the stream and followed a trail up a small tributary, through a narrow, rocky canyon which
could have given "an excellent place for the ambush." They later
learned that this spot, with its rocks and scrub oak on the "left hand
side" of the canyon was "where the Indians made a desperate stand,
but were driven from it." The report of the editor continues:

> . . . Crossing over a precipitous bluff at the head of the canon [we
> encountered] a high ridge . . . and on the very summit of this back-
> bone lay a dead horse, evidently an Indian pony. This was the
> first conclusive evidence which showed that we were on or near
> the scene of action. . . . Coming down from the ridge about sun-
> down, we descended to a high mesa, running out some distance
> towards Little Castle Valley and breaking into a canon. On this
> promontory we camped for the night, and two of the boys . . .
> found a shovel and a rubber overcoat, and we were led to believe
> that the fight must have been in the canon just below.

A description of the terrain and the reflections of the editor, sitting in
the twilight in that foreign land, follow. The verbal pictures he drew
are still seen today, for the country has changed little. At daybreak, they
started into the canyon:

> . . . Finding nothing of consequence here, the party crossed over
> into a wide, open valley and it was the battleground. To the

right of the trail, about fifty yards, completely hidden by the brush, lay the body of a squaw. She was probably fatally wounded in the early part of the fight and crawled away to die. The head was uphill and the blanket was drawn lightly around the shoulders. Shortly afterwards we found where an Indian pack had been cut loose. The saddle which had been ridden by Jack Galloway and Wiley Tartar were thrown upon the bushes, being very poorly rigged. On the field was found the pocketbook of young Jimmy Heaton, one of the murdered. All that was in it when picked up was a photograph of this brother, one of himself, and a letter. A letter to one of the Tartar boys was found and several coats left. Some few Indian trinkets were picked up, including a comb, some arrows, and several jing bobs to ornament bridles.

After describing the terrain (detailed earlier in this chapter), the editor confesses to being mystified by the reason the murdered men had remained in the gulch. He knew that Dawson in vain had "used every method of persuasion to get his men to leave the place," and recounted the following which adds further insight:

> ...It is known that one of the men weakened at the commencement of the fight, and begged the others not to leave him there to die. He was not wounded, but seemed possessed of a terrible fear. The Tartar brothers left him once, and then went back and said, "We'll stay until the end." If it had not been for him, the chances are that none would have been killed. We found one grave, that of Dave Willis, which is about two hundred yards above that of the others. The graves of the other boys were in another arroyo to the left of the one in which Willis was killed, and our understanding was that the graves were in the same hollow.

The party kept a sharp lookout for Indians but found none "which would lead to the belief that many there were killed and wounded at from twenty to twenty-five." They finally encountered Captain Carroll with four companies of soldiers at Big Bend. Carroll was en route to the battlefield also. The story continues:

> ...They followed the trail of the Indians to the reservation and then returned to the Blue Mountains where they will establish a permanent post. They report that the Indians only traveled from six to seven miles each day, and at each camp were found bloody rags, where they cared for the wounded....On our return we found Capt. Rogers' mounted infantry on the road for Blue Mountains, escorting an immense lot of supplies....It is the declared intention to kill all Indians found off the reservation.

The Solid Muldoon (published weekly on Friday in Ouray by David F. "Dave" Day, a former Indian agent), takes an entirely different view of the situation. An editorial in July 1881[15] asked in large type "Will the Colorado Springs *Gazette*, Pueblo *Chieftan*, Denver *Times*, and other papers that have displayed a vast amount of ignorance in locating the Indian trouble, please be kind enought to inform their readers that the fighting took place in Utah, one hundred eighty miles from Rico, two hundred thirty-one miles from Durango, and two hundred sixty-four miles from Ouray?" Farther on in the same editorial is found: "Our Colorado exchanges in speaking of the Pah-Ute troubles should locate them where they belong, in the Castle and Grand River valleys, Utah. Don't credit them to Ouray and Rico." Excerpts from the June 25 edition of the *Dolores News* are then printed, together with quotations from its June 24 and June 28 "extra" newspapers. In reading the editions of the Ouray newspapers, one finds a friendly attitude toward the Ute Indians in Colorado.

IN SUMMARY, there are perhaps many observations which might be made. When covering the battleground, one cannot but wonder how supposedly trained and experienced Indian hunters would have been led into the trap...as they evidently were. Why they remained there to be slain is another question that is difficult to answer. There are many stories and legends which have been preserved. The author is certain of the victims and acknowledges persistent legends, but leaves the reader to decide between fact and fiction.

The victims of the so-called Pinhook "massacre" were Hard Tartar, John Galloway, Wiley Tartar, Hiram Melvin, Jimmy Heaton, and George Taylor of Rico; Tom Click of Dolores, Dave Willis of Mancos, and Alfred and Isadore Wilson of Moab. Three were severely wounded: Jordan Bean, Jim Hall, and Harg Eskridge.

The bodies of Hiram Melvin and Dave Willis were moved October 1881 by their families. Willis was interred at Mancos and Melvin at Dolores. Two other victims of the Indian slaying are also buried at Dolores: Dick May and John Thurman. The remainder were buried in common graves at the battle site. A monument (Figure 9.2) has been erected to their memory; it was dedicated November 11, 1940, by William R. McConkie. This marker can be seen if one is willing to walk a little distance from the road over some rather rough terrain.

It was thought by old-timers that Indians Posey, Poke, Hatch, and Wash — renegade Ute Indians — were the leaders of this uprising, but no one knows for certain. The perpetrators were never punished by the government because the settlers were unable to identify them. Polk was

[15]*The Solid Muldoon*, Ouray, Colorado, July 1, 1881, vol. III, no. 26, p. 2.

Figure 9.2. Marker Erected at 1881 Battleground, 1940

said to have boasted that he had killed white men in this battle, but this has not been substantiated despite its general acceptance by many old-timers.

During the battle, when Dawson sent the courier to Rico to secure help, he must have known that it would be long in coming, for Rico is 140 miles from the battleground. Yet the courier, who changed horses many times (the settlers gladly furnishing him the best along the way), was able to reach Rico in 22 hours. Quickly the news was given out that the Rico–Disappointment Valley men were trapped by the Indians on the northwest side of the La Sal Mountains. Rico at that time was a lively mining town of about fifteen hundred people, mostly men. Its population was comprised of miners, prospectors, teamsters, saloon-keepers, and merchants. The news, spreading like wildfire, elicited excitement as men gathered in the streets to learn the latest developments and to determine what could best be done.

John Clark, then the sheriff, a tall former miner and prospector, told the townspeople that they must organize and go at once to help those who were trapped or killed. They were told to get horses, food, a "good" gun, and cartridges as soon as possible and assemble on Main Street. "Remember, get good horses that are fast, regardless of who the owner may be."

Thus, men emotionally aroused, bent on revenge, set out to do battle. Looking back, one might ask: Did they seek justice or did they take justice into their own hands? Furthermore, if Poke and Posey were part of the renegade band involved in the Pinhook "massacre," one must add another chapter, for they grew up to cause problems many years later when again soldiers were called out to control them.

Chapter 10

Regional Outlaws: Fact and Fiction

The folk history of the West, preserved for us through the legends of its badmen, holds great fascination for young and old. This is evidenced by the number of books written about these bandits on the trail, and by movies and television programs. The term "folk history" is used because somehow the legends that are told and retold as fact often have little semblance to contemporary literature or reporting. Perhaps one way for a bandit to preserve his story with himself as hero is to outlive the other members of his gang and dictate his own biography (for example, Wyatt Earp and Matt Warner).

Oddly, most outlaws of the West approach the romantic and chivalric traditions of Robin Hood. The outlaw was often a bandit but not a badman. He did not rob the "little man." He often robbed to help the less fortunate. Because he made friends wherever he went, one of the major difficulties in capturing these early outlaws was that of obtaining cooperation of farmers or ranchers along the outlaw trail. Many farmers and ranchers would supply horses, food, and shelter without question to the bandits, but would not supply information to their pursuers. Doors were opened to the outlaws socially; they were made welcome in homes. This is demonstrated time and again in accounts of these people. A few of them were killers, but this was the exception, not the rule. Mostly they killed in self-defense, not wantonly.

The heyday of the western outlaw spanned the period from post-Civil War to after the turn of the century.

The Far Country: Moab and La Sal

Probably due to its location, the Moab–La Sal area was often the "hideout" for early outlaws such as Butch Cassidy, Matt Warner, Mont Butler, "Kid" Jackson, Al Akers, "Kid" Parker, Bert Madden, and locally known Tom Roach. They were outlaws, but also cowboys and ranchers. The McCarty's, of course, lived at La Sal during part of their outlaw career.

The citizen who today walks down the well-ordered main street of Moab has difficulty picturing a time when one virtually "took his life in his hands" to casually walk down the same street. But Moab, like most every western town, experienced a period of "wild and woolly" days when the gun was law, and sometimes discretion was flung to the winds by means of too much hard whiskey. Cowboys rode through the streets shooting at first one side and then the other, or trailing bolts of yard goods which they had appropriated from some hapless merchant. The "romantic days" of the early West were often in reality somewhat unromantic. But with a saloon on each side of Main Street and whiskey brought in by barrel lots and sold without license or restriction (at 95 cents per gallon wholesale), brawls were not uncommon. At times the dances became free-for-alls, and often the patrons made a hasty exit via windows or any other means of escape.

There were numerous engagements with guns — perhaps not so many as the romanticizers of the West would have us believe — and men and sometimes women were killed. Many of the old-timers relate chilling experiences of those early days. The name of Tom Roach, for example, although known only locally, could elicit fear in many. Most old-timers could tell how Roach killed Indian Joe on October 24, 1888. Tom Trout told the author that he was standing slightly in front of Roach when the fatal shot was fired, and that the bullet "singed my whiskers as it went past my face" to strike its mark.

Indian Joe had been taken captive after the Indian war and was raised by Branch Young of Mona. Eventually he found his way to Moab with a drive of cattle and started working for J. H. Shafer. He was a peaceable man except when under the influence of whiskey. But in 1887 he killed Bill Gibson, and from then on was morose and troublesome. He seemed to be constantly seeking trouble, and when he challenged Roach he was too slow in drawing his gun. Roach was one of the Blue Mountain cowboys who had come into the area from Texas.

One sees two personalities in Roach; there is the "badman" side as depicted by Lyman[1] who tells of an unfortunate incident when Roach, reinforced with whiskey and gun, went to a dance. Because of a large

[1]Albert R. Lyman, *Indians and Outlaws* (Salt Lake City: Bookcraft, 1962), pp. 108–13.

crowd, each participant was given one of the numbers that were called out so that the dance floor might not be overcrowded. Roach had a number, but he also had a bottle of whiskey hidden outside the dance hall and often found it necessary to repair to the bottle for refreshment. Upon returning from one of these trips, he found that he had missed his turn to dance but insisted on dancing anyway. The floor manager tried to put him off the dance floor. A fight ensued in which Roach threatened the floor manager and entire assembly. He ordered them at gun point out of the room, and swore he would shoot anyone who tried to leave the crowd. Joe McCord tried to convince him that the floor manager was only trying to be fair, and to see that everyone had an equal opportunity to dance.

Roach threatened to kill McCord, but Joe, relying on the fact of their friendship, attempted to reason with him. To the horror of the captive crowd, Roach shot his friend McCord to death and threatened to do the same to anyone who interfered. Someone slipped out a window and went for a gun. In the resultant exchange of shots, Mrs. Jane Walton, mother of two grown daughters and a son, was shot through the heart. Someone brought Roach a horse and he fled into the night. He was never apprehended although he was reported by friends to be in the area. He openly visited at the homes of some friends at Moab.

But Roach was not a terrorizer in the strictest sense, for others tell of how he often came into their homes, never carrying a gun beyond the portal. He would, like the others, hang it on the peg outside the door and enter unarmed. He was welcome in many homes and spent much time with his friends, the O. W. Warners. They were such good friends that the Warners named one of their sons "Roach," thus creating a legend: When Tom learned of this he was disturbed and told the Warners that they should not have named the child for him because the boy would consequently die with his boots on. While still a small child, the boy ran round the corner of the house where his sister was engaged in target practice. She accidentally shot him dead.

The remoteness, the proximity to the famous hideout at Robbers Roost, the McCartys at La Sal, and its location as one of the major crossings of the Colorado (Grand) River probably all contributed to the number of outlaws who used the vicinity as a hideout or escape route. Some of those known to settlers in the Moab–La Sal vicinity are today legendary outlaw heroes: the McCarty brothers, Butch Cassidy and Matt Warner, and a few members of the Wild Bunch. These notorious outlaws were sometime partners and close associates who spent considerable time in the area, particularly at La Sal, where the McCarty's had taken up ranches in the late 1870s, and at Robbers Roost near Green River. Baker tells us:

That high desert country in southeastern Utah, around the heads of the side canyons of the Green and Colorado on the east and south and the Dirty Devil on the west, had been called Robbers Roost long before Butch Cassidy drove his stolen horses there in 1884....With the exception of a few out-of-the-way grazing areas, such as the Bull Pasture, Sam's Mesa Canyon, and Twin Corral Box, the trails ridden today are those laid out by the men who rode away from the main highway — looking back.[2]

It is difficult to assign dates to many activities of these outlaws. Their biographies and autobiographies are conspicuously lacking in specific dates. Newspaper items and known dates establish a certain relativity, but exactly when certain events happened is hard to pinpoint, and when the careers of these men as outlaws began is conjecture.

As STATED IN chapter 5, Dr. McCarty and his family came to La Sal in 1877 as pioneers. Within a few years Dr. McCarty and his son George moved to Haines, near Baker, Oregon. He left his ranch to his sons Bill and Tom. Bill had already married Letty Maxwell and Tom married Teenie, a sister of Willard Christiansen (Matt Warner), while George found an attractive French-Canadian girl in Marysvale named Nellie Blanchett.[3]

According to Kelly, the McCarty brothers were affluent for the times. They had fine herds of cattle and horses located on some of the best range in Utah. Had they remained in the stock business, they might eventually have become wealthy. But for some reason they, and others at La Sal, sold their holdings to the Pittsburg Cattle Company in 1885, reportedly for about $35,000. Accounts vary somewhat. Some indicate that Tom (Figure 10.1) was already an outlaw, others say Tom and George were hiding out when Dr. McCarty wrote for George to assist him in moving back to Oregon, and still others contend that Tom and Bill turned outlaw after the sale of their outfit. We do know that Tom was one of those who robbed the Telluride bank in June or July of 1889, and that Bill and Fred were killed at the time of the Delta bank robbery in 1893. We assume their careers had begun considerably in advance of these dates. Kelly quotes from a copy of Tom's autobiography, *History of Tom McCarty*,[4] which, although giving accounts of his activities, does not give a clue as to when or why he turned outlaw:

---

[2]Pearl Baker, *The Wild Bunch at Robbers Roost* (Los Angeles: Westernlore Press, 1965), pp. 15–16.

[3]Charles Kelly, *The Outlaw Trail* (New York: Devin-Adair, 1959), p. 17.

[4]*Ibid.*, p. 18. The autobiography of Tom McCarty is in the possession of Charles Kelly, Salt Lake City, Utah.

The fore part of my life I will say little about. I was born
and raised by as good parents as anyone can boast of, but fortune
never seemed to favor me, which I suppose was my own fault.
My downfall commenced by gambling. Horse racing was the
first, then other gambling games and as we all know the company
one comes in contact with was of all the wrong kind for teaching
honesty. . . . After losing about all I had I commenced to cast
around for something else.

That something else, of course, was cattle rustling. Many old-timers
related that Tom McCarty worked from Brown's Hole, an outlaw hideout at the meeting point of Wyoming, Utah, and Colorado.

Kelly says that Bill McCarty (Figure 10.2) joined the Cole
Younger group in Missouri. He admits that Bill's name does not appear
on any roster of the gang, but bases his opinion upon statements made
by Billy's eastern wife, Anne Perry, about Billy, Tom, and Matt Warner.
This is the only reference the author has found to the eastern career
of Billy McCarty, but there seems no reason to doubt Kelly's research,
particularly since it is substantiated by the fact that Billy was sentenced
to the penitentiary at Stillwater, Minnesota, for the murder of his
partner O'Connor in a quarrel over the loot from some holdup. About
this time friends of the Younger gang had been successful in getting
some legislation, making it possible for the governor to release criminals
who agreed to leave the state. On his promise to do so, Billy was released
after serving a short term.

Kelly further says that Billy left the state but returned to visit his
seriously ill wife whom he believed to be dying. He was rearrested, but
upon appeal was freed on a legal technicality. After this, his eastern
wife left him, and he returned, now a full-fledged bandit, to his old
range and his first wife, Letty, on the La Sal Mountains.

His return is substantiated by considerable evidence, including
reports of old-timers. Baker[5] relates that Tom McCarty, following the
Delta bank robbery (1893) in which Billy and Billy's son Fred were
killed, was in hiding at the McCarty cabin in the La Sals. Gene Grimes
went there to collect some horses he had earlier bought from Tom, and
during the visit Tom told Gene much of his life story. Again the element
of time is confusing, but Baker relates the coming of the McCartys with
the Rays and Maxwells, their selling out to the Pittsburg Cattle Company, the return to Oregon, and then "but we drifted back last spring."[6]

Tom and Billy seem to have operated together for some time in
Utah, stealing horses and cattle in some of the older settlements. On

---

[5]Baker, *op. cit.*, pp. 183–95.
[6]*Ibid.*, p. 187.

one expedition to Nephi, Tom was caught with a stolen herd and placed in jail. Jumping bond, he went back to the Blue Mountain area, near the La Sals, where no officer cared to follow.

It appears that within a year or two Billy left Tom and went to Oregon where he bought a ranch near his brother George and settled down to ranching, intent upon ending his outlaw career. He was, however, after financial reverses, lured back onto the outlaw trail by Tom McCarty and Matt Warner.

In the meantime, Tom went to Arizona and New Mexico where he and various unnamed partners operated as large-scale cattle rustlers. He took some of his profits to purchase fast horses which were to serve him well during the remainder of his outlaw career. The McCartys had been lovers of good horse flesh, and Tom purchased only the best for use on the trail.

As did most of the early outlaws, Tom graduated from cattle rustling to bank and railroad holdups. Baker says[7] that Tom's first holdup was so easy it almost ruined him. She says it was in Denver where one of the banks refused to cash a check. Tom, angry (he hadn't known the check wasn't good), decided to hold up the bank. Dressing in ministerial clothes he went into the bank with a pint flask of water which he showed to the teller with the statement that it was nitroglycerin and if the teller did not give him the money he would throw the bottle on the floor and blow everyone to "kingdom come." The teller was warned to be quiet and the bottle, reinforced with a gun, was convincing. Tom made quite a haul of cash and, quickly shedding his costume, returned to the street before the alarm had been broadcast. Ironically, he even helped in the search for the bandit, making it a point to talk face-to-face with the teller who did not recognize him. A preponderance of evidence, however, indicates that Tom's career had begun much earlier than this.

He was joined, probably in 1884 or 1885, by his brother-in-law, Matt Warner, who under Tom's tutelage became one of the most daring operators of the McCarty gang.

MATT WARNER, born Willard Erastus Christiansen at Ephraim, was the son of a Mormon bishop and his fifth and youngest wife. Matt was born in 1864, and shortly afterward the family moved to Levan. Kelly[8] describes him as "stockily built [who] bubbled over with uncontrolled energy. When he was in good humor he was a pleasant, likeable boy, when in a fit of temper he was a wildcat" (Figure 10.3).

---

[7] *Ibid.*

[8] Kelly, *op. cit.*, p. 20.

Figure 10.2. Bill McCarty

Figure 10.1. Tom McCarty

Figure 10.3. Matt Warner, 1933

While in his early teens, Willard fled from home, believing he had killed another young man in a fight over a girl. He headed for Brown's Hole, then headquarters for a gang of rustlers. He did not know for several years that he hadn't killed the boy (whose name was Hendrickson). Having previously driven cattle into the Uintah Basin, Willard knew the trail and headed in that direction, eating at various cattle camps along the road. On this trip he assumed the alias of Matt Warner by which he became known throughout the West.

He had not worked long before he discovered his boss (name unknown) was a cattle rustler. Accepting a few cattle, he became a rustler too. After working a couple of years, he had accumulated enough stolen stock to start a ranch of his own, which he did on Diamond Mountain.

Learning that Hendrickson was not dead, he wrote to his parents and, as a result of that letter, Tom McCarty's son Lew went to visit Matt and stayed with him for some time. Together with Elza Lay, a later member of the Wild Bunch and close associate of Butch Cassidy, they planned the first holdup in which any of them had taken part. This was a peddler who had come to Brown's Hole with a wagonload of goods. Following this incident, Matt joined with Tom, and together with others they set out on a trail of rustling and robbery that kept officers chasing in circles.

Matt and Tom decided to part company for a while. Tom rode to Ely, Nevada, and other points where he temporarily disappeared. Matt returned to Diamond Mountain for a short time; when he learned officers were after him, he tried to start another ranch on the White River, but had to leave hastily. Then he moved to the La Sal Mountains near the former ranch of the McCartys. Here he trained some fast horses for racing and later went to Telluride, Colorado, to pick up some easy money.

Matt Warner related[9] that he had a racing mare he called "Betty," which was very fast. He and his jockey, Johnny Nicholson, took the mare to Telluride where they had heard a man named Mulcahy had a horse he thought could not be beat.

The match was arranged. Matt said that when the arrangements had been made, a neatly dressed cowboy came up to him and told him the Mulcahy colt had never been beaten. This was Robert (George) LeRoy Parker (later known as Butch Cassidy), a lad from Circleville, Utah. The two men became friends and when young Parker lost his outfit to Matt on a bet, they joined up and became friends and associates

---

[9]Murray E. King, *The Last of the Bandit Riders* (New York: Bonanza Books, no date), pp. 105–16.

for many years. Starting out as racing partners, they traveled throughout Colorado, sometimes winning, sometimes losing.

Near Cortez, as the two made their racing rounds, Matt again met his former partner, Tom McCarty. A celebration followed, and this, so far as is known, was the first meeting between Tom McCarty and Butch Cassidy, who was to become the third member of that notorious triumvirate destined to become legendary throughout the country as "The Invincible Three."

BUTCH CASSIDY was perhaps the most colorful of the outlaw leaders of the last three decades of the nineteenth century. As leader of the Wild Bunch (Figure 10.4) he proved his ability time and again, especially in view of the fact that he never killed a man until the legend of the last hours of his life when he was allegedly engaged in a gun battle with Bolivian officers. Later, we shall be able to weigh good evidence which will militate against the validity of this time-honored legend. Kelly[10] sums up this outlaw leader vividly when he says:

> ...By ancestry he was as English as Robin Hood, by environment a typical American cowboy. To him, monotony was deadly and adventure the tonic of life. He entered the Outlaw Trail looking for excitement, with his eyes wide open, and followed it to the end, with few if any regrets. He had a sense of fair play even when robbing trains and banks. He made many friends and few enemies. While he never consciously robbed the rich to feed the poor, he did perform many acts of generosity. So far as we know, he never killed a man during his entire career, until his last stand. That in itself makes him outstanding among outlaws.

Writers agree that Cassidy was a friendly, gay, reckless, coolly daring young man whom everyone liked, including the sheriffs who chased him. He had so many friends along the outlaw trail that he literally thumbed his nose at pursuing posses. Yet he put the utmost fear into law officers for hundreds of miles, took thousands of dollars from express cars, banks, payrolls, yet apparently never robbed an individual except as a prank, and as previously said, did not kill one man in his holdups. As he broke bronco horses along the Sevier River, or punched cattle in the dreary deserts of southern Utah before he became an outlaw, there was nothing about him to distinguish him from other hard-working, hard-living cowpunchers of the 1880 breed. He did not seem to go to excess in gambling, drinking, or womanizing, and always kept command of his emotions and faculties.

---

[10]Kelly, *op. cit.*, p. 299.

Robert LeRoy Parker came from pioneer Mormons on both sides of his family. His grandfather, Robert, a convert from England, was a weaver. He and his wife had crossed the Plains with one of the hand-cart companies. Butch's mother, Ann Campbell Gillies of Beaver (Kelly gives it as Ann Campbell only), came across the Plains in another hand-cart company. The Gillies family settled in Beaver where the elder Robert Parker eventually set up a woolen mill.[11] He was then called to Washington, in Utah's Dixie, but his son Maximilian remained in Beaver, marrying Ann Gillies. Their eldest son, Robert LeRoy, was born there April 6, 1866.[12]

Most of the books about Butch Cassidy give his name as George LeRoy Parker, but Neal Ray, Tom Trout, and Frank Silvey — all of whom knew him well at La Sal, and all of whom knew the McCartys (and who were interviewed by the author) — give his name as Robert, saying he was known to them as "Bob" when he was in that vicinity with the McCartys and Matt Warner. Baker explains the discrepancy thus[13]: "Why Butch took the name of George LeRoy Parker in Wyoming is inexplicable. It was apparently an error when he was arraigned and he let it stand. He was known as George LeRoy Parker from that time on." Baker knew two of Butch's sisters and obtained much of her family information about Butch from them. This should give some authenticity to the name; and she had made a plausible deduction as to explanation.

Matt Warner, in his memoirs, was looking back across many years and there were frequent discrepancies in incidents which he related upon numerous occasions. When the Parker lad was still small, the family moved to Circleville. Here they settled on the Marshall ranch and experienced the usual vicissitudes of frontier life, the good times and bad. During one of the bad times while the father was away, one of the cowboys who came to the ranch and spent considerable time was a well-known rustler, Mike Cassidy. An affinity sprang up between man and boy, the young lad greatly admiring the outlaw who taught him to shoot and rustle cattle. When the older Parker bought the ranch, Mike Cassidy stayed on in his employ. Old-timers say the Marshall ranch had been headquarters for a gang of rustlers and horse thieves. It was not far from Bryce Canyon, an almost inaccessible section of country.

Mike Cassidy was one of the most active members of the gang and had already made quite a reputation for himself. Other members continued to stop off at the ranch from time to time as they passed through, and from them and Mike young Parker secured an education

---

[11]There are members of the Gillies and Parker families living in Beaver and vicinity at the time of this writing.

[12]Baker, *op. cit.*, p. 223.

[13]*Ibid.*, p. 226ff.

in the finer points of cattle rustling and horse stealing. He also learned to ride, rope, brand, and shoot and before he was sixteen had gained a reputation as the best shot in the valley.

If one can believe the tales of old-timers in any cattle country in the West, about half the inhabitants, at least most of the cowboys, had a long rope and a running iron and from this got for themselves a good start in the cattle business, often ending up better endowed economically than those for whom they worked.

After young Parker became an outlaw he took the name of Cassidy, apparently because of his admiration for Mike Cassidy. Again, there are differences of opinion as to how he decided on the name of Butch. Matt Warner says that he (Matt) once owned an old needle gun with a terrific kick, which he called "Butch." One day he maneuvered young Parker into firing this gun while seated with his back to a waterhole. The recoil knocked the boy sprawling into the water and from that day he was called "Butch." Matt seems to be the only source for this account. Baker and other writers say that Parker acquired the nickname as a result of some time spent working in a butcher shop in Lander,

Figure 10.4. The Wild Bunch, 1900 (left to right: Harry Longabaugh, Bill Carver, Ben Kilpatrick, Harvey Logan, and Butch Cassidy)

157

Wyoming. The name Butch sounded well with Cassidy and he accepted it. (One must remember that Matt Warner had a propensity to exaggerate and make himself the center of many of his stories. This was not unique with him. This, and the years intervening between the event and the dictating of his memoirs, may account for the discrepancies.)

Parker (Cassidy) had been engaged in some rustling and horse stealing, but became famous as an outlaw after he joined with Tom McCarty and Matt Warner.[14]

Matt Warner once said, "I taught Butch Cassidy everything he knew about bank robbing." This is one of Matt's exaggerations. As a matter of fact, both Matt and Butch were amateurs when they assisted Tom McCarty in the Telluride affair. Tom was a cool, clever, bold outlaw who was never caught by the law. Matt was brave but reckless, with an uncontrollable temper which often got him into trouble. Doubtless Cassidy learned from both these men, but he was a much more cool and calculating man than either and apparently believed that sooner or later Matt's dashing recklessness would bring him disaster. For that reason, he ceased operations with the McCarty gang and started out on his own. He was more careful with money than his companions, and when he left Tom and Matt on the Wind River, he is thought to have had most of his share from the Telluride bank robbery.

MANY VOLUMES have been written about these outlaws, but here we will concern ourselves only with some incidents which specifically relate to the locale of Moab and La Sal. One of these events was the Telluride bank robbery, planned and executed by Tom McCarty, Butch Cassidy, Matt Warner, and Bert Madden. The bank they planned to rob was the San Miguel Valley Bank at Telluride, Colorado, known to handle large mine payrolls.

This was Butch's first full partnership. He had worked in Telluride and knew the town well. He went there about a month before the holdup and spent the time training one of Tom's fast horses to stand motionless while he approached at a full run, vaulted into the saddle, and galloped a full mile before stopping. The miners, thinking this was just another crazy cowboy, paid little attention.

Kelly says that while Butch was training the horse, Tom and Matt visited the Carlisle Cattle Ranch near Monticello, Utah, where "Latigo" Gordon, a foreman, remembered seeing them make buckskin bags in which they later carried loot. They probably also scouted the routes of escape and arranged for relays of horses at necessary intervals. Butch's younger brother Dan, later called "Kid" Parker, was working at

---

[14]Kelly, *op. cit.*, p. 51.

Carlisle at this time. Tom and Matt decided to take him along as horse wrangler.

Posing as placer miners, they returned to Tom's cabin about eight miles from Cortez. Here they trained their imported horses as Butch was doing in Telluride. In Mancos they contacted Bert Madden. There seems to be some disagreement as to the date. Charles Kelly and Frank Silvey give it respectively as June 24 and July 3, 1889.

In his notes, Frank Silvey says that he knew all three of the men who committed the robbery in which they escaped with some $21,000. (Kelly puts it at $10,000.) Silvey also says that in March 1936 he interviewed the only living survivor of the robbery. This was probably Matt Warner who died in 1938.

Silvey says that he knew Bert Madden and Tom McCarty especially well. All of these men had fine horses and trained them for six weeks at Mancos. According to Silvey, he (Silvey) was working on a ranch for Judge Milton T. Morris at the time and had a white race horse which could not be outrun in the district, and Tom McCarty urged him to go to Telluride with them and they would win all the races there on the Fourth of July. In those days the mining camps of western Colorado offered liberal prize money for racing, drilling, and so on, which was a temptation to the young man. His race horse, with Tom McCarty riding him, had won all of the races at the celebration the previous year (1888) at Cortez, Colorado. In 1889 the celebration honored the arrival of the first water from the Dolores River through a long tunnel and flume to Cortez and the Montezuma Valley. Thus the trip to Telluride was indeed appealing to a 22-year-old man, and Silvey "came near going along" with McCarty and his friends. But Judge Morris advised him not to go, for if he went along, the others would get him into trouble. He finally decided not to go, and in retrospect was pleased he had not done so because it was later learned that the bank robbery had been planned at Mancos weeks before.

The morning of the robbery, the cashier stepped out to make some collections, leaving only the bookkeeper in charge. Tom McCarty, Matt Warner, and Butch Cassidy then entered, leaving Bert Madden in charge of the horses. With guns drawn they covered the bookkeeper and helped themselves to all of the money in sight. Backing out, they mounted their horses and were literally off in a cloud of dust before anyone in town was aware of what had happened. The whole thing was done so quietly and smoothly that considerable time elapsed before an alarm was spread and a pursuit organized. The robbers, on their fleet horses, were soon lost in the brushy hills between the Dolores and Mancos rivers, where a posse found it impossible, or inadvisable, to follow.

The bold bandits managed to lose the posse and then continued on to the Carlisle ranch near Monticello, where Kelly says they showed Latigo Gordon the proceeds of their exploit, which were considerably less than they had expected. (The mine payroll had left the bank just prior to their arrival.)

Although the Telluride posse had given up the chase, the three could not be sure, so continued north to Moab. Mrs. Lydia Skewes, daughter of A. A. Taylor, reported to the author that she and other members of her family saw the three riders racing toward the river. (The Taylor home, now known as the Parriott house, was on the road to the ferry.) She said they had no idea who the horsemen were, and her grand-father later told them about ferrying three men across the river who seemed in a hurry and paid a $10 gold piece instead of the regular charge of fifty cents per horse and rider. Later it was learned why the men were in such a hurry.

Matt Warner tells a more dramatic story of waking the ferrymen, whom he refers to by name, and how he bribed them to transport the fleeing outlaws. If the men were known, it is unlikely that it would have been necessary to bribe the ferrymen, and more unlikely that Taylor would have shown the gold piece to his family and told them his story.

Many years later at a racing meet in Moab, Matt Warner was betting heavily and several people in the crowd called to him, "Where did you get so much money, Matt?" and he shouted back, waving currency in the air, "At the Telluride bank, years ago!"

The outlaws went on to Thompson and the Hill Creek country, then on to the White River, and finally to Brown's Hole, where they stayed in one of Charley Crouse's cabins. After a rest, more rumors of officers sent them south to Robbers Roost. Following this, Tom and Matt went into Star Valley (Wyoming) for the winter, and indications are that Butch went to the general vicinity of Lander.

Billy McCarty, his wife, and seventeen-year-old son Fred had left Utah for Oregon with considerable money, but times had been hard in Oregon and when Tom and Matt came, after the Star Valley interlude, Bill was almost broke. It took little persuasion to induce him to join them, replacing Cassidy. Their activities in Oregon, Wyoming, and Idaho attracted considerable attention. The pressures were great; they left Oregon after the daring holdup of the Baker (Oregon) bank and the intense activity of officers.

Matt Warner, who later served a term in the penitentiary for another offense, was pardoned and retired to a quiet life on this ranch. Tom and Bill McCarty, with young Fred, realizing the close call they'd had after the Baker bank robbery, made a long ride from Oregon to Nevada, then to Manti, Utah, where they rested, then to Robbers Roost where they planned the robbery of the Farmers and Merchants Bank at Delta, Colorado. This robbery proved fatal to two members of the McCarty gang, and evidently ended the outlaw activities of Tom McCarty.

On September 6, 1883, Tom and Bill McCarty rode into Delta and registered at a hotel under assumed names. The next morning Fred came in with their horses, which he tied in an alley behind the bank. At 10:15 a.m. Tom and Bill stepped into the bank and held up the tellers. Fred came in from the rear and held a gun on a bank official named Robertson who was in his office. When the tellers refused to give them the cash, Tom and Billy jumped over the partition separating the cages from the lobby, and Tom grabbed all of the money in sight. One of the tellers shouted for help and Tom shot him in the head, killing him instantly.

An alarm was shouted outside the bank, and the robbers, afraid to delay although they had secured only several hundred dollars, raced outside. Fred rushed to the horses, quickly followed by the other two men, and they hastily fled the scene.

But fate intervened when a hardware store owner across the street, W. Ray Simpson, hearing the shot suspected a holdup at the bank. Grabbing a repeating Sharpes rifle and a handful of shells, he rushed into the street just as the McCartys were mounting. Instead of joining the crowd, he ran down the street, loading the gun as he ran, to intercept the robbers as they emerged from the alley. Billy was shot and fell from his horse. Fred turned back to his father and was also shot. Both were killed by the shots of Simpson. Tom's horse was shot in the leg, but with horses waiting outside town, Tom managed to escape. Although a posse was organized within a few minutes, it was unable to overtake and catch him.

ON SEVERAL OCCASIONS posses from Grand County, usually led by Sheriff Jesse Tyler, went to the Robbers Roost area seeking stolen horses. Many of these expeditions are reported in the *Grand Valley Times* and give contemporary views and reports. Several of these are cited here.

After Jack Moore was killed, "Silver Tip," "Blue John," and "Indian Ed," all regular outlaws of the Robbers Roost country, returned from Wyoming with horses they had stolen, taking them to Colorado to sell.[15] Returning to the Roost they acquired more horses as they traveled, ending at the Roost with some choice animals. From Monticello they

---

[15]Baker, *op. cit.*, p. 164.

had taken one of Latigo Gordon's horses, one from Mons Peterson at Moab, a mule from the Court House way station, and two horses, one of which was a little gray racing horse, from Andrew Tangren at Moab.

Tangren started out, determined to trail the outlaws. Sheriff Tyler was out of town following a man who had broken out of jail; but upon his return, Tyler organized a posse and soon overtook Tangren near Green River. For local flavor, the *Grand Valley Times* is quoted here[16]:

> Sheriff Tyler and posse, Andrew Tangren, J. C. Wilcox, H. Day, William Wilson, and R. W. Westwood, returned from a twelve-day trip into the San Rafael country after horses stolen from Andrew Tangren two weeks before. They did not get the horses they went after, but found two that were taken from Joseph Taylor and Thomas Larsen last summer.... In trailing... the horses... they lost the trail on the other side of Green River. Believing they could get assistance in learning the trails from people farther west, they went to Hanksville, but failed to secure any assistance there, and went on as far as the Henry Mountains. On their return... they saw a fresh trail leading into the San Rafael country and followed it up.

When the posse realized that it was getting near the outlaws, the pursuers decided to wait until night so that they could find the horse thieves by the light of any campfire they would make. The bandits, however, were in a "side canyon under shelving rocks" and the posse was unable to approach undetected. The account continues:

> ...They kept watch until morning when one of the group [outlaws], a half-breed Indian, came out into the open and was ordered to throw up his hands, but instead commenced shooting and the sheriff's party opened fire on him. He dropped and was last seen crawling behind the rocks. The others came out into the open and one fired a shot into the air and yelled to the sheriff's party to drift, but was answered by a volley. A battle then commenced and lasted for nearly two hours, a hundred or more shots were fired on both sides as far as known without damage. Fire from behind the rocks finally stopped, and the sheriff's party, being nearly out of ammunition, withdrew.

This is from the point of view of the posse, of course, but illustrates some of the problems encountered in trailing outlaws into their hideouts.

Further installments in the search for these horses are found in the pages of the *Grand Valley Times* as follows[17]:

---

[16]*Grand Valley Times*, Moab, March 3, 1899.
[17]*Ibid.*, March 24, 1899.

Sheriff Tyler with H. Day, Andrew Tangren, Wm. Littel, and Harvey Hancock left the first of the week to look for stolen horses in the San Rafael country. It was reported Wednesday that Tyler had located the parties with which they had the fight some weeks ago, and had sent word to the sheriff of Carbon County for aid. It was learned that the Indian was seriously hurt in the first fight.

And again in a later report of the incident[18]:

Sheriff Tyler and posse returned Wednesday evening from a trip into the San Rafael country after stolen horses and horse thieves. They brought in eight horses and one mule. The mule had been stolen from Mr. Young at the Court House Rock Stage Station, one horse from Mons Peterson and one from W. E. [Latigo] Gordon at Monticello, the others an owner is wanted for.

A description of the horse was then given.

Later the sheriff realized that all of his problems did not lie with the outlaws, for he was sued by Mrs. Jack Moore for having taken the two unidentified horses, which were hers. A search of the files does not reveal the outcome of the trial. The following summer, Sheriff Tyler and deputy S. F. Jenkins were slain by rustlers as a posse pursued the outlaws. They were slain by Harvey Logan ("Kid Curry") to avenge the killing of "Flat Nose" George Curry.

A wild young cowboy, Tom Dilly, became involved in a couple of fights at Castle Dale in 1899 or 1900. Warrants were issued for his arrest, but he fled to Robbers Roost. Then rumors began circulating that he was stealing cattle in the vicinity of Green River, Utah. Sheriffs Preece of Vernal and Tyler of Moab went in search of him.

Meanwhile Fullerton, manager of the Webster Cattle Company north of Thompson, discovered a man altering the brand on one of his cows. He rode to Green River to notify Sheriff Tyler but met Preece who immediately took up the chase, sending Fullerton on to get Tyler.

Sheriff Preece found a rustler at the place which Fullerton had described, and started in pursuit. A running fight for six miles followed, then the rustler crossed the river and took up a defensive position behind large rocks on the far bank. Preece continued to fire at him sporadically. This exchange permitted Sheriff Tyler to ride up from the opposite direction (on the rustler's side of the river), take careful aim, and shoot the outlaw through the head. Both men were surprised to find the dead

---

[18]*Ibid.*, April 1, 1899.

man was not Tom Dilly, but Flat Nose George Curry, a wanted railroad holdup man.

Curry had been leader of the Hole-in-the-Wall gang when the Logan brothers first arrived, and when Harvey Logan ("Kid Curry") learned of George's death, he immediately started north to avenge his former leader by killing sheriff Tyler.

Tyler and Preece were angered because Sheriff Allred of Price did not arrest Dilly who had a ranch near Woodside that was stocked with several hundred head of cattle. Learning that Dilly was out after more cattle in the vicinity of Hill Creek, some fifty miles north of Thompson, Sheriff Tyler went after him in company with Sam Jenkins (whom Dilly had at one time assaulted with a six-shooter), Herbert Day (a deputy), and Mert Wade (a young boy). Again the contemporary account in the *Grand Valley Times* tells the story[19]:

> The residents of Moab were inexpressibly shocked and startled last Sunday about noon when word was received here from Thompson that Sheriff Tyler of Grand County, and a member of the posse, Sam Jenkins, were killed by outlaws. The killing took place about forty-two miles above Thompson in the Book Mountains.... The posse had been out in that country for the past three weeks looking for some cattle rustlers that are badly wanted.
>
> The story of the killing as told by Deputy Sheriff Day who was only about fifty yards away when the shooting occurred is as follows: The posse had divided, one under Sheriff Preece of Vernal leading the Grand County group. The Tyler posse had ridden about half an hour when they discovered a camp they believed was Indians. Tyler and Jenkins turned west toward it to investigate. They dismounted and approached the camp, which was among some willows, leaving their rifles on their saddles. When within a few yards of the outlaws, Sheriff Tyler spoke to them, saying, "Hello, boys."...The reply made could not be heard by Deputy Sheriff Day, but immediately after it was made, Sheriff Tyler and Jenkins turned toward their horses, evidently having discovered their mistake. As soon as their backs were turned, the outlaws shot them through the back, the bullets coming out of their breasts, killing them instantly.
>
> Mr. Day was a witness to the killing, but was in such a position that he could offer no assistance when the outlaws turned their guns on him, shooting twice but missing him.... Mr. Day then started in search of Sheriff Preece and posse of four men who were three miles away. As soon as he found them, they decided to come for assistance as there were supposed to be quite a number

[19]"Killed by Outlaws: Sheriff Jesse Tyler and S. F. Jenkins Murdered on the Book Cliffs," *ibid.*, June 1, 1900.

of outlaws in the party, they having about twenty horses with them.... They left the bodies of Sheriff Tyler and Jenkins where they fell and came to Thompson, arriving at eleven o'clock Sunday morning.

Upon the arrival of Deputy Day at Thompson word was wired to Governor Wells who sent a posse from Salt Lake to assist posses from Moab and Price in the search of the outlaws. Sunday morning it was learned that the outlaws had passed the Turner ranch, about twenty miles farther north, where they had taken fresh horses. Sunday night Messrs. Fullerton and King brought the bodies of the dead men to Thompson. A posse of eleven left Thompson Monday morning with Day and Westwood and in the afternoon a posse of fifteen left with Sheriff Preece to follow up the trail. Sheriff Howell and posse of Salt Lake and Allred of Carbon are with the latter.

The death of Tyler and Jenkins went unavenged, and the *Grand Valley Times* of June 8, 1900, carries a simple announcement: "R. D. Westwood appointed to fill vacancy caused by death of Tyler."

Jane Warner Peterson recalled[20] that when she was a young girl some men robbed a train at Thompson, then came to Moab taking one of her father's horses and another that belonged to one of the Wilson brothers. The Warner horse was taken up to Blue Hill and shot; the Wilson horse was taken to Dolores and left there. The loot taken by the robbers from the train had been cached at Court House, and when the men were caught they showed officers where they had hidden the cache, and the officers took the money into their possession.

Moab had its share of local crime, much of which went unsolved. For example, an assassin waited all day on the stairway at the Taylor Mercantile, later La Sal Mercantile, for Jess Gibson to appear. The bullet missed Gibson, but struck the frame of the door and, glancing off, entered the victim's body. It was never known who fired the fatal shot, although there was much speculation.

There was always a great amount of excitement when the cowboys from the ranches came into the town of Moab. Drunken brawls were frequent, but no more than might be found in any frontier settlement. Law and order quickly supplanted anarchy and the law of the gun. With county organization came sheriffs to enforce the law, and courts of justice were soon established.

The outlaws who survived the period of open range found it difficult to adjust to the well-ordered life of the settlement. Some did

---

[20]Interview given by Mrs. Peterson to Arnel Holyoak, in files at Utah State Historical Society, Salt Lake City, Utah.

make that adjustment and became "solid citizens," some became wanderers, some fled to South America, and still others became victims of violence.

INASMUCH AS THERE HAS BEEN a recent surge of interest in Butch Cassidy and the Wild Bunch, as well as other famous outlaws of the West, and since much of the activity of Cassidy and various members of his band took place in the Moab–La Sal area, one recognizes a responsibility to add recent research in this fascinating story of the West. It is one of the ironies of history that those who settled the West and built for succeeding generations often remain unnoticed, while the colorful figures, some of whom lived outside the law or made their own law, are well remembered and romanticized.

A popular movie and many written accounts end with Butch Cassidy and his South American associate, the Sundance Kid (Harry Longabaugh), being riddle with bullets in a gunfight with two hundred Bolivian soldiers (in 1909). In an interview with Cassidy's surviving sister, Mrs. Lula Parker Betenson, by a Los Angeles *Times* reporter, Mrs. Betenson states[21]:

> That's the story the Pinkerton Detective Agency and the Bolivian government [were] supposed to have given out....But everyone in the family and a few others have always known my brother was not shot down and left for dead in South America. ...He visited me years after his reputed death. We heard from him from time to time through the years until he died. It's my secret where he's buried.

An Associated Press story of January 21, 1973,[22] from Spokane, Washington, reports that there is a theory that Cassidy survived the gun battle with Bolivian troops and made his way back to the United States where he lived out his life as a respectable Spokane citizen under the name of William T. Phillips. The article further reports that one promoter of the theory was Robert Longabaugh, who died in 1971 in a Missoula, Montana, hotel fire. The 71-year-old Longabaugh said that he was the son of the Sundance Kid,[23] Cassidy's sidekick, who died in the South American battle. He also claimed that he was a pallbearer at the 1937 Spokane funeral of Phillips (often confused with Cassidy).

---

[21]Charles Hillinger, "Butch Cassidy's Sister Tells All," Los Angeles *Times*, April 3, 1970, p. 12.

[22]"Outlaw's Death Still a Puzzler," *Arizona Republic*, January 21, 1973, p. A-15.

[23]"Sundance, Jr.," gives many conflicting statements. He is cited in a later segment of this chapter.

Figure 10.5. Butch Cassidy, 1894
COURTESY UTAH STATE HISTORICAL SOCIETY

But the statements of Longabaugh (Jr.) are so at variance within themselves that it is difficult to tell fact from fiction.

Newspaper obituaries, the city directory, and other sources (says the Associated Press report) confirm that a William T. Phillips died in 1937 and was cremated following the funeral. A copy of his death certificate indicates that he had been born in Michigan on June 22, 1865. Cassidy (Robert LeRoy Parker) was born in Beaver, Utah, one year later.

The first substantial research claiming that Cassidy lived and died in Spokane, Washington, came from Mark T. Christensen who, before his death, was a Wyoming state treasurer and secretary of state. Christensen's findings were published in the Cheyenne *Tribune* in 1940. He said that Phillips went from Spokane to Lander, Wyoming, in 1934[24] and was positively identified as Cassidy by officials who had known the outlaw. Cassidy went to Lander, Christensen said, to find money he had buried in the Wind River Indian Reservation in the 1890s. Cassidy's picture (Figure 10.5) was taken at the Wyoming state penitentiary on July 5, 1894, when he was age 27.

Kelly, in his *Outlaw Trail*, reported hearing from numerous sources that Cassidy lived and died in Spokane under the name of W. T. Phillips. He said that he interviewed Phillips' widow after hearing the story, but the widow stated that Cassidy and Phillips were close friends and that it was Phillips, not Cassidy, who went to Lander to look for the lost loot.

There have been ample controversy and lack of cohesion in stories about the demise of Cassidy. Considerable research for this book has

---

[24]So far as the author has been able to deduce, it would have to be 1933.

been done in an effort to find a definite date for his death, to resolve the conflicting accounts that have been handed down through the years regarding where he lived and died and where he actually reappeared upon his return from South America. There seems to be an abundance of evidence which denies the story that he was killed in Bolivia, as reported by the Pinkerton agency, and which supports the story that he returned to the United States and lived for many years in comparative seclusion under a new identity. Other research is continuing, and perhaps someone will one day be able to piece together the puzzle and document where he died and the identity of Butch Cassidy at the time of his death.

In 1972–73, after presenting a paper on Cassidy before the Westerner's Corral in Phoenix, Arizona, the author met Sam Adams (then of Phoenix but originally from Rawlings, Wyoming) whose brother George had known Cassidy. Shortly thereafter, Adams traveled to Wyoming and, upon his return, reported that he had again talked with friends who had been invited in 1933 to attend a get-together which Cassidy was arranging for his friends. Adams had talked with men who assured him that Butch Cassidy had been in Lander, Wyoming, at that time. The two men, George and Al, were sons of John B. (or R.) Smith, a rancher in the Wyoming Hole-in-the-Wall area.

John Smith had not only known Cassidy well when he was there, but had been a member of the rustlers' group in the Johnson County war. Both Sam Adams and his brother George feel confident that the Smith brothers knew Cassidy too well to be mistaken in his identity. They were certain that it was Butch Cassidy, not William Phillips, who came to Lander in 1933, searching for caches. This is borne out by Lula Parker Betenson (Cassidy's sister) when she said regarding her famous brother[25]:

> For over forty years, sworn to silence, I have quietly listened to and read of the controversy about my brother Butch Cassidy and whether or not he and the Sundance Kid were killed in South America in 1909. My brother Butch has emerged into a bigger-than-life image because of his winning personality — quite inconsistent with his brutal life. He was a rare composite of good and bad, which has made him a dream-hero of young and old alike, and so the stories have expanded in number and imaginative detail.

Research prompts one to agree with Baker[26] in her letter of June 14, 1973, in which she advises the author of her belief that it was

---

[25]*Deseret News*, Salt Lake City, Oct. 3, 1975.

[26]Baker, *op. cit.* Letters in the possession of the author.

Cassidy himself who returned to Lander. She suggests the possibility that Phillips had been closely associated with the Wild Bunch in their halcyon days and therefore knew a lot about them — perhaps had ridden with them in their early days. It is possible that Cassidy, to whom names meant nothing, did use the name of William Phillips on many occasions. It may even have been a private joke between Phillips and Cassidy. Baker believes that Cassidy died in North Hollywood or Long Beach in 1944, but of course does not know under what name. She has done extensive research in this area and has worked with many others who have also been researching this material. She indicates that there were probably two visits to Lander, one in 1933 and one in 1934. The latter may have been made by Phillips.

Baker states in her letter that she made a trip to Tropic, Utah, and talked to a man who had visited with Cassidy at the home of a man named Lige Moore, after Cassidy's return from South America. Some of the stories which Butch told while in Tropic he alone could have known.

On a trip to Lander, Wyoming, and vicinity in 1970, Baker interviewed a number of old settlers, many of whom had known Butch Cassidy well. Their stories seem to agree in several points: There was something of a hero worship of Butch Cassidy as an honest Robin Hood outlaw, a man who never killed another man. They also agree that he did make a trip to Lander in the 1930s and that he was seeking caches which he had left there. (According to reports gathered from various sources, Cassidy did find two or three of these caches, but the one he came for in 1933 he did not find.) According to one of those interviewed, he did not find some $65,000 in silver and gold which he had buried in an iron pot with a lid. He had hung four muleshoes in different trees and buried the pot in the center. This was after a train robbery when the outlaws fled through South Pass with a mule pack. The money was heavy and the posse close on their heels. Heading for the Hole-in-the-Wall hideout with his band, he had ingeniously contrived the hiding place. But when he returned, a fire had destroyed the trees and Cassidy was unable to find the iron pot.

There seems to be some controversy concerning the number and identity of those who fled to South America. Some stories relate that there were three men and a woman named Etta Place. Cassidy, the Sundance Kid, and Kid Curry are sometimes reported as being the three. They went to Argentina first, according to some versions, after picking up Etta Place in Mexico. There does seem to be evidence that Sundance also returned to the states. His son, Sundance, Jr. (who went under various names), tells conflicting stories. In a lecture given at the Weber County (Utah) Library, June 25, 1970, which was taped and transcribed by Pearl Baker, the then Harry Longabaugh, Jr., states that the four named above fled to Argentina, then to Chile, and finally to Bolivia.

Longabaugh, Jr., states that the first time he met his father was in 1940 and the last time in 1947. He says that he finally located the grave of his father who was buried in Casper, Wyoming, having died there in 1958 at the age of 98.[27]

Barbara Baldwin Ekker, of Hanksville, Utah, who has done some research and writing on this subject, tells us in a letter of June 21, 1973, that Longabaugh, Jr., came to visit her in Hanksville on his tour west to retrace his father. Ekker wrote an article from the information furnished by Longabaugh, from which the following is taken[28]:

> Harry Thayne Longabaugh, son of the famed western outlaw, Harry Longabaugh or better known as the Sundance Kid, visited Mrs. Mart Robison and Mr. and Mrs. Jess Ekker Tuesday collecting data on his father. [Jess Ekker's mother knew the Cassidy gang when they bought supplies from her father, the late Charlie Gibbons.]...Mr. Longabaugh relates that his parents were married in Price, Utah, in 1899. His mother, Anna Maria Thayne, was teaching school in Idaho and had come into Carbon County to visit her parents, Howard Harold Thayne, and met Longabaugh and they were married. Miss Thayne was half-sister to Etta Place who was also one of the women to ride with the Wild Bunch. Etta Place was an alias as her real name was Tryon. She was married to a Johnnie Johnson who ran a sawmill in the Castledale area of Emery County. Etta died in 1940 in Marion, Oregon....After Sundance and Butch Cassidy were reported killed at San Vincenta, Bolivia, they returned to the United States, and Sundance and Harvey Logan hid out at Fort Bottom (20 miles below the Bow Knot on the Green River) between 1913-1916....In 1897, Longabaugh (Sundance), Bill Carver, and Kid Curry are reported to have had a shootout with a local posse at the old Palmer House which was south of the railroad tracks and later burned, in Green River, Utah. [Brackets mine.]

On another occasion Longabaugh, Jr., states that he was named for Butch Cassidy, "Robert" Longabaugh. He still further confuses his stories when he states to a reporter in Missoula, Montana (where he died in a hotel fire in December 1971), that his mother was Etta Place. On yet another occasion, he states that his mother Etta was not a schoolteacher. Thus we see many inconsistencies in his stories. Before the fateful fire, he was writing a book and claimed to have been an outlaw

---

[27]In Missoula, Montana, he gives the date as August 28, 1967.

[28]Barbara Ekker, "Son of Famed Western Outlaw Visits in Hanksville Area," Moab *Times-Independent*, July 9, 1970, p. A-1.

in his own right, to have found some of the caches of Cassidy and Sundance, and to have in his possession maps of other caches. Whatever material he had gathered was burned with him in the hotel fire.

Again, the reader is left to ascertain between fact and fiction. However, more recent research does indicate that Cassidy and Sundance were not killed in Bolivia, that they did return to the United States and lived out their lives, probably under assumed names and in a more law-like manner, or at least on the fruits of their earlier labors. And with this we turn our attention in the ensuing chapters to the real and unsung heroes of the West — those who conquered the wilderness and carved out an enduring civilization. They may not have been so colorful or notorious as the outlaws, but they left a more lasting impression on the pages of history.

Chapter 11

Livestock and
Agricultural Goods

Many years before Escalante and Dominguez brought cattle with them on their expeditions across Utah (to supplement the food transported on muleback and to furnish meat),[1] another Spanish priest, Father Kino, had developed the cattle industry in Arizona. Borrowing a few cattle for a nucleus herd, Kino taught the Indians how to breed and care for cattle, and subsequently from this stock he furnished the beginnings for herds at many missions throughout the Southwest. He is known as the "first cattle king" of Arizona. Therefore, the Spanish are responsible for the development and extension of cattle throughout the Southwest, including Utah.

Early in the nineteenth century, before the coming of the Mormons, the "mountain men" and the immigrants to Oregon are reported to have wintered a few cows in northern Utah.[2] Perhaps the real start of this industry must be attributed to the Mormons who early saw the need for dairy cows and cattle. In 1847–48 Brigham Young sent Captain Jefferson Hunt on a difficult trip to southern California with orders to explore the route and to bring back cattle and supplies from what

---

[1]Herbert E. Bolton, *Pageant in the Wilderness* (Salt Lake City: Utah State Historical Society, 1950), pp. 1–50.

[2]Don D. Walker, "The Cattle Industry of Utah, 1850–1900," *Utah Historical Quarterly* (Summer 1964), pp. 182–83.

was known as the Santa Ana del Chino Ranch.[3] And thus the cattle industry came to Utah.

Fanning out across the Great Plains and into the West, the cattlemen often became the first permanent settlers; Utah, settled by the Mormons, was an exception. But some of the individual settlements were not: Both Moab and La Sal fit the pattern, for their first settlers were cattlemen lured by grazing lands. At first they were small, individual operators, but before many years some of the largest cattle companies in the nation ranged their stock on lands near Moab and La Sal.

The first were the Green brothers, George and Silas, who came from Chicken Creek (now Levan) in Juab County. They probably had heard of the grazing possibilities from members of the ill-fated Elk Mountain Mission. Sometime in the mid-1870s, they brought an estimated four hundred head of cattle into the valley. The disappearance of these brothers is recounted in chapter 4.

With the arrival of Tom Ray and his family at La Sal, the ranching history of the area really begins. Ray brought with him some sixty head of Durham milk cows.[4] Soon the Maxwells and McCartys came with two thousand head. They settled on Coyote Creek, also on the south slope of the La Sal Mountains.[5] Then came the Taylors and John H. Shafer, driving some three thousand head of cattle to the northeast side of the mountains.

By the late 1870s, large herds of cattle had reached the Blue Mountain area, including those belonging to the O'Donnels, "Spud" Hudson, and others. Frank Silvey says that in the summer of 1879 Hudson, a wealthy cattleman of the "Picket Wire" district (near Trinidad, Colorado), bought several thousand head of cattle in the settlements of Utah and drove them to the virgin range on the eastern side of the Blue Mountains, where he settled and established headquarters at what became called the "Double Cabins," but is now known as Carlisle (situated about six miles north of Monticello). He made a trip from his ranch to the settlements in 1879. Passing through the Blue Mountains, he saw the virgin range and decided to stock it with cattle.

When he reached the settlements he found that a good grade of cattle could be purchased for approximately $10 a head. He bought about two thousand head at that price.

On this trip he became acquainted with John E. Brown, Dudley Reece, and William Green Robinson, whom he hired to help him drive

---

[3]Milton R. Hunter, *Brigham Young the Colonizer* (Salt Lake City: Deseret News Press, 1940), p. 32.

[4]Frank Silvey, *op. cit.*; Neal Ray interview, 1935.

[5]*Ibid.*

the cattle. A few months later a man by the name of Peters moved his cattle (about two thousand head) to the Blue Mountains.

Arriving at the Blues, Hudson located his first camp on the Vega near a large spring, and here he built the two cabins end to end which became known as the Double Cabins.

Hudson left his cowboys to look after the herd, returned to his cattle camp on the Picket Wire, and sold his stock there at a good price. He then returned to the Blue Mountains, hired a few more cowboys to look after his cattle, and in company with John Brown, Dudley Reece, and Green Robinson left for the settlements to make further purchases. They bought about two thousand head. Hudson loaned Dudley Reece and Green Robinson $5,000 each to buy cattle, which they drove to the new range on the Blue Mountains.[6]

At this time Peters came in with about two thousand head and built a cabin about two hundred yards west of what, since 1880, has been called Peters Spring.

In 1880, Hudson made several trips to the settlements, returning after each with larger herds of cattle; thus the range was becoming fairly well stocked. The "L. C." (Kansas and New Mexico Land and Cattle Company, Limited) interests came in during this time and ranged their cattle southward and eastward from South Montezuma Creek. Thus the greater area of San Juan County had become stocked with cattle, and the little colonies of Bluff, La Sal, and Coyote were the only towns within the county. Moab cattlemen ranged their cattle on the northeast side of the La Sals.

It has often been said that Utah has more cattlemen and fewer cattle than any other state. This might be said to hold true in the early Moab–La Sal period. Although the number of cattle ranging on the mountain grazing areas of San Juan County was in the thousands, each cattleman was a complete entity, usually owner, manager, and cowboy. The stock had an endless hunger for grass. Sheep were not introduced until shortly after this time. The time was ripe for economic changes, both on the plains and in the western canyons.

The Durango (Colorado) newspaper in 1883 carried a story about an activity which would greatly affect the range history of the upper Colorado River. Two English capitalists, Eli Iliff and Harold Carlisle, had just returned from the Blue Mountains where they had purchased seven thousand head of cattle.[7] Behind the purchase were $720,000 of British capital invested in the new company.[8] The Kansas and New

[6]*Ibid.*

[7]Durango *Daily Herald*, May 31, 1883.

[8]Don D. Walker, "The Carlisles," *Utah Historical Quarterly* (Summer 1964), p. 270.

Mexico Land and Cattle Company, Limited, was just one of the many large companies which put British money into the range industry of the American West.

Carlisle previously had been in London a few months helping to organize a new company, to be known as the Carlisle Cattle Company. Sometime before 1883 he and his brother Edmund Septimus Carlisle had acquired some ranching property in Kansas. This property, plus the improvements, became part of the new company. The Carlisles sold their holdings in Kansas, taking in exchange shares in the new company which Harold had helped to organize. The company also picked up rights to a vast area of land along the south side of the San Juan River.

Thus the beef bonanza had become internationally known. It was evident that fortunes were to be made in southeastern Utah.

ACCORDING TO Frank Silvey, in the summer of 1883 (at the Blue Mountains), Spud Hudson, Peters, Dudley Reece, and Green Robinson sold their cattle interests to an English syndicate headed by the Carlisle brothers. The small operators got $35 a head for yearlings, range delivery, for the greater part of seven thousand head. Silvey explained the brand this company used — three vertical bars, one on the left hip, one on the side, and one on the shoulder — thus it became known as the "Hip Side and Shoulder" (see chapter 19 for greater detail). From then on, all of the increase in the herd were branded with this mark, and the Carlisle Cattle Company became the largest in eastern Utah and western Colorado.

Soon after selling his cattle, Spud Hudson left for his old home near Trinidad, Colorado.[9] Green Robinson went to the settlements in Utah and bought about a thousand head of cattle which he drove to Coyote (La Sal) where he lived for a short time. He employed John E. Brown as a company cowboy to help him look after his interests.

According to Silvey, in the spring of 1885, he (Silvey) was hired as a cowboy for Mack Goode, Carlisle cow foreman. Mack was an old Texas cowboy and his crew was largely made up of Texans. This crew included many names which were to become important in the establishment of institutions in southeastern Utah — such names as Tom Trout, Harry Green, Frank Allen, Tom Roach, Jim McTurner, Hickory Dennis, Jim Moore, and others. Later came Latigo (W. E.) Gordon and Bob Kelley, making a total crew of about a dozen men.

Early cowboy Harry H. Green became the first mayor of Moab, and was organizer there of mercantile and banking institutions. He was a man of great personal courage. On one occasion he allegedly trailed

---

[9]Silvey, *op. cit.*

some Indians who had stolen a few head of his horses. When the Indians refused to let him have them peacefully, Green rode into the herd, cut out his horses, and drove them away. The Indians admired his courage and let him go unmolested.

Another incident is told of how Green accused John Brown of having stolen several head of his cattle. With Brown holding a gun aimed at him and threatening to kill, Green cut out his cattle and drove them away. Such stories illustrate the courage and toughness of many of these men who came to southeastern Utah as cowboys and stayed on, many of them, to become leaders.

Latigo Gordon, foreman for the Carlisle Company during the decade 1887–97, perhaps best epitomized the tough, colorful man who rode for the British interests in Utah. Handsome and intelligent, ordinarily kind and peaceable, he had a streak of wildness. He had no fingers on his right hand which, according to local tradition, he had lost to a rope loop while showing some novice cowboys how to throw a cow. He is thought to be Zane Grey's leading character, Lassiter, in *Riders of the Purple Sage*. His employees included such outlaws as Butch Cassidy, Kid Jackson, Mont Butler, and others of the Robbers Roost gang. Other well-known Carlisle riders included D. L. Goudelock, H. C. Goodman, and many others, some of whom later became cattlemen in their own right.

In talking to old-timers, one gains the impression that at times the Blue Mountain cowboys were somewhat arrogant, lawless, and wild. This varies with the telling, and is usually illustrated by some tales of their wildness when they came to town, drank their fill, and became demanding, boisterous, and loud. And sometimes, as in the instance of the dance hall shooting in which Mrs. Walton died owing to Tom Roach's ugly mood (chapter 9), sweeping generalizations are made.

Cattle were driven out to Dry Valley about the first of May 1885, according to Frank Silvey. The final drive ended near the foot of Peters Hill. On this roundup it was estimated that there were nearly ten thousand head of cattle on the "bunch ground" (herding area), and during the "drift" in Dry Valley, many calves and 250 head of mavericks were branded. The calf tally that year was 5,300.[10]

During the first decade of its operation, the Carlisle Cattle Company felt most of the tensions and became involved in many of the conflicts of the rapidly changing frontier. The first of these conflicts came as a result of the application on the rangeland of a new American invention of that day...the invention which perhaps more than any other changed the world of the cattleman — barbed wire.

---

[10]*Ibid.*

THE HISTORY OF the cattle industry in the West can logically be divided into two periods: B.B.W. (before barbed wire) and A.B.W. (meaning obvious). The first patents to barbed wire were granted in 1874 to Joseph F. Glidden, who then began placing his product on the market. The use of this product increased rapidly, and its use was not limited to the homesteader, for the cattleman himself recognized the advantages. The wire helped to exclude homesteaders and small cattlemen from the vast ranges needed for the large herds. Had sufficient range and water existed, there probably would have been no problem resulting from the use of barbed wire.

How much of the Carlisle range was fenced is not known; nor do we know what measures were taken to resist the fencing. But the range was sufficiently large to result in antagonism and enmity. Whether Utah cowboys rode armed with wire cutters (as their Texas counterparts did), along with their Winchesters, also is not known.

Another problem which the Carlisles shared with other western ranchers was the conflict with Indians. There was a natural resentment between the cattleman and the Indians. The latter saw the cattleman taking away their lands — saw themselves losing their way of life. There were incidents of violence, many of which befell the Carlisle riders. One particular episode in 1884 attracted considerable attention.[11] A Carlisle cowboy thought he saw one of his own horses in an Indian herd. The resulting conflict ended with two wounded cowboys and three dead Indians. There were of course many other incidents of violence.

But the cattlemen resented sheepmen perhaps even more than they did the Indians. When the cattlemen encountered the herds of sheep of New Mexico there was unpleasant action. This resulted in an exchange between the Carlisles and the governor of New Mexico when it was charged that Carlisle, not even an American citizen, was denying the right of New Mexican sheepherders who had for many years grazed their sheep in the contested area. Carlisle retorted that he was a citizen, and that the range was not the traditional pasture of the New Mexicans.

The conflict between the Carlisle people and the settlers became real, and often the settlers accused the Carlisles of being determined to intimidate them. Early settlers claim that under orders, company gunmen sometimes shut off the stream flowing into the town, fired pistols indiscriminately, and generally disturbed the peace in a rowdy manner. They were said to race about the streets shooting wildly.

The Carlisles were not the only adventurers fascinated with the dream of making a fortune in cattle in this vicinity. In 1884 a group of Pennsylvania investors became so intrigued they organized the Pitts-

---

[11]Salt Lake *Daily Herald*, July 8, 1884.

burgh Cattle Company. During the summer of 1884 Charles H. Ogden and Jim Blood, representing the company, came to La Sal and, after some delay, bought the cattle and ranch interests of Philander, Tom, and Cornelius Maxwell, Billy McCarty, Green Robinson, the Rays, and Niels Olson.[12]

The cattle were tallied and branded with two circles on each rib (Billy McCarty's old brand), which was changed two years later to the Cross H (this brand is still used by the La Sal Live Stock Company, the "Redd Ranches"). At that time Ogden was manager and Blood the range foreman.

Acting upon the advice and recommendation of his uncle, Thomas Davis Cunningham (of Blairsville, Pennsylvania), John Mendell Cunningham accepted a position with the Pittsburgh Cattle Company as assistant manager and established himself with the cattle camp at La Sal, Utah. (He left his wife and young son Wallace behind on this first expedition.)[13]

In the latter part of 1888 Cunningham was made manager of the company. He and his family, whom he had brought from the East, then lived at the cattle camp for approximately a year. The following year they moved to Montrose, Colorado, 150 miles distant, occupying a house built for them by the company.[14]

Cunningham reported that the company had ranches and ranges in the mountains, some fifteen or twenty miles from Montrose, where cattle were fattened for market and his time was largely divided between the camp at La Sal and these points.

Another stockholder in the company had a nephew who was eminently fitted for a job with the company at La Sal. Thomas B. Carpenter, who had come to Utah about 1887, had had considerable experience in the Dakota territory, which qualified him to serve as ranch foreman. As a team Carpenter and Cunningham were a profitable combination, for they were able to improve the holdings of the company and acquire new range.

THAT THE LA SAL COMPANY produced good livestock and received wide recognition is shown by a humorous report in the *Grand Valley Times*[15]:

> At the stockmen's convention in Denver this past week, J. M. Cunningham & Company of La Sal received a silver medal

---

[12]Silvey, *op. cit.*

[13]James L. Cunningham, *Our Family History Subsequent to 1870* (Pittsburgh: Private printing, 1943), p. 67.

[14]*Ibid.*

[15]*Grand Valley Times*, Moab, February 3, 1899.

for the best load of calves from the northern division and a special prize of a jug of whiskey, a box of cigars, and a lantern. The lantern is supposed to be of a necessity after the use of the first.

About 1890, the Pittsburgh Cattle Company decided to go out of business due to low market prices. J. M. Cunningham, T. B. Carpenter, and Fred Prewer became associates in buying out the company.[16] Prewer was a cowboy "able and honest but without the vision of John and Carpenter."[17] Included in the purchase was the company house in Montrose in which Cunningham's family had lived. Prewer later sold his holdings to these two men, who continued the company until they sold to the La Sal Live Stock Company in 1915.

In 1896 a large, white, frame ranch house was built which became and still remains the headquarters, although it changed ownership for nearly seventy years. Before he left on a trip, Wallace Cunningham, then owner of the ranch, instructed his men to dig a foundation. Upon returning he found that the foundation was not quite "square with the compass" (or the world), but inasmuch as he had invested as much time and labor as he had, he decided he would go ahead with the building.

In its early years, the ranch house served as headquarters for the La Sal area. It served as living quarters for Cunningham as well as cookhouse and dining area for nearly thirty ranch hands. Old-timers in La Sal still remember the bell which rang each day at 6:30 a.m. and 12:30 noon, calling the long line of men to meals.

The ranch house underwent extensive renovation in 1970, its 75th year.[18] Hardy Redd, manager of Redd Ranches, reported that when it was completed the building would serve as a hospitality house for visitors at Redd Ranches. A modern kitchen was to serve the large crowds which attended bull sales and Christmas parties each year at the ranch. Office space and bedrooms were also added.

In early days, the ranch served as a post office and general community meeting hall. The building was first used as an office after a fire in 1953 destroyed the original office building. The west end of the ranch was then converted into office space and enlarged.

During the years 1890 to 1899, in October or early November, Cunningham shipped the cattle for marketing at Kansas City or Omaha stockyards.[19] The cattle were driven across the country from the ranch

---

[16]Cunningham, *op. cit.*, p. 68.

[17]*Ibid.*

[18]"Historic La Sal Ranch Home Being Renovated," Moab *Times-Independent*, April 30, 1970, p. C-1.

[19]Cunningham, *op. cit.*

to Thompson, Utah, a distance of approximately 75 miles, where they were loaded into the cattle cars on the Denver and Rio Grande Railroad and shipped to their destination. In 1912 cattle shipments requiring 27 cars were made. These were the maximum loads that the locomotives then in use could haul over the existing grades.[20]

Carpenter lived on the ranch and ran it in the winter, while Cunningham remained with his family in Montrose from mid-December until early in March when he drove to the ranch and returned for his family in June. For almost ten years this regimen was followed.

In 1899 the Montrose bank, of which J. M. Cunningham was a director, failed, wiping out all of his savings and making him responsible for notes on which he had given security. Under the law of that time, as a director of the bank, he was additionally responsible to the depositors. He was long in recovering from these losses. The home in Montrose was sold. He worked steadily and conscientiously to recover the losses and overcome the indebtedness. This was finally accomplished, and in 1915 he retired after selling out to the La Sal Live Stock Company.[21]

DURING THE LATE FALL of 1885 D. M. Cooper and Mel Turner, with small herds of cattle, settled on Indian Creek near the mouth of Cottonwood at the Dugout.[22] A trapper and prospector by the name of George Johnson Wilbourne (the original Indian Creek Johnson), had trapped some there, but had made little attempt at any permanent improvement. Thus Cooper and Turner were the first to attempt a bona fide settlement. Shortly after this came V. P. Martin, two men by the names of Davis and Wilson, Harry Green, Lee Kirk, Henry Goodman, and others. In 1887 John E. Brown settled there, planted a fine orchard, and built good cabins and a corral, with a sturdy fence surrounding the crop. The second year he had considerable ground planted in hay and soon afterward had large haystacks for the winter months.

After 1895 D. L. Goudelock settled at the head of Cottonwood where he started a ranch. After a number of years Goudelock, Cooper, and Martin merged and formed what was called the Indian Creek Cattle Company. This was dissolved and sold to Scorup-Somerville Cattle Company in November 1936.[23] With the sale fifteen thousand acres of grazing lands in the Geyser Pass section were transferred.

---

[20]*Ibid.*, p. 68.

[21]*Ibid.*, pp. 69–70.

[22]Silvey, *op. cit.*

[23]Moab *Times-Independent*, November 19, 1936.

Redd[24] points out that when the Hole-in-the-Rock Company undertook the task of getting the resources of the country into their hands, they learned they had come into a country which was occupied by strangers and enemies to their appointed mission, enemies "who were sheltering and employing thieves and outlaws, making it quite impossible for the people to achieve their purpose." Remaining to them was the poorer part of the country. Then came a Texas cattle outfit which crowded in on them with a big herd of longhorned, narrow-hipped cattle, and with a gang of gunmen calling themselves the Elk Mountain Cattle Company.

This company scorned the attempts of the Bluff colonists to buy them out. Finally, however, this purchase was accomplished, with L. H. Redd, Jr., figuring prominently in the deal. Behind him stood such strong men as Hanson Bayles, Kumen Jones, Hyrum Perkins, John Adams, the Nielson brothers, J. F. Barton, and Willard Butt, some of whom were to play a part later in the cattle companies of Carlisle and La Sal.

In 1905 L. H. Redd bought the valuable part of the mountain, the Dark Canyon country on Elk Mountain, from Cooper and Martin.[25] In 1911, Redd was stake president of the LDS church and took the initiative on the part of the stake in the purchase of the Carlisle Ranch, then owned by Harold and Esther E. Carlisle and William E. (Latigo) and Mary Gordon.[26] Others involved in the purchase were Hyrum Perkins, John E. Adams, and H. D. Dalton.

In 1917 fifteen men formed an association to buy the La Sal Ranch and the Cunningham and Carpenter interests. The purchase price was $220,000.[27] The fifteen persons making the purchase were: L. H. Redd, Jr., Jens P. Nielson, Hanson Bayles, Lemuel Burton Redd, Wayne H. Redd, Francis Nielson, Ida E. Nielson, Kumen Jones, J. A. Scorup, Joseph F. Barton, Fletcher B. Hammond, Sr., John P. Larsen, and William G., Andrew, and James Somerville.

L. H. Redd then traded his interest in the Bar Cross Cattle Company, which he owned in partnership with J. M. Bailey, to H. D. Dalton for Dalton's quarter-interest in the Carlisle Ranch properties. This transaction made Redd half-owner of the Carlisle Ranch.[28] As superintendent of the Elk Cattle Company, he was instrumental in disposing of

---

[24]Amasa Jay Redd, *Lemuel Hardison Redd, Jr.* (Salt Lake City: Private printing, 1967), p. 49.

[25]*Ibid.*

[26]*Ibid.*

[27]*Ibid.*, p. 50.

[28]*Ibid.*

the Texas longhorns and in stocking the range with good quality Hereford cattle.[29]

After the purchase of the La Sal Company, Carpenter continued to manage the ranch for three or four months until organizational details for the new company could be worked out. Charles Redd from Bluff, a son of L. H. Redd, Jr., came to La Sal as manager of the La Sal Land and Live Stock Company in 1915. He applied his managerial talents so successfully that the company expanded and improved. Ownership has undergone a number of changes, and at this writing Charles Redd and sons own the property which is called Redd Ranches.

ANOTHER YOUNG MAN set out to make his fortune in cattle and managed to transform his dreams into one of the largest cattle ranches in the United States. As a young man John Albert Scorup of Salina earned four hundred lambs helping his father with a cooperative, but he traded them for cattle.[30] When he was sixteen he used part of his summer wages to buy a new suit of clothes and the remainder to buy steer calves.[31]

Gaining a reputation as a good cattle hand, Scorup worked in trail herds and helped ship cattle to market. Finally he went to work for Claude Sanford, which led him into the San Juan country. Here he met Franklin Jacob Adams who was to be a future partner. He also met Emma Bayles who was to be his future wife.

J. A. Scorup persuaded his elder brother James (Jim) to go with him to San Juan; they started out with a herd of about three hundred head of cattle.[32] The next few years were a struggle for survival. Severe winters, lack of feed, shortage of money — all contributed to the problems of operating a small herd. But pluck and determination won out. Finally in the winters of 1897–98 and 1898–99, Al Scorup made nearly $10,000 gathering wild cattle for the Bluff Pool (cooperative cattle association). He rounded up more than two thousand head at $5.00 each.[33]

This provided the brothers with sufficient funds to operate without selling. Further, they were able to shop around for good buys, and when the Bluff Pool collapsed later that year (1898), the Scorups bought it out. The following year they bought cattle from the Indian Creek

---

[29]*Ibid.*, p. 51.

[30]Stena Scorup, *J. A. Scorup: A Utah Cattleman* (Private printing, 1944), p. 23.

[31]Neal Lambert, "Al Scorup: Cattleman of the Canyons," *Utah Historical Quarterly* (Summer 1964), p. 302.

[32]*Ibid.*, p. 305.

[33]Scorup, *op. cit.*, p. 34.

Company and from Monroe Redd; the second year they bought from Bob Hott.[34] Thus their interests began to increase. The need to improve their stock resulted in the purchase of blooded Hereford bulls in 1901–02.

By 1912 the Scorup brothers had developed a rather large cattle business. Their "Lazy TY" brand appeared on thousands of cattle ranging over tens of thousands of acres from the Elk Ridge of the Blue Mountains to the junction of the San Juan and the Colorado rivers.

Because of their growing families, the two brothers sold their Wooden-Shoe–White Canyon interests in 1918 to Jacob Adams and his brother, and the remainder of their holdings to other San Juan cattlemen, and then they bought their brother Pete's Lost Creek Ranch in Salina.[35]

Learning that D. L. Goudelock was willing to sell the Indian Creek Cattle Company, J. A. Scorup began bargaining for it. He approached Bill (William) and Andrew Somerville of Moab to join as partners, which they agreed to do. J. A. Scorup signed his brother's name to the agreement (much to the anger of his brother, he says). The sale price was $426,000.[36] This was in 1918, during World War I, when prices were high.

In addition to the Scorup brothers and the Somerville brothers, Joe Titus of Moab became a fifth partner, selling out his interests within the year. Controlling interest was held by the Scorup brothers. It was the largest and most daring venture J. A. had yet made. He had hoped he might buy out the controlling interest in the La Sal Company, which at that time was worth $236,000 and included cattle, sheep, horses, and fine range rights. But the asking price was too high.[37]

The winter of 1919–20 was a difficult one. Severe storms made heavy losses in stock, and Jim Scorup died. The personal loss of his brother was a severe blow to John Albert. The cattle market was down, feed on the range was buried under three feet of snow, and there was no hay to be bought. Cattle were dying everywhere. During this winter the company lost nearly two thousand head of stock. Scorup managed to salvage only some of the hides which were sold for 28 cents a pound.[38] The company managed to hold on, although cattle companies all around were failing.

When prices began to climb, the Indian Creek Pool (cooperative) was still in business. In 1926 J. A. Scorup, the Somervilles, and Jacob

[34]*Ibid.*, p. 35.

[35]*Ibid.*, p. 41.

[36]*Ibid.*

[37]*Ibid.*, p. 42.

[38]*Ibid.*

Adams combined to form the Scorup-Somerville Cattle Company; the majority of the stock was held by J. A. Scorup. In 1927 the company held a U.S. Forest Service grazing permit for 6,780 head of cattle, the largest ever issued in the United States up to that time. In 1928 Scorup sold over four thousand head for $194,000 and paid Goudelock the remainder of the note — $100,000.[39]

The company managed to pass through the years of the Depression without ever again experiencing financial hardship. Each year seven thousand to ten thousand head of cattle wandered over their range which covered a giant triangle from the Blue Mountains to the junction of the San Juan and the Colorado, an area of almost two million acres.[40]

In 1944 Scorup reported[41] seventeen stockholders in the company. He said they were running about seven thousand head of well-bred Hereford cattle and owned 32,000 acres of grazing land and about two thousand acres of farmland. Their grazing permit under the Taylor Act was for seven thousand head of cattle, probably the largest grazing permit issued to a single cattle company. They also had a four-thousand-head forest permit. Their summer pasture took care of some two thousand head of cattle, and they fed about two thousand head during the winter.

John Albert Scorup retained active management of the company until a short time before his death. Following his death (he was the last of the partners to die), the company was sold in September 1965 to Charles Redd of the La Sal Live Stock Company. The Scorup-Somerville interests have become a part of Redd Ranches. This enterprise is presently the largest livestock company in southeastern Utah and one of the largest in the United States.

THE IMPORTANCE OF the cattle industry in the area as late as 1973 is indicated in what locals call "Best Ever" (for "best ever bull sales held by Redd Ranches").[42] The sale was held in Paradox, Colorado, and involved 109 performance-tested bulls that sold for a total of $129,150, an average of $1,184 each.

Also sold were eight registered Red Angus bulls for a total of $6,725, an average of $840 each, and eight Charolais bulls sold for a total of $4,850, an average of $606 each. Buyers came from Utah and Colo-

---

[39]*Ibid.*, p. 46.

[40]*Ibid.*, pp. 52–53.

[41]*Ibid.*, p. 53.

[42]Moab *Times-Independent,* May 10, 1973, p. B-1.

rado, and the auctioneer moved 125 bulls through the ring in record time.

A personal touch to the cattle business is added by B. W. Allred in his account of a cattle roundup.[43] He prefaces his story with this description:

> In principle, the cattle roundups in my home country in San Juan County, Utah, were similar to those historically famous in the Great Plains. The roundup was a voluntary cooperative institution where ranches worked together to gather semi-wild cattle from the great unfenced free grass range....Great Plains open ranges disappeared under settlers' fences before 1880. But in the Rocky Mountains in 1930, a rider could, by dodging a few towns, drift from Big Piney, Wyoming, to Phoenix, Arizona, without opening a gate unless he pulled into a ranch for the night.
>
> Our cattle ranged with those of twenty other ranches from Hatch Point on the Colorado River to the west, Indian Creek on the south, to the Dolores River on the east, and the La Sal Mountains on the north. The cattle summered in the high country in the La Sal National Forest and wintered in the low country on the public domain.
>
> Two roundups were made each year. During the major one held in early June each year, cattlemen pooled their forces, gathered cattle from the low country, and drifted them [allowing the cattle to drift leisurely] to the high country to summer. Before the stock [were] left on the summer ranges, calves were marked and branded and steers and dry cows were separated and sold to local buyers or shipped to middlewest markets.
>
> At the first snowfall in late October, the cows left the high country and headed toward old stomping grounds in the low country to winter. They were intercepted on the way down, calves were weaned, slick-eared calves were marked and branded, and marketable animals were cut and sold. (Brackets mine.)

Allred tells us that the winter and summer ranges combined were more than three thousand square miles, providing forage for "about two cows or two horses per square mile." The winter forage, though sparse, cured naturally on the stalk, and full-grown cattle would easily subsist on this forage if grass had been plentiful through the summer months. The ranchers paid the U.S. Forest Service 20 cents a cow per month for summer grazing, but the grass in the public domain on the lower slopes was free. There was one stipulation, however: Those cattle owners who

---

[43]B. W. Allred, "Cattle Roundup Mountain Style," in *Corral Dust: Potomac Corral of the Westerners* (Arlington, Virginia, winter and spring editions, 1966), vol. XI, nos. 1 and 2.

wished to use the Forest Service lands must also have "winter feed-growing land" before they could qualify to get summer grazing permits. His account continues:

> Each year our ranchers elected a roundup foreman.... Most of our saddle horses were out of big Steeldust studs and tough, wiry, broomtail mares. Quick and speedy, they had the bottom to take a hard day's ride.... It was a pleasant jog across Blue Hill, Cane Springs, Flatiron and to West Coyote Wash where we nooned.... Roily snowmelt from Lackey Basin had the creek running twenty feet wide and a foot deep. The water looked like pale coffee but tasted of the thousands of cow tracks it had washed over.... Pups in the prairie dog towns chirped as we dusted along. We saw lush blue grama in the flats, sego lillies tossed their white blossoms, and Indian ricegrass and needle-and-thread on sandy ridges waved their seeding heads. The abundant grass was the product of our wettest spring in years.... We pulled up at Abiqui Springs two hours before dark and the others who had beat us in were swapping yarns and drinking coffee by a smoky fire. They joshed us about being late.

Allred and his trailmates unpacked their food, and everyone ate a pot-luck dinner. The first few days they "lived high on the hog," eating the baked goods and the jams and jellies that their wives had sent along. From then on they were forced to "settle down to the sowbelly, spuds, baking powder bread, canned tomatoes, and Farmer Jones Molasses." They made camp near firewood and water each time; the more accessible these items were, the better. Before going to bed each night the men learned to shake their "sougans [quilts]...to check for sidewinders." One year a cowboy had found a small sidewinder in the folds of his bedroll.

The men pulled rainproof canvas covers over their bedrolls. Some complained of the hard ground. Because of the constant hard work, there was "no time for poker, no one owned a guitar, and not a soul could sing better than a coyote." Even in those days, the western song was synonymous with the western cowboy. There was some merriment on the cattle drive, however:

> A few brought a bottle of White Mule to cure snake bites and other outward infirmities that could be relieved with internal treatment. Few cowboys drank on the job, but when they did, the White Mule gave even a timid man the courage to swat a mountain lion with a short stick.... Our nearest approach to a social hour came when we gossiped around the fire at suppertime. We listened open-eared to every man's comedies and tragedies, about the latest shotgun wedding, and recent fights at country dances.

187

... By now we'd had the opportunity to size up each other's clothes and riggings. All wore [jeans] and jumpers. No one would have been caught dead in anything but a [ten gallon] hat. High heel boots all came from John Silcot's famous cowboy boot shop in Grand Junction, Colorado. Everyone had batwing chaps and a Manila hemp lariat. Spurs and bridles varied according to choice. Most spurs had long shanks and sunset rowels.... Spur straps were buckled on the inside in tune with western custom. Buckling inside is risky, as a buckle catching on the cinch could get a rider dragged to death. However, only a greenhorn would show up at one of our roundups with spurs buckled on the outside. Curved bits were standard on bridles. All used double-rig saddles with swelled forks.

According to Allred, several men had brought Winchester rifles "in scabbards fitted under the right leg," and there were a few with six-shooters "out of sight in saddle pockets." However, Allred had never witnessed "a cowboy pull a gun on anyone."

In his discussion of branding irons, he tells us that although they were considered the "tool of a cattle rustler" in the Plains area, they were the legitimate tool of the cowboys who carried them in an accessible location so that they could easily get at them if there was a calf or two in need of a brand. The techniques used in roping cattle are told in typical cowboy linguese:

We were all tie-fast ropers, a style needed in a brushy or rough country where the cowboy had few opportunities to throw his rope on a critter and when he latches on he needs to have his catch firmly anchored. For our hard-and-fast knot, we used a spliced-in snug slip knot that fitted firmly around the saddle horn. On the other end was the honda that tightened or enlarged the loop. This spliced-in loop or eye was larger than the tie-fast and served as a nonrevolving pulley for the rope to slip through.... The ropers worked the cattle easily, waiting until they saw a cow claim a calf, then roping and dragging the bawling calf to the branding fire. We calf wrestlers took turns flanking. The flanker grabbed the calf's right flank in his right hand, lifted the calf off the ground, and dumped him on his side. The other wrestler grabbed the downed calf by the upper front leg, took a half-nelson, and pinned down his neck with one knee. The flanker rammed the bridge of one foot across the hock of the calf's lower hind leg straight back. Two expert wrestlers can handle any calf while the brander and marker do their work.

Allred's account shows the cowboy as the hard-working man he was. But the cattle drive was not all hard work, for there were moments of serenity:

Before noon we turned the cows and calves onto summer range. Cows with their calves and little groups that ganged together divided like the Ten Tribes of Israel and drifted toward the particular range where they'd summered every year. Some headed for Lackey Basin and Deer Creek, some went to La Sal Pass, others chose Pine Ridge and Ray Mesa, and most of ours worked their way to Hangdog and Two Mile.... We topped the cedar-covered hill and looked back at the quiet ranch scene below. Gone were the hot fires and smoking irons. Gone [were] the banter, jibes, and profanity of hardworking cowhands. Gone were the bawling cows searching for newly wounded calves crying in agony for their mothers.... The cowboys were gone too. Some went to other roundups, others were heading into the mountains with salt for the summer range. Some were going home on a layoff, others left to spend a wad at poker, see the bright lights, and go to a dance. But all would be back for the fall roundup.

Heywood gives an interesting account of a cattle roundup from information furnished him by J. A. Scorup[44]:

On roundups, a calf was killed every day, and they used only the hindquarters. Twenty-five or thirty men would handle up to fifteen hundred or two thousand head a day. The Cross Canyon Pool cattle were driven east and the L. C. cattle west. The cattle would be driven to Dodge Spring, and when fifteen hundred L. C. cattle were gathered, they would take the herd to Dolores, Colorado. They gathered around twenty-two thousand head. The Cross Canyon Pool was from Mancos, Colorado. Irv McGrew was the foreman and Lew Blecher was strawboss. The company had fifteen or twenty owners.... Cowboys were paid thirty dollars per month, and a good hand got $1.25 per day.

The material which follows his account repeats much of that given in the Allred discourse above[45]:

The oldtime cowboy remembers that the country was a wave of grass, with no sheep or prairie dogs to speak of to destroy it. The pioneer settlers of 1877 to 1878 had plenty of grass and water for all their cattle. Then came drout [*sic*] and overstocking of ranges. Then in 1895 came sheep (one herd) to the north end of the La Sal Mountains. Many cattlemen sold out and the cattle were shipped to Montana. Many of the oldtime cattlemen invested in sheep. Wyoming, New Mexico, and Arizona sheepmen came, bringing thousands of sheep into Grand County and San

---

[44]Leland Heywood, "Historical Information about La Sal National Forest, 1940," unpublished notes, pp. 58–59.
[45]*Ibid.*, p. 57.

Juan County. Today we have comparatively few cattle and real cowboys. . . . Hudson, Green Robinson, Dudley Reese, and Peters owned Durham cattle. In 1885 the first Hereford came. I assisted in driving seventy-five head of yearling herefords from Colorado to the Blue Mountain range in 1885 for the Carlisle Cattle Company. . . . In 1886 I went to work for the Pittsburgh Cattle Company with John E. Brown and we drove steers via Paradox to Horse Fly Mesa and to Montrose, Colorado. We drove forty-five head of Hereford bulls from Montrose, Colorado, which had been shipped from Kansas City to La Sal. They cost $85 per head for yearlings and $145 for two-year-olds. There were only two-year-olds.

Silvey was a partner with D. L. Goudelock from 1890 to 1894. They had approximately four hundred head of cattle ranging in Dry Valley and vicinity. One of the largest cattle owners in Grand County in the early 1900s was John Brown. From 1905 to 1910 he did well. He had about eight thousand head ranging from Kirk's Basin to Sinbad Valley and on the desert west of Court House.

What had once been an exclusive cattle land was transformed into an important sheep country, probably as a result of drought, low cattle prices, and rustlers.

The Taylors were the first to bring sheep into this country. Arthur A. Taylor[46] told the author that he, Nels Yorgensen (from Santaquin), and Buddy Taylor brought the first two herds of sheep into the country. He said it was in 1882, though it may have been later. Taylor bought a half-interest with Yorgensen. Lester and Buddy Taylor bought a herd in Nephi.

Realizing the antagonism harbored by cattlemen for sheep, they brought U.S. Deputy Marshal Joe Bush with them for protection. More herds of sheep followed, and like the Taylors, several cattlemen went into the sheep business. Within a few years sheep outnumbered cattle in the vicinity many times over. Cunningham and Carpenter followed the trend when they brought about four thousand sheep into the range country in 1900. As early as 1896 the newly founded newspaper reported[47]: "Over one hundred fifty thousand pounds of wool [were] shipped out of this valley via Thompson this spring."

The Heywood historical notes furnish the following information from C. R. Christensen[48]:

> The first sheep in San Juan County was a herd owned by McAllister, trailed from New Mexico in the fall of 1895. He got

---

[46]Arthur A. Taylor, interviewed by author, 1936.

[47]*Grand Valley Times*, Moab, May 30, 1896.

[48]Heywood, *op. cit.*

caught in a snowstorm on McCracken Mesa and wintered there. In the spring of 1896 he sold to the Bluff Cattle Pool. L. H. Redd and Hansen Bayles took them to Colorado to summer. There was no sale in the fall. The other members of the Pool did not approve of sheep so they insisted on Redd and Hansen keeping them. Later, Lester Decker, Joseph F. Barton, and Hyrum Perkins purchased part of the sheep, and about 1897 sheep started to range on the foothills near the Blue Mountains.

THE LA SAL NATIONAL FOREST was created in 1902. (It is now part of the Manti–La Sal National Forest.) Part of this reserve is in Grand County and the remainder in San Juan County. Supervised and limited grazing under Forest Service regulation protects the plant growth and in some measure saves soil erosion caused by overgrazing. Moab and La Sal stockgrowers find their summer range principally on the La Sal and Book mountains and use the adjoining deserts and river bottoms for winter range. A brief history of the Manti–La Sal Forest and its importance will be presented in chapter 12.

Livestock continues to be an important industry of this area, though not so exclusively as once was the case. There are a number of individual owners of cattle and sheep in this section of the state, as well as the one large company.

Recent years have seen the industry of poultry production develop into significance. The dairy industry has not been extensively developed, but there is a local dairy at Moab serving the needs of the community.

Virgin soil and an abundance of water for irrigation gave rise to a thriving agricultural society which still survives. Fortunes were made in the fruit industry at Moab in earlier days, with the fruit that was grown of an unusual quality.

The first settlers in the valley found the Indians growing corn and squash. The Elk Mountain Mission men grew many vegetables — corn, squash, turnips, melons, potatoes, and so forth. Later settlers found the Frenchman and the mulatto growing delicious melons, squash, corn, and the like. When O. W. Warner brought his family to the valley in 1881, he brought many fruit trees with him, which he not only planted for himself but distributed among other families. This became the nucleus for the future fruit industry of the valley. Randolph H. Stewart developed the Stewart peach and was active in developing the fruit industry. The Warners, the Lances, J. P. Miller, and others became widely known for their fruit production. They shipped carloads of apples and pears great distances. Several carloads of the latter were shipped to England where they were favorably noticed. Although many of the orchards were permitted to die out because of shipping problems, there has been some recent activity, particularly in the production of peaches.

The old-timers of Moab insist that no better watermelons are produced anywhere. Again, remoteness from a large market has resulted in a decline of commercial production.

In the preparation of this book, the files of the *Grand Valley Times* during the productive fruit years were researched and a summary of some of this production is given without listing each individual issue of the paper.

During the month of July 1896, O. W. Warner shipped, via Thompson to Colorado, three hundred crates of peaches. In 1907 J. P. Miller shipped two carloads of Easter pears, one going direct to the New York market and the other to Liverpool, England.

Grapes three and one-half inches in circumference and Bartlett pears weighing a pound each from the O. W. Warner orchard were on display at Moab in September 1896.

An item in the *Grand Valley Times* for November 15, 1907, tells of 25 carloads of winter apples that were shipped to Colorado, largely from the orchards of John Peterson and Myron Lance. The cars contained five hundred boxes each, making a total of 12,600 boxes. At the contracted price of $1.25 per box, the fruit paid the growers $15,750. The newspaper's editor conservatively estimated that six thousand boxes of summer apples were shipped out and growers received an average of $1.00 per box for them. This made a total of $21,750 brought into the valley for apples, in addition to the several thousand dollars paid for peaches, prunes, and so on.

The above statistics give one an idea of what the fruit crop meant to Moab when the industry was at its best. It was the boast of people in "Sunny Moab" that they produced fourteen-ounce peaches and twenty- to 25-ounce apples as everyday products.

During the Eleventh National Irrigation Congress at Ogden in 1903, a Moab grower received the gold medal for the finest display of peaches. In 1905 Utah received the grand prize for the best fruit display at Boise, Idaho. Much of this fruit was grown in Moab. In 1907 at Sacramento, California, another grand prize was received for the best display of grapes. The prize-winning grapes were grown in Moab, and much of the other fruit was also Moab produce. At Albuquerque, New Mexico, in 1908, Utah received the grand prize for the best display of fruit. Moab contributed 42 varieties for that exhibit. A Moab grower received ten first prizes for the fruit he displayed in the 1908 Colorado state fair.

Only the most signal honors accorded Moab fruit growers have been mentioned here. The reputation for local fruit was widely known as the following quotation from a Denver and Rio Grande Railroad publicity pamphlet of this period will show[49]:

> Moab...has been famous for a quarter of a century for the apples that have been sent out from the orchards of Mr. Warner and others to a market that absorbs them ravenously and then cries out for more. The apples of Moab are without doubt the juiciest and the most delicious in the world. Something in the climate and soil must be there that cannot be found elsewhere, or there would be more apples like the apples of Moab. In 1909, two hundred sixty pounds of Moab apples carried away ten blue ribbons at the Denver Apple Show....They raise grapes, too, that have won prizes in California and peaches that have held first place in every national irrigation congress where they have been exhibited. Elsewhere mention has been made of several carloads of pears that were shipped from Moab to England and remained in perfect condition until the last one was sold....Strawberries bear in Moab twice a year, in May and in the fall, and have been picked from the vines as late as November 26. Moab Valley is fifteen miles long and two miles wide, and is irrigated from Mill and Pack creeks.

Grand County was Utah's leading county in corn production, and Moab corn won renown throughout the country. During 1913 a local grower, J. P. Larsen, raised the largest number of bushels per acre in Utah. In 1915 Larsen was awarded a bronze medal at the Panama–Pacific Exposition at San Francisco, California, as first prize for corn production in the state of Utah. His yield averaged 156 bushels per acre.

Moab corn was awarded four out of five possible places at the International Hay and Grain Show held at Chicago in 1925 as follows: John Peterson first, Dale M. Parriott second, Henry Cole fourth, and Birt Allred fifth prizes.

Numerous state prizes have been won at shows by Moab corn growers, and corn is one of the most important soil crops in Moab. It is mainly used locally for consumption by livestock.

The valley is largely self-supporting in the production of fruit and garden products, a very negligible amount of these products being shipped in from outside markets during the season. Exports are not presently an important industry in the valley.

Some Moab growers are experimenting with new developments in agriculture, and it is possible that the town may regain some of its past reputation as a producer of fine fruits and vegetables.

------

[49]Denver and Rio Grande Railroad pamphlet, pp. 11, 14.

193

Chapter 12

Creation of
La Sal National Forest

The conservation-ecology movement in the United States in the 1960s and '70s recalls vividly the conservation movement of the Progressive Era in American history at the turn of the century. One's thoughts immediately turn to the name of Theodore Roosevelt whose name is virtually synonymous with conservation, although there are many others which should be added to the list.

The formation of a national Forest Service preserve was a part of this early Progressive Era. We find that the La Sal Forest Reserve was established by proclamation on January 25, 1906. The Monticello Forest was established by proclamation on February 6, 1907; and the La Sal and Monticello were consolidated on July 1, 1908.[1]

Although a definitive history of the Manti–La Sal Forest Service Reserve has been written by Dr. Charles S. Peterson, a history of Moab and La Sal would be incomplete without some information regarding this reserve and its impact upon the area. With the permission and cooperation of Dr. Peterson, a brief summary of the history is presented here, together with some interesting information related to the Moab–La Sal area.

Leland Heywood, a former supervisor of the La Sal National Forest, did considerable research on the area, gathering material for

---

[1]Heywood, *op. cit.*, p. 8.

a history. This, together with the microfilm "Echo,"[2] the writings of ranger Riis in his book,[3] and personal researching of the files of the *Grand Valley Times* and the Moab *Times-Independent*,[4] furnishes the sources of information.

The conflict between miners and cattlemen is indicated in a report of September 1900 in the *Grand Valley Times*:

> A miners' meeting was held at Mill Creek in the La Sal Mountains, and resolutions were adopted protesting against the efforts of the state to secure for school lands vast tracts of public lands in the La Sal Mountains by claiming the land was non-mineral and valuable only for grazing purposes.

In a later edition, we find the mention of devastating floods in Castle and Mill creeks, which would indicate that overgrazing was an early problem. Note of this came to the attention of national conservationists as is indicated in the *Grand Valley Times* under the date of December 1, 1905:

> News report from Washington says the La Sal Mountains will be made a forest reserve in the near future. This will be of great benefit in the long run, though it may immediately affect a few adversely. The water supply depends on maintaining the forests. The matter of cutting timber will then come entirely under the inspection of a government officer, as well as the amount of stock that may be ranged therein.

A specific report on the creation of a forest reserve on the La Sal Mountains is reported in the *Grand Valley Times* under the dateline February 2, 1906:

> The government has created a forest reserve on the La Sal Mountains...covering 152,000 acres. It takes in all the mountain peaks coming down on the west side to about the Gardner ranch on the Wilson Mesa and goes north to near Harpole ranch. On the east it takes all the land not sold or taken by the state and from the southeast slope extends over into Colorado. The timber on the mountains will be subject to cutting new, only under special permits. The reserve does not interfere with mining or prospecting, but the cutting of timber even for mining purposes is more a matter of government regulations than when not a reserve.

---

[2]"Echo," *op. cit.*

[3]John Riis, *Ranger Trails* (Richmond, Virginia: The Dietz Press, 1937).

[4]Since the research for this chapter covered the years in which these Forest Service lands were being set aside as national preserves, the individual editions of these three newspapers will not be cited. However, the dates are noted in the text.

The report on the consolidation of the La Sal and Monticello reserves was clarified by Heywood in his manuscript[5]:

> Allowance letter dated December 13, 1910, approved division of the forest into five general grazing districts. District one included the west part of the forest and south to Lackey Basin. District two was the south (La Sal allotments) and all the west side, including Paradox and Sinbad allotments. The south division of the forest consisted of districts three, four, and five. District three (Baker) was the range north of Bull Dog Draw and north from the top of the mountain and east from Indian Creek. District four (Grayson) was south and west of Bull Dog and South of Notch, including the Allen Canyon drainage. District five (Cottonwood) was north of the Notch following the rim from Hammond Canyon north to the head of Cottonwood, thence following the rim east to West Mountain, thence north on the west side of Indian Creek.

In chapter 1 of this book, a referral was made to reports of some of the districts as found in the microfilm "Echo" (a publication which provides copies of the report of the forest reserve as published for administration and employees). Some of the interesting descriptions from this record[6] are again cited:

> From a historical standpoint, district five is perhaps the most interesting in the La Sal Forest. It was in this country that Joe McCoy of Kentucky, a member of the famous McCoy family of McCoy-Hatfield feud fame, made his home for several years. From all accounts, Joe McCoy, while he may have "got his man" in other parts of the country, led a thoughtforward [sic] and upright life around Indian Creek and Cottonwood. He was a typical Southerner, speaking with the southern accent, and he retained all the Kentucky mountaineer's fearlessness of all earthly things. He died in 1898, and now lies buried in Cottonwood Canyon, a short distance outside the forest boundary, with a large monument of sandstone over his grave....It was to Mormon Pasture, years ago, that Brigham Young [probably Jr.], a son of the president of the Latter-day Saints church, came to escape prosecution for polygamy during the early 90's. Young Brigham, together with another Saint named Stevens, established a dairy at this place, and their old milk vats and cheese press can still be seen at the cabin, which is now used as a cow camp. The [Mormon] Pasture is used by the Indian Creek Cattle Company as a horse pasture, and is one of the best in the mountains.

---

[5]Heywood, *op. cit.*, p. 8.
[6]"Echo," *op. cit.*, pp. 35-36.

(The latter part of the above was written by ranger F. W. Strong.) The La Sal National Forest met a vital need in the prevention of the overgrazing which resulted in damaging floods.

THOSE WHO SERVED as rangers had many interesting experiences. One of the early rangers, assistant ranger John Riis, son of the famous Jacob Riis, American journalist and social reformer, worked with supervisor Orrin C. Snow in connection with the La Sal and Blue Mountain Forest Reserve. Snow was the first supervisor for the La Sal and Monticello National Forest, serving during 1906 and 1907. He was succeeded by John Riis as acting supervisor on December 1, 1909. Riis, telling of his experiences while with the Forest Service, writes a particularly interesting chapter[7] which he titles "Strange Trails and a New Ranger," in which he gives the reader a glimpse of his concept of the job, the country in which he worked, and the reactions of the people with whom he came into contact:

> From Coyote on the slopes of the La Sals, the Blue Mountains are visible twenty miles or more to the southwest. They held a strange fascination for me. Often my eyes turned toward their mysterious bulk and I wondered just what sort of country slept there in its isolation. I was keen to know.
>
> Late on a February afternoon I rode down the wide lane between the barb-wire fence that marked the main street of Monticello, seat of San Juan County....I had come to "look after the trees." In my saddle pocket was an appointment as Assistant Forest Ranger, a copy of the Use Book, or "Rangers' Bible," and a miscellaneous assortment of blank forms.
>
> Monticello was in truth merely a wide place in the road. Some thirty Mormon families made their homes there, tending their little farms, grazing their cattle and sheep on the Blue Mountains in the summer and out on the great dry desert to the east in the winter or herding them lower in the canyons along the banks of the San Juan River....There was no hotel. Few strangers ever came that way, so I was not surprised when they told me at the first house in the village that they were "not fixed to keep strangers." I had better luck across the way at the substantial stone dwelling of Ben Perkins, a squat little Welchman who surveyed me calmly and critically from head to feet. Reluctant to take me in at first, he finally provided stable rooms for my horse and a comfortable room for myself.

---

[7]Riis, *op. cit.*, chapter 4.

The news that a government man was in town spread rapidly through the little village.... They were frankly suspicious of all "government men."... We were all in a hard place. They did not know the new forest laws and I did not know the country. They had settled it and it was theirs. I was here to tell them they must pay hard cash for the use of the range and their herds must be limited to the capacity of the range.

The respectful and courteous Mormons made me feel keenly that I was an alien in the land and my presence was on sufferance only. As far as social functions and the little intimacies of the village hospitality were concerned, I was completely ignored. It was not an easy task; that of being the first Forest Ranger in the San Juan country.... Much of my time was spent on the mountain ridges posting fire notices and familiarizing myself with the country. At night I sat alone in a cold room working up reports, or ventured into the big living room and took a silent place on the edge of the Perkins family circle. In later years I came to know the true worth of these rugged Mormon settlers, an industrious, law-abiding, and loyal people whose friendship, once won, was well worth the price.

Early in the twentieth century, devastating floods were reported in Castle and Mill creeks. Despite this, in a letter dated July 29, 1907, supervisor Snow stated that the people of the region were very unfriendly toward the policy of the Forest Service in the beginning.

All forest rangers were not so fortunate as John Riis. One who met a tragic death was Rudolph E. Mellenthin (for whom Mount Mellenthin is named), appointed as ranger of the La Sal district in 1911. As a forest ranger and federal officer, he was sent to apprehend a draft deserter and was shot and killed on August 23, 1918.[8]

One of the big issues, so far as the Forest Service was concerned in the La Sal–Blue Mountain area, was the matter of boundaries. The duties of the Forest Service entailed many functions, including supervision of timber and so forth. The sawmill history on the Mesa–La Sal district is very interesting.[9]

A report by Owen M. DeSpain, ranger, indicated that although there was never any great amount of timber cut, the number of old mill settings was equal to other areas of greater production. The early mills followed the mining booms and other activities that created a demand for labor. Few areas were ever entirely cut before the mill was moved to

---

[8]Two Mexicans were charged with the murder — Ramon Archuletto, the deserter who was wounded, confessed; and Ignacio Martinez, who was present, was held for complicity.

[9]Heywood, *op. cit.*, p. 108.

a new location due to the closing of the nearby market, and it was easier to move the mill than to transport the lumber.

The actual dates of operation, especially prior to the creation of the national forest, are difficult to accurately determine. The early sawmill men had vanished long before anyone began gathering this information.

From available sources, it appears that the Mont Hill sawmill, 1881, was the first in this area. It was located at what is now known as Mont Hill Spring, just under the high rim northwest of Paradox Valley and west of the present Buckeye. There were a number of sawmills from the last decade of the nineteenth century through the first four decades of the twentieth century.

It is indicated that floods and erosion began about 1900, but were not outstanding until about 1912. From then until 1920 most of the large floods occurred. Before 1905 both Pack and Mill creeks were small, and old settlers remember when it was possible to jump across either of them.

The original flood at the head of Pack Creek occurred between 1902 and 1905; the exact year has not been determined. These were not large floods and caused relatively little damage. The later floods, from 1918 to 1920, were the most destructive, with the greatest cutting taking place in 1918. Prior to this time the area at the head of the drainage had been seriously overgrazed. This area was closed to grazing in 1920; although the sheep have been kept off it, there has always been some cattle in the area.

The damage from floods led to another contribution of the national forest during the Depression years of the 1930s. The La Sal National Forest was assigned a Civilian Conservation Corps (ccc) camp in the spring of 1933. The ccc men and boys camped at Dill's Knoll on Brumley Creek until they could establish a camp at Warner Ranger Station. In the fall, the camp was established at Moab. During the summer of 1934 the La Sal did not have a camp. A spike camp was established at Castleton during the winter of 1934–35 to work on the Pack Creek–Castleton Road. The main camp worked on Pack Creek flood control, settling the Mill Creek bank protection.

The next assignment of a ccc camp was in September 1936, and the camp was disbanded in the fall of 1937; thus the La Sal Forest had a camp for three winter and two summer periods.

Later, a camp was established (September 1936 to February 1937) at Baker Ranger Station pasture, then moved to Moab. The camp members returned to Monticello in April 1937. A spike camp was established at Moab during the entire winter of 1936–37. These men returned to Monticello in April 1937. The Moab camp was then transferred to the

Soil Conservation Service in the spring of the same year, and the Monticello camp in the spring of the following year.

The major contributions of the ccc camps under the direction of the Forest Service were flood control work, access roads, and recreation areas. The benefits from work done under this program are inestimable.

The La Sal National Forest began as a part of the Manti National Forest, then became an independent unit, and reverted later to the Manti Forest. In 1976 it is known as the Manti–La Sal National Forest. Its functions in conservation continue, and it meets with both approval and disapproval of the citizenry, as have all efforts at conservation and control of natural resources throughout human history.

Chapter 13

Development of Mineral Resources

The industry of mining has played a prevalent role in the development of Moab and La Sal; but changes have taken place. In the first edition of this book, the significance of coal mining was pointed out in the following statement[1]:

> Coal mining has been and will continue to be one of the leading industries of Grand County. [The town of] Sego is the center of the coal industry in Grand County, and enough coal is supplied for all county use, some being exported. Although coal is not mined at Moab, this industry has a great influence upon the town, for it not only furnished coal for consumption at a reasonable rate, but for labor and a source of revenue.

Time and progress have changed the needs, and most of the local fuel used at present is natural gas. Until recently, coal was no longer the imperative source of energy that it once was, nor does the above 1937 projection apply to the 1960s and early '70s, as the author had boldly predicted. But with the current energy shortage, coal is being touted as the number-one resource in the United States. The projection may yet become truth once more.

During the 1960s, long-distance transmission of ultrahigh-voltage electricity and the use of pipelines to carry a slurry of water and coal to

---

[1]Faun McConkie Tanner, *A History of Moab, Utah* (Moab: Times-Independent Press, 1937), p. 48.

expanding California industries increased the demand for more energy — coal can supply that energy. Other solutions are also being developed, but the demand for coal,[2] according to economists and industrial experts, will be 75 percent higher than it was in 1961.[3]

During the recent (and still current) energy crisis, development of large coal deposits in the four corners area seemed to be the solution. But the pollution created by electric plants which operate on coal caused the reservation Indians and ecologists to protest the release of dirt and smoke into the air, pollution that could cover the entire area. The result was government action in which development of these deposits was curtailed. Perhaps scientists will yet develop a process whereby coal can be used in the production of energy without the resultant pollution. If this occurs, the future of the area will be assured.

But coal is not the only natural resource with which the area is endowed. Gold and silver were found in small quantities in the La Sal Mountains; the Colorado River near Moab yielded a few of the "fascinating flakes." Although these precious metals were not found in sufficient quantities to be of great commercial value, the quest for the metal had much to do with the building of the region — there are those who still hope that they will someday strike rich ore. (Early in this century one group of miners on the La Sal Mountains, who had enjoyed only marginal success, at one time refused an offer of $75,000 for their holdings.)[4] But with the high price of gold on the current market, it would be possible for a prospector to make a living even in the insufficiently productive precious metals that exist in the southeastern Utah area.

As one turns through the early issues of the *Grand Valley Times*, one finds the pages full of enthusiastic reports and prophecies of the future of the gold mining industry in the La Sal Mountains. In fact one wonders if the prime purpose of the paper was to promote mining in the La Sals. Items related to mining possibilities seem to take precedence over what would today be considered more highly newsworthy items, whereas the mining future might be regarded as only a hopeful dream.

As early as 1896, Editor Corbin wrote[5]:

> The recent finds of exceedingly rich float on the La Sal
> Mountains is beginning to attract attention from practical miners.
> They have been quietly coming in until at this time there are at
> least one hundred prospectors at work in the mountains.... Every

---

[2]Thomas G. Alexander, "From Dearth to Deluge: Utah's Coal Industry," *Utah Historical Quarterly* (Summer 1963), p. 246.

[3]*Ibid.*, p. 247.

[4]*Grand Valley Times*, Moab, April 8, 1910.

[5]*Ibid.*, August 20, 1897.

practical miner that has ever passed over the mountains has been convinced that as rich lodes as were ever discovered lay hidden in them. Some samples of quartz were recently shown in this office holding gold in nuggets as large as grains of wheat. These, certainly, are from mineral bearing veins.

Activity in the region is indicated in a news item dated June 11, 1897: "O. D. Loutsenheiser was in from Miners Basin this week for supplies.... He reports between forty and fifty men at work in the basin."

The following month, on July 16, another report related that "Winn and Wheeler of Westwater shipped last week six hundred dollars in gold taken from their placer ground below Westwater. This was taken out in six weeks by four men working with a rocker." The report further stated[6]:

> O. D. Loutsenheiser brought down from Miners Basin this week some ore taken from the Little Dot mine that is a rich pointer of what the La Sals can produce. This ore assays a thousand dollars to the ton in copper and silver. There is a five-foot vein that will average one hundred dollars to the ton separate from the rich streak which is from twelve to eighteen inches wide.

These items illustrate the indefatigable optimism of the miners and the newspaper publisher. The activity is further evidenced by an item in the paper on July 21, 1899, which indicated that Sam N. McGraw had opened a general merchandise store at Miners Basin. An item the following week indicated the population of Miners Basin[7]:

> The camp of Upper and Lower basin now presents a very city-like appearance, there being twelve cabins in the Upper basin and fifteen in the Lower basin. There are twelve ladies in camp, and fifty-five men at work prospecting and mining.... There is one well-stocked grocery store, two restaurants, two saloons, a livery and feed stable, a shoemaker's shop, mining office, mining recorder's office, deputy sheriff, Dr. Richmond's office, post office, and a well-attended Sunday School.

The editor continued farther on in the newspaper account:

> The past week McGraw, Miles, and Howell, working on the Clear Crystal claim, laying [sic] between the head of Little Castle Valley Creek and Beaver Basin, right on the "backbone" of the La Sals, uncovered a two-foot vein [lying] between granite walls, from which an assay of the average of the vein gave two hundred eight dollars in free gold to the ton. The richness of the

---

[6]*Ibid.*

[7]*Ibid.,* July 28, 1897.

vein can be seen with the naked eye, as it was cut at the end of an eighteen-foot tunnel cut through solid granite. . . . This claim [lies] nearly parallel and just southeast of the Green Mountain, Little Dot, and Bryan claims, owned by McGraw and Loutsenheiser, from which they have taken some thousand dollar ore in silver and copper.

Mineral Mountain, the name of the peak at the head of Miners Basin, on which, and in close proximity to, [lie] most of the rich claims discovered this year on the north end of the La Sals, is certainly well named. On this mountain, northwest of the Little Dot, [lies] the High Ore, also owned by McGraw and Loutsenheiser, from which ore just taken to the Ouray smelter netted eighty-three dollars in gold and copper. Still father north-east [lies] the M.I.F. claim owned by Fowler, Hepburn, and Wolf, who have followed the other discoveries with one or two and a half foot veins of ore assaying one hundred seventy-nine dollars in gold.

Such reports show not only a keen enthusiasm but at least some reason for the interest. This kind of news brought many people and eastern capital in search of gold, and a fair-sized settlement developed at Miners Basin. A post office was established there in 1899.

ONE MINERS BASIN gold seeker, obviously a persistent man, worked his mine for 38 years and sold $18 worth of ore! But Gordon Fowler, who termed himself "the luckiest miner in the business," was undaunted, even though his search had taken such a long time, with varying degrees of disappointment and success.[8] When he was interviewed at his Miners Basin kingdom on the La Sal Mountains, he expressed himself as having everything a man could want from "a pot of uranium at the end of a tunnel."

The prospecting fever hit the man when he spent two summers at the Miners Basin camp as a teenager, visiting an uncle. He followed a devious route for several years, but eventually returned to take over the mine. The La Sal Mountains gold rush, in full blast on his youthful visit, had subsided by the time he returned to Miners Basin as a man. He remembered a lively town with a saloon run by blind Sam McGraw; a store, boarding and rooming houses, and enough people to cast more than forty votes at election time. On Saturday nights people saddled up their horses, put their children in the panniers (leather bags — a larger version of saddle bags), and traveled for miles to the Miners Basin dances.

---

[8]"Years Fail to Dim Hope of Values of Historic La Sal Mountain Basin," Moab *Times-Independent*, April 27, 1967, p. B-1.

At the time of his return all six major mining areas of the mountain were ghost towns. The story was the same in every area. Ore had not been rich enough to feed the mills, and eventually the scores of prospectors, most from Colorado, left for more lucrative fields. Only a few diehards remained at Miners Basin, including Gordon's uncle, M. E. Fowler, and his partners, Billy Price and George Hepburn (a Harvard graduate whose brother was president of the Chase National Bank).

Gordon went to New York in an unsuccessful attempt to sell his uncle's property. A lot of lower grade ore had been taken out of the La Sal Mountains mines, and despite the disbelief of potential buyers, he was convinced there was a mother lode somewhere; thus he bought the mine himself.

In 1929, Gordon Fowler began his 38-year tunneling project. He mined for gold, for copper or silver, until the Moab uranium boom of the 1950s, when he began looking for uranium. His studies led him to Mineral Mountain, where he found low-grade gold. For seventeen years he packed supplies into the basin by mule train until he built his own road in 1946.

His "gold mine" turned out to be a tourist hotel which he built. Miners Basin is a popular tourist haunt, but the rewards are esthetic, not commercial. His hotel is the beautiful mountain basin where visitors spread their own camp equipment; there are no room fees. He keeps accurate logs, and his guests represent every state in the union and many foreign lands.

When people have visited the mountain miner, they are able to understand his patience with the enterprise. Mineral Mountain is situated on the green slopes of the La Sals, surrounded by pine trees and white-barked quaking aspens, overlooking the grass-covered basin. It is high enough to be cool all summer, and has its own built-in ice plant (where Fowler cuts and stores ice). Visitors can hike, rock hunt, or just bask in the natural resort. By the time they leave, most of them envy Fowler his peaceful mode of life.

His home is a log cabin built in 1898, and although it now wears its fourth roof, there is no reason to believe it will not last his lifetime. Although his ore production has been a bit slow, he never seems to grow discouraged or impatient.

BOTH TUNNEL AND placer gold mining existed in the La Sals. Neither was highly productive of a great amount of gold, and activity has dwindled to a small scale.

The anonymous "Bard of Gold Basin" in February 1966 wrote a poem commending two women for cutting wood and keeping the mill furnace going "on a 30-below night...Of course there are things in which men excel, / Such as drinking and raising up — well; / If good common sense & courage we need, / Men score a big failure, when women succeed."[9]

Located some forty miles southeast of Moab is the Big Indian copper mine which was of some importance to the region, and is still productive. The low-grade copper is difficult to extract, and the paramount reason for inactivity of the mine is the expense of milling and the problem of transportation. Until these problems can be solved, or until the demand for copper becomes more acute, there is not much hope for this industry to become highly significant. But here again the optimism of early miners played a part in the development of the region. In 1899 the *Grand Valley Times* reported[10]:

> The promoters of the Huntsman copper mine in the La Sal Region are pushing development of the property with wonderful vigor. Meanwhile the stock is selling readily on one of the New York stock exchanges from fifty to seventy-five cents a share. The property was incorporated for one million shares, and at the rate stock is going, places the value of the mine at considerably over half a million dollars. Professor Tibbals and associates, who bonded the property to the representatives of the promoters a few months ago for ten thousand dollars, are of the opinion the bond will be taken up and the money deposited long before its expiration, which is January 1, 1900. A few days ago eleven thousand shares of the stock was disposed of on the New York board at sixty cents a share, and sales have been noted daily ever since....At the mine a new boarding house and assay office has been completed, while a large force is at work developing the property and extracting pay ore.

The following month another report was given[11]:

> Mr. Thomas Daly, the veteran prospector and miner of the Lisbon district, was probably the proudest man in Moab today when he walked into the *Times* office and exhibited a copper ingot that had been run from precipitates obtained by the leaching process that is being experimented with at his mines at Lisbon.... The furnace used for melting had proved inadequate, the blast coming from an ordinary blacksmith forge, but they succeeded in

---

[9]*Grand Valley Times*, Moab, February 1906.

[10]*Ibid.*, July 21, 1899, cited from Salt Lake *Herald.*

[11]"The First Copper Ingot Reaches Moab," *ibid.*, August 25, 1899.

melting down about ten pounds into a bar containing with copper a fair valuation in gold and silver.

Frank Silvey tells the story of a silver stampede into Lisbon Valley of some three hundred men who prospected there for several weeks only to find they had followed a mistake. This was in 1880 when a prospector from Nevada on his way to Rico, Colorado, picked up a piece of ore that looked good to him near Lisbon Springs. Upon reaching Rico he had it assayed and it ran high in silver value. The several weeks of prospecting which followed revealed no rich lode and the man went back to Rico. It was later discovered that the piece of rich silver ore had dropped out of another prospector's pack and perhaps had come from some distant mine as a specimen.

Among the prospectors who came from Rico and stayed in the San Juan district for a number of years were Johnny Maloney, a man by the name of Case, the Martin brothers, Jack Wright, Doby Brown, Gus Manville, and others. Gus Manville and Jack Wright located what is now called lower Big Indian in 1881. In 1882 they got a Cincinnati, Ohio, company interested, and A. J. Kile was sent out to investigate. As a result a company was formed which secured a small diamond drill with which considerable prospecting was done round lower Big Indian and what is now known as Lackey Basin. They met with little success, and in 1883 all work was abandoned. At upper Big Indian, Matt and John Martin did considerable work on their claims. This today is known as the Big Indian Mining District and Milling Company.

After about two years the Martins abandoned their claims, but no one was interested enough to work them until 1893 when Can Young, Cap May, a man named King, and Judge Hall of Ouray took over the property and did some mining. In 1894 they shipped a carload of high-grade copper ore, which had considerable silver value, to the smelter near Salt Lake City. The shipment of ore made possible the sale of this mining property for $60,000. The property resold twice after the first sale, and a large reduction mill was built. It would seem that the process was wrong, for the mine never paid its way.

Johnny Maloney was the first prospector in the Lackey Basin area, but he soon became discouraged and left the district. About 1891 Tom Daly, M. H. Darrow, Rhone Higgins, Charles McConkie, and others came to Lisbon Valley and staked a number of copper and silver claims. Although they worked hard to develop their property, they finally abandoned it. Tom Daly stayed with his property many years and did a good deal of development work. He refused two good offers to sell but later had to abandon the property as valueless. J. W. Webb was another who went to the mesa to do placer mining.

THE NAME OF Moab, Utah, became known worldwide in the second half of the twentieth century, and people who had never heard of the community suddenly became aware of its importance. A town of a thousand population suddenly mushroomed into one six times that size. Stores and movies centered about the town, and its reputation began to resemble in many ways that of its ancient counterpart. The reason, of course, was the massive publicity connected with Charles A. (Charlie) Steen's discovery of his Mi Vida uranium mine and the resultant rush to stake out the mineral wealth of the area.

Even the word "uranium" was unknown or unused by many persons throughout the world until the early 1950s when the badlands of the Colorado Plateau became alive with prospectors and miners who searched feverishly for the precious uranium, much as miners and prospectors of an earlier century had sought gold and silver. Only those who have lived through a "rush" for one mineral can understand the generation that lived through the "rush" for another mineral or metal. As in the days of California, the searchers set out by any conveyance they could find. In this new rush, however, they came by jet as well as by "shank's ponies" (a western expression for "afoot").

Before the days of the Geiger counter and governmental assistance, there is a long history of the seekers of this metal. In fact, the search goes back beyond the turn of the century. Old-timers of Moab can tell of those who searched for and mined vanadium and carnotite. This is borne out by Frank Silvey, by representative quotations from the *Grand Valley Times* and the *Times-Independent*, and by Howard Balsley, who laughed at the term "new industry" in connection with uranium.[12] He had prospected and mined for almost half a century in southeastern Utah before the atomic bomb uncorked the profitable side of the industry.

One could not write a history, even brief, of the uranium industry surrounding Moab without mentioning time and again the man who perhaps has been active in the industry longer and more consistently than any other individual in southeastern Utah — Howard W. Balsley, who is the father of the uranium industry in southeastern Utah. Balsley took up residence in Moab in 1909 when he came as chief clerk in the office of the forest supervisor at Moab. In 1918 he resigned his position to accept an assignment with the Moab State Bank.

In a paper presented before the Moab chapter of the American Institute of Mining Engineers,[13] Balsley reported:

---

[12]Moab *Times-Independent*, September 8, 1966.

[13]Copy of this paper and permission to use it was given by Mr. Balsley.

210

In talking with the Talbot brothers, in Paradox Valley, just over the state line, in Colorado, in the early 1900's, when I was a forest ranger, I was told that, in 1879, they found a fissure vein carrying some odd mineral, which they assumed to be silver, and sent a sample thereof to the American Smelting & Refining Company's smelter, at Leadville, Colorado, to be assayed. However, the folks at the smelter advised them that they had no idea what the material was but they were sure it was not silver.

In October, 1898, this same fissure vein was rediscovered and located by a man by the name of Tom Dolan, also of Paradox Valley. A sample of this discovery was sent to the Smithsonian Institution, in Washington, D.C., for analysis. Word came back that the ore was high-grade uranium.

This alleged fissure vein was located on Roc Creek, just across the La Sal Mountains, in Sinbad Valley, in Colorado. Incidentally, the name of the creek above mentioned is spelled "ROC" and the name of the valley is spelled "SINBAD." Whoever gave that creek and that valley, as well as several other old landmarks in that part of the country, their names had unquestionably read a former very popular book entitled "Sinbad the Sailor," for these names were definitely taken from that book.

Well, this so-called fissure vein turned out to be the very famous Rajah mine which eventually produced thousands of tons of very high-grade uranium ore. On various occasions, while riding over in that general area, I have met strings of as many as fifty burros and pack mules, loaded on wagons and hauled to Placerville, Colorado. From there it was shipped by narrow-gauge railroad to Montrose, Colorado, where it was transferred to the broad-gauge railroad and sent on East, from whence most of it was shipped to France.

For many years, the Rajah mine was claimed to embrace the only fissure vein of carnotite (uranium) ore ever discovered. Just in case someone present should not know the difference between a fissure vein and a blanket vein: a fissure vein is presumed to stand up and down, sometimes called a vertical vein, but they are not always exactly vertical, whereas, a blanket vein lies more or less flat. All of the carnotite (uranium) ore I know anything about has come in blanket veins or in pockets.

Frank Silvey concurred with Balsley's statement and believed that because the assay report was not indicative of the kind of ore present, no claim was located at that time. But later Tom Dolan gave some samples to Tom Swain at Paradox. He also left some ore with Charles Pouilot and M. Voilique, two French chemists recently come from Paris, who were at this time doing assay work for the Cashin Mine on La Sal Creek. Tom Swain sent the samples Dolan had given him back to the Smithsonian Institution in Washington, D.C., for analysis. Almost simultaneously came the reply from Washington and the French chemists notifying Swain and Dolan that this ore was uranium.

Tom Francis, who was prospecting near the McIntyre claims in early March 1898, visited the Paradox district and saw some specimens of the uranium ore. He thought he knew of some near his camp. He found it, notifying Silvey and others. Several of the group staked a number of good uranium claims and were therefore among the pioneer discoverers of this rare material.

Balsley reported that in 1898 Messrs. Pouilot and Voilique visited southwestern Colorado and southeastern Utah, the territory surrounding the La Sal Mountains, and investigated the uranium deposits which by then were known to exist there. They proceeded to build and equip, so far as is known, the very first uranium concentrating plant in the world, on the Dolores River, at Camp Snyder, San Miguel County, Colorado, near the junction of State Highway 80 and the Dolores River.

In 1898, the noted Polish physicist and chemist, Madame Marie Curie, and her husband Pierre discovered the element "radium" in uranium ore. Madame Curie is credited with having been responsible for the coming of the two Frenchmen and the construction of the uranium-concentrating plant mentioned previously. She visited the mill in southwestern Colorado in 1899. She is also credited with having given the name "carnotite" to the type of uranium ore that has been produced in the area. The name was in honor of A. Carnot, French inspector general of mines. Carnotite occurs in the Salt Wash member of the Morrison foundation. This type of ore carries uranium, vanadium, and radium.

Soon after this, other discoveries were made in Long Park, Saucer Basin, Bull Canyon, and other districts. A few years later uranium was found (associated generally with vanadium) in the Yellow Circle district, at Yellow Cat and Temple Mountain, and in Dry Valley and many other places in San Juan and Grand counties.

Silvey said that in October 1901 he shipped a ton of uranium ore consigned to John C. Wiardy and Company, Brooklyn, New York, from one of his uranium claims in the McIntyre district (western San Miguel County, Colorado). He said that this was the first shipment out of the uranium belt.

The history is also recorded among the pages of the *Grand Valley Times* and *Times-Independent*[14]:

---

[14]*Grand Valley Times*, Moab, June 1, 1900; June 23, 1905; August 30, 1912; August 14, 1913; February 13, 1914; May 28, 1915; and Moab *Times-Independent*, August 12, 1920; June 4, 1925; October 16, 1930; January 14, 1942; February 11, 1948; April 27, 1950.

June 1900: T. L. Crapo left last Saturday morning for his uranium mines on the Delores [*sic*] river, where he will soon put on a force of men and commence shipping ore to the plant on La Sal Creek which is fast nearing completion.

June 1905: Whitman Cross in charge of the Government Geological Survey...reached Moab the first of the week with a company of six men and a pack train....They will go up the river as far as Richardson and examine uranium properties there.

October 1911: Uranium and vanadium deposits...a dozen miles southeast and west of Green River...had just been under inspection by Kirby Thomas of New York.

August 1912: The Vanadium Ores Mining Co....[is] making regular shipments...from [its] mines at Sayers....Mark Beeson and Albert Anderson, Moab freighters, have been employed by the company.

August 1913: A contract has just been closed...for the shipment... of four cars of uranium and vanadium ores [to European manufacturers] from holdings on Pack Creek. (Brackets mine.)

February 1914: That the interest of the mining world is centering on the rare metals fields uranium and vanadium of this section is...evidenced by the arrival of uranium experts and buyers. The quality and richness of the deposits in the Pack Creek, Dry Valley, and Brown's Hole fields are attracting unparalleled interest.

May 1915: Seven men from Salt Lake City were in Moab yesterday, and left today for Dry Valley, where they will be employed this summer on the Kearns uranium property. There are now about fifty men working on the Kearns holdings.

August 1920: The Moab Garage on Saturday was awarded the contract to haul a minimum of one hundred tons of carnellite ore a month from Dry Valley to Thompson.

June 1925: The United States Company's vanadium mill in Dry Valley is about ready to start operation.

October 1930: The largest payroll of southeastern Utah is now provided by the International Vanadium Corporation at its mill in Dry Valley, forty miles southeast of Moab.

January 1942: Million tons of vanadium within forty miles of Moab.

February 1948: Harold and Glen Lile, proprietors of the Moab Cash Grocery, closed out. Hope to engage in uranium mining.

April 1950: A group of officials of the United States Uranium Mining Corporation...[was] in Moab....[They] plan to erect a uranium mill [here].

In reviewing the history of the development of the uranium industry, one would agree with Sorenson and Bruyn[15] that we may see it as moving through three stages: (1) the radium era, ending in 1923, (2) the vanadium era, ending in the 1940s, and (3) the uranium era; that is, the modern-day period.

Indeed the prospecting of uranium and the mining and processing of the industry have been more than half a century in developing. Most of this history is related to a 100,000-square-mile area of the Colorado Plateau near the four corners area of Arizona, Colorado, New Mexico, and Utah, a region which has been sparsely settled and is almost inaccessible.

The Navajos and the Utes who roamed the plateau centuries ago were likely the first to use uranium ore in America. They used it to decorate their bodies with bright red and yellow war paints made from carnotite ores.[16]

Uranium mining in the West probably began indirectly in the gold and silver mining of the late nineteenth century — indirectly because the pitchblende which clung to the mining tools was thrown aside as worthless. It wasn't until 1871 that Dr. Richard Pearce, of Wales, recognized the presence of uranium in the mines of the plateau area and had two hundred pounds shipped to London. The following year he leased property near the Colorado Plateau area and for several years successfully mined small amounts of uranium.[17]

A dozen years later, uranium mining was under way on a small scale in the American Southwest. The mined ore was shipped to France and Germany where it was reduced and used as a coloring ingredient for ceramics and ink dyes, in the manufacture of glass and pottery, for experimentation in photography, and in the manufacture of steel.[18]

Although a number of sources of uranium-bearing ore veins were known to exist by this early date, there seem to be no indications that mining was done outside Utah and Colorado. Most of the discoveries of uranium-bearing ores were made while sheepherders and ranchers, familiar with various ores, were searching for what were considered more

---

[15]Don Sorenson, "Wonder Mineral: Utah's Uranium," *Utah Historical Quarterly* (Summer 1963), p. 281; Kathleen Bruyn, *Uranium Country* (Boulder, Colorado, 1955), pp. 1–2.

[16]*Ibid.*

[17]*Ibid.*, p. 282.

[18]*Ibid.*

important minerals.[19] Utah deposits occurred in the eastern and south-eastern portions of the state near the basic margins of the Green and Grand (now Colorado) rivers. The most valuable deposits, which were predominatly high-grade vanadium ores and carnotite, were found in the canyon of the Grand River at Richardson, Grand County. These had been discovered by a man named Welsh in the spring of 1898. They were prospected that year by James Lofftus and opened by the Welsh-Lofftus Uranium and Rare Metals Company. At first only small shipments were made for experimental purposes, but in 1902 Lofftus sent about five hundred pounds to Buffalo, New York, for processing experiments and analysis.[20]

The material was known to be radioactive by the fall of 1903, and some was sent to the Curies for tests. The company, incorporated in New York, conducted further experiments at its plant in Buffalo, affirming the presence of commercial-grade uranium minerals.[21]

New finds were widespread; deposits were reported on the west side of the La Sal Mountains (south of the Richardson locality) at Mill Creek, around Grand River north of Moab, near Cold Creek, twenty miles north of Price, southward between Price and the Henry Mountains, and on Temple Mountain. An estimated two hundred tons of ore were mined annually in Colorado and Utah by 1906.[22]

For a number of years after radium was isolated from pitchblende, uranium ores were not sold or evaluated in America by the quantity of radium they contained. But by 1911 the industry began to show the positive effects from the much publicized and mysterious element, more precious than rare gems. Interest in increasing development began to surface, and agents of ore-buying companies in the East, stirred by increasing demands for uranium, frequented uranium and vanadium fields. Foreign interests also became intrigued, thus tending to crystallize American purchase of the metal.

Higher prices brought impetus to the growing industry in south-eastern Utah, resulting in shipments of carnotite from deposits fifteen miles west of Green River, on the east side of the San Rafael Swell; from Professor Valley, north of the La Sal Mountains; from deposits near Richardson, seventeen miles southeast of Moab, in the neighborhood of Pack Creek; from newly opened deposits northwest of Moab near Court House and other places. Along with other new discoveries were the deposits found at the summit of Big Canyon at the head of Lisbon Valley, just over the state line from the McIntyre district in Colorado,

[19] *Ibid.*
[20] *Ibid.*, pp. 282–83.
[21] *Ibid.*
[22] *Ibid.*, p. 283.

and on or near the La Sal Mountains, on the San Rafael Swell (about seven miles northeast of Monticello), along the Green River (eight miles south of Green River), on the east and southwest sides of the Henry Mountains, and in Uintah County and around Independence, reaching into Carbon County on the west.[23]

High costs of mining, transportation, and extraction and the lack of sufficient technology resulted in slow progress in the development of the industry. But by 1913 two companies, the Standard Chemical Company (Pittsburgh) and the Radium Company of America (Sellersville, Pennsylvania), had surmounted the difficulties and radium had become a "wonder drug." Expectations now increased the demand.

THE OUTBREAK OF World War I in 1914 interrupted the American overseas market for radium salts and radium-bearing ores, and mining activities were almost halted. But the setback was only temporary, for the war increased the demand for vanadium as a steel-hardening agent, and for radium for illuminating watch faces, gunsights, compasses, and airplane dials of various kinds. Furthermore, with the normal Continental sources eliminated, this nation became a prime supplier of Britain and the other allies. Thus by 1918 the value of uranium and vanadium ores, mined in the areas of Montrose and Mesa counties in Colorado and the La Sal Mountains and Green River district in Utah, now reached nearly $1 million, with an estimated 27 grams of radium in the ores.[24]

In 1918, the United States Metals Reduction Company built a plant southwest of Gateway, Colorado, just inside the Utah line. Standard Chemical Company, the largest company engaged in isolating radium, employed about two hundred workers and had nearly four hundred claims in Colorado and several dozen in Utah.[25]

After the war, discovery of exceptionally rich deposits on the Utah-Colorado border started a rush to stake out new locations. Considerable uranium was used for watch dials, the manufacture of luminous fish bait, and glowing eyes for toy dolls and animals.

More efficient mining procedures were developed, greatly increasing the output. But the optimism and new way of life were short-lived. Foreign competition and the Depression began to slow down the American radium industry. As the Depression deepened, it was natural that ore production should slow down; most of the mines were closed by the fall of 1921. Then a deathblow came by way of the discovery of

---

[23]*Ibid.*, pp. 284–85.
[24]*Ibid.*, p. 286.
[25]*Ibid.*

rich uranium ores in the Katanga Province of the Belgian Congo in 1923. Easily worked, this new source drove the price of the metal downward almost overnight; the mines of Utah and Colorado were unable to compete.

To further add to a depressing situation, newly discovered vanadium deposits in Peru began to dominate the market at about the same time. Without a profitable market for radium or vanadium, the mines of the West had little cause to produce. Thus the radium era came to an end in 1923.

When Madame Curie returned to the United States in 1922, the U.S. government, in recognition of her singular contribution to the science in discovering radium, purchased one gram of the precious metal and presented it to her. The cost was $80,000 wholesale. Radium at that time was retailing for $120,000 a gram.[26]

Howard W. Balsley, cited earlier, reported that as nearly as he had been able to ascertain, the first uranium ore discovered in the immediate vicinity of Moab and La Sal was by old-time prospector Albert M. Rogers, a member of the Rico posse in the Pinhook massacre (chapter 9), who in later years lived for some time in the Balsley home. Rogers had found ore on a famous old uranium property near the base of Brumley Ridge, not far from the turnoff to the M-4 ranch, in upper Spanish Valley (designated for many years as "Poverty Flat" or "Bueno"). This mining property was later patented under the name of "Blue Goose." Ore from the Blue Goose was mined and shipped to France, and (it is said) to Madame Curie's laboratory in Paris.

Rogers was grub-staked on many occasions by Balsley. (Grub-staking is a custom that has long prevailed in all mining areas in the West. It means that someone buys enough food, supplies, and tools to last a prospector for some time — say, thirty days — together with grain for his pack and saddle animals [or, in the case of Charlie Steen, fuel for automotive equipment and so on]. When the food and supplies are used up, the prospector, if he wishes to continue, must then return to the same grub-staker or find another who is willing to take the risk. However, during prospecting excursions, if one or more promising claims are located, both the prospector and the grub-staker share equally in the profits.) Rogers was lucky (perhaps even shrewd) enough to find a number of good uranium claims to share with Balsley.

But Rogers was not the only investment Balsley made, for he tells of grub-staking another prospector, Charles Snell, because of a dream that Snell had experienced about a uranium mine with a yellow circle in a block of sandstone in the Upper Cane Springs Wash area.

[26]Balsley, *op. cit.*

Within ten days, Snell had located the yellow circle in the block of sandstone.[27] Later claims in this area produced vast amounts of good uranium-bearing ore. More than $1 million in ore was taken from these sites, yet the claims sold for a neglible amount in later years.

Balsley's initial ore shipments were processed and used as coloring agents for ceramics. By 1934, he had entered into a contract with Vitro Manufacturing Company (Pittsburgh, Pennsylvania) in which he agreed to supply its requirements for uranium ore, with the stipulation that the ore would contain at least 1.5 percent vanadium. During these years, Balsley owned seven warehouses, spaced over the area, where he collected ore from many mines — enough to ship 54 carloads.

All production of uranium in Utah and the nation was negligible from 1923 to the 1940s. Then activity on the Colorado Plateau was again spurred by World War II, vanadium being essential to the hardening of steel. Roads were built, ore-purchasing depots opened, and new plants erected in Blanding and Monticello, Utah, and several locations in Colorado. The government aided in discovering new deposits of the ore and stepping up production, and the nation soon led the world in the production of vanadium during the war years (1943-45).

In May 1942, Balsley began stockpiling carnotite ores for the Metal Reserve Company (as its agent).[28] By 1949 he was operating one of the largest vanadium mines in the western Colorado–eastern Utah region. He played an important role in petitioning the federal government to raise prices on vanadium ore in 1949.[29]

The war also stimulated the demand for uranium. It was in demand for use in the now-famous Manhattan Project. A covert but intensive attempt was made to reprocess low-grade tailings at the vanadium mills in Utah and Colorado. As a result of this activity and other needs, the Defense Plant Corporation constructed an improved mill at Monticello.

ALL SUCH ACTIVITIES were suspended when World War II came to an end. Mines, ore mills, and chemical plants were closed. But the period of inactivity in this case was a short one. National security prompted the passage of the Atomic Energy Act, with the result that resumption of uranium production was on a far larger scale than ever before. There was a step-up in exploration; new processing plants were built; the out-

---

[27]*Ibid.* Although this was a case of dreams literally coming true, Balsley does not give the name of Snell's mine. There were several mines in the area of Yellow Circle, Yellow Cat, Temple Mountain, Dry Valley, and others.

[28]Moab *Times-Independent*, May 28, June 4, September 17, 1942.

[29]*Ibid.*, February 3, 1949.

put of ore soared to unprecedented heights. Uranium was no longer a minor industry — it became the most sought-after mineral in the world.

At that time there was an exciting aura about uranium. The crucial role it must play in the Cold War gave it significance beyond mere necessity. Patriotism was somehow involved in it. Thousands flocked to the Colorado Plateau region — amateur and professional prospectors, mining engineers, trained geologists. There were fortunes to be made; each man sure that he would find his own personal "bag of uranium" at the end of the rainbow. And indeed many did find those bags of uranium. Until then, a number of people had been collecting royalties of considerable size for some time, but doing it rather secretively. Then there were the sensational discoveries of people like Pratt Seegmiller, the humble retailer, who discovered the famous Marysvale deposits in 1947; Paddy Martinez, the Navajo, and Joy Sinyella, the Supai, who, without Geiger counter or drilling rig separately discovered the rich deposits in Grants County, New Mexico; Vernon Pick, who found his Delta bonanza while flying over the area; Joe Cooper and Fletcher Bronson and their "Happy Jack" mine; and the young geologist, Charles A. Steen, who, with a Geiger counter under one arm and a bundle of Geological Survey bulletins under the other, found the wondrously rich Mi Vida deposit in the Big Indian district near Moab in the summer of 1952. He formed the Utah Exploration Company that year, and it was only a short time before he had literally made his way from rags to riches.

Nothing stimulates like success. Such discoveries as those cited above, plus the stimulus of lucrative government contracts, induced formation of virtually thousands of new companies — to explore, mine and mill, or promote.

Selected issues of the *Times-Independent* between March 1941 and February 1952[30] tell how the government raised uranium prices as much as 300 percent and offered a major bonus for initial production. A million-dollar access-road project was authorized. In September 1951 the *Times-Independent*[31] reported the first five mines to receive the special bonus from the Atomic Energy Commission for ore production and said "three are located within a stone's throw of Moab."

It was the spectacular discovery by Steen which triggered the boom and sky-rocketed Moab into national and international prominence. Steen's story has been written many times, but pertinent facts seem appropriate here: Charles A. Steen was a professional geologist,

---

[30]*Ibid.*, March 6, 1941; January 15, February 19, 1942; August 16, 1945; March 1, September 13, 1951; January 3, February 7, 1952.

[31]*Ibid.*, September 13, 1951.

receiving his degree at West Texas College of Mines.[32] Employed by a Texas oil company, he read an article in the *Engineering and Mining Journal* about uranium in southeastern Utah and left Houston to come to the Moab area.[33] According to his own story, he was a "ragged prospector, often broke...usually hungry." He and his wife Emelle and their four boys lived first in a tent and then in a house trailer. He had a second-hand jeep and "a battered old drilling rig."[34] In December 1951 they were living at a mining location in the Yellow Cat district several miles from Cisco and sixty miles from Moab.

At some time in the spring or summer of 1952 he left the Yellow Cat and Cisco area and traveled south through Moab to the head of Big Indian Canyon. Here he set up his drilling rig on claims he had staked the previous year. According to the Salt Lake *Tribune*, the following events occurred[35]:

> This is to report that "Steen's Folly" today is a going concern....When Charles H. (Hard-luck) Steen first started digging around at the head of Big Indian Canyon...they all said he was crazy. Most of the major companies had already prospected the area and were convinced that it was barren....He set up a drilling rig and his first hole hit pay dirt....[He] struck a mass of pitchblende type ore, "primary ore" — the kind of stuff that's needed for atomic defense.

The *Tribune* may have given Steen the initial "H" so that it could justify the nickname "Hard-luck."

Both Moab and La Sal grew and prospered with the uranium industry. Moab in particular experienced many of the pains of a rapidly growing city where it is impossible to keep up with new building construction, the need for additional zoning and regulatory ordinances, and the lack of adequate law-enforcement personnel. But the populace soon settled down to the serious business of accepting change and making the most of it. More orderly expansion was soon managed: Newly passed zoning ordinances were enforced, and the inhabitants made every possible effort to feed and house the heavy influx of people.

The uranium boom lasted for several years. According to Sorenson,[36] Salt Lake City became the locale for the wildest "speculative mania in the nation since 1929 — the 'investment' in penny uranium

---

[32]*Deseret News*, Salt Lake City, October 11, 1954.

[33]"Moab, Utah, Modern Day Boom Town," *Intermountain Industry* (June 1961), vol. LXIII, p. 9.

[34]*Deseret News*, Salt Lake City, December 20, 1958.

[35]Salt Lake *Tribune*, May 3, 1953.

[36]Sorenson, *op. cit.*, p. 290.

stocks during the years 1953, 1954, and 1955. For months on end, the demand for stock kept brokers at work around the clock."

But by 1956 the Atomic Energy Commission announced that the supply of uranium had reached a saturation point. Producers were advised not to expand further. Steen sold out to the Atlas Corporation and moved to Nevada. However, the reduction mill which he had constructed and the railway spur from Thompson (built to serve the potash plant) have remained in production.

But again (and this is the third revival), there is recent renewed activity — perhaps even more than in the first boom period. There are several reasons for this: New demands for the use of radium for electric power generation have lowered the stockpile much faster than had been anticipated. The 1985 estimates have now been lowered to those of 1970. There may be a demand for new discoveries and more production.[37] What the future holds is still uncertain. The Rio Tino discoveries in Canada could well dwarf the Steen deposits. But what will be the demands? The future, at least, looks bright.

Nuclear power is now in competition with coal generation of power. It has many advantages: It is cleaner and there is no danger of total blackouts (as there is with coal power). With nuclear generation, each plant can have its own generator and thus any blackout would be limited to those served by one plant. In addition, nuclear power produces no air pollution, one of the most thorny problems facing this nation today. (Natural gas is the only fuel at present which can compete with nuclear power insofar as cleanliness is concerned, but its supply cannot last forever.)

One must assume, then, that the problem lies in the economics of power production. It is costly to reduce uranium ore to produce sufficient quantities of radium for nuclear power, and it is economically impractical on a large scale. The author is a historian, not a scientist, but optimism must be maintained that a more economical reduction process may be developed, thus greatly increasing the demand for uranium ore. At present, the demand is sufficient to revitalize the activity in southeastern Utah. The future indeed looks promising.

THE REDUCTION MILL near Moab, built during the boom, is economically important to the city, for it carries a large payroll and plays a key role in the economic stability of the community. The plant concentrates copper ore as well as uranium. Copper ores must be shipped from outside

---

[37]Interview with Samuel J. Taylor, state senator and editor of the Moab *Times-Independent*, May 1968.

because there are insufficient high-grade copper-bearing deposits in the area.

Another major mining industry in Moab's and Utah's post-World War II period is that of fertilizers, including potash. In 1963 a significant amount of potash was discovered in the Cane Creek area near Moab. Utah is the only state in the nation to produce all three primary plant foods: nitrogen, phosphate, and potash. Except for small potash operations during World War I, the industry didn't actually get its start until after 1940; major developments weren't made until after 1948.[38]

The search for potash in the United States was necessary when, as a result of World War I, shipments from Germany were cut off. This instigated the search in Utah. When domestic prices rose from $35 to $500 per ton, the impetus to find this mineral was real, especially in light of acute agricultural needs for the fertilizer. Although the precious mineral was found in Utah, the fields near Moab were not explored at this time, and the war-stimulated production terminated in 1921. However, interest continued, and exploratory work led to future developments.

When oil wells were drilled south of Thompson, near Moab, potash was discovered in the salt section of the Paradox formation. The *Times-Independent* reported in 1926[39] that the world's richest potash bed had been discovered in Grand County, near Thompson, at the Crescent-Eagle well. This and later drilling led the Defense Plant Corporation to drill a carefully controlled test well, the report of which described a rich section of potash salts at a depth of over three thousand feet. Federal and state lands were leased for intensive exploration and development by the Delhi Taylor Oil Corporation. An intensive and successful drilling campaign was begun in 1956 in the Seven Mile area, just north of Moab. This was later extended to the Cane Creek area. Testing and evaluation were carried out until 1960, when Delhi Taylor made a deal with Texas Gulf Sulphur Company to take over development and operations. Plans were announced for mine development and processing facilities.

A mill has been built in Moab and deep mining is conducted. A large number of people are employed by Texas Gulf Sulphur, which is economically important to the area. At this writing Canadian potash is highly competitive, but Texas Gulf is getting improved reduction and the demand should increase. The company is filling its warehouse, expecting a short period of recovery. It is optimistic about the future, and the residents of the Moab area are also hopeful. The company has a $40 million investment in its mining and milling complex.

---

[38]ElRoy Nelson, "The Mineral Industry: A Foundation of Utah's Economy," *Utah Historical Quarterly* (Summer 1963), p. 190.

[39]Moab *Times-Independent*, January 7, 1926.

The initial excavation was six feet in depth and 23 feet in diameter.[40] By the end of 1962 the shaft had been sunk to a depth of 2,977 feet where a station was established. From this station several cross-cuts were made that extended into the 11,400-acre body of ore.[41] By late 1963 a mill had been completed. This modern mill, ten miles down the Colorado River from Moab, rests on a vast cushion of potassium salt.

This successful operation of the Cane Creek potash development has been effectively aided by the construction of a $7 million Denver & Rio Grande Western railroad spur which extends some 32 miles between the main line at Crescent Junction near Thompson, Utah, and the Texas Gulf Sulphur Company mill. The story of the building of this spur is one of superb engineering and modern construction. The spur and a siding north of Moab serve not only the potash plant, but will provide the community with an adjacent railway service and lend substantial support to future industrial expansion.[42]

As late as March 2, 1972, the *Times-Independent* noted that there was a revival of potash production at Cane Creek as a result of the use of the new solution mining method. Texas Gulf Sulphur Company was again producing potash with the conversion from conventional mining to solution mining.

THE VOLUME AND different varieties of hydrocarbon compounds found in the Colorado River drainage basin probably cannot be excelled. In the Moab country, these take the form of oil deposits which have been prospected sufficiently to determine their presence and location.

Since near the close of the nineteenth century, a search for commercial quantities of oil and gas has been carried out in southeastern Utah. As early as 1891 a well was drilled on the Green River desert, about forty miles northwest of the Moab district. The distinction of drilling this first Utah well belongs to Simon Bamberger and a man named Millis.[43] Early in the year, Bamberger (later Utah governor from 1916 to 1920) financed the drilling of this hole near the Denver & Rio Grande Western Railroad on the east side of the river south of the town of Elgin, in Grand County. A stratum of gypsum was penetrated at just over a thousand feet. Drilling was stopped, and the well shut down with no reported oil production.

---

[40]*Ibid.*, March 2, 1961.

[41]"Moab, Utah, Modern Day Boom Town," *ibid.*, p. 6; and "Texas Gulf Sulphur Company Annual Report, 1962" (Houston, Texas, 1963), p. 23.

[42]Moab *Times-Independent*, December 17, 1964, and July 8, 1965.

[43]Osmond L. Harline, "Utah's Black Gold: The Petroleum Industry," *Utah Historical Quarterly* (Summer 1963), p. 293.

Because the results were discouraging, no additional wells were drilled for oil or gas in this locality for about a decade. Then three more wells were drilled in 1899 and 1900 with the same result. But ten years later, 1910 to 1914, there was a revival of activity in the area of the Green River desert, during which time several more wells were drilled. None of these found more than a trace of oil, though some went to depths ranging from fourteen hundred to eighteen hundred feet. However, some gas was found.[44]

In the 1920s important developments were made in the Moab district. Drilling was begun in the vicinity of Crescent Junction, a few miles west of Thompson, and several wells were drilled in 1920. Oil and gas evidence was encountered in the wells of the Crescent–Eagle Oil Company and the Crescent syndicate. The Western Allies–Big Six well (1920) was sunk to a depth of 2,450 feet in the Moab Valley. This yielded oil and gas evidence. Later the same year the Big Six Oil Company started another well in the valley which was located on the west side of the Colorado River. The drillers encountered several signs of gas and oil. None of the drillings resulted in the production of oil wells.

Considerable excitement was created in October 1924 when the Utah Oil Refining Company's well, about ten miles northwest of Cisco, "blew in" on October 11 with an immense flow of gas of hydrocarbon origin. This was encountered at a depth of 1,960 feet. The gas was ignited by lightning on October 13, and the fire could be seen for miles. It required the services of an expert to extinguish it. It was estimated that the pressure generated by the escaping gas was around 2,500 pounds and that the flow would measure 150,000 cubic feet per day.

The gas field near Cisco was found to have commercial value and a carbon-black mill was built. The gas was used in the manufacture of carbon black (a dense carbon deposited in gas retorts). It also furnished light and fuel for nearby houses, but activity of the mill was soon suspended.

Perhaps the most disheartening of the exploratory attempts was the Frank Shafer No. 1 well, which was located on the Cane Creek anticline. The well was begun in the winter of 1924–25 by the Utah Southern and the Midwest Exploration companies. On December 8, 1925, oil was found at a depth of 2,028 feet. This was excitement! The well had blown in with the greatest oil gusher in the state's history — Utah's first oil gusher. The well, spouting like a geyser two hundred to three hundred feet high, was estimated to be producing in excess of five hundred bar-

---

[44]Arthur A. Baker, "Geology and Oil Possibilities of the Moab District, Grand and San Juan Counties, Utah," United States Geological Survey *Bulletin 841* (Washington, D.C., 1933), p. 80.

rels a day. Later a news report in the Moab *Times-Independent*[45] carried the headlines: "Big Oil Gusher Blows In. Midwest Well on Big-6 Dome Spouting Excess of five Hundred Barrels." But the oil burst into flames almost immediately, demolishing the derrick. The fire was extinguished after a ten-hour battle.

This well produced a large quantity of high-grade oil (estimated to flow at the rate of 1,400 barrels daily)[46] before it was brought under control. The well attracted wide attention because of its unique location at the bottom of the river canyon and because the oil was coming from a salt formation in the lower Pennsylvania series.

Within a few days after the gusher blew, there was considerable activity in the vicinity of Moab, with evidence of a real oil boom. The interest lasted for some time. However, because of failure to secure a successful water shutoff, the well was drilled to a final depth of five thousand feet with several evidences of oil and gas, but inability to solve the casing problems made it impossible for operators to determine the real worth of the discovery. Several flow tests indicated, however, that the production was approximately fifty barrels per hour. Sufficient oil was produced for the drilling of another well on the flank of the same structure. The first well was plugged with cement and lead in 1928 after the casing had collapsed and production had been shut off by the recrystalization of salt in the well and tubing.

After a full year of periodic drilling, with oil and gas encountered again at lower depths, the operation was suspended. Others undertook additional wells in which oil showings were found, but no gusher.[47]

Economic conditions — the Depression years followed by World War II — prevented new drillings for several years. Although 25 wells were drilled in the state during this twelve-year period, no producers were found.

With the end of World War II, interest in Utah's oil and gas possibilities was renewed. Commercial oil was found in the Vernal area. But the big find, which was to move the state from anonymity of the "all other" column in national crude-oil production reports to a separate listing, was to be in the Greater Aneth location — in the complex of fields located on either side of the San Juan River in the Paradox Basin in the extreme southeast corner of the state. While these fields are some distance from Moab and La Sal, they have led to more activity in the field of exploration, and Moab and La Sal have benefited economically from related activities. The discovery of the Lisbon field, south of Moab,

---

[45]Moab *Times-Independent*, December 10, 1925.

[46]*Ibid.*, January 7, 1926.

[47]Harline, *op. cit.*, p. 297.

in 1960 is an example of the beneficial results of commercial strikes in a near area.

Pure Oil Company drilled its Northwest Lisbon No. 1 (later changed to No. 1 USA)[48] in August 1959. The attention of the entire industry was turned to the Paradox Basin when the well became a producer in early January 1960. It was designated "discovery of the year"[49] by the national petroleum industry because of the size of the field and because the area had heretofore been considered a poor prospect for oil and gas exploration. The oil is piped to Los Angeles, California.

It was not until the pipelines were built that oil production in quantity from Paradox Basin oil fields could be achieved. With these pipelines, Utah is in the unique position of being able to transport Utah-produced crude oil from the Paradox Basin to both the Pacific and the Gulf coasts for refining.

With the existence of an energy crisis in the United States, there may well be an important future for this area in the wealth of "black gold." Early in 1973[50] oil and gas drilling activity in southeastern Utah's Grand and San Juan counties continued to move along at a steady pace. Several wells were under way in the Cisco area of Grand County, and significant exploratory wells were being drilled in San Juan County.

Work has been centered round several oil fields. The future for this industry also looks promising.

---

[48]*Ibid.*, p. 301.

[49]*Ibid.*

[50]Moab *Times-Independent*, January 18, 1973.

Chapter 14

Transportation and Communication

If one were to reduce the West to a brief appellation, perhaps "vastness" would be appropriate. The illusion of proximity has been the undoing of many a traveler in the West, even in recent years. Recognizable landscape seems near and yet is so far distant that it has caused people to die of thirst pursuing that which appeared near at hand. The very ruggedness of the topography has been a handicap to travel. Indeed this has been true of the canyonlands area around Moab and La Sal.

Earliest travel was of course by foot, then by horse. As discussed in an earlier chapter, the Old Spanish Trail was never a wagon road. Trade transported over this route was by pack horse or mule. No wagons went over any portion of the trail in Utah until the Elk Mountain Mission men cut a road and pioneered with a few wagons in 1854–55. The Escalante-Dominguez expedition of 1776, reaching almost to La Sal, was by horse and foot.

Any historical study of the slowness or rapidity of development of the West is related to the availability of streams for transportation. Although there are several rivers — the Dolores, Colorado (Grand until 1921), Green, and San Juan — in this vast area of southeastern Utah and western Colorado, they were not practical for transporting long distances. Rapids, strong currents, shifting channels, and inaccessibility are not conducive to using anything but small crafts. During the summer, the water sometimes is at such low ebb that sandbars make successful travel difficult (if not impossible), whereas during flood season, there are contrasting problems. But the early settlers' eternal optimism caused them to test river crafts of varying sizes, as will be evidenced from the following discussion.

Major John Wesley Powell's now-famous expeditions down the Green and Colorado rivers — especially those of 1869 and 1871–72 — have been thoroughly documented by others. Not so well known, perhaps, is that in July 1869, he entered and traversed the Moab area. His records indicate that he entered Desolation Canyon on July 8, 1869, near Flaming Gorge (alongside Green River) where he found this inscription: "Ashley, 1825." William H. Ashley had preceded Powell by 44 years when he took his fellow fur trappers through this part of the Green River in boats that were covered with buffalo hides.[1]

Another traveler of this northern section of the Green River was William Manly who had taken a group of California-bound prospectors down through the canyons in 1849.[2] Both Manly and Powell, with their respective parties, had left the Green River at the junction of Yampa, Colorado. Powell was the first to scientifically negotiate the remainder of the wild, unknown river. He traveled through the pristine northwest corner of Grand County where it joins with three other counties, Emery, Carbon, and Uintah, in approximately the center of Desolation Canyon.

Almost without exception, explorations of the Colorado River by boat have started at some point on the Green River. An exception to this, however, was the expedition of Frank M. Brown in 1889. He led a party down the upper Colorado River to make a preliminary survey for a "water-level" railroad route from Colorado to California. Dellenbaugh,[3] in the account of this expedition, says that a new railway was proposed from Grand Junction, down the Colorado River, through the canyons to the Gulf of California, a distance of some twelve hundred miles. At that time, coal was difficult to obtain on the Pacific Coast, and it was thought that this water-level railway, crossing no mountains, would be profitable in bringing the coal of Colorado to the Golden Gate. When an abundance of coal was subsequently located in the Puget Sound region, the reason for constructing the Grand Canyon railway no longer existed. Since there was nothing to support a railway through the three hundred miles of canyon to the junction of the Green and Colorado rivers, with the exception of tourist travel and the possible development of mines, the plan was no longer feasible.

---

[1]Moab *Times-Independent*, July 3, 1969.

[2]*Ibid.*

[3]Frederick S. Dellenbaugh, *The Romance of the Colorado* (New York and London: G. P. Putnam's Sons, 1909), pp. 342–70.

The Brown party that had set out from Grand Junction encountered little difficulty in the Moab area, as shown by this account from Dellenbaugh[4]:

> The boat party continued down Grand River to the head of the canyon, 24 miles, and then more slowly descended over rougher water, averaging five or six miles a day. At a distance of 43 miles from the start, the rapids grew very bad, and at one place they were forced to make a portage for twelve miles. At the end of one hundred miles they came to the little Mormon settlement of Moab. From here to the junction of the Grand and Green was a distance of sixty miles, and the water was the same as it is just above the junction, in the canyons of the Green, Stillwater, and Labyrinth, that is, comparatively smooth and offering no obstacles except a rather swift current. Nowhere had the cliffs risen above one thousand feet, and the river had an average fall of five feet to the mile. This was the first party on record to navigate, for any considerable distance, the canyons of the Grand River.

Below the junction, Brown was swept to his death in the Soap Creek rapids. The reorganized party continued to Needles, California, and reported the route to be impractical because of periodic flooding.

Early-day pioneers took a dim view of any type of travel strictly for pleasure. But since transportation was a necessity, a hot, dusty wagon or buggy ride over rough, primitive roads was the only access from Moab to the nearest railroad at Thompson, 35 miles distant. A real spurt of interest in water transportation between Moab and Green River, from the passengers' point of view, developed about the turn of the century. Several pleasure boats were built at Green River to make the run, but their success was discouraging because the river fought back with a supply of natural weapons — sand, rapids, and ever-moving sandbars that constantly changed river channels.

Beginning with the launching of the Major Powell, a 35-foot boat with eight-foot beam, in 1891, unsuccessful attempts were made to establish navigation service between Moab and Green River. The Major Powell had an upright wood-burning boiler, two y-horsepower engines, and twin screws. It went only as far as Wheeler's ranch at the mouth of San Rafael River where a broken screw discouraged going farther. Later the wood burner was changed to an oil burner; but after a trip or two, the boat was dismantled in 1894 for lack of power. Thus ended two unsuccessful attempts to establish navigation service between Moab and Green River.

Yet the route was used by a few men, as witnessed by the story of Frank (Francis M.) Shafer of his arrival at Moab, who related that,

---

[4]*Ibid.*, p. 346.

with his brother Will and others, he had come to Grand Junction by train from Colorado Springs.[5] At Grand Junction they loaded their belongings onto a heavy wagon and started westward behind a team of mules. Eventually the party came to a point on the Colorado River south of Cisco Wash. From there most of the party went on by team, but Shafer and his brother built a log raft, six by twelve feet, and started down river with five hundred pounds of supplies. "Rapids and cataracts — there were plenty of them," he recalled many years later. "Each seemed a little worse than the last. We finally reached our destination, the mouth of Little Castle Creek."

ATTEMPTS WERE MADE to establish a commercial route, as evidenced by the ill-fated boat, the Undine (Figure 14.1), which was planned to carry freight and tourists between Green River and Moab (and points between). The boat was 56 feet long and eight feet wide and had a 22-horsepower, coal-burning steam engine and a paddle wheel in the stern. Commanded by Captain Frank Summeril, it made its initial voyage in February 1902. On May 21 of that year, on its return trip from Moab to Green River, it overturned at Big Bend, about eight miles north of the Moab ferry[6] (7.5 miles upstream from the present Highway 163 bridge). Its captain had tried to steer through the first riffle using the wheel only, causing the Undine to overturn.

Lydia Skewes[7] later told of being with a group of young people who were horseback riding when the report of the sinking reached them. They rode up river to Goose Island where they saw the pilot of the Undine on a large rock near the opposite shore, calling for help. Others from the boat had worked their way down river and were safely ashore. Mrs. Skewes said that her group reached the site before a rowboat (manned by J. A. Gavette of Gunnison, Colorado, and another man named Miller) arrived at the scene.

Another boat, the Black Eagle, had a short but merry life. Built in 1905, it was powered by a twenty-horsepower, water-tube engine. The Black Eagle left Green River amid immense fanfare on its first voyage, but near Anderson Bottom, its copper tubes clogged with silt, melting the copper, which caused the engine to blow up. The remains of the Black Eagle were abandoned at Anderson Bottom, the crew leaving the canyon on foot.[8] (Figure 14.2 shows a typical transport boat in 1927.)

---

[5]Moab *Times-Independent*, September 29, 1955.

[6]*Grand Valley Times*, Moab, February 21, 1902.

[7]Interview, May 1968.

[8]Moab *Times-Independent*, July 8, 1965.

COURTESY MOAB MUSEUM

Figure 14.1. The Undine

COURTESY BARBARA EKKER

Figure 14.2. Equipment Being Transported by Boat
to Oil Wells on the Colorado River, 1927

231

Many other boating ventures were tried but failed. In May 1905 still another boat called the City of Moab, a double-decker about fifty feet long and eighteen feet wide, failed to reach Moab from Green River and was remodeled and renamed the Cliff Dweller, but it never made a full trip. It was eventually sold and again renamed — this time, the Vista — and used as a pleasure boat on the Great Salt Lake.[9] The Wilmont had a short career hauling drilling machinery; the Marguerite hauled mining supplies but was forced to bow to the railroad. The Paddy Ross, the Colorado, the Navajo, the Ida B, and the Utah were smaller craft used for private transportation up and down the river by trappers, miners, prospectors, and hunters.[10]

THE MOAB GARAGE COMPANY, founded in 1917, had what was probably the most lasting successful commercial enterprise on the Colorado River during the 1920s. Light freight and passengers were transported down river in its Punkinseed, so named because of the boat's shape,[11] during that decade. The Punkinseed was a twenty-foot-long boat with a four-horsepower outboard motor. Later the company used other boats and barges as commercial transportation for freight and passengers. It also owned the Black Boat, twenty feet in length with a 4.5-foot beam, which was powered by an automobile engine. Other motorboats, several row-boats, and some outboard-motor canoes were counted among its holdings.

The Baldwin brothers, Virgil, Clarence, and Dennis, owners of the Moab Garage Company, let their boats out for hire to the Mid-West Exploration Company. Personnel from the exploration company made several trips up and down the river, collecting data. When a location was finally chosen, on the John L. Shafer Dome about eighteen miles downstream from Moab, a contract was made between the two companies to ship two hundred tons of drilling equipment from the railroad station at Thompson. (In Figure 14.3, one of the Moab Garage Company boats is seen with its cargo; rails are for carrying the cargo to the drilling site.) The equipment was to be moved from the railhead by truck and then by boat to the well on the river.

A larger scow was built, measuring 75 feet in length and sixteen feet in width. It had a depth of three feet, a forty-horsepower automobile engine, and an eight-foot paddle wheel. The scow had a draft of four inches when empty and twelve inches when loaded with twelve tons of

---

[9]*Ibid.*

[10]*Ibid.*, July 8, 1965.

[11]Barbara Baldwin Ekker, "Freighting on the Colorado River: Reminiscences of Virgil Fay Baldwin," *Utah Historical Quarterly* (Spring 1964), p. 122.

Figure 14.3. Side View of a Moab Garage Company Boat

COURTESY BARBARA EKKER

freight. It took all of January (1925) in the building. Because the river was frozen over, it was possible to use a sled and team to haul lumber to the site for building bunkhouses and other necessary buildings. It wasn't until March 2 that the barge was launched and the finishing touches completed for its initial voyage.

From the outset, the barge made three round trips a week to Shafer well Number 1, each time taking a load from twelve to fifteen tons. The return trip from the well was accomplished at a respectable six miles per hour, but the journey back to the well, fully loaded, was done at a much slower pace — approximately three miles per hour. Yet within two weeks a hundred tons of equipment had been transported. In April a pointed prow was added, enabling the boat to part the waters for a freer gliding movement, thus shortening the round trip to about nine hours (including the unloading of the equipment).

The Moab Garage Company also freighted on the Colorado for Snowden and McSweeny who drilled across the river from Shafer well Number 1. Between March 1925 and June 1927, the scow made about two hundred trips each month. For transportation of freight alone, the oil companies paid about $250,000. In addition to this, many passengers were carried.

After 1930 there was little boating on the river. It was after World War II, when boating boomed as a major recreational activity, that the rivers came into use again. Commercial sightseeing tours on the Colorado are still popular today. One of the larger of these excursion river-boats was announced as soon to be in operation in 1972.[12] It was believed that this tourist attraction would be unique in the continental United States west of the Rockies.

"Tex" McClatchy, owner of Tex's Tour Center, a Moab-based river tour operation, announced that he was "laying the keel" for a 93-foot, double-decked, stern wheeler excursion boat for use in the scenic Colorado River gorge downstream from Moab. It was to be called the Canyon King and would be available for charter use and other activities.

To RETURN TO the earlier days — by the time the Elk Mountain Mission entered the valley, a ford across the Colorado had been well established. But in high water this was a frightening and dangerous experience. An account has been given of the difficulty the missionaries experienced in getting their cattle across. They had to resort to tying the cattle to the boat for the purpose of swimming them across. Later, the Taylors also had difficulty in their crossing. It is understandable, therefore, that shortly after the arrival of the Taylors in the valley a ferryboat was built, which was operated by Norman Taylor. There is some disagreement as to the exact date the ferry was built, but it was in operation before 1885. F. A. Hammond, president of the San Juan (Mormon) Stake, on July 20, 1885, made the following notation in his journal[13] (he had paid a visit to the Moab Ward on his way to attend General Conference of the LDS church in Salt Lake City):

> *7:00 a.m.:* Hitched up and drove four miles to the ferry on Grand river. Kept by Norman Taylor. Paid four dollars for crossing five horses and one wagon. The river is some seven hundred fifty feet wide. Stream not very rapid. High bluffs each side. The valley here at the mouth is some four miles wide. Good deal of meadowland. Directly opposite is a dry wash we follow up on our way to Green River.

J. H. Johnson reported that when his party came through in 1883 they forded the river. Thus the ferry was built sometime between the fall of 1883 and the summer of 1885. Many old-timers said it was built a year or two after the Taylors arrived.

The first ferryboat at Moab was small, only 28 feet long. To cross the river, the settlers had to take the wagons apart. One man, John

---

[12]F. A. Barnes, "Large Riverboat Now under Construction in Moab for Service on Colorado River Tour Excursions Here," Moab *Times-Independent*, December 30, 1971, p. B-1.

[13]This journal is in the possession of members of the family.

Gordon, came to Moab to show Norman Taylor how to build a larger ferryboat. Thus a craft sixty feet long and eighteen feet wide was built (probably in 1884). It was operated for some time by Taylor. There were several mishaps with this larger ferryboat, but on the whole it was successful. At one time Taylor was thrown off the boat into the river. Unable to swim, he was rescued by his assistant just before being swept under the keel. At another time, when soldiers were crossing (at the time of Indian trouble farther south), the boat was too heavily laden and the captain cut the cable. He, too, was thrown from the boat, but drowned. Some of the supplies were lost.

The boat was later leased and operated by different parties. Several times the cable broke and the boat drifted downstream to a sandbar. A motto occupied a place of prominence on the boat at one time: "We accommodate to accumulate. In God we trust; all others, spot cash."

A newspaper item in 1897 reports the purchase of the ferry by the county commissioners.[14] The sale price was $300, which did not include the boat, for a new ferry was to be built and would be operated free of charge to patrons. Some time later[15] the newspaper reported that the new ferryboat was completed and had been accepted by the commissioners. It was 55 feet long and sixteen feet wide and drew two inches of water unloaded. Figure 14.4 shows an old ferry across Grand River near Moab. This was later superceded by a steel bridge. The photograph shows the navigable size of the river.

THE CITIZENRY DEMANDED more and better service. A bridge across the Green River, at the town which bears its name, was dedicated on December 16, 1910,[16] and the people of Moab began pressing for a better way of crossing the Grand (Colorado) than by ferryboat. In January 1911, Congressman J. P. Miller introduced a bill in the state legislature asking for $45,000 with which to build a steel bridge across the Grand at Moab.[17] An amended bill, authorizing $35,000, was passed in both houses and signed by Governor William Spry.[18] Work started on the bridge early in September of that year and was completed in late January 1912. The Board of County Commissioners accepted the bridge in February.[19] The bridge, 620 feet long, with three spans, had been built at a cost of $45,000. (See Figure 14.5. The photograph was taken in

---

[14]*Grand Valley Times*, Moab, June 18, 1897.

[15]*Ibid.*, September 17, 1897.

[16]*Ibid.*, December 16, 1910.

[17]*Ibid.*, January 27, 1911.

[18]*Ibid.*, March 10, 1911.

[19]*Ibid.*, February 16, 1912.

Figure 14.4. Old Ferry across Grand River near Moab

COURTESY UTAH STATE HISTORICAL SOCIETY

Figure 14.5. The 1912 Three-Span Bridge over the Colorado River near Moab

July when the river was at flood stage. Note that this photo was made at almost the exact spot where the photographer had stood when photographing the old ferryboat of Figure 14.4 years before.) The completion and dedication of the steel bridge were fittingly celebrated with a barbecue banquet and program on April 8, 1912. Approximately thirteen hundred were in attendance at the ceremony and "bash." In 1920 the bridge (pilings and floor with its superstructure) was raised an additional four feet at a cost of $70,000.

Construction of the bridge greatly facilitated travel and transportation. It served well until the uranium boom of the 1950s, when it became inadequate and was declared a hazard (it had not been constructed substantially enough to meet the demands of the heavy equipment which now must traverse it; nor was it wide enough). Meeting the exigencies of the time, government officials declared that a new bridge should be built (the new one was erected at a cost of $1 million and now serves southeastern Utah). The old structure was removed when the new bridge was completed. Now local inhabitants and tourists alike can drive over the streamlined bridge and have an unimpeded view of the scenic landscape. Figure 14.6 shows the modern Colorado River Bridge at Moab on U.S. Highway 163. Utah has more than three hundred miles of the mighty Colorado within its borders. Regular boat trips are scheduled from this point to Lees Ferry, Arizona, a distance of nearly 270 miles.

TODAY'S WELL-GRADED canyon roads and smoothly riding automobiles make stories of the early settlers' drudging tasks of bringing wagons and teams of mules, horses, and oxen into the valley seem like a myth. Yet these hardy men and women calculated and improvised until they were able to conquer the difficulties they faced. The journey from Thompson to Moab, which took the pioneers two days, is now accomplished in less than an hour. Hardships endured by the indomitable old-timers are sometimes looked upon with amusement by modern-day generations, but the humor of reality often exceeds that of the imagination. For example, there was the British woman who kept the station-hotel, known as Court House, at the halfway point between Thompson and Moab. As weary, dusty travelers ate her salt bacon, she would apologize, "If only I'd known you were coming, I'd have cooked a chicken." But somehow the chicken dinner never materialized.

U.S. Highway 163, which connects with U.S. 50 at Crescent Junction (near Green River), is a surfaced superhighway. No longer is one subjected to the spine-tingling "suicide curve" that marked the old narrow, quick-descent road into the valley.

COURTESY MOAB *TIMES-INDEPENDENT*

Figure 14.6. Modern Bridge Spanning the Colorado River at Moab, on U.S. Highway 163

The first automobile to come to Moab made its appearance September 21, 1909. A contemporary report[20] states that

> ...W. E. Cameron and son C. C., Tecumseh, Nebraska, who were en route to Los Angeles, were stopping at Thompson a few days while repairs for one of their machines arrived from Kansas City, and were employed by Messrs. Meyer and Sproutt, traveling salesmen to bring them to Moab. The trip from Thompson was made in three hours and 45 minutes. They had twelve-hundred-pound Ford cars and were traveling from 75 to two hundred miles a day according to road conditions.

The Moab Garage Company, discussed earlier in connection with shipping by river, was also in the transportation (via land) business. Those chiefly concerned with the organization and operation of the company were R. C. Clark; Clarence, Virgil, and Dennis Baldwin; R. J. Fletcher; and C. S. Thomson. The company had branches in Monticello, Green River, and Thompson and did a large business in freighting as well as repair and general service. It operated freight service from Grand Junction, Colorado, to Salt Lake City, from Price to Moab and San Juan County, and from Moab to Grand Junction.

For many years the Moab Garage Company held the mail contracts for the vicinity and also furnished passenger service. There was perhaps one personal service of which many people were not aware. The then First National Bank of Moab was, for many years, the only bank in southeastern Utah. San Juan County merchants used the services of this bank, and each day Albert Beach, mail driver, would bring deposits from the merchants and take change to them for their next day's business. Those who worked at the bank were instructed not to lock up the cash until after Albert had arrived, regularly between 3:30 and 4:00 p.m. Confidence of bank officials in the integrity of this mail driver was never once betrayed.

In more recent years the Moab Garage Company sold its interests to Garrett Brothers, a large nationwide trucking firm. There are of course numerous other garages, truck lines, and service stations serving the greatly increased needs of the community and area. But the Moab Garage Company was an important pioneer in transportation. The service rendered by this company in freighting on the Colorado River and by land can never be properly weighed.

When the Denver & Rio Grande Western Railroad began operating throughout southeastern Utah — Grand Junction to Salt Lake City through Thompson and Crescent Junction — many of the transportation problems of the vicinity were solved. Whereas it had taken many days to

---

[20]*Ibid.*, September 24, 1909.

go from larger centers to the settlements at Salina and Richfield, service could now be obtained from these larger centers in a short time. In more recent years trucking firms and bus lines also furnish local service. A spur of the Denver & Rio Grande Western hauls ore into and out of Moab to the railhead at Thompson. Individual automobiles have solved many problems of transportation, and the citizens no longer are totally dependent upon public transportation.

A DECIDED ASSET to any community is a lively newspaper. Social psychologists tell us that one of the most vital organs of public opinion is the newspaper. An editor of even a small paper may have a great influence on the opinions and progress of the community he or she represents. Many civic activities and developments in Moab may be directly traced to continued efforts of this medium. The "power of the press" is a positive force within any community. A newspaper serves many functions, not the least of which is reporting the news.

From its earliest days, Moab has enjoyed the benefits of this positive force within the community. The significant date was May 30, 1896; the publisher, J. N. Corbin. He had spent $300 to purchase type and had come to Moab from Denver. In the first edition, the editor makes the following comments for his readers[21]:

> In making our appearance to the people of southeastern Utah, we have no apology to offer. The newspaper has become a necessary factor in the civilization of the age. The only question that has puzzled the writer, since becoming acquainted with this section, and seeing the evidence of thrift and enterprise that is fast making this naturally beautiful valley an Eden is, why has not the local newspaper been established before?...It can only be accounted for by the fact that the hardy pioneer settlers have been too busy ploughing, planting trees, and irrigating to look after themselves, or to discover to the outside world the necessity for such an addition to the valley.

Then, after five years of publishing, Editor Corbin noted[22]:

> With this issue the *Grand Valley Times* completes five years of voyaging in the newspaper seas. Perhaps the most that it can be credited with is the fact that during its life it had never missed an issue. Considering the location, distance from supply points, population of the surrounding country, the fact that all labor connected with its appearance has depended on the energy of one

---

[21]*Ibid.*, May 30, 1896.
[22]*Ibid.*, May 24, 1901.

man, and he having to depend largely on the result of his labor in other lines for the necessaries of life, means much. No newspaper ever before existed so long under similar conditions. In many parts of the state, with many times the population, the paper that started died young.... The *Times* man has faith in the natural resources of this section (but man cannot live on faith alone).

Corbin goes on to exhort his readers to move for more and better circumstances: "more developers [probably of mining and of land], better newspapers, more prosperous merchants, farmers" and so forth. He felt that waiting and "murmuring will not do it, *doing* is all that will do it." (Emphasis in the original.) In the next paragraph, his remarks seem almost prophetic:

> There is but one industry that can possibly advance this section and that is mining. There is not sufficient agricultural land in [the section] to maintain a large population, outside the possibility of the irrigation of the desert lands, and that [lies in an] uncertain number of long years in the future, with prosperous mining that would quickly follow, mining is the lever that must move it all.

His next probing comments along the same line appeared a few days later[23]:

> Eastern Utah is likely to become as famous an oil-producing section as western Pennsylvania. Coal fields surround all this district, and every indication points that Nature has some of her great oil storehouse here. The great future possibilities from the mineral wealth of this region can scarcely be imagined at the present time.

Corbin edited the paper until 1926 when Edgar L. Beard became the editor and publisher. In 1907 C. A. Robertson acquired the *Grand Valley Times*[24] and incorporated the publishing company in 1908.[25] Loren L. Taylor succeeded Robertson (his brother-in-law) in 1911.[26]

A second newspaper made its appearance in 1917–18, which served the community for about one and a half years. The paper was known as the Moab *Independent*, with Howard Cherry as the first editor, serving for about three months. He was succeeded by Fred Strong. In September 1919, the *Independent* was purchased by L. L. (Bish) Taylor, who changed the name of the publication to the *Times-Independent*, by which name it is still known. Taylor was a grandson of Norman Taylor,

---

[23]*Ibid.*, June 7, 1901.

[24]*Ibid.*, March 22, 1907.

[25]*Ibid.*, April 3, 1908.

[26]L. L. Taylor interview.

Moab pioneer (who also ran the ferryboat); thus the ownership of the newspaper had come full-cycle, which always seems to be pleasingly fitting. "Bish" Taylor's career in the communications media began at an early age: When he was thirteen, he began "riding the mail" from Moab to Cane Springs on the route to Monticello.[27] Taylor gave up active operation of the newspaper in 1951, leasing it to H. R. "Red" Halliday. Within a few years (1956), the operation was taken over by his son, Samuel J. Taylor, who is at present editor and publisher.

As editor and publisher of the Moab *Times-Independent* for half a century, Bish Taylor made untold contributions to Moab and Grand County. He dedicated his newspaper and his career to promoting the area and serving in many public offices on a local and state level. Taylor has often been called the "Father of Grand County" because of the service he has rendered through his newspaper, making it truly the community's voice. He is probably best remembered for his editorials, which pulled no punches, and which promoted interest and activity in community-building projects. He once said, "I never wrote one [editorial] unless something needed saying." And he supported his words with his own service. He, probably more than anyone else, is responsible for such new developments as a courthouse building, a new school-building, a new water and sewer system, and an expanded, improved hospital during the Depression years. He urged the citizens of the city and county to vote in favor of bonds and to apply for PWA and WPA funds[28] to obtain these necessary improvements. His editorials and news reporting probably developed the incentive and the action resulting in the securing of them.

For twelve years he was chairman of the Grand County Commission; for fifteen years he served in the (then) no-pay position of city clerk. Also gratis was his fifteen years as Grand County hospital administrator. He was a member of the State Industrial Commission for six years, and chairman and charter member of the Division of Grazing when it was first organized for San Juan and Grand counties, serving for fifteen years.

Through his efforts, the first automobile road into the Arches (later a national monument) was built. When Editor-Commissioner Taylor failed to get an audience with the governor, he waited in the lobby of a prominent Salt Lake City hotel for him; he got a $30,000 road for the now-popular Arches National Monument which draws a hundred thousand visitors per year into the area.

---

[27]Moab *Times-Independent*, September 29, 1955.

[28]Public Works Administration and Works Project Administration — federal monies were loaned to cities and counties under these acts. They were offered as recovery acts during the Depression by the F. D. Roosevelt Administration.

When the county needed a new high school, Bish interceded with the Denver & Rio Grande Railroad through its president. The high school was built and later remodeled as a junior high school building.

More than one football coach in early-day Moab admits that he would have given up the fight except for the support of the *Times Independent.*

When Taylor acquired the newspaper from Robertson, he was nineteen years old. It was a coincidence that he turned the editorship over to his own son when he too was nineteen years of age.

After his retirement in 1961, he became the second man in the state to receive the Utah State Press Association's Master Editor Award — the highest honor extended to those of his profession in Utah.

Samuel J. (Sam) Taylor, who is presently editor-publisher, carries on his father's way of publishing a newspaper that is an important organ of the community. With a computerized press, business has enlarged and expanded.

Sam Taylor has followed well in the footsteps of his father. He has a genuine interest in promoting the communities which he represents. Having served as a member of the Utah state senate, young Taylor is aware of the state and local problems, and as editor of the paper at Moab, he keeps his readers well informed. He has replaced the "hot metal" linotype with new computer equipment which will electronically and photographically set type for the newspaper at the rate of about thirty lines a minute. This is in contrast to a speed of approximately six lines a minute on the old linecasting machines. Although the equipment is new, the style and interest in southeastern Utah remains the same. Under Sam's guidance, the newspaper promotes the development of the area and reports the news on a weekly basis.

PUBLIC REPORTING of the news alone is not sufficient for the communications needs of a settlement. In today's world, the telephone is an essential commodity. The Midland Telephone Company today furnishes local and toll service over its 320 miles of toll line to the incorporated towns of Moab, Monticello, and Blanding and to the unincorporated town of Dove Creek in Colorado. Midland also serves the following unincorporated towns in Utah: Thompson, Bluff, Mexican Hat, and La Sal. The company serves six dial and two toll-only exchanges. The main office is located in Moab, and the corporate office is in Grand Junction, Colorado.[29]

---

[29]Since members of the Corbin family have managed the company since its inception, unless otherwise indicated the information for the history of this important medium of communication was given by J. Wallace Corbin, vice president and general manager of the company, 1968.

The first telephone line in Grand County was built from Moab to Thompson in about 1900. This connected with the Denver & Rio Grande Western Railroad and the Western Union Telegraph Company and was the only means of communication in this section of southeastern Utah.

In June 1903, the La Sal Mountain Telephone and Electric Company was organized with the following officers: Harry Green, president; John Welsh, vice president; V. P. Martin, treasurer; J. N. Corbin, secretary and manager; and F. B. Hammond, director. It was organized for the purpose of building and operating telephone and electric light and power lines.[30] The first step, according to the news report, was to construct a telephone line from Moab to Castleton and thence to Miners Basin and camps of the La Sal district. It was their intent to put in a local exchange at Moab and connect their lines with Thompson.

A line, constructed from Moab to Monticello, took more than two years to complete. Most of the labor was done by the late J. N. Corbin, with the help of one man and two pack horses. This line was completed in January 1908.[31] Another line was constructed in the same manner from Moab to Castleton, a small mining camp with a population of approximately a hundred people. At that time, Castleton had two saloons, one hotel, and two grocery stores.

About 1908, J. N. Corbin sold his interest in the company to a group of cattlemen (who were stockholders) and moved to Fruita, Colorado (where he entered into another type of business), and remained there for seven years.

In the spring of 1915, Corbin saw the need for communication west from Fruita, Colorado, to Price, Utah. Thus, with the help of a group of his friends, he organized and incorporated the Midland Telephone Company, and began building a line from Mack, Colorado, to Green River, Utah. The company was incorporated under the laws of the state of Colorado in September 1915. J. N. Corbin was made manager.

When the company got as far as Cisco, the cattlemen who had purchased the La Sal Mountain Telephone Company were anxious to get rid of the telephone business. They talked Corbin into taking the line back and it was then operated (under lease) in connection with the Midland Telephone Company for a period of ten years, after which all of the property of the La Sal Mountain Telephone Company was purchased by the Midland Telephone Company. In the fall of 1923, upon Corbin's death, the general management was taken over by his son, J. W. Corbin, who at that time was exchange manager at Monticello, Utah.

[30]*Grand Valley Times*, Moab, June 5, 1903.
[31]*Ibid.*, April 3, 1908.

Following World War II the company began to expand and increase its service. It switched to the dial system in 1948. The business enjoyed a steady growth from 1949 to the fall of 1953, at which time the uranium industry was barely getting under way. The rapid growth of the communities quickly rendered inadequate the telephone facilities. The communities surrounding Moab had experienced the same rapid growth which placed a general overload on telephone services.

J. W. (Jack) Corbin served as vice president and general manager under the president, M. N. Due, until Due died in 1960. Corbin was then elected president and general manager and remained in this capacity until January 1, 1965, when he retired as general manager. He has served as head of the Midland Telephone Company for a total of 44 years and until recently held the office of president.

J. W. Corbin first worked in his father's telephone company as a lineman in 1916, and after his father's death, took over managership of the company. It was under J. W. Corbin's direction that the company increased from a telephone system of a 150 hookups to over five thousand. He also added such modern facilities as microwave, radio, teleprinters, and TV signals.

Corbin saw his company through Moab's two most crucial economic upsets — one when the town was at its lowest ebb and the other when it was at its peak. The first crisis occurred during the Great Depression of the early 1930s, when most of the nation was out of food, and Moabites were out of money. He could not collect enough cash to pay his help, and he and his family moved into the Center Street telephone building for cheaper operation. The $25 per month rent they got from their home helped tide them over.

Corbin worked lines by day and operated the switchboard by night, his wife Ila taking over the switchboard each day. A few cash customers helped pay the wages of one $40-a-month assistant (usually a young woman). The rest of the Midland telephone users paid their accounts with a side of beef or a sack of potatoes. Somehow the Corbins and other Moabites managed to survive the crisis.

The second crisis was somewhat opposite of the first. It began in the early 1950s, a few months after Charlie Steen made his famed Mi Vida uranium strike near Moab. The phenomenal growth of the town left the telephone company — equipped to handle a hundred calls a day — with the problem of dealing with fifteen hundred calls. With only five long-distance circuits east and west, calls had to be accepted on a waiting-list basis. Sometimes several days went by before a customer's call could be completed.

Employees worked round the clock installing new lines. The force grew from ten to 65 and still a four-party business-service line was as good as could be offered. Customers were lucky to get one of these. Outside the city limits, all lines were kept to a ten-party minimum.

Had Corbin foreseen his company's rapid growth, he would no doubt have refused to run for the office of mayor. With this added responsibility, including a population increase from twelve hundred to well over five thousand within a few brief months, all areas of the city's business were affected. The marvel is that development progressed as orderly as it did.

On January 1, 1965, J. Wallace Corbin was named general manager of the company. He had previously been with the company since May 1946, serving in various capacities.

In 1971 the company began a building program which, under the direction of the general manager, J. Wallace Corbin (son of J. W.), will extend service to the community and surrounding areas.

The Midland Telephone Company (now Continental Telephone) serves one of the largest areas in the Continental system, with approximately 11,200 square miles in southeastern Utah and a thousand square miles in Colorado. The population of the area serviced is approximately sixteen thousand. The largest town is Moab with about 7,500 population.

The planning of a further expansion is indicated by a 1968 headline[32] which announced a multimillion-dollar building program. In 1973 the building in Moab was under construction.

There are in today's world many forms of mass media of communication. Moab has of course kept abreast of the times and has its own television station. In addition to this, other stations have been made available to serve the community through a television tower.

Faded into the past are the days of horses and carriages, and multiparty telephone lines which made it possible to spread news faster than the weekly paper, or, if one wanted to "straighten someone out" who was not on his line, he needed only call a neighbor and be assured the word would be delivered first-hand.

---

[32]Moab *Times-Independent*, May 30, 1968.

Chapter 15

Additional Industry and Business

For many years the inhabitants of Moab and the surrounding region were forced to do their banking either with distant institutions or in the proverbial "sock." Seeing the need and seizing the opportunity, a group of far-sighted local businessmen undertook the organization of a local bank. The *Grand Valley Times* in December 1911 reported that a representative of the Utah National Bank of Salt Lake City was in Moab to meet with local businessmen for discussion of the matter of establishing a bank. However, no immediate action resulted, for it was not until 1915 that the Moab State Bank was chartered and capitalized at $25,000. F. B. Hammond, Sr., was elected president; R. L. Kirk, vice president; Knox Patterson, secretary; Glen J. Hudson, cashier; and as additional directors, W. E. Gordon, J. P. Miller, C. A. Johnson, Glen J. Hudson, and John Jackson. The bank opened July 10, 1915.[1] Advertising itself with the slogan "The Bank with a Heart," it served the community until 1921 when it closed its doors, failing to reopen thereafter.

Early in 1916 twenty citizens made application for a charter of a First National Bank of Moab with a $50,000 capitalization.[2] The charter was granted in December of that year and 44 stockholders elected the following officers[3]: D. L. Goudelock, president; H. G. Green and

---

[1] *Grand Valley Times*, Moab, June 25, 1915.
[2] *Ibid.*, March 10, 1916.
[3] *Ibid.*, December 8, 1916.

D. M. Cooper, vice presidents; V. P. Martin, cashier; and William R. McConkie, John E. Pace, and Don Taylor, additional directors. From the closing of the Moab State Bank in 1921 and the Green River Bank in 1933, until 1962 this was the only bank operating in the state east of Price. The First National Bank purchased the assets of the San Juan State Bank in 1934.

In 1917 a bank building was erected. This historic stone building, on the corner of Center and Main, though earlier remodeled, has been razed (1973) and a larger, more modern building was under construction at this writing.

By 1955 the First National Bank's deposits had sufficiently increased so that it was necessary to open a branch bank at Monticello. The bank faced the uranium boom. Screening requests for business financing became a responsible task; in the frenzy to capitalize on Moab's boom "before it went away," many loan applicants wanted 100 percent financing.

The demand for housing in Moab grew with the town, and soon subdivision plans went on drawing boards. In its then present capacity, it was apparent that the First National Bank could not handle the business. Loans were limited to 60 percent of time deposits, which would not have financed one of the proposed housing projects.

The dilemma was resolved with a stock exchange, and the First National Bank became a branch of the First Security Bank of Utah.[4] This meant that unlimited funds were now available for loan in Moab, and loans were guaranteed by FHA. By 1960 federally insured loans through the Moab bank topped the $3.5 million mark. Savings accounts increased from $25,000 to $3.5 million.

Glen Carlson, who became manager of the First Security Bank after the death of William R. McConkie in 1956, stated that it was a marvel that Moab's boom proved such an orderly one.[5] With a cross-section of every type of person coming into the town, there was the constant threat of holdup. But people were too busy seeking bigger spoils to fool with such stoic money-making schemes as bank robbing during the wild search for uranium ore.

Economic chaos might have followed the subsiding of the uranium boom, but fortune smiled on Moab. Two subsequent big business eras followed: Oil and gas exploration began in earnest, and at one time eighteen seismograph crews, each employing thirty to forty men, used Moab as drilling headquarters. The huge payroll took up the slack of the declining uranium business.

---

[4]Moab *Times-Independent*, February 9, 1967.
[5]*Ibid.*

But when the Texas Gulf Sulphur Company began construction of its multimillion-dollar potash facilities at Cane Creek near Moab in the early 1960s, Moab was doing well economically. In many areas the Texas Gulf Sulphur Company construction boom netted more returns than uranium, and the production era which followed established and stabilized the economy.

As business demands increased, a branch bank was opened at Blanding. The Monticello and Blanding branches were under the management of Robert Dalton, who began his bank career at Moab and at this writing is manager of the Moab bank.

There was excitement in Moab in May 1923[6] when three burglars looted the safe of the First National Bank, taking $7,000 cash. The robbery was interrupted by the bank's bookkeeper (H. Brumley Green) who passed by the bank on his way home from an evening call. Just as he passed the building he heard an explosion. He turned back to investigate and was accosted by one of the robbers. The robbers tied his hands, gagged his mouth, and wired his feet together. However, they evidently did not observe that he was wearing cowboy boots. Completing their business of taking currency (they left the heavy silver and gold), they placed him in the vault. After some discussion about whether or not to close the door tightly, they decided they would not leave him to smother, and left the door open a crack. Green managed to work his feet out of the wired boots and went to a nearby hospital where his gag was removed and his hands were released. He was then able to give the alarm. The robbers were captured 37 hours later. An alert Moab Garage Company mail driver spotted a money wrapper in the road as he drove from Thompson to Moab. The men were trailed by a posse into the desert near by where they were hiding in a gully awaiting the coolness and darkness of night to take up their travel.

They managed to escape jail by killing Deputy Sheriff R. D. Westwood and fleeing. But they found Moab to be a "big jail." Hiding in barns and haystacks, they maintained their freedom briefly, but were soon recaptured and made secure. Convicted of robbery and murder, they were sent to the penitentiary.

The Moab National Bank was chartered in February 1962.[7] The chief organizer and prime mover was William R. McCormick, who at that time was president of Standard Metals and the Dove Creek State Bank. Directors elected were: McCormick, Jerry Havel, William G. Aldeck, K. E. McDougald, Loran L. Laughlin, Frederick G. Stover,

---

[6]*Ibid.*, May 3, 1923.
[7]Information supplied by an officer of the bank in an interview May 1968.

E. J. Claus, C. O. Keller, and John W. Corbin. The bank was capitalized for $400,000. It is a unit bank.

THE FIRST GENERAL STORE, owned by the Taylors, was known as Taylor Mercantile. Mr. and Mrs. Philander Maxwell built the first hotel at Moab in 1885, which they operated for many years.[8] Mrs. Maxwell ("Aunt Add") also owned and operated the first millinery shop in the early days (Figure 15.1), and in more recent years operated a Navajo rug and curio shop.

The second hotel was the Darrow House. The land on which this hotel was built first belonged to Leonidas L. Crapo, who in 1883 made application for it to the United States government.[9] He later (1884) sold the property to Randolph H. Stewart and O. W. Warner. In 1885 the land passed to William E. Peirce (Moab's first postmaster) and he sold it to George W. Stowell in 1886. Marcus Henry Darrow and his wife, Mary Adeline Lee, bought the property November 29, 1886, for $250, and the Darrow House was built. According to Lydia Taylor Skewes, it was a big house with a balcony and served as a hotel and rooming house from the time it was erected. It was made of local sun-dried adobe brick, with walls that were eighteen inches thick. The hotel was closed sometime in the 1890s. While it was in operation, it housed many outlaws.

Frank Hall, who had married a daughter of the Darrows, reopened the hotel December 24, 1897, operating it as manager until July 10, 1903, at which time Mrs. Darrow took it over again. The following month the D. L. Goudelocks bought it for $12,000, and it served as their home until the death of Goudelock and his wife. Many motels now serve tourist needs.

All of these businesses operated during the early years of the permanent settlement. Tom Farrar had a store in 1882, which Randolph Stewart operated. In 1884 Billy Peirce managed it. Farrar had a big store in Green River, and the Moab establishment was a branch.

With the expansion and growth of Moab, there was also an expansion of mercantile institutions and other services. Today the face of Main Street has been lifted (Figure 15.2). As in all modern cities, the business center has fanned out.

After the community had become stabilized, there were several general merchandise stores to supply the needs of the population. The early Taylor Mercantile and the La Sal Mercantile have been mentioned. The La Sal Merchantile Company, Inc. (Figure 15.3), occupied the site of the present Saveway Store in Moab. It was here that Jess

[8]Moab *Times-Independent*, July 11, 1940, p. A-1.
[9]*Ibid.*, October 24, 1968.

Figure 15.1. Addie Maxwell's Millinery Shop

Figure 15.2. Main Street in Moab, Looking South

Figure 15.3. La Sal Mercantile Company, Inc.

Gibson was shot. (His killer was never apprehended.) But later old-timers will recall the Moab Cooperative (later known as the Moab Co-op), Hammond's General Store, Peterson's Market, and Cooper-Martin Company. The two largest were the first and last named. There were vegetable and meat markets and a ready-to-wear section.

Perhaps the Miller stores are an illustration of the imagination and determination of Moab merchants. This business reaches back into the century when J. P. Miller, a Moab farmer, in 1913 organized a farmers' and ranchers' cooperative.[10] Stockholders were J. T. Loveridge, John Peterson, Daniel Holyoak, Robert Thompson, J. E. Brown, J. E. Snyder, Henry Grimm, Mark Walker, and perhaps others.

Upon the death of the senior Miller in 1929, management was assumed by his son, Ralph Miller, Sr. The Depression put the store on shaky ground and in 1930 it went into receivership. Ralph Miller (Sr.) bought out the shares of the other investors and somehow managed to survive the Depression, making new innovations during these years. He introduced a new line in his store — refrigerated items such as fresh meat, cheese, butter. He installed a six-foot refrigerated showcase and walk-in box, and put in his own line of meat. Later he installed the first locker plant in Moab to accommodate local stockraisers.

Just as things were going well, the store burned to the ground. The fire started with an oil furnace explosion in the basement, and the entire stock, new locker plants, accounts receivable, and all went up in smoke.[11] Two days later he bought the Cooper-Martin Store, now Family Budget Clothing, on the corner of Main and Center.[12]

In 1954, Miller expanded again, buying the Golden Peterson grocery on Main Street. There was a continual upswing in business, and by the 1950s Moab was in the throes of the uranium boom, which turned the village of a thousand into a city of five thousand in an unbelievably short time.

In 1957, Miller built a major supermarket at the Pack Creek crossing on Main Street. Refusing to be discouraged by bankers who felt the location was not good, he finally managed to obtain financing and his supermarket was followed by a clothing store and other buildings; the site is now a large shopping center. The city had followed the new store outside Moab on the south highway. Today it is a major portion of the Moab business area, surrounded by subdivisions and a new high school. In the 35-year span of his business career, Ralph Miller, Sr., had seen a small $3,000 inventory store grow into a business which topped

---

[10]*Ibid.*, December 22, 1966.

[11]*Ibid.*

[12]*Ibid.*

a volume of $2 million each year. His enterprises include a chicken ranch and a federally inspected packing plant at Delta, Colorado. Other stores and shops help to supply the populace.

MOVEMENTS TO INSTALL an electric light system in Moab finally resulted in the granting of a franchise to the Moab Light and Power Company in 1914. Water power from Mill Creek was used, and early in 1915 Moab boasted electric power. During the following years severe floods brought considerable damage to the plant at various times, even taking out the dam, thus leaving the town in darkness for significant periods. In 1919 a large concrete power dam was built to remedy the constant danger of the dam's being washed out by floods. Utah Power and Light Company purchased the plant from the local company and has furnished power to the community through the years. The use of natural gas piped in from Texas has largely replaced coal and wood as fuel.

As LATE AS 1896 an open ditch furnished culinary water for the town. The editor of the *Grand Valley Times*, J. N. Corbin, in the first edition, wrote an editorial on this subject urging early action in installing a water system. However, it was not until 1907 that any definite action was taken. At that time the stockholders of the Moab Irrigation Company voted to mortgage property to install a pipeline. This company (Utah Pipe Line Company) served the community for many years. In 1935 a municipal water system was installed under a PWA grant. This has since been expanded. Simultaneous with the PWA grant for the water system was one for installation of a sewer system in Moab. This action modernized the town and updated the sanitation.

THERE WERE WELL OVER two hundred businesses in Moab in 1967.[13] V. P. (Krug) Walker reported that from his Main Street shop he had seen all but one of them set up. His Walker Barber Shop, at that time, was the oldest business in the city with the exception of the *Times-Independent*, which his cousin, L. L. Taylor, was publishing before Krug began his barbering career.

Krug began his profession one day when he was visiting the only barber shop in Moab, then operated by Earl Harris, who asked the young man if he'd like to learn to cut hair. "Guess I'll try it," Krug answered, and casually began his fifty-year profession.

His parents were early-day pioneers. His mother was Augusta Taylor who had lived in the old fort by the Colorado River with her

---

[13]*Ibid.*, February 2, 1967.

parents when she first came to the valley. She was a twin to Judge Taylor, prominent in early Moab history. Krug's father, as a sideline to his trade as carpenter, worked with Don Taylor in the sheep-raising business and, among other things, helped build the first Moab Co-op Store building.

An examination of the advertising in the *Times-Independent* today indicates the broad spectrum of business services which now entice and supply the community.

AT LA SAL, the company store supplies all of the needs of the people living in that area. Except for one brief period, this has been adequate to the needs. If, at some future date, the population of La Sal becomes sufficiently large to see the need for incorporation, the institutions and services will increase according to the demands.

Chapter 16

Education, Religion, Social Growth

Moab's beginnings were religion-oriented. Two colonizations of the Church of Jesus Christ of Latter-day Saints were made — the first in 1855 was short-lived; the second in 1881 was permanent. This was the church colony that had Randolph H. Stewart as its bishop. Contemporary with and prior to the second settlement were cattlemen. Conversely, La Sal was first settled by cattlemen, and it was not for some years that an ecclesiastical organization was effected. Thus settlement of these two communities did not follow the pattern of most settlements in Utah. Moab was made an ecclesiastical ward in 1881. From that one unit, it was expanded until at present the Moab–La Sal area has several LDS wards which make up the Moab Stake.

Another early religious denomination of the community was the First Baptist Church, organized on March 21, 1905, by the following citizens: Helen B. Kirk, Mattie E. Turner, Annie R. Green, E. Gertrude Neff, Sarah Allred, M. Louise Goodman, Smith M. Davis, Ruby E. Davis, and Queenie M. Wheat, all of whom were charter members. On May 19, 1905, a call was extended to J. P. Berkley to become pastor for three months, and plans were made for building a chapel that was subsequently dedicated on August 28, 1910. A new church building was begun November 25, 1916, under the pastorate of the Reverend R. W. Spencer at a cost of $4,950. The building was dedicated February 24, 1918. In 1917 the parsonage was remodeled and a garage built for nearly $56 (left over from the funds for church building). In 1928 a new parsonage was built. Members of the two religious denominations cooperated in community activities for many years, working for the interests of all.

The churches in Moab today represent a cross-section of American churches in any region. The population which rapidly followed the lure of the mushrooming city found its place of worship, or provided one. There are many fine modern church buildings in Moab today.

UTAH IS NOTED in the annals of American history for the early and profound interest in education as evidenced by the pioneer fathers and mothers. One of the first acts of Brigham Young after the pioneers reached the Salt Lake Valley was to establish schools. The first schoolteacher in Utah, Mary Jane Dilworth, later became the wife of an early southeastern Utah pioneer, F. A. Hammond. He was called to preside over the San Juan Stake in 1884. Some of her children and grandchildren have been prominent in the settlement and development of Moab, La Sal, and southeastern Utah.

The settlers of Moab and La Sal, like the first Utah pioneers, began early to think of schools for their children. Tom Ray, La Sal's first settler, hired a teacher for his children. At first the children were taught in his home by his wife; later a teacher was cooperatively employed by the families at La Sal. At Moab, Laurana, wife of Norman Taylor, became the first teacher. School was held in the homes. Jane Warner Peterson, who started going to school in Moab in 1882, says the first school she attended was held in a tent and the children sat in spring seats. Augusta Taylor was her teacher. The only text she could remember was the *Wilson Reader.*

When Moab was yet in swaddling clothes, when the valley comprised a portion of Emery County and the population was meager, School District Number 1, in which the Moab schools are situated, was established August 8, 1883.[1]

The first school board was made up of O. W. Warner, chairman; W. H. Allred, treasurer; and Hiram M. Taylor, clerk. The schoolbuilding under their management was by no means an imposing structure. It was built of unhewn logs, and a mud roof protected the students from sun and rain. Rough benches took the place of desks.[2]

J. Alma Holdaway was the first teacher in this building.[3] He received $30 a month for his services; his contract included a provision

---

[1]"Something about Moab's Public Schools," *Grand Valley Times*, Moab, April 29, 1910.

[2]*Ibid.*

[3]*Ibid.*

allowing him to "board round" among the patrons of the school. Augusta Taylor Walker succeeded Holdaway as instructor. She taught for a ten-week term. George W. McConkie was another of these early teachers. He came to Moab each day from Bueno (Poverty Flat) to meet the students in class. Salaries, of course, were not high. Hyrum Allen, in 1885, taught a three-month term.[4]

J. H. Johnson related that when the district schoolhouse was built, he and Jens Nielsen hauled lumber from Thompson. He said they forded the river both ways for as long as they could and then took wagons apart and hauled them across in a little skiff. (This was the first ferry.) The contract for building the schoolhouse was held by Messers W. Nix and W. Small.

As early as 1887, the log schoolbuilding, which was private property and was located on the Lutz corner (diagonally opposite the present school site), had become inadequate for the needs of the growing community and the board elected to build two schoolhouses. There were then more than eighty children of school age in the valley.

One of these schoolhouses (the lower school) was built on what is now known as the Beeson property, in the lower end of the valley, and the other (the upper school) on the present school lot in the center of town. These buildings met the requirements for some ten years. By 1896 more room was needed; thus largely through the counsel of Superintendent Alma Molyneaux, a central school was decided upon. Under the central plan, mixed grades in one class were superseded by single grades in separate classrooms, schoolwork of the entire valley was placed under the personal supervision of one principal, and more effective teaching and learning were made possible.

Molyneaux served as superintendent until 1907 when Ida M. Wells replaced him. In 1908, William R. McConkie became superintendent. Many others have held this position since that time — some were local, some imported.

The Central School, completed in 1898, required some later additions and improvements, but was in use (Figure 16.1) until 1934 when it was razed to give way to the new modern structure erected at that time. An item in the *Grand Valley Times* reflects the editor's enthusiasm over the original Central School[5]:

> The new schoolbuilding is rapidly approaching completion. The bell has been hung the past week, and its clear tones can be heard all over the valley. The new furniture is being put in place and by the time school opens...the children of this district will have a beautiful place [in which] to assemble.

---

[4]*Ibid.*
[5]*Ibid.*, August 26, 1898.

Knowing youth in general, one wonders if the students felt the same enthusiasm as the editor.

Grand County High School (at Moab) had its beginnings in 1901 when high school-type lessons were given in the Moab district school according to the grade each boy or girl was in. In 1902, the high school was formally organized and Professor B. H. Jacobsen employed as instructor.[6] In the spring of 1904 the contract for a separate high school was let and a two-room structure completed in time for use in the fall. To the surprise of most of the taxpayers, the building was paid for when it was completed. No bonds or special taxes were required to meet the expense. Some years later a large addition was made to this building (Figure 16.2) which served the needs of the community until the erection of the new building in 1934.

The citizens of Moab and Grand County had availed themselves of the opportunity for a Public Works Administration grant from the federal government for the construction of a new schoolbuilding which cost approximately $136,000. This modern brick structure housed the Moab District Elementary School and the Grand County High School. Part of the old high school building was renovated and used as a section of the new complex. But in 1967 this old schoolbuilding was destroyed by fire. The new building is thoroughly modern and adequate to serve present needs of the community. In addition, there is a modern junior high school (Figure 16.3), now called the "middle school."

In 1955 an additional elementary school was built — the Helen M. Knight School (she was a long-time teacher, principal, and superintendent). It was found that the facilities were no longer adequate because of the great influx of people into the community during the uranium boom. There are of course schools in outlying districts such as Cisco, Thompson, Sego, and wherever population requires.

The schools furnish not only educational opportunity, but form an excellent means of community cooperation and recreation. This was especially true during the first decades of the settlement. Classes were held only a few months out of the year, for children were needed at home during "the growing season." Often the members of the class were in the same age group as the instructor.

Many anecdotes of early regional history are related to teaching experiences. For example, one young man, diligently studying his geography lesson, came up to the teacher's desk and protested vigorously: "Russell, this damned book says that Rio de Janeiro was discovered on a fine summer's day in January." After all, who had ever heard of a summer in January!

---

[6]*Ibid.*, May 13, 1910.

COURTESY MOAB MUSEUM

Figure 16.1. Central School before 1934

COURTESY MOAB MUSEUM

Figure 16.2. Early High School in Moab

263

The high level of regard for education is indicated by the report that in 1970 the median number of years of schooling completed by all adults, 25 and over, in Moab was 12.3.[7] A private research organization, Utah Foundation, in its analysis of education and income levels in Utah, reported that 8.2 percent of Moab adult population had completed at least four years of college, 60.6 percent had finished twelve or more years of schooling, and only 2.3 percent had completed less than five years of formal education.

According to the report, Utah has led the nation in the median number of years of formal schooling completed by its adult population in every decennial census since 1940. Utah also leads the nation in the percentage of its adult population who have completed high school and ranks third among the states in the proportion who have completed four or more years of college.

Accounts of early schools at La Sal parallel those at Moab, and were common throughout the frontier country. As previously stated, Thomas Ray was responsible for the first school at La Sal. Unable to read or write himself, he was especially proud that his wife had acquired these skills from a neighbor woman in Tennessee by sandwiching in a few lessons amid her responsibilities on the farm while Tom was away in the Civil War.[8] He wanted his children to learn the fundamentals. He had a large family and its members were far removed from established schools. The first school was held in his home. He hired a Miss Lulu Ivie to teach a six-month term, and he alone paid her salary. This was the second school in San Juan County; Bluff had the first.[9]

In September 1884, Tom Ray again took the lead and urged the erection of a community schoolhouse, which was subsequently built of yellow pine logs near his own ranch. The lumber for this building was "whipsawed" by Neils Olson, Neal Ray, and Will Silvey. The senior Silvey and son Jack were carpenters who laid the floor and built the desks and a crude blackboard. Mrs. Ray, as postmistress, had a plentiful supply of black ink which was used to make the blackboards. The Maxwells and McCartys, with six children, moved from Coyote and built cabins near the schoolhouse, making a total of fifteen children to attend the school.

A Miss Stair of Philadelphia, Pennsylvania, was employed to teach a six-month term of school. Her salary was paid cooperatively by all parents of children attending the school.

A year or two later, when the first settlers sold their ranches and cattle and moved away, the schoolhouse was abandoned. It was not until

[7]Moab *Times-Independent*, July 19, 1973, p. B-1.
[8]Neal Ray, interview, 1935.
[9]Silvey, *op. cit.*

Figure 16.3. Modern Junior High School in Moab

about 1916 that another school was built at La Sal (old La Sal). This school served until 1941.

The first county library was established in 1914.[10] Some 425 books were contributed to get it into operation. The library opened to the public the week of February 19, 1915, with Miss Edna Bankhead serving as librarian.[11] The following week the library trustees were appointed by the town board as follows: C. A. Robertson, Howard W. Balsley, Mrs. Helen B. Kirk, Mrs. Helga Humphrey, D. A. Johnson, C. A. Hammond, and W. R. McConkie.[12] The library for many years was in the county courthouse, but after the completion of the new schoolbuilding, was moved to facilities there. Most of the books were saved during the fire which destroyed that part of the school in 1967. A fine new building on First East Street now houses the library which has been expanded.

IN AN ACT approved March 13, 1890, the territorial legislature created Grand County from portions of Emery and Uintah counties. The boundaries of the county were changed in 1892 when a portion of the northern boundary was added to Uintah County. The name of the

---

[10]*Grand Valley Times*, Moab, December 18, 1914.

[11]*Ibid.*, February 21, 1935.

[12]*Ibid.*

county was derived from the Grand (Colorado) River which flowed through it. The boundaries established were as follows: on the south by San Juan County, on the east by the state of Colorado, on the north by Uintah County, and on the west by Emery County.

A government was organized in May 1890 in accordance with an act of 1865, with the naming by the legislature of a probate judge and three selectmen to serve until the general election in August. The probate judge and selectmen met as a county court on May 5 and appointed the following county officers to serve until after a general election August 28, 1890: clerk and recorder, assessor and collector, coroner, prosecuting attorney, treasurer, surveyor, and sheriff.

Officials appointed to serve until the general election were: John H. Shafer, Richard C. Camp, and Hansen Walker, selectmen; Sylvester Richardson, prosecuting attorney; Walter Moore, sheriff; George H. Wade, county clerk and recorder; Orrin D. Allen, assessor; Marcus H. Darrow, road supervisor; William Allred, coroner; John Shafer, O. D. Allen, and George H. Wade, school trustees. O. W. Warner was named selectman when Hansen Walker failed to qualify.

At the general election the following were elected: John H. Shafer, Nathan J. Turner, Sylvester Richardson, selectmen; A. A. Taylor, treasurer; George H. Wade, county clerk and recorder; C. J. Elliott, surveyor; F. A. Manville, assessor; R. D. Westwood, sheriff; R. C. Camp, prosecuting attorney; and M. H. Darrow, coroner.

After the first general election the following were appointed by the newly elected officials: Caleb C. Aldrich, game commissioner; Leonidas L. Crapo, United States Commissioner for Territory of Utah; Lilliston B. Bartlett, probate judge; Robert A. Kirker, appointed selectman to fill the unexpired term of Nathan J. Turner, deceased; Royal A. Jacobs, road supervisor; and Mark R. Walker, justice of the peace for the Moab precinct.

When the county was first organized, George H. Wade, clerk, rented his home for a courthouse. However, Wade sold his home in 1891 to Tom Trout, and the county was required to look elsewhere for a place to conduct its business. In January 1892 the county purchased from O. D. Allen a lot on which was located a small house. They built an addition to this house and also a jail on the property, which served until 1903.

Construction of a new courthouse was started in 1902 and was completed in 1903 at a cost of about $10,000.

This old stone county courthouse was replaced with a new modern one in 1937,[13] constructed at a cost of $65,000. Dedicated in July 1938,[14]

---

[13]*Ibid.*, October 16, 1903.

[14]Moab *Times-Independent*, July 1, 1973.

Figure 16.4. Grand County Court House

the building was said at the time to be the most modern in Utah, completely housing all departments of county government and district court (Figure 16.4).

Moab was proclaimed a third-class city by Governor Henry H. Blood in December 1936.[15] It had been an incorporated town since January 1903.[16] H. G. Green, former Blue Mountain cowboy, was Moab's first mayor.

IT IS INTERESTING to read of simple home remedies used by pioneers. One marvels at the ingenuity and knowledge of the simple remedies concocted from what was available, such as the prickly-pear salve prepared by Mrs. Wilson for the treatment of Joe's wounds. Old-timers will recall how "Uncle Horace" Johnson was called to set broken bones or pull teeth, and how midwives "brought babies" in their black satchels. But Moab was fortunate in December 1896 when Dr. J. W. Williams arrived. The county commissioners had hired him to serve as county physician[17] for $150 a year, "on condition he qualify by February 1, 1897."[18] He served for many years, not only as physician, but as a civic-minded

---

[15]*Ibid.*, December 17, 1936.

[16]*Grand Valley Times*, Moab, January 2, 1903.

[17]*Ibid.*, December 4, 1896.

[18]Moab *Times-Independent*, September 29, 1955.

citizen greatly interested in Moab and the surrounding area. He campaigned for many years, promoting the Arches and calling the scenic wonders of the area to the attention of the world. His life spanned more than a hundred years, during which time he lived to see his dream of an Arches National Monument fulfilled.

During the ensuing years, as the population increased, other doctors came to serve the people of the region. The Moab Hospital Company was organized in September 1919 by a group of citizens. The hospital was voted (by the citizens) a county hospital in January 1925. The present hospital, much enlarged and modernized, is today in the same location as the original.

A contribution to the cultural activities of the community was made in October 1902 when a Literary Club was organized.[19] This club has been in existence continuously since that date and is today a civic force.

The Literary Club celebrated its diamond anniversary in 1972.[20] Minutes of the meeting of March 9, 1898, report that several women of the community met to organize a women's club to be known as the "Busy Women's Club." Miss S. J. Elliot was elected president; Mrs. Helen Kirk, vice president; and Mrs. Melissa Stork, secretary. The club was to be a study group, and the first subject considered was Alaska. Each member was required to answer roll call with a quotation. Names appearing on the roll call on April 20, 1898, were Miss S. J. Elliot, Mrs. Helen Kirk, Mrs. Lissa Stork, Mrs. Annie Green, Mrs. Lula Goodman, Mrs. Addie Maxwell, Mrs. Mildred Williot, Mrs. Effie Taylor, Mrs. Sadie Wilson, Mrs. Annie Loveridge, Mrs. Clara Savage, Mrs. Vera Olson, Mrs. Susan Ray, Mrs. Sena Taylor, Mrs. Lydia Watts, Miss Lula Stork, Mrs. Essie Shafer, Mrs. Emma Empey, and Mrs. Augusta Walker.

For the first several years the club was a study group taking up current events, literature, geography, and other such interests. On June 7, 1898, it became a member of the Utah Federation of Women's Clubs and the General Federation of Women's Clubs and began to follow federation lines. The name was changed to the Women's Literary Club on October 28, 1914.

Active in promoting many community programs, its present project is the nursing home that is to be developed by the county. It promoted the bond election for this project.

WE OFTEN take for granted the inventions and conveniences of modern living and find it difficult, unless we have been a part of something

[19]*Grand Valley Times*, Moab, October 25, 1907.
[20]Moab *Times-Independent*, October 12, 1972.

different, to believe that there exists the paradox and contrast of customs and traditions of not-so-long-ago and today.

With paved highways, roads, and a modern city, it is difficult to picture the valley as its pioneers first knew it — sagebrush so tall a man could ride a horse unseen through it, grass belly-high to a horse, Mill Creek and Pack Creek beds deep with channels so narrow one could step or lay fence planks across them, not a tree or a house in sight. The sagebrush roots were so large they had to be pulled out with teams of oxen, and one root could be split into four stove-length pieces to stoke the kitchen stoves or the heating stoves (the former many times serving the role of both cooking and heating).

Floods early began to widen the channels of the creeks in the valley. As early as September 1896, reports of floods were carried in the newspaper[21]:

> Grand valley has experienced a washing this week that has never been equaled before as to the amount of damage done. In 1884 similar floods were experienced but there was not as much damage.... The heavy rains the early part of the week thoroughly saturated the ground and then came the heavy rains of Wednesday and Mill and Pack creeks began to deepen and widen their channels. Just before noon Wednesday the bridge near the Darrow house went out, and the channel there was soon twice the former width. For several hours all attention was directed to save the Darrow house, as the banks were fast cutting toward that building. Many of the trees about the house were felled and placed against the bank to break the force of the stream and did much to finally save the bliss [*sic*]. The river [rose] about ten feet in 24 hours.

The following week the paper reported that the floods had disappeared but the channels of both Mill and Pack creeks had deepened and in some instances cut three times the former width. A flood in Mill Creek a year later took the life of Carl J. Boren.[22]

Flood is frightening to anyone who has experienced it. The author recalls many experiences of cloudbursts on the slick rocks and the resultant floods in the creeks. One could hear the flood coming for some time before it reached town. The huge boulders made cracking sounds as the water roared and crashed down the bed of the creek. There was always ample time for townspeople to walk to the side of the creek to watch the wall of water come in. One could smell the muddy, pungent water rushing down the channel. In front would be only the small rivulet, then approaching, that huge wall, several feet high, rolling in, carrying with

---

[21]*Grand Valley Times*, Moab, September 25, 1896.
[22]*Ibid.*, October 1897.

it boulders weighing tons, trees, farm buildings and even, at times, animals and chickens. The author well remembers the terror of a young child at the terrible flood of August 1919, when the newspaper carried these headlines: "Water system out of commission for a week"; "Main Street bridge carried away"; "Many homes and farms damaged"; followed by this account of the flood[23]:

> Coming without warning, and coursing down from the mountains at a terrific speed, the largest flood ever seen in Mill Creek overflowed its banks and swept through the south part of Moab Valley Saturday night [August 2]. Damages estimated at [$25,000] were sustained. . . . The power plant dam at Mill Creek was taken out, and the power house, which was situated near the creek, was undermined by caving banks. The house was carried away by the flood and some of the machinery was lost. . . . Nearly one thousand feet of the Moab Water System [pipeline] was carried away leaving the town without water for a week. Moab irrigation dam in the creek was taken out. The new Main Street bridge over Mill Creek, recently constructed at a cost of fifteen hundred dollars, was carried out by the first impact of the flood. A number of homes and farms were badly damaged. The flood hit Moab at approximately 10:30 Saturday evening.

Flood control projects during the 1930s made the town safe from a repetition of this disaster. But today control and protection exist and more bridges span the streams.

During spring months each year the Colorado River rises, and in early years the lower end of the valley was covered with flood waters. During 1884 much damage was done to cultivated acreage in the lower valley by the unprecedented floods of August of that year. Unusually heavy and protracted rains throughout the mountains in the watershed of the Colorado sent such immense volumes of water down the stream that it was possible to go from the river to the fort, a mile and a half from the banks of the stream, in a rowboat. The entire lower valley was a lake. This stage of high water holds the record in the memories of, whites and Indians.

IN EARLY DAYS the materials for laundry were all made in the home — lye, soap, and starch. Lye was made from cottonwood ashes and starch from potatoes. Each family had its large soap kettle.

Sugar cane was raised for molasses. Because money was scarce, a piece of sugar cane made an excellent substitute for a piece of candy.

---

[23]"Cloudburst Does Twenty-five Thousand Damage — Electric Light Plant Taken Out," *ibid.*, August 8, 1919.

Some cotton was raised, although it had to be combed by hand. Yarn was made from this cotton. Very early, sheep were brought into the valley and the wool used for homespun cloth. Wheat straw was often used for the making of hats.

Life was primitive in comparison to today, but a family was a unit and a community worked and played together. Children had their pets. William Peirce brought the first cats into Moab. He traded one to Mrs. A. G. Wilson for a pig.

Shortly after the solidification of the community, in 1881–82, a public house was built. This served as a church meeting house, a school, and a recreation center for the community. Pioneer life did not lack for interludes of fun and recreation. Dances were a popular form of recreation and were often held in private houses. The Stocks family, for example, had a hall and would furnish music for dances. Warners soon had one too. There was no lack of music. Addie Taylor Maxwell had an organ. She and her husband, Philander, took the organ with them to community functions. While she played it, her husband played the violin. Angus Stocks, a mason and blacksmith by day, became a fiddler by night to play for the dances. He had learned to play by ear, but was accurate in note and rhythm and is said to have stopped dancers if they were out of step, coming down onto the floor to show them how the dance should be done. Alma Lutz, a veteran of the Black Hawk War, would shake his "bones" (a kind of rattle held in each hand) in rhythm to the music. Old-timers tell of his humorous side. His favorite expression was "Ai hell." The story is told that on one occasion he took one of his daughters to a dance, and (displeased with the conduct) called out to her, "Ai hell, Hat, get your hat and let's go home."

George and Viry Gibson were good step-dancers. Since there were no wooden floors during this early period, they put the end gate of a wagon down and danced on that.

In 1888 a new LDS meeting house was constructed. Construction continued in 1889 and an adobe structure 32 feet by 22 feet was erected. Later on the same lot was built a recreation and dramatic hall. This was, and is, known as the Star Hall and community theater. Drama supplied entertainment for many years. This hall, which now belongs to the school district, has recently been remodeled and renovated (Figure 16.5) and will again function for the purpose for which it was erected.

One item worthy of mention, which is really a business but also an essential medium that fits into the social activity of the community in its entertainment, is the movie theater. The first films were a far cry from the technicolor extravaganzas later produced in and around Moab. A building was erected for the purpose of producing movies. The motion picture theater was operated by Robert C. Clark and his wife Elberta.

The first movies were silent flicks starring Fatty Arbuckle, Rudolph Valentino, Mary Pickford, and other great names of that vanished era. They were shown in a makeshift theater in the old Woodman of the World (W.O.W.) Hall, now the Arches Building on Center Street.

The theater was named the Ides[24] after its blustering March opening day. In the mid-1930s a theater building was erected. The Ides remained a family operation. Mrs. Clark sold tickets, Neva (Kirk), a daughter, pumped background music on an old player piano from an elevated nook just large enough to hold her, the piano, and the hundreds of piano rolls.

Matinees were the most trying of the silent movie days. The W.O.W. Hall was surrounded by an apple orchard, and young theater goers went armed with fruit. If the show was interesting they ate the apples; if not, they threw them. Many a Moab youth was helped out of the matinee via his suspender straps.

Moab was without a theater for a time after the W.O.W. Hall burned. All that the volunteer firefighters managed to rescue was the player piano. It was hoisted out of the box with a rope and pulley, and survived to play for the next theater when it reopened in the new W.O.W. Hall.

Al Jolson's "Sonny Boy" was the first talking picture shown at the Ides. All through the film, sound and picture were unsynchronized, but not a fan left the building.

Background music (then an electric record player) was played, and during this early period of "talking pictures," the record custodian assisted the operator in synchronizing the sound and film. Somehow it seemed a hopeless task. But one of the fond memories of the intimacy of a small community is of a lovely German lady in the town who placed a bag of chocolates on the record player, quite often, with a kind little note. Perhaps that helped to compensate for the frustration of the failure to synchronize the film and sound, or when the sound track jumped or slipped, or a film had lost too much footage in a splice.

Since the W.O.W. Hall served as a dancehall, the benches were folding ones that could be stacked against the wall. The building also served for political rallies and for Lyceum Theater circuit productions. Children looked forward to the activities provided for them on July 4th and 24th[25] celebrations. Os(mer) Elmer and his bottomless wooden barrel of lemonade was a memorable treat.

One of the most memorable evenings of the year was election night. The movie was presented on schedule, but was halted several

---

[24]Moab *Times-Independent*, October 27, 1966.

[25]A holiday peculiar to Utah, commemorating the arrival of the Saints into the Salt Lake Valley, July 24, 1847.

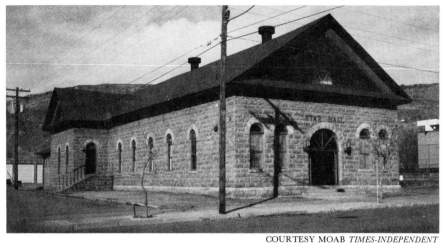

COURTESY MOAB *TIMES-INDEPENDENT*
Figure 16.5. Star Hall in Moab

times during the evening when editor Bish Taylor rushed over from the *Times* office to read the latest election returns reported to him by telephone.

After Clark's death, Mrs. Clark and John Leaming pooled resources for a new Ides Theater, later the Holiday, on Main Street. The new theater was the pride of Moab, sporting plush carpets, upholstered seats, and a velvet-curtained stage. During the uranium boom the pressure was so great that Mrs. Clark sold her theater and, after almost half a century of service, went out of business. Other movie houses replaced the Ides.

HORSE RACES were another source of entertainment and an occasion for celebration. This was particularly true at La Sal where the Rays, Maxwells, and McCartys loved horses, and although their best were just better-than-average cow ponies, the excitement aroused by what usually began as casual wagers had an effect for miles around. Frank Silvey gave a good account of this sport. He told that the Rays had a horse named "Tobe" which they thought was fast. The McCartys, in turn, were just as proud of their horse "Selim."

One day a friendly argument developed over which horse was the faster. So sure was Billy McCarty of his horse's fleetness that he offered to bet $1,000 and twenty head of horses that his horse could beat Ray's over a quarter of a mile. The Rays accepted the challenge, and a date five weeks hence was set. The horses were carefully "fitted," and a good race track was laid out, Indian style, on the ridge above the Ray ranch, near the pines. Several days before the race a number of families from

273

Moab arrived in their old-fashioned wagons with bedding and plenty to eat. A few came from Paradox on horseback. All camped out and had a jolly time; during this festive period they held a dance each night.

When the day of the race arrived, there had been considerable bets made in the way of stock and money upon the outcome. There was much excitement when the Ray horse, "Tobe," won easily.

Neal Ray had a trim looking sorrel mare which he matched against Eck McCarty's. Eck was a mere boy at that time. He weighed about 105 pounds, and Neal weighed 165. This was somewhat of a handicap, but Neal won the race by a length. The Maxwells and McCartys were good losers and offered to run Philander Maxwell's "Bally" pony in four weeks against "Tobe" for any amount. Another match was arranged on the spot.

Another race track was agreed on and it was laid out just below the Ray's field on Deer Creek. George Gibson of Moab was the crack rider of the county in those days. He was engaged by the Rays to ride "Tobe," and Eck McCarty was to ride "Bally." Gibson was the mail carrier from Green River to La Sal once a week, and it took four days to make the round trip. Frank Silvey carried the mail on one trip so that Gibson might become familiar with his mount. The race was a close one, "Bally" winning by half a length. Thus the Maxwells and McCartys won this round. But again sportsmanship prevailed, and the losers took their loss gracefully. These races were always well attended with excitement running high, but there are no written or oral reports of fights or lack of sportsmanship.

It would be impossible to relate all forms of entertainment and all who made contributions to the communities. Life was not simple and unexciting as it might appear to many today, surrounded as we are by so many activities pulling at us that we must constantly make decisions. The social activities of a community kept it a closely knit unit. There were cabin raising bees, corn husking bees, quilting bees, apple cutting bees, peach peeling bees, and other group activities in which neighbors shared in joys and sorrows. Perhaps the fact that professional insurance had not reached its present necessary proportions and that the doctors, lawyers, publishers, and other servants were tried over the quilting or paring bees, the energies were released without frequent recourse to the courts. And homemade ice cream and cake could be served, which tended to enhance the mood of the participants.

Some of these customs have been taken into the cities and retained, others have been lost. But Moab and La Sal had their share of community activity and sharing.

Chapter 17

Scenic Beauty and Natural Wonders

How does one describe the beauty that nature has wrought in the Moab and La Sal area? As a world traveler, the author has seen many of the touted scenic spots both in the United States and elsewhere in the world; has motored along the Skyline Drive overlooking the Shenandoah Valley and the tidelands; has stood on the summit of Mount Pilatus in Switzerland and looked down upon Lake Lucerne; has driven through the Black Forest of Germany and the Vienna woods which inspired Johann Strauss to write his lovely waltzes; has visited Capri, Hawaii, Greece, Rome, Egypt, and innumerable scenic spots, all of which leave one breathless at the handiwork of nature and humankind. Each is unique in its own way — and each is indescribable.

Indescribable and unique also is the scenery round and about Moab and La Sal — and just as breathtaking. As one stands looking at the meandering Colorado River at Dead Horse Point and sees where it has slashed the massive sandstone into deep, vertical canyons, one stands in awe at the vastness, the beauty of sand and water. Or one can play games with oneself, endlessly attempting to visualize how many statues the wind and water and sand have carved in the Arches, Fisher Valley, or the canyons of the Colorado. The red sandstone backed by the blue and white of the La Sal Mountains, its color shifting with the lights and shadows, is a memory worth storing. Or as one stands on the mountain itself, fascinated with the blazing glory of the sun's descent, one's thoughts turn to the lines of that poet of intense nature love who said[1]:

---

[1]William Wordsworth, "Tintern Abbey."

> For I have learned
> To look on nature, not as in the hour
> Of thoughtless youth; but hearing oftentimes
> The still, sad music of humanity,
> Nor harsh nor grating, though of ample power
> To chasten and subdue. And I have felt
> A presence that disturbs me with the joy
> Of elevated thoughts; a sense sublime
> Of something far more deeply interfused,
> Whose dwelling is the light of setting suns....

How one longs for the insight and expression of the poet that she might do justice to that which she sees.

Standing on Bald Mesa on a clear July day and gazing down at Warner Reservoir and the mountains in the background, one realizes that the majesty of this sight which has caught the vision minimizes all human tribulation. Fields of wild iris — a riot of color — gently wave in the mountain breeze. And again one thinks of Wordsworth, who stored up his daffodils for some pensive mood when his recollection might envisage their golden glory again. One is moved to exclaim, "Hosts of wild iris on the hills!"

Or to stand on Bald Mesa and look over the panorama to the west and northwest is almost overpowering. Castle Rock can be seen in the foreground, then farther back the Book Cliffs and Henry Mountains, the canyon of the Colorado, and the red cliffs stretching endlessly ahead into a magnificent kaleidoscope of ever-changing interest and color.

Numerous deep emotions have been expressed in descriptions of this land of many facets. Gifford Pinchot in his introduction to *Ranger Trails*,[2] expressed the feelings of early settlers when he wrote, citing a common description of the area: "We cowmen came into this country before Uncle Sam even thought it worth lookin' at. When God finished makin' the world, he had a lot of rocks left over an' he threw them down here in a pile in Utah."

When Riis came to this western picture country from the east, he too was overwhelmed with its magnificence and described it as follows[3]:

> Somewhere in the uninhabited jumble of rocks the Green River and the Grand River joined to form the Colorado. Two hundred miles to the north and to the south the country was impassible, useless and barren. Yet as the sinking sun drew distorted shadows across its twisted face, there was an odd and impossible beauty about it.

---

[2]Riis, *op. cit.*, "Introduction."
[3]*Ibid.*, pp. 62–63.

Nothing lives there except horned toads, lizards, mountain sheep, and an occasional coyote. It is fit for nothing else. Here and there across its deep canyons hide the cliff-built homes of a race that lived a thousand years before, and etched on their walls are the undecipherable record of their history. Men penetrate this desolate region only in the winter when there is water in the canyon sinks. In the summer they are hell holes of heat!

Here are canyons whose walls rise for hundreds of feet yet so narrow one can toss a stone from rim to rim with ease. Needle-like spires shoot from their depths into a turquoise sky. Row after row of serrated rock formations with mushroom tops or capped by delicately balanced slabs of rock stand like long files of Egyptians bearing burdens on their heads.

It is a land to dream over, for in some indefinable way it seems to present the story of creation, to hold locked in its rocky fastness tales that have been lost among the centuries. Long I watched as the sun sunk lower and creeping shadows spread over that still and lonely land. Dead it is and has been for thousands of years, yet it seemed to me that here the Creator had painted a vivid picture of time eternal that was good for man to see; a picture that has lived for centuries, and will live for countless more.

Two decades later, another ranger — this time in the Arches National Monument — was to experience a similar emotion as he gazed over the vast wasteland and wrote[1]:

> ...I put on a coat and step outside. Into the center of the world, God's navel...the red wasteland....The sun is not yet in sight but signs of the advent are plain to see. Lavender clouds sail like a fleet of ships across the pale green dawn; each cloud, planed flat on the wind, has a base of fiery gold. Southeast, twenty miles by the line of sight, stand the peaks of the Sierra La Sal, twelve to thirteen thousand feet above sea level, all covered with snow and rosy in the morning sunlight. The air is dry and clear as well as cold; the last fogbanks left over from last night's storm are scudding away like ghosts, fading into nothing before the wind and the sunrise.

He then describes the "dark gorge of the Colorado River...carved through the sandstone mesa" and, to the south, the "Moab valley between thousand-foot walls of rock, with the town of Moab somewhere on the valley floor, too small to be seen from here." His vista ranges as far as the Blue Mountains fifty miles to the south. To the north and

---

[1]Edward Abbey, *Desert Solitaire: A Season in the Wilderness* (New York: McGraw-Hill Book Company, 1968), pp. 4–6.

northwest, he can see the Roan and Book cliffs, "the two-level face of the Uinta Plateau." He can see the highway and the railroad tracks; to the west, mesas, canyons, red cliffs, arid tablelands "extending through purple haze over the bulging curve of the planet to the ranges of Colorado — a sea of desert." He continues:

> Within this vast perimeter... are the 33,000 acres of Arches National Monument of which I am now sole inhabitant, usufructuary, observer, and custodian.... What are the Arches?... These are natural arches, holes in the rock, windows in stone, no two alike, as varied in form as in dimension. They range in size from holes just big enough to walk through to openings large enough to contain the dome of the Capitol Building in Washington, D.C. Some resemble jug handles or flying buttresses, others natural bridges but with this technical distinction: A natural bridge spans a watercourse — a natural arch does not. The arches were formed through hundreds of thousands of years by the weathering of the huge sandstone walls, or fins, in which they are found. Not the work of a cosmic hand, nor sculptured by sand-bearing winds, as many people prefer to believe, the arches came into being and continue to come into being through the modest wedging action of rainwater, melting snow, frost, and ice, aided by gravity. In color they change from off-white through buff, pink, brown, and red, tones which also change with the time of day and the moods of the light, the weather, the sky.

Abbey shares with his readers his feelings of a "ridiculous greed and possessiveness" in the land, his desire to "know it all, possess it all, embrace the entire scene intimately, deeply, totally, as a man desires a beautiful woman." His description of the sunrise is especially stirring:

> The now-covered ground glimmers with a dull blue light, reflecting the sky and the approaching sunrise. Leading away from me the narrow dirt road, an alluring and primitive track into nowhere, meanders down the slope and toward the labyrinth of naked stone. Near the first group of arches, looming over a bend in the road, is a balanced rock about fifty feet high, mounted on a pedestal of equal height; it looks like a head from Easter Island, a stone god, or a petrified ogre.

MOAB IS LOCATED at the heart of the Canyonlands (Figure 17.1). By highway, it is fifty miles from Green River. By river, it is 182 miles of fantastically colorful scenery. To the east lies the La Sal Mountain range. Six miles to the north is Arches National Monument headquarters. A scenic road leads to the rock formations located in the park. If one likes to hike, there are many trails and thrilling sights ahead.

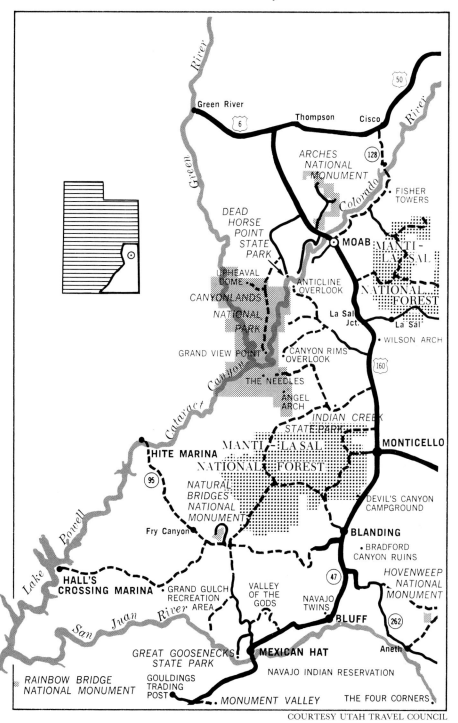

Figure 17.1. National and State Parks and Forests
in the Moab–La Sal Area, Southeastern Utah

Arches National Monument is well named. There are more natural stone arches, windows, and pinnacles than in any other section of the nation. Nearly ninety arches have been discovered, and others are probably hidden away in remote and rugged parts of the area.[5] But there is far more to the monument than the arches. "Spectacular towers, sweeping coves, shapes resembling figures of men and animals, balanced rocks, and other weird forms resulting from the combined action of running water, wind, rain, frost and sun form a setting to which the arches are a majestic culmination."[6] In the country sweeping to the west and to the south the concentration of scenery is all-engulfing.

Lohman[7] states that the vivid and varied colors of the bare rocks and the "fantastic buttes, spires, columns, alcoves, caves, arches, and other erosional forms of Arches National Park result from a fortuitous combination of geologic and climatic circumstances and events unequalled in most other parts of the world." He points out that these events were the piling up, layer upon layer, of thousands of feet of sedimentary rocks under a wide variety of environments. He further indicates that the sedimentary rocks of the region are composed of clay, silt, sand, and gravel carried and deposited by moving water, or silt and sand transported by wind with some materials precipitated from water solutions; some of the beds were laid down in shallow seas that once covered the area or in lagoons and estuaries near the sea. Other beds were deposited by streams in inland basins or plains, a few were deposited in lakes, and some were carried in by the wind.

The rock in which these arches were formed was deposited as sand some fifty million years ago, during the Jurassic period. The three-hundred-foot layer, called Entrada sandstone, is believed to have been laid mainly by wind. Its characteristics indicate that it first accumulated as a vast coastal desert, which in time was buried by new layers, and then hardened into rock.[8]

Geologists tell us that the rock was then lifted up, twisted, and severely cracked a number of times. Then after erosion had stripped away the overlying layers at some later time, the Entrada sandstone, exposed to weathering, began the formation of the arches. The water which entered the cracks in the sandstone dissolved some of the cementing sand, and cracks were widened into narrow canyons separated

---

[5]"Arches National Monument, Utah," National Park Service, Department of the Interior (Washington, D.C.: U.S. Government Printing Office, 1966).

[6]*Ibid.*

[7]S. W. Lohman, "The Geologic Story of Arches National Park," Geological Survey Bulletin 1393, U.S. Department of the Interior (Washington, D.C.: U.S. Government Printing Office, 1975), p. 20.

[8]"Arches National Monument, Utah", *op. cit.*

by fins. Because softer areas were more vulnerable, the vertical walls resulted from the undercutting by rapid weathering. Water and frost enlarged the "windows." All stages of development and decay can be seen in this area. The rock matrix of the Arches is generally some forty million years old.[9]

A tour of world-famous Arches National Park is a must on any visit to Canyonlands. The question is, as aptly stated on a poster in the Visitor Center, "How long can you stay?" The park is open year-round, but, like most high deserts, it gets rather hot in the summer and cold enough in the winter for occasional snows, and is sometimes closed temporarily because of heavy snowfall. The weather generally is ideal during the spring and fall. Even though summer daytime temperatures often exceed 100° F (37.8 C) which tends to slow down hikers, the nights are cool enough to make comfortable sleeping beneath ample covers.[10]

Officially set aside as a national monument in 1929, Arches lies only six miles from downtown Moab. In 1956 the National Park Service conceived a new program that changed Arches National Monument from an unimproved and unknown scenic area into a spot of national prominence.[11] The program, called "Mission 66," designed to complete (insofar as possible) ultimate facilities to designated public parks and monuments by the National Park Service's fiftieth anniversary in 1966, was enthusiastically backed by President Dwight D. Eisenhower. Congress indicated its approval of the project by appropriating more than $1 billion during the ten-year period.[12]

As a result of this program, the Arches received the first significant government money designated for improvements, and dusty wagon trails and roads built by Grand County have been transformed into 21 miles of paved highways leading to major scenic centers in the park. There is a wide, surfaced road leading through the confines of the park where many of the main features may be viewed from a car, and an endless assortment of unique sights may be seen from short hikes on foot trails leading off the main road. In addition to stabilized trails built into remote areas, there is a water well nine hundred feet deep and an electrical generator added to supply light and water to comfort stations in the Devil's Garden campground area.

A visitors center with exhibits and displays, an information desk, audiovisual slide show, and a museum, boasting a bust of founder Dr. Williams, for public enjoyment have been added. Park personnel have

---

[9]Jack Breed, "Utah's Arches of Stone," *National Geographic* (August 1947), pp. 452–61.

[10]Lohman, *op. cit.*, p. 51.

[11]Moab *Times-Independent*, July 8, 1965 (scenic supplement).

[12]Lohman, *op cit.*, p. 4.

been increased, with modern housing provided for them. The investment of nearly $3 million has resulted in increased interest and tourism. In 1964 over a hundred thousand visitors registered at the center.

Arches graduated to a full-fledged national park in November 1971 when President Richard M. Nixon signed a congressional bill authorizing the action. However, the change in status was accompanied by boundary changes that reduced the area to about 114 square miles. The loss of most of Dry Mesa, just east of the 1974 boundary, was offset in part by gains of new land northwest of Devils Garden.[13]

Arches National Park consists of five sections — Court House Towers, the Windows, Devil's Garden, the Fiery Furnace, and Klondike Bluffs — each with a distinct variety of scenery to offer. All but the Klondike Bluffs area are available by way of the two-lane surfaced road through the park. This area can be reached by a seven-mile dirt jeep road, usually passable to passenger cars.

Guided foot tours into the Fiery Furnace are conducted by Park Service personnel. Visitors could easily become lost in the maze of intricate red rock canyons, spires, and fins without the services of a guide familiar with the trails. This tour may be made in cool comfort, even though hot weather persists elsewhere.

The tenderfoot coming to the West should become informed about water, trails, and distances before undertaking a hike into the Park. It is easy to underestimate distances in these wide-open spaces, and the heat is more intense than one realizes.

Approaching the park, one first passes through the Court House Towers section. Here the huge, silent sandstone skyscrapers look down on travelers as they make their way toward the "Great Organ Rock" at the far end. The monoliths in this section have been named by the people of Moab who have explored the area, and one can readily recognize such formations as Sausage Rock, the Three Gossips, Sheep Rock, the Tower of Babel, and many others. Park Avenue, if one wishes to take an easy hike of one mile, resembles the skyscrapers of a great city with towering red-rock walls topped by an orderly array of towers and spires.

In what is known as the Windows section, eight immense arches and many smaller windows, passageways, coves, pinnacles, spires, and balanced rocks have been carved. Here are Double Arch, Parade of the Elephants, Cove of the Caves, North and South Windows, Balanced Rock, and other erosional features.

It requires a hike of a mile and a half to view the famous Delicate Arch, which is probably the most photographed arch in the world (Figure 17.2). The sight is well worth the effort as a climax to the scenic

---

[13]*Ibid.*, p. 5.

COURTESY MOAB *TIMES-INDEPENDENT*

Figure 17.2. Delicate Arch

features of the monument. It is an example of isolated erosion, and one leg of its lofty 65-foot span is no more than six feet thick at the narrowest point. The pastel colors of the arch change continuously throughout the day as the sun moves toward the west. On a clear day the arch is a perfect frame for the entire range of the La Sal Mountains twenty miles to the southeast, and at any time an inspiring and thrilling view of the valley below may be seen. Its setting against cliffs and massive "slickrock" domes is unsurpassed. The gorge of the Colorado River and the snow-capped peaks of the La Sals complete the background.

Early-day cowboys had a more colorful name for Delicate Arch — they called it "Schoolmarm's Bloomers." However, there did not seem to be the indignation among the local inhabitants at the official adoption of the name "Delicate Arch" such as was expressed when a state highway sign indicated the name of the Wilson Arch (on U.S. Highway 163) as "Window Arch." The misnomer lasted for several years because, when it was first posted, it was officially listed under this name by the U.S. Board on Geographic Names in Washington, D.C. With the typical fierce pride that Moabites have in their pioneer heritage, they protested, requesting the state to restore the original name.

It nearly took an "act of Congress" to accomplish this, however, for bureaucratic red tape had to be surmounted before the federal agency would approve the preparation and installation of new signs. It was because of the efforts of (state) Senator Sam Taylor, editor of the Moab *Times-Independent*, with a copy of the 1937 edition of this book in his hand, that the authorities were convinced an error had indeed been made, and the original (proper) name was restored. Joe Wilson, for whom the arch had been named, was a local pioneer in the valley. The government wasn't entirely too far wrong when it dubbed the arch "Window Arch," for the window cut by erosion was large enough that a helicopter was flown through it in 1968.[14]

The Fiery Furnace, an intricate maze of narrow passageways and high stone walls, gets its name from the glow in the light of the setting sun. This area has not yet been fully explored.

Nine miles north of the Balanced Rock the road ends in the Devils Garden section. From the end of the road near Skyline Arch, trails lead to Fin Canyon, Tunnel Arch, Landscape Arch, Double-O Arch, and many others found in that part of the monument. Sixty-four of the monument's known arches are found in the Devil's Garden area.[15]

Landscape Arch (Figure 17.3), 291 feet long, is believed to be the largest natural stone span in the world.[16] Perhaps one can better visualize

---

[14]Moab *Times-Independent*, August 8, 1968, and September 19, 1968.

[15]Breed, *op. cit.*

[16]National Park Service, *op. cit.*

COURTESY MOAB *TIMES-INDEPENDENT*

Figure 17.3. Landscape Arch

the length of this arch when it is pointed out that the arch is just nine feet short of the length of a football field. It has been eroded down to six feet at one point.

The official width of 291 feet had to be increased by a few feet recently because a section of stone fell from under the arch at one end. Many are concerned that Landscape Arch, which is more "delicate" by far than Delicate Arch, will be destroyed by sonic booms created by military aircraft that fly over the area periodically.[17]

Tower Arch and Klondike Bluffs lend further interest and awe, although the Klondike Bluffs area has not been extensively investigated because of the rough terrain.

Fisher Towers, those knifelike pinnacles of deep ruddy sandstone, are isolated in a remote canyon, hidden away along Utah Highway 128. This forty-mile scenic byway connects Moab and Cisco, Utah, and is a winding canyon road up a streambed noted for its quicksand. Many motion pictures and some television advertisements have been filmed in this beautiful setting. Here are some classic examples of vertical erosion with buttes, mesas, and other characteristic canyon-country formations. Viewers are limited in what they see only by their imagination.

Also up the Colorado one finds the great Castle Rock and the scenery of Castle Valley. Castle Rock, too, has been used in television advertising.

The arches are not limited strictly to the Arches National Monument boundaries. Small arches are found in several places. For example there is a small arch in "Nigger Bill" Canyon north of Moab; and about the same distance to the south of town is another. On U.S. Highway 163 after one passes the La Sal junction, there is the famous "Looking Glass Rock" and the Wilson Arch. In Pritchett Canyon there are several, including the well-known El Arco bridge. Following the Potash Road (Utah 279), one finds Corona Arch, Jug Handle Arch, and several other small ones. It would seem that Nature was in an impish mood as she carved these many and varied arches and figures. The entire vast area of Canyonlands is an awe-inspiring kaleidoscope of primitive nature.

One wonders what the uninitiated remarked when they first saw this vast array of sand and stone. One is reminded of Bryce's comment when he first saw the canyon bearing his name — "It's a hell of a place to lose a cow."

Dr. J. W. Williams had been promoting the setting aside of the Arches area as a park for many years, but he had not been successful. Dr. Laurence M. Gould, who had written his doctoral dissertation on the geology of the La Sal Mountains, and who had later headed two expeditions to the Antarctic, was visiting in Moab in 1933. He told the

---

[17]Moab *Times-Independent*, October 14, 1971.

author[18] that Marvin Turnbow guided him on a tour of the Arches area, and when Dr. Gould waxed ecstatic over the formations and sheer beauty of the region, Turnbow mused, "I didn't know there was anything unusual about it."

This acceptance by those familiar with the country as not having unusual appeal probably accounted for the difficulty Dr. Williams experienced in getting recognition for it. Dr. Gould made some contacts with park officials and people who could act. He told the author that he felt one of his greater achievements in life was the part he had played in calling the region to the attention of important people in Washington, D.C. He in no way wished to detract from the work of Dr. Williams and his associates, but was happy that he, too, had a part in getting proper recognition and action.

The early history of the Arches area is associated with the livestock industry. During the Battle of Bull Run, a soldier by the name of John Wolfe (of Ohio) was wounded in a leg. After doctors gave him six months to live, he moved to southeastern Utah in 1888, built a cabin along Salt Wash where he established a ranch and lived 22 years in spite of those gloomy prophecies.[19]

The Wolfe ranch, consisting of 150 acres, carried the DX cattle brand. It was in the heart of what is now Arches National Monument. In 1906 Salt Wash flooded and washed Wolfe's cabin away. Undaunted, he built a new one farther away from the creek. This still stands, near the start of the Delicate Arch trail, as a historical relic in the monument and is known as the "Turnbow cabin."

After operating his ranch for 22 years, Wolfe sold the homestead to Marvin Turnbow, whose heirs sold it in 1947 to a sheep rancher named Emmett Elizondo. Elizondo in turn sold it to the U.S. government to be included in Arches National Monument.

Many stories have been handed down about the ranch — that broomtail (wild) horses ran unmolested in the grazing lands, using the now-famous Arches country as a hideout when cowboys herded cattle in the confines and gave the rock formations amusing titles, little knowing their trails would one day be a famous tourist mecca.

In 1923 F. A. Wadleith, passenger traffic manager for the Denver & Rio Grande Railroad wrote a letter that was to immortalize the ranch. He wrote to Stephen T. Mather, director of the National Park Service, urging him to establish the area as a national monument.

It was a long seven-year grind from the date of Wadleith's recommendation for the Arches National Monument to its official establish-

---

[18]Dr. L. M. Gould, personal interview, April 1968.

[19]Moab *Times-Independent*, July 8, 1965, scenic section.

ment in 1929. The fight was headed by the Moab Lions Club, Dr. J. W. Williams ("Father of the Arches"), and Dr. Laurence M. Gould.

The original monument consisted of only 4,520 acres. More extensive exploration and discovery of additional arches and other scientific features resulted eventually in the expansion of the park to its present size of 33,770 acres.

Until 1936 the Arches National Monument had been seen only by those sturdy outdoor people who could ride horseback or a jolting wagon through its primitive trails. The first automobile trip was made in 1936 by Dr. Williams and several other Moabites. They followed the wagon trail to Balanced Rock and pioneered a trail to the Windows section. The trip was dusty and rough, compared to the comfortable tours now available through the park on the wide, surfaced highways.

How do the various formations found in the Arches National Monument get their names? And how does one distinguish between an arch, a tunnel, a bridge, or just a hole in the rock? A ranger from the Arches National Monument gives some explanation of this problem in the following paragraphs (quoted material is from his article)[20]:

> Visitors to the sandstone wilderness, called by geologists the "Colorado Plateau," are all too frequently faced with a minor but irritating problem. Longtime residents of the "Canyonlands," as such people tend to call the Colorado Plateau, also have the problem, but they have simply learned to live with it. Indeed, experts, or those who should be experts, have likewise not solved this persistent and annoying dilemma, but, unlike visitors and local residents, their very occupations make ignoring the situation a shameful, unprofessional response.... This curious and universal problem is best stated allegorically. A person, either visitor, resident, or expert, stands staring upward at a piece of sky surrounding the chunk of sky itself, asks "Is the rock surrounding the chunk of sky an arch or a bridge? Or maybe the thing is a window? Or perhaps just a simple hole in rock? A tunnel, maybe?"

Barnes concedes that if someone has put up a sign to tell the viewer that this is "a bridge, arch, or window," the problem is solved because the "little sign says so ... [and] little signs are always made by world authorities, aren't they?" Then he asks, "But what about those other hundreds ... of gaping voids ... that are not graced by authoritative little signs?" His list of criteria used by the "Arches experts" for determining the proper identification of these phenomena? Simply these:

(1) A *window* is a hole in a wall of rock.

---

[20]Fran Barnes, "An Arch, Tunnel, Bridge – Or a Hole in the Rock: Experts Even Disagree on the Proper Definition," Moab *Times-Independent*, July 1, 1971.

(2) A *bridge* is a hole through rock that has water running through it.

(3) An *arch* is like a bridge, only without any water running through it.

(4) Holes that don't fit these definitions have no right to exist.

He then asks some questions that cast doubt upon the value of these definitions:

> How big does a hole in a rock wall have to be to be called a window? A foot wide? Six feet? Twenty feet? Or is height the critical dimension? Does the top of the wall have to be level? What if it's humped up, is the window then an arch? If so, how high a hump? How thick must the rock be above the hole before it is a window, not an arch? Why is Skyline Arch in Arches not a window? And how thin must the wall be to create a window, not a tunnel? What if, during infrequent rainstorms, some water runs through the window, but never otherwise? Is it then a bridge? If not, why not?...Maybe the method of formation of the span is the key.

After more chiding of the "experts," he concludes with:

> ...The whole subject is very confusing, and shows every sign of staying that way....The upshot of it is that as of now, there simply aren't any recognized authoritative experts on definitions pertaining to natural rock spans and holes. So rather than assume blithely that there are, or innocently believe the signs you see, or even ignore the problem altogether, why not be your own expert? At least until a better one comes along? It's more fun that way!

Well, there you are. Is there anyone who would care to take on this responsibility? (It's too cumbersome for this author.)

ANOTHER "TREASURE" of southeastern Utah is the Utah State Park's Dead Horse Point. Josephine Fabian[21] tells a dramatic story of the importance of historians on the Green and Colorado rivers. She says that their task is to roll back history by cutting away the outside surface of the earth until some of the first layers of the earth's skin are reached. This they have done to reveal the secrets of the earth's formation, its turbulent youth, and its maturation.

Ms. Fabian points out that explorations in recent decades have brought to light many facets of history. Caves and deep recesses along

---

[21]Josephine Fabian, "Dead Horse Point in Rainbow Land," *Utah Historical Quarterly* (July 1958), pp. 239–45.

the canyon walls and riverbanks have revealed the habitations of human-kind, some said to be more than fifteen thousand years old.[22] Petroglyphs and pictographs have been uncovered, and excavations have disclosed evidence of prehistoric human existence stretching back eons in time. Dead Horse Point, one of the most singularly spectacular spots in south-eastern Utah, is, she says, like an index finger pointing to the vast country which holds these and many other wonders in its embrace.

Dead Horse Point, an overlook on a broad mesa three thousand feet straight up from the Colorado River (Figure 17.4), commands a view of a canyon unsurpassed even by the Grand Canyon in Arizona many miles to the south. The earth seems to end at this precipice. Below is the mighty Colorado, winding and twisting its way to meet the Green forty miles downstream — unhurriedly meandering through immense goose-necks before continuing a less circuitous pattern to its juncture with the Green. The brilliant colors of the sheer, rugged walls of the canyon prompt many a camera buff to "shoot on sight."

The scene from below, on the floor of the canyon looking up to-ward Dead Horse Point, is stupefying in its immensity, with the sprawl-ing river cutting its way through weathered canyon walls that have been chiseled out for millions of years. Paths through the valley floor's vege-tation have been worn by automobiles and the feet of countless hunters, lovers of the sport of fishing, sightseers, and (more than likely) Indians. Park guides caution that only the hardiest of souls have attempted the route from the top of the mesa to these paths and roads which can be seen from the vantage point of Dead Horse.

If, while viewing these vistas from Dead Horse Point, travelers allow their gaze to lift upward, they are treated to the sight of an almost limitless expanse of land. In one sweeping view there is unfolded some five thousand square miles of one of the largest, relatively roadless areas in the United States. To the east are the La Sal Mountains, where one can see Bears Ears, the buttes that pinpoint the location of the Natural Bridges National Monument and directly beyond them Monument Valley and Navajo country. Also to the south are the Henry Mountains guarding the entrance to Utah's little-known Wayne Wonderland; to the west are the Boulder and Thousand Lake mountains; and the High Uintas are to the north. Southwest is another commanding promontory, Grand View Point, which is at the junction of the Green and Colorado rivers.

Here in one magnificent vista lies one of the largest areas of in-completely explored country remaining in the United States, forbidding, colorful, silent, and inaccessible. And hidden in this expanse are many of the wonders of the world — the Valley of the Goblins, Circle Cliffs,

---

[22]*Ibid.*

COURTESY UTAH STATE HISTORICAL SOCIETY

Figure 17.4. Dead Horse Point with the Goosenecks of the Colorado River in the Background

Cathedrals in Stone, Capitol Reef, the San Rafael Swell, the wondrous and weird Upheaval Dome, rainbridges, arches, colorful monoliths and monuments, and always the canyons made by the rivers while simultaneously writing the story of the earth.

The naming of Dead Horse Point is almost a legend in itself; and, like all legends, it has its variations. The time goes back to a day prior to the turn of the century when wild horses were rounded up and sold for domestication. Because of the peculiar terrain of the point area, according to one version, it was often used by cowboys in this vicinity as a natural corral for the wild horses. Some were roped and broken for personal use and others were taken to an eastern market. The point is some four hundred yards at the widest place and thirty to sixty yards at the neck.

On one occasion, the horses were culled and a small herd of wild mustangs ("broomtails") was left on the waterless point. Whether or not they were somehow fenced in is not known, but they must have raced around looking for a way to get to the water in the river three thousand feet below. They died either from exhaustion or thirst within sight of the water they could not reach.

Another version concerns two rustlers who penned a group of horses on a little island of land left standing hundreds of feet above the Colorado River. The rustlers fenced off the narrow access and then spent considerable time trying to outrun a local posse. By the time they eluded the posse and made their way back to the Point, the horses had grown so thirsty on that hot and dry island that, one by one, they had jumped toward the river far below.

A more logical answer is given by livestock raisers who had lived in the area when there were large, natural water holes near the Point, which collected rain and snow during the winter and provided water for stock in the spring. As the hot season progressed, water levels dropped in the potholes until they became death traps for animals that had slid down their steep sides and were unable to crawl out. Because of this hazard, the potholes were filled in long ago, but the name "Dead Horse" remained.

There must, of course, always be a more entertaining version — a Paul Bunyanesque story to fit the occasion. This account describes how a cowboy's pinto horse named "Paint" accidentally went off the cliff with the cowboy's expensive new chaps fastened to the saddle. It took the cowboy several days to climb down to the base of the cliff so that he could recover his chaps. But when he reached the floor of the canyon, neither horse nor chaps were to be found. Looking up, he saw Ol' Paint drifting downward, the chaps billowing out like the wings of a glider plane, the cliff's updrafts lifting and swinging the horse and his accoutrements as easily as the leaves of a tree. Paint was eased gently to the ground where he collapsed, dead of thirst from the long, slow fall. The grieving cowboy recovered his chaps but went away mumbling, "Poor ol' dead horse Paint." Thus, as will sometimes happen, "dead horse Paint" became "Dead Horse Point."

Another story, more grim than humorous, tells of a gang of thieves who stole some Moab horses and headed around below the lofty point along what is now called the White Rim Trail. A pursuing posse pressed the rustlers so closely that they shot the stolen horses, thus "destroying the evidence," and then tried to escape. The posse, coming upon the dead horses below the point, were so enraged they took a shortcut across the Island in the Sky and waylaid the thieves in a canyon near the Green River, shooting them all dead. Thus Dead Horse Point and Horse Thief Canyon got their names.

And so the stories go — along with others too filled with improprieties to print. However it came by its name, the Point is a tourist attraction that offers a full circle of scenic splendor. The area has been preserved as a state park, has a readily accessible road, and is a scenic wonder that should not be missed.

> I FOUND MYSELF looking down on the most fantastic colored jumble of natural wonders I had ever seen. There were arches, spires, rugged canyons, crevasses and fins, stitched together with little green grabens. A large number of still-intact prehistoric Indian ruins were visible as I looked down upon this rainbow-hued land. To a park service official, it was the proverbial pot of gold.

In this manner Superintendent Bates Wilson described his first glimpse of Canyonlands National Park (prior to its establishment as a national park).[23]

Wilson was custodian of Arches National Monument when he boarded a small plane with a local bush pilot and took off from an eerie dirt landing strip on the flight that started his quest for recognition of the Canyon Country. Subsequently, Cayonlands National Park was established on September 12, 1964, by President Lyndon B. Johnson.

Southeastern Utah had been surveyed in the early 1930s for a more ambitious project: the proposed Escalante National Park. The name "Escalante" was chosen as a working title for the early-day park proposal after Frederick Law Olmsted, a son of the Olmsted who de-

---

[23]Maxine Newell, "Canyonlands," in a special edition of *Naturalist* (Summer 1970), vol. 21, pp. 40–47.

signed the great Central Park in New York City, discouraged the use of the name Canyon Lands.

Former Secretary of the Interior Stewart Udall unintentionally disputed Olmsted's objections some thirty years later and is credited with naming the new park. After an extensive tour of the lands, in 1961, which had once again been proposed for park status in the late 1950s, Udall made an enthusiastic comment[24]: "A national park in the 'canyonlands' of southeastern Utah is an investment for the future.... Acre for acre the canyonlands of Utah are the most spectacular in the world." The name "Canyonlands" captured the imagination of the press, and Canyonlands National Park was named. Perhaps this name for the park might have been scorned had it not been presented spontaneously. It is ironic, too, that the park encompasses much of the territory in the proposed Escalante National Park. Canyonlands National Park was officially established on September 12, 1964, under the signature of President Lyndon B. Johnson. The President's blessing was the final stamp of approval to set aside for posterity one of the last uninhabited frontiers.

The new 250,000-acre park is the core of a vast and rugged scenic acreage in southeastern Utah. It is one of the largest and most spectacular parks in the nation, famous for its esthetic beauty long before park status was attained.

The first bill to authorize establishment of the park was entered in both the U.S. House of Representatives and Senate in 1961. The proposals were met with mixed emotions in Utah, and a lively controversy, over a three-year period, enused. The opposition to the establishment of the park was made by organized mining and cattle interests. Areas surrounding Canyonlands had netted rich finds of oil, uranium, potash, and other valuable resources.[25] Their question was "Why so much?" — to which Secretary Udall replied that although there might be some quibbling on details by those who would strive to assign a priority of magnificence and who would remove from consideration all but what they might judge the finest of the fine, the flaws in their approach were obvious and would have resulted in the discarding of all but the geyser basins of Yellowstone and, by comparison, such parks as Zion Canyon, and others. He stated that he felt the area should be conserved and protected that it might have electrifying appeal and magnetic recreational and economic potential for the region.

The publicity resulting from the controversy cast a national spotlight on the proposed park, and sightseers flocked to the area. Traffic became so heavy that it was necessary for the Interior Department to

[24]Moab *Times-Independent*, July 8, 1965 (scenic supplement).
[25]*Ibid.*

arrange for guards and guides as a safety measure for both tourists and artifacts. The enthusiasm of the visitors left little doubt in Utah of the tourist potential of the proposed park. In the end, a compromise was made and only 257,640 acres were set aside.

Chief credit for legislative impetus in gaining approval in Congress (1964) must go to U.S. Senator Frank E. Moss, a Utah Democrat, who promoted the Canyonlands bill for three years in the Senate; and to Representative Laurence J. Burton, a Utah Republican, who effected compromises which gained final approval in the House.

The spectacular, unique beauty of Canyonlands National Park was doubtless the lifesaving factor that allowed it to survive the feuds involved in its creation.

The future of the park is easy to predict. Surely no one, after a tour of the rugged lands which offer a new view from every turn, a change of color with the moving sun, will challenge Secretary Udall's description of the park — "acre for acre, the most beautiful country in the world." Countless tourists have agreed with Secretary Udall.

THE AREA HAS three major separate scenic attractions, isolated from each other by the Y-shaped Colorado and Green river canyons surrounding the confluence of the two rivers (Figure 17.5). The largest area, and one traveled now only by jeep, is the Needles segment, reached by entering the south entrance of the park on U.S. Highway 163, forty miles south of Moab, through Cave Springs and Indian Creek.

The second level of the park is the Island in the Sky section south of Big Flat, which features the official northern entrance of the park at Grand View Point, reached from an offramp of U.S. Highway 163, north of Moab. This level features such highlights as Upheaval Dome, Shafer Trail, and Monument Basin.

According to Rowe Findley,[26] every property owner in Moab would be a millionaire if salt became dear, for only three feet or so of alluvial deposits separate their basements from solid salt. A salt deposit as big as Maryland and as much as two and a half miles thick underlies southeast Utah and part of Colorado, a legacy of landlocked seas. Lighter than the rock above it and like putty under pressure, the salt rises into faults or other weakened areas, warping the surface upward. Where subsurface water invades the salt, it dissolves, letting the surface drop. The vast cracks in the surface make it vulnerable to the erosive forces of sun, wind, rain, and the two great rivers, creating the land's fantasies in stone. Thousands of columns, spires, buttes, arches, alcoves, and head-

---

[26]Rowe Findley, "Realm of Rock and the Far Horizon Canyonlands," *National Geographic* (July 1971), vol. 140, no. 1, pp. 71–91.

standing stones pepper the map with curious names — the Doll House, Angel Arch, Six-shooter Peaks, Paul Bunyan's Potty, Land of Standing Rocks.

Salt, Findley says, is responsible for Moab's valley; welling up along a fault, it lifted and fractured the surface. The salt later receded, leaving a vast sheer-walled trench.

But the salt's most spectacular creation is a three-mile-wide bull's-eye called Upheaval Dome. "Some scientists thought it was a meteor crater," Dr. Richard B. Mattox told Findley. Dr. Mattox, Professor of Geology at Texas Tech University, has been studying Upheaval Dome and similar salt structures since 1958. They hiked up an ovenlike canyon and into the tortured heart of the dome, a sunken geological garble that made them feel they had somehow stepped onto the moon. Dr. Mattox pointed to the walls of red cliffs towering above them and said, "See the curves in their strata? That means warping under tremendous pressures. There's not enough shattering to support the meteor theory."

The warping thrust came from below, from a huge column of salt pushing upward into an area of weakness, bulging the surface into a mountain that cracked open and eroded into a crater of concentric stone strata, their jagged edges twisted upward. Hence the three-dimensional bull's-eye effect.

The central monument in this big hole is a lofty stone stiletto that stands within two degrees of vertical. "That's a piece of the White Rim, a sandstone formation that's generally about eighteen hundred feet lower than it is here, and it usually lies horizontal," Dr. Mattox said.

Most Canyonlands visitors hear about or see the steep switchbacks of the famous Shafer Trail, and the tortuous beauty of the White Rim Trail. One such was Joseph Wood Krutch, well-known writer, who was imbued with a great love of and appreciation for the Southwest. On a visit to Canyonlands, he became familiar with this particular sight and wrote the author early in 1969 for further information about Shafer Trail in particular. He planned to write an article on the subject, and was interested in knowing if it were named for John H. Shafer, early pioneer of Moab, and what other information she could give about its history. She furnished him with available material and further contacted John L. Shafer of Moab (son of John H.) for the history. John L. confirmed her opinion that it had not been named for his father, and that his father had never seen the country except from atop a high rim.

In Shafer's letter,[27] he related that his brother Frank bought John Jackson's cattle interests from him in 1914. Jackson had a few head on White Rim at that time. There was an old Indian trail and Frank hired

---

[27]John L. Shafer, letter, February 12, 1969.

COURTESY MOAB *TIMES-INDEPENDENT*

Figure 17.5. Confluence of the Green and Colorado Rivers

Vern Bliss (who was a good rock worker) to do some work on the rough trail. At one time horse thieves working through that area had used the trail to cross the river about three miles above the mouth of Indian Creek. From there they would get on White Rim, come up the Neck Trail, go down Horse Thief Trail across Green River, and on to Robbers Roost.

John L. Shafer went into the area in 1916 and he and Ray Cook camped at the foot of the trail and worked on it during the spring of 1917. Improvement of the trail was necessary so that cattle might be taken into the area. Shafer then took over and worked alone, staying through 1922, at which time he suffered financial reverses. By that time he had only a rather bad stock trail.

In 1918 he began to study geology as it relates to oil deposits. He made his first oil locations in 1919, and more during the ensuing several years.

He stated that he did a lot of work getting around the first point on White Rim, which he referred to as "beautiful country" that he began "boosting for a park" as early as 1916. He mentioned the beautiful monuments visible from Grand View Point. He camped and hunted the old trail, wintering cattle there. "At best it was hell both places. The

297

choice was swim the river in early March before the river got up and down making lots of bog — that was hell. The feed was dandy for the fellow who knew enough to only stock the water." He stated this took a lot of work to protect and he had to do this alone.

He pointed out that the trail picked up that designation in 1917 or '18 and has been thus named ever since.

During the early days of the uranium interest (1953, Shafer recalled) Nate Knight, Jr., Nick Murphy, and young Felix Murphy went into the area with a tractor and a four-wheel-drive truck to make the first road. A few years later the Atomic Energy Commission came in to survey it. This agency then contracted and built a good road, considering the terrain.

The third level of Canyonlands Park is the most isolated of the three sections. It is the river bottom country itself, and the land west of the confluence of the rivers, known as the Land of Standing Rocks. For decades it was the domain of the vast Scorup-Somerville Cattle Company. Few people saw the Needles area until the advent of four-wheel transportation in the western states in recent years.

It is situated south and east of the confluence of the Colorado and Green rivers. Varicolored spires, grass-filled valleys, canyons filled with ancient archeological ruins, and challenging jeep roads have destined the area for national prominence.

Best known of the Needles area is Chesler Park — a green panorama surrounded by red and white spires thrusting into the sky. Chesler Park is reached by taking four-wheel-drive vehicles over tortuous trails winding from Dugout ranch on Indian Creek. Southeast from the park, Salt Creek and Horse Creek canyons wind to their headwaters in the Abajo or Blue Mountains. The two canyons, along with lesser intermittent watercourses, are filled with prehistoric Indian ruins and writings. In the upper reaches of these canyons are located Angel and Castle arches; and majestic Druid Arch is situated in the upper end of Elephant Canyon, near Chesler Park. Druid Arch, whose 360-foot height dwarfs a man, is reminiscent of Stonehenge in profile.

Other Needles features include Devil's Lane, Junction of the Rivers Overlook, Elephant Hill, Beef Basin, and Squaw Park. Squaw Park is the projected headquarters for the Needles district of Canyonlands National Park and can now be reached fairly well by car.

At Cave Springs, a point near the entrance to Needles, protective overhangs in white mushroom-shaped rocks guard springs that have supplied cowboys and ranchers since the late 1800s. This is the point where jeep trails head out for the Salt and Horse canyons side trips. Only a few hundred yards from Cave Springs, the first Indian ruins appear, high on canyon walls. The two canyons, filled with quicksand during rainy seasons, carry heavy floodwaters at times, obliterating the traces of past vehicle travel.

On toward Chesler Park, Elephant Hill presents a formidable barrier to all but the sturdiest vehicles. Crawling over stone steps, inching round hairpin curves, and at times putting the drive in reverse when sufficient turning space is not available, the four-wheel-drive vehicles get a quick indoctrination in what lies ahead. Beyond Elephant Hill are junction trails that lead to Beef Basin, Chesler Park, and the confluence of the Green and Colorado rivers.

At present the best developed of all the Canyonlands areas, the Island in the Sky, is situated between the Green and Colorado rivers west of Moab. It is reached by traveling over the Seven-Mile Canyon road leading to Dead Horse Point. Entrance to the Island is the Neck, where a thirty-foot brush fence, built years ago by ranchers, blocks off fifty thousand acres of land that is bordered on either side by the two rivers.

Upheaval Dome is the first feature south of the Neck, and this circular-shaped, exposed salt dome stands out clearly from its symmetrical surroundings. At the end of the Island in the Sky, Grand View Point overlooks the confluence country and scenic Monument Basin, nearly a thousand feet below. Monument Basin, an eroded area in the White Rim country, is filled with totem-pole spires reaching for sunlight from the canyon floor. The White Rim itself is a white sandstone formation halfway between the levels of the rivers and Grand View Point. It is now traversed by jeep roads built when uranium prospectors during the early 1950s explored Shinarump formations situated on the canyon walls only a few hundred feet above the White Rim. For variety and color, the nation's newest national park excels them all.

The La Sal Mountains themselves provide good fishing, some hunting, and scenic enjoyment. The lakes, streams and reservoirs, basins and mountains make available activity to please the outdoor lover. As the pressures of urban growth increase, doubtless more and more people will avail themselves of the quiet coolness of the mountains.

There are two excellent books with which the prospective tourist of the Canyonlands country should become familiar. One is the very artistic and informative work of Dr. Gregory Crampton, *The Standing Up Country*. The other is *This is Canyon Country*, by Dick Wilson. Copies of the latter may be obtained from the Times-Independent Press at Moab. Here, in a convenient paperback, are outlined automobile routes, jeep trips, and bicycling and hiking adventures. As a guide for scenic wonders and opportunities, it is excellent.

However much or little time one can spend enjoying the scenic wonders, one and all will say it was well worth it.

299

Chapter 18

Economic Development in the Area

Tourism is fast becoming a much sought-after form of business in all but the most primitive parts of the world. Lucrative to residents of an area, to small and large businesses, and to state and local governments, it is considered a major vehicle for providing economic stability. Income derived from tourism, both private and public, has helped to "bail out" many small communities stifled by lack of funds. Yet only within the past two decades has southeastern Utah been converted from an agricultural, ranching, and mining area into a "scenic wonderland" for tourists. To compete in this new market, the people of Moab, La Sal, and nearby communities early recognized that the marvels of nature which they harbored at their doorsteps would need nationwide exposure in order to attract tourists. To this end they pressured the governor and the Utah legislature to do something for the benefit of all.

Early in the 1960s, because of this press by local far-seeing residents, Governor George D. Clyde requested that the Bureau of Business and Economic Research at the University of Utah do an in-depth study of traffic patterns in the canyonlands area of southeastern Utah. The request followed the findings of a committee, consisting of legislators and lay citizens, which painted an unbelievably rosy picture.

The findings of the study, which was to project the patterns over a ten-year period, indicated that between ten thousand and twelve thousand tourists would visit the canyonlands area the first year. Moreover, if proper developments were made, it was predicted that "Canyon-lands," as it was named by then, would host more than a million tourists a year at the end of the decade. These predictions were glowing and promising indeed. Yet the projection has proved to be remarkably correct, for tourism in the first decade and a half has borne out the predictions.

The "proper developments" have consisted of new roads being built; hotels and motels being made available; and restaurants, cafes, rest and recreation spots, guided tours, and tourist needs of all kinds being provided. Businesses unheard of in pioneer and early twentieth century times now dot the highways: rocks for the rockhound, western Americana books for the reader and collector of Western lore, novelty shops where one can stroll through a collection of artifacts and hand-crafts of many times and many peoples; trading posts; camera shops; curio shops and others to please the taste of even the most discerning tourist.

The Moab Chamber of Commerce announced that the tourist season would be open year-round, and transportation is available through airlines, railroads, buses, and of course private automobiles, jeeps, and campers. Scenic places along or near all of the highways are well advertised by signs, placards, and road maps. And for out-of-the-way attractions (such as described in chapter 17) there are guided tours, the Chamber of Commerce hastens to point out.

Among prominent highlights are such activities as the River Marathon Race and Pleasure Cruise — the 196-mile, two-river cruise through wild canyons on smooth water. This junket, called the "Friendship Cruise," is held annually in June and takes the sightseer from Green River to Moab. Jeep and pack trips are routinely and regularly arranged; horseback riding and exploration expeditions on surfaced paths are provided for the less rugged tourist.

Flying services provide air tours of Canyonlands and nearby Arches National Park. The tours take the sightseers over Dead Horse Point, where one can see the meandering Colorado River with much more clarity than at the Grand Canyon farther down. (Descriptions and stories of Canyonlands State Park are in chapter 17.) Sightseers are taken to the Maze and the Land of Standing Rocks where tourists can see one of the most thoroughly eroded areas in the entire canyon country[1] — located in the portion of the plateau between Happy Canyon, draining into the Dirty Devil, and Millard Canyon, draining into the Green River. They also visit the confluence of the Colorado and Green

---

[1]Crampton, *op. cit.*, p. 23.

rivers where the once-placid and leisurely flowing rivers enter Cataract Canyon where the cliff walls grow higher and the canyon becomes narrower and there are more than forty rapids[2]; and Angel Arch, a magnificent natural bridge in the Needles country, and one of the most notable arches to be seen, for it is one of the largest of such formations in the world, with an estimated height of 190 feet and a span of 160 feet. It is formed out of chiseled, buff-colored sandstone in the outline of an angel, with folded wings and bowed head, standing over the intricate and little-known wonderlands of which it is a part. Jeeping parties can see ruins of the ancient Anasazi, the prehistoric Indians common to the Four Corners and the builders of Mesa Verde in Colorado.[3] Other sights include formations such as Delicate Arch, Landscape Arch (see chapter 17), and other indescribably magnificent designs of nature.

One may either fly over the area or travel by car or jeep on a tour where, by traveling southeast from Arches National Park, one can find the Colorado running through a canyon at the base of the La Sal Mountains. Where it opens onto the Richardson Amphitheater and Castle Valley, there are the exquisitely eroded Fisher Towers — a thousand famous columns of banded, rich-red Moenkopi rock rising hundreds of feet into the air. There are buttes, mesas, and other characteristic canyon country formations, all near the red-walled, deeply entrenched Colorado River.

Tex's Colorado River Cruises invite the tourist or local nature lover to join the jet set in taking one of the daily jetboat adventure trips down the Colorado River into exciting Canyonlands Park. Mitch Williams conducts daily "Tag-a-Long Tours" — scenic trips in special air-conditioned tour cars and motorized rubber boats. Kent Frost, with his Canyonland Tours, provides transported tours of the area. Ottinger Tours (and others) and camping trips can be arranged. There are special "Jeep-O-Ramas" planned and conducted. Fishing, hunting, and recreation of many kinds lure vacationers to the La Sals.

Sound and light productions have become a popular tourist attraction. Especially striking at nighttime, they combine light and sound to bring the viewer a thrillingly imaginative panoply of beauty. Many travelers in European, Asian, and African countries have witnessed these kinds of productions — in the forum of Rome, in the Parthenon at Athens, at historical landmarks in Cairo — taking them back to a time when ancient civilizations flourished and permitting the observers to give full play to their fantasies. And on the Colorado River at Moab, light

---

[2]*Ibid.*, p. 39.

[3]Dick Wilson, *This Is Canyon Country* (Moab: Times-Independent Press, 1968), p. 18.

and sound have been used in an equally impressive production, bringing Canyonlands at night international recognition. Barnes has said that "no place on this continent is better deserving of that name."[4] He also tells us that Moab has two principal assets — the wild beauty of the country that surrounds it, and the mineral wealth that can sometimes be wrested from its tortuous canyons and towering mesas — and adds, "Thus uranium and a few other minerals, plus tourism, provide the basis for Moab's prosperity."

He delineates the various types of tours provided for scenery lovers, but has indicated his feelings that the most unusual of the water tours is Canyonlands by night, created by W. B. "Skinny" Winn[5]:

> ...[T]he boat works its way up the river....As darkness gathers, a darkness that is sometimes made ever more intense by clouds blocking even the faint starlight, the setting becomes more eerie by the minute. The river's shallow, silt-laden waters grow dark and mysterious. The silent, ghostly forms of shoreline trees and brush and gigantic boulders drift by on parade. And looming high above, dominating everything, the massive black-on-black silhouettes of gigantic, ominous cliffs block off half or more of the sky. It's a scene that could stir up deep, instinctive fears....After about thirty minutes of travel, the pilot nudges the ungainly craft against a midriver sandbar, swings it around to face a particular section of the pitch black cliffs, turns off even the dim running lights, and everyone grows still, waiting. Only the faint mutter of the boat's idling engine breaks the gathering silence.

His description of the river does not belie the feeling one gets of its overwhelming magnitude, with its formidable cliffs, in the onrushing darkness. But he has more surprises in store, as he continues:

> The stage is set, and the audience is ready....Out of the black silence an awesome voice booms, rolling across the dark water and echoing from the canyon walls: "In the beginning, the earth was without form and void; and darkness was upon the face of the deep. And the spirit of God moved upon the face of the waters. And God said — 'Let there be light.'"...And there *is* light! The immense rock dome that the boat faces is suddenly, dramatically ablaze with brilliant light.

The light and sound production continues with a tape, professionally recorded, playing over a hi-fi sound system in "perfect coordination with

---

[4]F. A. Barnes, "Canyonlands by Night," *Travel* (August 1970), pp. 64–66.
[5]*Ibid.*

a battery of powerful lights on shore." Sightseers are transfixed. Barnes again continues:

> ...As the program unfolds, the boat drifts slowly with the river current, guided by its idling engine. The lights pace the boat, following a road that parallels the river at the base of the towering cliffs, lighting the changing scenery, and dramatizing and illustrating the recorded narrative....A unique story is told by the lights and sound, from the early development of life on this planet through the geological formation of the canyonlands and the history of the Indians who inhabited them, to the recent entry of the Mormons and other settlers who brought civilization to this wild country. The coordination between the tape-recorded sound and manually controlled lights is perfect.

This particular show that Barnes so vividly describes is done only in the summertime. But many tours are planned for all seasons of the year, such as the one taken along Utah Highway 128, a short distance northeast of Moab.[6] Towering due south of the highway, the 12,500-foot La Sal Mountains can be seen. Snow capped much of the year, the majestic La Sals stand in direct contrast to the desolate splendor of the desert landscape at their base. Closer at hand are the reddish-purple Fisher Towers rising like a big-city skyline as high as seventeen hundred feet above the valley floor. The Colorado River is in the foreground.

UTAH HIGHWAY 128, a rough dirt road, heads northeast out of Moab, generally following the course of the Colorado for 31 miles. There the road crosses the river via Dewey Bridge, a sixty-year-old cable suspension structure. The bridge is but one car-width wide, and is named for a tiny settlement of log houses that once prospered at the crossing. A short distance upstream the Dolores River empties into the Colorado. From the bridge the road leads another twelve miles to U.S. Highways 6 and 50. The stretch from Moab to Dewey Bridge is the longest drive along the Colorado River in Utah. Other than Highway 128, there are no riverside roads upstream from the bridge. Downstream from Moab, the Colorado carves through untracked and inaccessible canyonlands.

During the flood season, much of Highway 128 is covered with water and therefore impassable. Before the floodwaters peak, negotiating the road is thrilling but hazardous — an experience not recommended for the tenderfoot who is unschooled in the vagaries of the Colorado. During heavy rains the first ten miles of this trip are sometimes referred

---

[6]"The Best of the Southwest," Denver *Post* (August 2, 1970), pp. 16–17.

to as "Moab's waterfall route." Approximately thirty waterfalls pour off the seven hundred-foot sandstone cliffs, many times forming veils of spray and in other places muddy, raging torrents. There is great danger from rocks falling on the highway at the time of a cloudburst.[7]

Canyonlands country, though mostly remote and wild, offers something for everyone who travels there.[8] Some areas are best left to sturdy four-wheel-drive vehicles or for backpackers, but many others are open for exploration in a passenger car.

With Moab as a base of operation, there are vast areas which should be on a "must see" list. Most of these spots can be reached within an hour's time, although adequate time should be allotted to fully enjoy them.

The annual Friendship Cruise, the Jeep-O-Rama, the annual rodeo, and the more recently proclaimed "Butch Cassidy Days" all add to the lure of the adventurer and the excitement of a vacation spent in this vicinity. For the rock hunter there is endless search, for the hunter and the lovers of fishing there are streams and game in good supply, and the beautiful La Sal Mountains offer a variety of attractions. The towering peaks are capped with snow nine months of the year. Below timberline are forests of spruce and fir, and at lower elevations there are the pines.

The rocks and their geological structure are unique in the world. In the mountains the brilliantly colored formations, so characteristic of the canyonlands, have been thrust up in steep stratification and form huge structural domes on each of the three mountains comprising the La Sals. These domes were formed by the forceful intrusion of igneous rock that was molten, like lava, and pushed upward by the same kinds of forces that cause volcanoes. Most of the molten rock "froze" solid when it neared the cooler surface of the earth. Subsequent erosion removed the earth's crust from the domed formations. The results are not only magnificent but fascinating to study.

Within half a mile of the Utah-Colorado border, on the Colorado side, is Buckeye Reservoir, a blue jewel set among tall pines on the eastern slopes of the Alpine–high La Sals. At an elevation of more than 6,600 feet, this area offers a cool respite from the summer heat of the canyonlands and other areas. The cold mountain waters of the reservoir furnish an ideal home for trout and other pan fish, and those who fish the lake report excellent catches. The lake also offers excitement for swimming, boating, and just plain beauty.

---

[7]Wilson, *op. cit.*, p. 18.

[8]"Moab Is Base of Operations for Tours into Varied Mountain-Desert County," Moab *Times-Independent*, June 28, 1973, p. B-1.

Administered by the Forest Service, recreation areas are provided in the region. It may be approached either from Grand Junction, Colorado, or from Moab.

ANOTHER "MUST" TOUR is that of the La Sal Mountain Loop Road (except in flood season). This is a convenient and comfortable route to the forested slopes and above-timberline heights that dramatically rise above Moab. The tour begins with a right turn at the Colorado River bridge north of Moab and ends in upper Spanish Valley a few miles south of Moab. The fifty-mile route includes unpaved portions which can be muddy in wet weather. With its thirty alpine peaks, the La Sals rival in grandeur many better known areas. The vertical difference between Moab (four thousand-foot elevation) and Mt. Peale (over thirteen thousand feet and seventeen air miles from Moab) is more than nine thousand feet, one of the greatest vertical differences in America. (Pike's Peak is only eight thousand feet higher than its base.)

To follow the loop, one travels upriver for the first paved portion of Utah Highway 128 and turns south into Castle Valley, another sunken valley lying parallel to (and almost a twin of) Moab's Spanish Valley. The famous Castle Rock towers some 2,256 feet above lower Castle Valley and was made nationally famous as a location for several television commercials (which involved a helicopter-placement of an automobile on top). Adjoining formations are known as the Priest and the Nuns.

The loop route makes a sharp right turn about thirty miles from the turnoff point at Moab. If the traveler continues east up the valley, the road leads to Fisher Mesa and Polar Mesa and on to Beaver Basin, a former mining camp. There are lakes and recreational possibilities on the eastern slopes of the La Sals. But the auto route turns south at this junction. The pavement ends within a short distance; the road is rough and narrow in spots, but negotiable. From Castle Valley one can, if interested, follow to Harpole Mesa and the battleground site of the Pinhook massacre. If one desires to see the monument erected to the pioneers killed in this battle, one must make a short hike over rough ground and brush on foot. But it is worth the time and effort.

After the battleground is crossed, there is a road leading to Warner Ranger Station and Warner Lake. Here one may engage in trout fishing, camping and, if it is spring, see beautiful fields of wild flowers; or if it is fall, witness superb fall colors when the aspens don yellow robes. No traveler should go this far without climbing to the top of Bald Mesa and (as described in chapter 17) viewing the panorama from the ridge. It is breathtaking and thrilling. And, it is hoped, one will camp in the early evening so that one of the most gorgeous sunsets may be witnessed through the aspens. The Egyptians insist that their sunsets surpass anything in the world, and it is true that the reflection of the sun's rays through the dust of the desert is enough to make one speechless, but indeed the setting of the sun, as seen from the La Sal Mountains, cannot be surpassed.

The last stage of the La Sal Mountain Loop Road descends Brumley Ridge, south toward Pack Creek Ranch. The La Sal Mountains provide high-altitude relief from the summer's heat. Wildlife includes grouse, deer, wild turkeys, rabbits, porcupines, skunks, and sometimes bears. Quaking aspen, spruce, pine, and alpine fir are the common trees on the high slopes. Since the La Sals are an isolated mountain group far removed from the major mountain systems of the Rockies, they indeed bring delight to a weary traveler and offer respite from the noise and confusion of urban life.

Another scenic trip is to go south from Moab on U.S. Highway 163, through Spanish Valley, approximately ten miles long, two miles wide, observing the thousand-foot cliffs of the Moab Rim (also called The Rocks) on the right, which demonstrate the fault escarpment formed when the valley sank into cavities caused by the dissolving of great subterranean salt beds.[9] (Moab lies in the narrow cliff-lined valley.) The ascending highway begins as one leaves Spanish Valley and begins to climb Blue Hill. Here one follows near the Old Spanish Trail site where early Spanish and Indians traveled with their caravans of supplies and Indian slaves. There are rest and picnic areas at Kane Springs Park and Hole 'N the Rock (a fifty thousand cubic foot home hollowed out of solid rock and open to visitors).

A short distance beyond one arrives at La Sal Junction where, by following Utah 46, one finds an access road to the backside of the La Sal Mountains and to the Colorado high country. It is beautiful country and one can see where early settlers in the area built their homes and the cattle industry, through "The Ranch," became the headquarters of one of the great cattle companies of the West, and where some of the famous outlaws of the West stayed at various times.

RETURNING TO La Sal Junction, the sightseer then travels about a mile to another junction that leads down a small side road to Looking Glass Rock, a magnificent arch two miles off the highway, which has a large, hollowed-out amphitheater. Here is an area suitable for camping at any

---

[9]Wilson, *op. cit.*, p. 15.

season. But one must again return to the highway to travel about two more miles to Wilson Arch (along the highway), named for Joe Wilson (chapters 8 and 19) who had a cabin near by. There are many other rock formations which permit travelers to allow their imaginations to create visages of their own.

If one is interested in mineral deposits and desires to see the Mi Vida Mine location of Charles Steen (which made Moab famous), there is a marked junction in the road where a traveler can turn to visit this location. And about two miles farther along the highway, one may take a 22-mile side trip to Canyon Rims Recreation Area to see the Needles Overlook. To reach this area, however, the traveler must pass Windwhistle campground, a worthwhile stop, and then on some distance farther to Hatch Point campground, both of which figured in the Pinhook massacre (the Indians and posses followed this route).

In the Needles area, one may view special sights of interest such as Newspaper Rock (a huge, firmly imbedded boulder with centuries-old Indian carvings — petroglyphs — on its smooth, vertical face), Dugout Ranch, and other sites all worthy of a visit. The tour then proceeds, via Highway 163, to Monticello, a lovely city that is recognized as one of the healthiest places in the United States to live. Then proceed down the highway where a good view of the Blue Mountains may be seen (if one is lucky, a vision of the Horse Head [chapter 19] may be seen). Passing through Blanding and Bluff (famous for the end of the renowned Hole-in-the-Rock expedition of the early Mormons), where many pioneers located before coming to the Moab and La Sal areas, there are side trips to view the Natural Bridges National Park and the goosenecks of the San Juan.

Then follows the trip across Monument Valley where there are many rock formations, some with names but many left to the imagination of the viewer. In this tour a visitor may see landscape in extremity — from mountains and streams, trees, and rich agricultural lands, to desert and rock formations. Easily understood is the old cliché that when God finished creating the earth he shook his hands to free the fingers of earth and so was born southern and southeastern Utah.

All along the way, motels and hotels, campsites and rest areas have been built to provide for the growing tourist industry. By no means are the tours that have been described the extent to which one may find pleasure. There are as many tours and views as one cares to see. One might well spend years in the area and never see all there is to see and enjoy. The Moab Chamber of Commerce, as well as Sam Taylor of the Moab *Times-Independent*, and Miles Turnbow of the Monticello *San Juan Record* are ready and willing to be helpful and enthusiastic in assisting tourists with information and arrangements for tours.

ONE OTHER INDUSTRY should be mentioned, for it, too, has grown out of the scenic wonders of the region — it is that of movie production. Since 1946 a number of Hollywood movies have been filmed in the vicinity of Moab. The locale is rich in background for any type of Western. Indeed within a short time, one can have any western background desired — mountains, hills, sand dunes, river, streams, lakes, timber, underbrush, terrain, red sandstone, monoliths and rocks of all types, canyons, space. The possibilities are phenomenal, and variety and kind unlimited.

Although this industry has sometimes interfered with tourist facilities, the demand is short-lived, and new housing and restaurant facilities have been constructed to meet the growing need. The movie industry probably should not be relied upon as a steady source of income inasmuch as the whims of Hollywood are susceptible to many pressures. But when the production crews descend on Moab, the townspeople know that it means many thousands of dollars for the community coffers, and employment for many who might otherwise be without remuneration. Merchants and business people share in the profits; every phase of community life is affected. A few of the transplanted movie production staff and often the stars themselves return for vacationing and hunting.

For many years the beauties of the area and the opportunity to secure an economic base because of the scenic wonders, which lay relatively unexplored and unappreciated, went unnoticed. But once the populace became aware of its vast potential in these modern times and began to capitalize on them, the communities have taken on new life and have accepted a new challenge. They now realize the potential economic opportunities to be developed in southeastern Utah as an outcome of the natural beauty and variety of the entire area.

Chapter 19

A Characteristic Touch of Spice

History tends to perpetuate the phenomenal, the colorful, and the sensational. We may recognize the names and may have heard about the exploits of outlaws, robber barons, industrialists, rulers, and leaders in all phases of the development of a community or civilization, but we sometimes forget, or have never heard of, the names and accomplishments of those who furnished the foundations, the studs, walls, roofs, and mortar of whatever it took to hold the group together — in short, those who were the bulwarks of the historical figures. But these people also have contributed to history...and to legend.

Many who set out to cut a niche for themselves, a place in the order of things, or to confront the challenges of life on the frontier were unable to endure. Their unmarked graves could fill a cemetery. Countless others returned to the land whence they came and have gone unnoted in the annals of history. Life on the frontier was not easy. Many left homes and families whom they would never see again.

Whether one accepts the Turner Thesis of the lure of free lands, with the return to a state of savagery, followed by the birth of democratic institutions on the frontier, or an escape valve — or the Webb-Strickland Great Plains–Dry Desert Thesis, with its lure of adventure and riches in which the desert shaped the people and institutions — or the Germ

311

Theory[1] with its development of democratic institutions brought with the immigrants, one finds the settlement of the West a unique and fascinating subject.

Life on a frontier is a serious matter of survival against incredibly long odds. Work is difficult. To survive, the settlers must play as hard as they work — but the secret is in knowing when to do which. Humor plays a vital part in the lives of those who challenge the wilderness. Returning once more to the microcosm theory: The humor that was manifest in the southeastern Utah pioneers is a trait they held in common with other frontier societies — when the most that people have to look forward to is hope, they laugh away many heartaches.

In presenting some of the characteristic humor and the people who provided it in this region, the author recognizes that it is impossible to include everyone's contributions to this needed element of our society, for one could write a book on this subject alone. Persons written about in this book have not been intentionally singled out; nor have others been deliberately neglected. Those who have appeared in these pages — as a microcosm of history — have, it is hoped, given insight into that which has made Moab and La Sal unique yet similar to other settlements of the West. Much of the material herein is common knowledge to the people who have lived in this area for many years.

In almost every country in the world, nature has cunningly and capriciously produced magnificent, sometimes grotesque, often bizarre, but nearly always sculpturesque scenery that takes the breath away. Inhabitants in every corner of the globe have furnished names to fit their impressions of these natural phenomena: the Tetons (French for "breast") in Wyoming; Amah (Chinese for "nursemaid") Rock in Hong Kong, a rock formation in the shape of a woman praying — for a lost child; the Teapot Dome (self-explanatory) in Wyoming. And as their counterparts are wont to do throughout the world, local people in the vicinity of Moab and La Sal have given names to their particular landmarks: Mule Shoe, Bald Mesa, Mount Haystack, the Three Gossips, Deadman and Horsethief points, Yellowjacket Canyon, Matrimony Springs (on Utah 128), Organ Rock, Parade of the Elephants, and many more.

---

[1]When the 1890 U.S. census announced the closing of the frontier, Frederick Jackson Turner presented his thesis that the frontier had produced a unique American democracy. In the 1930s opponents advocated the Germ Theory that immigrants brought these institutions with them. Later Walter Prescott Webb and Rex W. Strickland presented the Great Plains–Dry Desert Theory that the desert had shaped people and institutions.

312

Many of the rock formations in Canyonlands have such names as Elephant Hill, S.O.B. Hill, the Needles, the Maze, and innumerable formations and names of interest. But even more colorful appellations were supplied by the cowboys and miners: Amasa's Back, Amasa's Crack, the Nipples, Brown's Hole, Kissing Cousins, Walking Rocks, Paul Bunyan's Potty, and many more.

On the Blue Mountains, an isolated range towering above a seven-thousand-foot mesa at the juncture of the Colorado and San Juan rivers, is a natural outline of a horse's head created by spruce trees on an otherwise sparse slope. Called "Horse Head" by the old-timers, it has been a conversation piece since early pioneer days. Local inhabitants have pointed it out to newcomers and tourists until it has become famous. But, as with all fantasies, one must be endowed with the right kind of imagination to identify it. For example, a local salesman took great pride in showing it to his customers who were either new arrivals to the community or were just passing through. One day, after many years of pointing it out, he was trying to pinpoint it for an interested listener, saying, "See? Right where I'm pointing — right there in that swale.... My God! It *is* there, isn't it?"

Fred Keller, erstwhile lawyer in Monticello and an "old-timer" with an exceptional memory for facts, wrote a song about the pioneer cowboys of this area (reproduced in part in Figure 19.1). In a narrative[2] accompanying the song, he tells of the circumstances that prompted its writing. Keller had settled in Monticello after his discharge from the U.S. Army in 1919, where he set up his law practice. While serving on a committee that organized the annual party given for all inhabitants over sixty years of age, he wrote the lyrics of "Blue Mountain," filled with cowboy lore, to entertain these "old folks":

> ...My friend, Tom Evans, helped me with the music. Together we made some variations to suit my lyrics from an old Texas cowboy song which I think bears the title "Bound Down in the Walls of Prison." At its first rendition it was sung as a duet by myself and a cowboy friend by the name of Pat Adams. We were dressed as cowboys and undertook to spice the rendition by jingling our spurs between verse and chorus. Tom played the accompaniment. Our audience was familiar with the characters and life which I hoped the song would commemorate. They liked it, and I have had some satisfaction from the fact that it became one of the songs that was sung at the farewell parties held in Monticello for the boys summoned from that locality to the Armed Forces of the United States in World War II.

---

[2]Excerpts from the narrative are used with permission of Fred W. Keller, Monticello, Utah, 1975.

According to Keller, the first white settlers in the area were cattlemen and cowboys. Among the first pioneers were two "young English brothers with the surname of Carlyle" (Carlisle)[3] whose brand was three bars — one on the hip, one on the side, and one on the shoulder; hence the name "Hip Side and Shoulder." The "L.C." brand in his song refers to a competitor cattle company "with headquarters on Recapture Creek." The "sleeper calves on the side" provides a vignette almost unknown even to modern-day Westerners[4]:

> Many of the cowboys who did punching for the Blue Moun-
> tain cow outfits were young men of the adventurous type who had
> been in difficulties with the law in Texas and took sanctuary in
> the remoteness of the Blue Mountain. Some had the ambition to
> acquire herds of their own. The easy way to get into the cow
> business was by the process of what was known as "sleepering"
> calves — a refined type of larceny....A cowboy finds a young calf
> with its mother grazing in a secluded canyon that isn't ridden very
> often. He takes down his rope, catches the calf, and with his run-
> ning iron burns a line that may become part of the finished brand
> which the mother of the calf carries or may be used as part of the
> brand that the cowboy making it claims.

The cowboy then leaves the calf for the mother to raise to the weaning stage. When he returns at a later date, if the owner of the cow and calf hasn't noticed the partial brand and completed his own branding of it, the cowboy "completes what he began in his own brand, and thereafter the calf belongs to him. During the time the calf was first caught and the completion of its brand, it was referred to as a 'sleeper.'" The "hand with a long rope" refers to this same cowboy if, while he was performing his "larceny," another cowboy was in on the secret. Keller concludes this part of the narrative with, "As you might surmise, a cowboy with a 'long rope,' if in the employ of the LC outfit, got along better with his foreman if most of the 'sleepers' were from the Hip Side and Shoulder."

"Laddie-Go Gordon" was Bill Gordon, roundup foreman of the Hip Side and Shoulder, who had been nicknamed "Latigo." He owned the Blue Goose Saloon, "which ranked in importance with Mons's Store as a rendezvous for the cowboys." Mons Peterson had established a general store "in a rambling log cabin with a dirt roof." The front door was riddled with bullets by celebrating cowboys, and once a cowboy rode his horse into the store, grabbed up a bolt of calico, and rode through the streets, trailing the calico behind him.

---

[3]Spelling of the name varies in usage.
[4]Keller, *op. cit.*

Figure 19.1. Fred Keller's Song "Blue Mountain"

The man called "Slick" in the song was a cowboy whose name has not been recorded, but he was also part of the lore:

> ... "Slick," a cowboy who neither gambled nor drank hard liquor, but saved his money, married a good-looking grass widow who came on to the frontier. She lived with him just long enough to get hold of his roll and then left for parts unknown. The efforts of Slick to catch up with the widow were matters of jest around the Blue Goose Saloon and Mons's Store. Slick was slow to realize that his lover had gone forever, but lived on and on through the years with the hope that she would some day return.

Keller refers to one of the Texas cowboys as "Yarn Gallus with gun and rope." The nickname was given him because his mother (in Missouri) sent him a present each Christmas "of some knitted galluses" (which, according to Webster's dictionary, means "suspenders," though the narrative does not explain its meaning). "Yarn Gallus" (in reality Henry Goodman) is remembered by others in the Monticello region, for he became a prominent cattleman in Moab. One of his favorite sayings was "You can get tired doing anything — even kissin' a purty gal."

But the man about whom history has more recorded facts was "Doc Few Clothes." Keller tells us that there are "conflicting versions about how he acquired this name. Some say that it was on account of... a very scanty wardrobe and [he] was not overscrupulous in matters of sanitation." Doc Few Clothes was Tom Trout, who rode the ranges of southeastern Utah as an early-day cowboy. A native-born Texan, he traveled to Moab in 1885 where he later married a local girl and took up residence. He retired from the cattle business around 1920 and engaged in farming. Born on Independence Day, 1863, he worked as a cowboy on the Texas plains and accompanied several cattle drives from Texas to Kansas along the Chisholm Trail. In 1885 he made the trip from Amarillo, Texas, to Durango, Colorado, by train. He accepted a job as cowhand for the Carlisle outfit in San Juan County, riding horseback from Durango to Monticello where he worked for several years. Then he entered the cattle business as an owner of stock (not as wrangler) and prospered, ranging his cattle on Indian Creek and in Dry Valley.

On his first visit to Moab (Christmas 1886) he arrived in time to take part in a celebration that was being staged, with several race horses, and won $10 on a race. Approached by a local citizen, he was asked if he would like to buy some property in the town. His reply was, "I might as well invest my money in town lots as anything I know of," and he purchased one lot for the $10 he had won, and left town. It was a year later before he saw either the lot or the deed to it. He was then informed that the town wanted to build a $1,000 schoolhouse and his ground had been selected. He immediately conveyed the property to the county without charge.

Although he had a gruff exterior, few men were more active in charitable work. When sickness or death made its appearance, Trout was always among the first to offer his services. Practical and given to humor, he often quipped, after a death, "Well, there will be two more shortly. The devil always wants to wait for three to load the chariot." For some reason he did not want the world to know of his kindly nature. This is borne out in the story that, despite his love for children, when asked where he lived, he would point in the general direction and say, "Oh, over there on 'Incubator Row.'"

Trout had a phenomenal memory. Knowing the interest of the author in the history of the area, he would often greet her with, "Well, seventy (or eight, three, 26, or whatever) years ago today (such and such an event) happened." One day he went into the local bank and greeted the president with "Fifty years ago today Harry left Texas. But he can't go back." (Harry was also a Blue Mountain cowboy.) Harry retorted, "In 1885 Tom left Texas. They wanted him to stay so bad that two sheriffs followed him to the state line." Such were the exchanges between old friends who enjoyed their private jokes throughout many years.

Two brothers who lived in Moab used different surnames. A favorite pastime of the people who knew them was to conjecture whether they were half-brothers or whether one had changed his name when they left Texas. One day while shooting a game of pool, they got into a heated argument. As was often typical in those days, they went outside to settle the dispute with a fistfight. After a violent, bloody, enervating contest, they got up off the ground, dusted themselves off, wiped off the blood, and returned to the game. Said John, "It's your shot, Bill," and the game continued.

SUFFERING AND DEATH were frequent callers on the frontier. Disease was easily obtained. Even in cities, medical knowledge was limited, and those who lived both long and short distances from such help had to rely on the experiences of others and on improvision and prayer. Midwives and practical healers were also in short supply but could nearly always be found. Some settlers, unusually gifted in the art of healing, relieved the suffering as best they could. Before medical professionals came to Moab, one of those to whom the pioneers looked for help was J. H. "Uncle Horace" Johnson. A veteran of the Blackhawk Indian War (during which he served as voluntary hostage), and one who had spent many years among the Indians (who, studies show, passed along much of their knowledge and expertise to whites), he had learned some of the skills and medicines of these people. When eventually a doctor came to Moab, many families refused to let anyone but Uncle Horace set broken limbs of family members.

When the Johnsons first came to Moab to settle (1884) they came with several other families — relatives and friends — who had passed through Moab on their way to New Mexico and then had returned to Moab to live permanently. Three years later the husband of one of the women in the group was in Mexico as she was approaching delivery of a child. She wished to go to her Mother who lived in Mona, Juab County. Her brother and his wife agreed to take her, and Johnson agreed to accompany them that the men might return to Moab with wagons loaded with flour and other supplies. But the baby was ready en route, and Johnson helped in the delivery of a boy who would one day marry the Johnsons' daughter — who wasn't born until two years later.

During a diphtheria epidemic in Mona and Moab, Johnson and two others, George W. McConkie and Bert Newell, went about ministering to the sick, burying the dead, and comforting the living. Others were too ill or too frightened by the disease to undertake the work.

Remedies such as bread-and-milk poultices and the "sticky gum" (resin) of pine trees were used to draw out infection. Mustard plasters were applied for chest infection. Johnson and his wife tell of an incident in which an Indian, whom neither knew, came to their home with a badly infected leg wound and a dangerously high fever. Their best efforts failed to reduce the infection or the fever. Finally, the Indian bade them go to the corral and get the fresh dung of a cow. When Uncle Horace returned with the "cow cake," the Indian asked them to place it on a cloth and heat it on a rock. This they did. Then the Indian had them put it, cakeside down, on the wound and wrap the leg until the dung was thoroughly dry. To the amazement of the pioneer practitioner, when he removed the cloth the inflammation was reduced, as was the fever, and the Indian recovered.

When Johnson was 77, he suffered a broken leg when he was thrown from a wagonload of hay that he was bringing from his ranch to his town home. The leg healed, but later on, he developed a serious heart condition. For many years before his death, his family lived in fear of any communicable illness, afraid that it might result in the death of "Grandpa." But he lived to the grand old age of 84.

ON THE FRONTIER, pioneers had no television, no movies — no "canned" entertainment. Their times of relaxation and play were largely community- or family-produced affairs. One early pioneer couple, who had numerous progeny, were honored with an annual celebration on "Grandpa's birthday" in June. All the clan gathered at the ranch for games, talk, and huge tables laden with food set up under the silver maple trees...a typical western "family reunion." Hungry children were shooed away to await their turn, because in those days the adults ate first. But nothing was kept from the little ones, for there was always enough to set up a banquet for them, too. (How different from today, when grownups must wait until the children have had their fill before being served.)

The menus in those early days were as flexible as they are at such gatherings today. Each household brought enough food for its own members and "plenty to spare," an open invitation to one and all that each dish was not meant exclusively for a certain family. One could heap fried (often wild) chicken, roast beef, venison, roast lamb or mutton, homemade bread of all shapes and sizes (and baking expertise), vegetables — anything that was in plentiful supply and near at hand for the women and girls to cook — on one plate and go back for seconds. A special treat on many occasions was the ten-gallon freezer of homemade ice cream — rich with real custard, lots of eggs, and frozen just right. When the beaters were pulled out of the reluctant mixture, there was a scramble of kids and near-kids grabbing for the delectable "first taste."

The parallelism doesn't stop with food, for the young lads of those days went "skinny dipping" in pools and creeks. Some even dared the Colorado (in places where the river was in a sleepy mood), but it generally was forbidden territory. Occasionally, someone disappeared, never to be found, for the ever-vigilant Colorado only appears to be sleeping. Yet many of the best swimmers took their lessons in the river.

LIFE ON THE southeastern Utah frontier was not all pleasure. Occasionally, the old-timers would grow serious and tell about the privations they suffered; but they nearly always ended their stories with a touch of humor — the spice that makes any situation bearable. For example, in the Plainfield (also called Bueno) area, drought and dust took their toll of farmers. With typical pioneer humor, they dubbed their abandoned farms "Poverty Flat," a name that still stands, despite the more dignified appellation of Spanish Valley.

One individual stands out in the story-telling era. Amasa (pronounced Am ´-uh-sa) Larsen had an innate sense of humor that enabled him to laugh at himself and to enjoy the stories told about him. He relished the type of wit employed at Crout's Saloon, such as the day he suffered the epitome of cowboy chagrin — his horse had thrown him. In telling the story on himself, he added (in his customary lisp): "Had a pig in one panniard and a thack of oatth in the other, an' the dang horth ran away and killed 'em both."

His lisp was famous. Cold sober he talked as clearly as anyone, but with a little "whithkey" under his belt, the lisp became pronounced. And his stories lose their flavor without the lisp. It worried him that some of his drinking sprees caused much comment in the religious little frontier town. "When I die at eighty, people will thay that whithkey killed Amathy," he prophesied. He did, it did, and they did.

Born in 1866, he was a cattleman who lived in Moab for approximately half a century. He changed little during his lifetime, although he did grow a bit morose. He was "head high to the saloon door when hunched, and he was always hunched" (the better to keep his balance on his high-heeled, runover cowboy boots). He was lanky, hardly wide enough to hide a bottle, long in the back, and his shirttail was always flying in the breeze. He was an avid imbiber. He walked on the outsides of his feet because of an old injury that had left him with somewhat less than a fluid stride. He acquired his identifying shuffle early in life. His horse had fallen on him in a rugged canyon near Valley City while he was chasing broomtails. His foot was crushed. His companion managed to get him home, then rode twenty miles to Moab for the town "bone-setter." But Uncle Horace had a broken wrist and was unable to set Amasa's leg. As best he could, he directed novice medics in the bonesetting techniques, feeling the break with his good hand and directing his helpers to "pull some more" until he "allow[ed] the foot is in normal position."

It was a less than successful treatment. Amasa ended up walking on the sides of his boots that were not meant to be walked on. Once, several years later, he almost landed in jail in Grand Junction, Colorado. The arresting officer, having hauled Amasa before the judge for drunkenness, reported that he was "wobbling down the street." When the judge asked Amasa how he pled, Amasa replied:

"Not guilty!"

Inquired the judge, "Then how does it happen you can't walk straight?"

Amasa reached down, pulled off his boot, shook it in the judge's face, and lisped, "Judge, if you can walk thtraight in that boot, I'll plead guilty."

He was released.

Tom Trout, of the "twenty years ago" fame, told the author of how he remembered Amasa: "...years ago today, Amasy [Amasa] came to town. We decided to celebrate his arrival so we bought a bottle of whiskey. Amasy took a drink, then I took a drink. Then Amasy took a drink and Bill took a drink. Amasy took a drink..." and on until "and Amasy got so drunk he has never been sober since."

Amasa could neither read nor write. He boasted about his two days of formal schooling: "The firtht day it rained; the thecond day the teathyer didn't thyow up." But he could outfigure anyone in the valley. His circle of friends in Grand Junction was large, especially among the newsboys. This latter friendship began on the street one day when a newsboy approached him to buy a paper. "Son," said Amasa, unwontedly sober, "I'd be wasting my nickel. I can't read." To which the enterprising young salesman responded, "You could smell it — it's all bull anyway." The quip fell on appreciative ears and Amasa bought the whole supply. From that time on word spread fast when the bowlegged Utah cowboy hit town. They liked his stories. "How long you been in Moab?" they would ask, and he would reply, "Why son, when I first came to Utah those La Sal Mountains were just ant hills, and Moab just a hole in the ground."

One day he dropped into his favorite barber shop. The barber slapped a hot towel on his face. Amasa reared up in the chair and bellowed, "Jethuth Chritht, Krug! When thith dod-damned towel getth cool enough tho you can thtand to take hold of it, would you pleathe take the dod-damned thing off my faith!"

So far as he was concerned, there were only two ways to travel — both of them on horseback. Once a year he deviated from this theory when he drove his steers to Thompson and rode the cattle train with them to the eastern market. He was perhaps more awed than the rest of the townspeople when the first bi-wing airplane flew over the valley. He moved into the street with the rest of the residents and squinted at the mechanized bird until it disappeared in the horizon. "Amasa, how'd you like to be up there with that pilot?" someone asked.

The old cowboy seemed to reflect a moment, then replied soberly, "I'd a dang thight rather be up there with him than without him!"

GERMAN-BORN Teucher (Tusher) was the first to introduce the thriving industry of wine grape vineyards which proved adaptable to Moab's sandy soil and warm climate. Teucher spoke fluent German and English, but when angered he lapsed into a broken combination of both languages. Teenagers of his day stole his fryers for their beach parties on the banks of the Colorado River, and played other pranks to annoy him. There were two frightened young people on one foiled raid. A sleepy hen squawked and alerted old Teucher. Suddenly there he was, shotgun in hand, silhouetted in his long johns in the doorway of his house. The two

321

young people headed for the nearest fence, but ducked to the safety of the coop when the shotgun blasted into the night.

"What are we gonna do?" one lad asked.

"I don't know about you," the other answered, "but I'm gonna try that fence one more time."

No one ever knew what inspired Amasa to initiate a raid on old Teucher's chicken coops, but Larsen's wife discovered the plot before zero hour. A born imitator, she slipped down the back path and hid by the henhouse before Amasa and his fellow prankster arrived. As they stealthily slipped into the coop, Amasa's wife went into action. In Teucher's voice she exploded, "You S.O.B.'s—feist ya drrrink my vine, then ya sh-steel my chickens!"

The would-be thieves vied for first place at the gate and took off in separate directions. When he arrived home, Amasa's wife was calmly churning by the fireplace. "Pleath thwear I wath here all night," Amasa pleaded as he burst into the room. "You gotta thwear I wathn't at Tutherth chicken coop or he'll thotgun me down!"

Of course Teucher did not come gunning — he wasn't in on the joke. Though he found out later, Teucher kept his knowledge to himself, and he and Amasa spent many evenings trampling the vine. They would climb barefoot into the big vats, and as the juice deepened, they rolled their pants up another turn. It kept Amasa's lisp in tune for many years.

Teucher cured his wine in wooden kegs; some he buried on the ranch for safekeeping. They were well concealed; seldom were would-be looters successful on a keg hunt.

Watermelons were a delicacy during season in Moab. To many young people, of course, melons from the farms of neighbors tasted much better than those grown at home. On one occasion, four young men, out on a lark, decided to raid someone's patch. They consulted together about whose patch to raid, and finally concluded that the best melons in town belonged to the parents of two members of the group. Since these brothers were rather large young men, the problem of hiding their bulk was a strategy they hadn't prepared ahead of time.

Just as they were in the act of getting their melons, the mother of the two young giants emerged from the house and let go with an extremely sharp tongue, emitting somewhat earthy language. All of the boys dropped into a dry ditch, but although they were not visible in the darkness, she knew they were there and started calling them every name she could lay her tongue to. Then she started on their pedigree. While she was still going strong, one of her sons stood up and said, "Yeh, Ma, I guess yer right." (Touché!)

Often young, inexperienced cowhands went to the mountains to learn the business of running cattle. Two such young men had been out riding and branding all day. When they came into camp that evening, ravenously hungry, they cast about for something that would be filling, easy to cook, and complementary to the inevitable beefsteak. They decided on rice, but when it came time to prepare it, neither knew how much they should use. They finally decided (because they were so hungry) that ten pounds would be about right. They later recounted, "We soon had filled every pot, pan, and dish in camp and then began burying the damned stuff."

Sometimes the naïveté was on another side. A sheepherder sent in to Phil (the German manager of the Cooper-Martin store) for a supply of groceries which were to last for several months. On the list was an item "ten pounds of your best cheese." To the German, the best cheese meant Roquefort, and he filled the order accordingly. When the sheepman came to town on his next trip, he came into the store to reorder. The manager inquired whether the previous list had been satisfactorily filled. The sheepman replied, "Yes, all except the cheese. That was rotten and I had to bury it."

Children who attended the large brick elementary school vied for the privilege of ringing the old bell which called the students to class. It was great fun to hold the rope when one pulled down, because as the bell swung in the opposite direction, it would lift the young ringer off the floor.

Humor is found even in the statements of those who managed to escape from the small brick jail, only to find true escape impossible because of the natural jail of the surroundings. One such escapee broke jail and headed over the hill for Grand Junction. As he looked down the sheer cliff into the river he said, "Moab is the biggest damn jail I've ever seen."

Sometimes justice went awry, as it often does, for strange reasons. In one incident in Moab, Sheriff John Skewes had arrested a man for illegal possession of alcoholic beverages and had confiscated a case of beer for evidence. When the jury went out they took the evidence, kept the bailiff busy to and from the rest room, drank up all the beer, and freed the defendant for lack of evidence.

Young people were pranksters, as they often are in all places and times. The excuse of Halloween Eve furnished an occasion for many pranks and much labor the following day restoring what they had displaced the night before. Picket fences were often removed and placed atop houses. On one occasion an "Abraham Lincoln" (outhouse) was set in the center of the main street. Across the front was nailed a borrowed sign, bearing the title "Moab Short Order House."

Every community has those who are very serious minded and who cannot understand why people laugh at the unconscious humor implicit in their remarks. The *faux pas* are of course unintentional, but certain personal characteristics of speech or manner of speaking tend to result in statements with humorous overtones. Such a person was a man called Jake. He spoke in all sincerity and simplicity and with an exaggerated drawl. Things just didn't come out the way they were meant to emerge. A successful cattleman, he was one of the first men in the area to purchase an automobile. Thus he was extremely popular whenever he made a trip "to the city" and had an ample supply of passengers.

On one trip, Jake stopped in one of the villages and told a friend of an experience he'd had when he got his car stuck in the mud. He'd had to lift up the back end of the car to get it out of the mud and place it on an unmired spot, hoping this would hold until the tires got traction. But by the time he ran round and got back into the driver's seat, the wheel was spinning and digging its way into the soft mud again.

Finally, he decided to get a large pole to put under the rear wheel to lend substance to the soggy earth. To make sure the pole remained in place, he asked the women to hold it, even sit on it. Then he wondered why they got so angry when, as he got the car started and drove out of the mire, they had fallen into it.

On another occasion, he was asked to speak at a church meeting. A man of utter humility, he started his speech with, "Before I begin my talk tonight, I think I will read a passage from the Bible. You know, I think we all feel better after a passage." And down came the house!

The British woman (Mrs. Farrell), who was proprietress of the halfway station between Thompson and Moab (discussed in an earlier chapter), rode along with Sam Hudson, a freighter who was on his way to Thompson. After he had loaded the wagon, they visited the local saloon and became more than a little inebriated. Somehow they managed to climb aboard the wagon and start on their journey. But before they reached their destination, Sam discovered that she had fallen off the wagon seat. He retraced his route until he found her lying serenely in the middle of the road, unconscious from the fruit of the vine. He circled the wagon so that he could lift her more easily onto the wagon seat. But his reflexes were not at their best, and he drove the wagon over her arm, breaking it. The shock was sobering to both of them.

PRIDE WAS AN important attribute of frontier people. Many lacked even the barest education, but their pride forced them to acquire ingenuity for hiding the fact that they could neither read nor write. Several incidents indicate this pride, although it was often a well-kept secret which their friends and acquaintances honored.

One man who was exceptionally talented but unschooled in even the rudiments of music, and who was the organizer and leader of fine choral groups, always insisted upon holding a book as though he were following the notes and instructions printed on the pages. No one had the heart to tell him that he sometimes held it upside down.

In another instance, a man worked in a store, and unable to read or write, kept a ledger in which he drew pictured items, such as yard goods, kinds of food, and so forth. His doodlings were readable to him, if to no one else. One day a farmer came into the store to settle his account, and the clerk got out his records. As he went over the bill, he itemized a "half roll of cheese" (about five pounds). The farmer protested that he hadn't purchased any cheese but the clerk had said nothing about the emery stone the farmer remembered buying. The salesman then exclaimed, "Oh, I forgot to put in the little hole," and promptly corrected his "cheese" to make it resemble an emery stone.

At a later time, when the salesman had grown old, he visited Salt Lake City, where friends took him to Hogle's Zoo. As he looked at the giraffe, he shook his head, clucked his tongue, and said indignantly, "Ain't no such animal!"

Children manufactued their own entertainment and fantasies. Where dolls were lacking, many hours were whiled away by young children making dolls of "corn in the silk" (during the corn growing season when the tassels and silk of the corn were soft and pliant). Arbors and trees provided play houses for imaginative youngsters who pretended that they belonged to the adult world. Such activities furnished at least temporary surcease from the chores that all frontier children had to perform — responsibilities undreamed of by today's youth. The girls cut paper dolls from the Sears, Roebuck and other catalogs (Figure 19.2). Pleasant play such as this occupied long and contented hours. Drama, dance, and other social events filled the life of adults, and picnics were popular with both young and old. Patriotic holidays were always a special occasion. Although those of us living in modern times feel sorry for the frontier people because they lacked recreation as we know it, it may be that they were more fortunate, for they provided their own social activities, thus developing bonds of unity that held them together in times of crisis, joy, and sorrow.

One never knew when to expect company, and beds were made all over the house. Many times visiting adults usurped children's beds, but it was always a lark to sleep on the floor or, weather permitting, in large beds on the ground out in the yard. This furnished an occasion for telling horror tales which developed into contests to determine who could conjure up the most terrifying story and who could hold out the longest before pleading for the storyteller to stop. Laughter and jokes were spontaneous. One can scarcely feel sadness for these people who made their own fun and enjoyment.

The high regard in which women were held on the frontier sometimes backfired on those who considered themselves as being gentry. On one occasion two men stood under the protection of a building, waiting for the rain to subside. From across the street they heard the screams of a woman calling for help. They rushed over to find that her husband was beating her. They interceded in her behalf, only to find her turn on them and call them every vile name she could remember. She informed them in positive terms that he was her husband and could beat her if he wished. It was none of their blankety-blank business and they should "get the h---" out of there. They beat a hasty retreat.

Two elderly gentlemen in Moab each had the idiosyncrasy of carrying on a conversation with himself as he walked along the street or path. Young children soon learned of this and followed at a discreet distance. On one occasion they witnessed one of the old gentlemen pick up a handful of red ants, address them solemnly, "Measly little critters!" and then pop them into his mouth. (They were his internal cleansing agent.)

A cattleman, needing barbed wire, asked another cattleman if he knew where some might be found. The second replied that there was an abundance in Dry Valley. The first man thanked him and went on his way. In reporting the story, the informer related that the next time he went to his cabin in Dry Valley he found a huge roll of barbed wire stacked against the wall. The man who had been informed of the fencing available there had taken down a plenitudinous supply of fences, had divided the amount in half, and had left a share for the man who had informed him.

On one occasion a Mormon bishop came to a cattleman and told him he knew of a poor family who needed meat. Could the cattleman help him? The latter replied that he would see what he could do. After thinking the matter over, the cattleman went by way of the hill near what was known later as the Wilcox place, found one of Walt Moore's steers and killed and dressed it out. He then sold half to Walt, gave a quarter to the bishop for the poor family, and kept a quarter for himself. In telling the story, he said that this act was the first big mistake he had made. He kept that family from starving to death, and he didn't feel it was worth the effort.

In Dry Valley there is one dome rock called Jail Rock (there were a number of these dome-like rocks which have water in them). They were well known to cowboys and ranchers. In some, such as Jail Rock, it was necessary to have help to get in and out of the hole in the rock. One of the Dry Valley ranchers one day wanted to go to Moab. His wife

Figure 19.2. Reproduction of a 1900 Sears, Roebuck Catalog

objected. The husband then found one of these water holes that would keep his wife under control, yet furnish water to slake her thirst, while he went to town to savor the beverage at the local saloon. He dropped her into one of these tanks, and from that time forward it has been called Jail Rock.

Tom Trout, in his typical fashion, once asked a young man in Moab if he knew why the Wild Bunch left the country. To the negative answer, Tom said, "Well, as they left town on one occasion during the daytime, they rode past the Lower School. They saw Peck Taylor, Lester Walker, and some of their friends outside and decided the country was too tough for them."

Moab and La Sal had their "spit and whittle" clubs. Men would congregate in front of the pool hall or the post office and, while their wives exchanged gossip and recipes at their quilting bees, the men discussed their problems and observations as they watched people pass by.

In these and in unnumbered thousands of forgotten episodes, it becomes clear that the frontier was neither humorless nor stale. Despite the conviction of many young people that frontier life was without zest, humor most assuredly obtained in a hard, uncompromising environment. Indeed it was often humor that made life endurable.

Chapter 20

The Future:
Land of Quiet Peace

Historians can relate the development of an area, a town, a region, a nation, an era. The task of projecting the future lies with the economists, the statisticians, the philosophers, and the sociologists. Historians can only put together a few writings and attitudes.

Daniel Keeler,[1] in his "Town on a Powder Keg," presents as his thesis three assumptions:

(1) An idea has persisted that Moab's economic birth and uncommon industrial renaissance might be directly or indirectly related to a geologic peculiarity; i.e., an ancient deposit of salt.

(2) Moab has been on the verge of an economic explosion more than once, and conditions bode well for future expansion.

(3) Local citizens of Moab (and other areas in Utah) must take hold of their economic potentials and opportunities in an effort to turn them into profitable realities.

What Keeler seems to be saying throughout his dissertation is that Moab and its vicinity have the potential for industrial development, that the area has been on the verge of an industrial explosion several times, and that the only way to ever achieve this industrialization is for the people

---

[1]Daniel Keeler, "Town on a Powder Keg: A Video Tape Production on the Industrial Emergence of Moab, Utah" (Provo, Utah: Brigham Young University, 1966), MFA thesis.

329

themselves to want this achievement to the point that they will make their dream a reality.

Keeler, an outsider, may be more objective than one who has his roots in the community and has perhaps a certain sentimental attachment for it. But reducing things to a formula does not always yield the full and true picture.

What are the physical facilities or limitations of Moab? Obviously space and resources would prevent the development of industry on a grand scale. The physical limitations of water are an unknown factor. This area, as a result of strikes in uranium, oil, and potash, has weathered a "boom" of some proportions, and these industries are marked "go" at this writing. The economic factors of a competitive market, cost of production, cost and availability of transportation are indeed keys to industrialization. The reason for the temporary regression in the uranium industry was not absence of initiative on the part of the local populace, but lack of demand on the market and of government support. Stockpiles, inaccurately estimated, suggested the provision of needs for many years hence. The mill, despite the slowdown, remained in operation during this period. Local ore was processed, and other ore was shipped into Moab. The mill was, during this slow period, an important economic factor in the community. The potash industry is at present operating at a loss but gambling on future needs. Oil shortages are stimulating new effort.

FROM THE BEGINNING Moab and La Sal have experienced a slow but steady growth. The area has known periods of regression and periods of rapid acceleration, but the overall picture has been steadily upward. Even when confronted with the uranium boom, the agricultural community managed to evolve into an industrial community and still retain the flavor of the past. The local citizenry has learned it need not fear outsiders — that these newcomers can quickly become a part of community life.

As the author moved about the town — interviewing, gathering, and verifying — she found as much enthusiasm for this book among the newcomers as the old-timers. All were proud of their city and anxious that the world hear of its advantages and opportunities. This civic pride has kept the community progressive. No doubt the presence of an alert, civic-oriented newspaper has much to do with this, and the recent addition of a local television station will likely expand that tradition.

A columnist of the Salt Lake *Tribune*[2] supports the author's position that it is the people themselves who, in the final analysis, are impor-

_____

[2]Dan Valentine, "Nothing Serious," a column feature, Salt Lake *Tribune*, June 1, 1973, p. B-1.

tant in what happens to a community. He says that unusual and unbelievable as it may seem over a period of some 25 years, he has never heard a resident or visitor say he did not like Moab. The columnist talks about the advantages and disadvantages of large and fascinating cities in this country. But, he continues, "every resident of Moab is a walking chamber of commerce for the community.... Every stranger leaves Moab an unofficial press agent for the town." He feels that Moab has a kind of magic; ethereal as it may seem, it does exist.

Moab, on the surface, is no better — certainly no worse — than thousands of other communities of its size round the nation. But it has something extra: "A mood, a spirit, a state of mind."

People who live in Moab are happy about it. In fact, there exists a sympathy for anyone unlucky enough not to live there. He sums up his discussion:

> I've tried to figure out what is so attractive about Moab, and I've come to a few conclusions: First, the setting is breathless. ... But it's the people that make Moab. They all seem content... and they all seem to have a live-and-let-live attitude. They don't worry about their neighbors, they just enjoy them.... Perhaps that's the secret.... Moab people don't worry about life — they just enjoy living it.

La Sal continues to be oriented to the ranch, but miners and prospectors have changed the flavor and are accepted as part of the growth.

The author agrees with Keeler that the citizenry will have much to do with the future, but she believes they will be limited by certain physical factors. It is not certain that the valley, with its limited acreage and water in some areas, could achieve significant progress in agriculture. The problem of transportation still exists as does the problem of seasonal production. One would hope that, with the increasing tourist industry, there will be retained the quietness of the wilderness, that there will be left a few places on this continent where one may seek retreat to the quiet beauty of nature, where the sound of a stone rolling down the canyon still echoes with a reverberating hollow sound, and where one can yet wonder about the "pasture on the other side of the hill."

If all other industry in the region fails, Moab and La Sal can serve humanity well in the industry of tourism. In these troubled times, with the increasing pressures of urban life — polluted air, noise, the rushing about — there will be an increasing need for the few remaining retreats where one can find quiet peace.

Selected Resources and References

Books

Abbey, Edward. *Desert Solitaire.* New York: McGraw-Hill Book Company, 1968.

Alter, J. Cecil. *Utah, The Storied Domain.* Chicago and New York: The American History Society, Inc., 1932.

American Guide Series. *Utah: A Guide to the State.* New York: Hastings House, 1945.

Athearn, Robert G. *Rebel of the Rockies: A History of the Denver and Rio Grande Western Railroad.* New Haven: Yale University Press, 1962.

Bailey, L. R. *Indian Slave Trade in the Southwest.* Los Angeles: Westernlore Press, 1966.

Baker, Pearl. *The Wild Bunch at Robbers Roost.* Los Angeles: Westernlore Press, 1965.

Bolton, Herbert E. *Pageant in the Wilderness: The Story of the Escalante Expedition to the Interior Basin, 1776, Including the Diary and Itinerary of Father Escalante.* Salt Lake City: Utah State Historical Society, 1950. Translated and annotated.

Carter, Kate B. *Heart Throbs of the West.* Second edition. Salt Lake City: Daughters of the Utah Pioneers, 1939.

Coyner, David. *The Lost Trappers.* Cincinnati and New York: Hurst and Company, 1894.

Crampton, C. Gregory. *Standing Up Country: The Canyon Lands of Utah and Arizona.* New York: Alfred A. Knopf, 1964.

Creer, Leland Hargrave. *The Founding of an Empire.* Salt Lake City: Book-craft, 1947.

Cunningham, Eugene. *Triggernometry: A Gallery of Gunfighters.* New York: The Press of the Pioneers, Inc., 1934.

Cunningham, James L. *Our Family History Subsequent to 1870.* Pittsburgh: Herald Press, 1943.

Daly, Denis: *Geographical Companion to the Bible.* New York: McGraw-Hill Book Company, Inc., 1963.

_____. *The Geography of the Bible: A Study in Historical Geography.* New York: Harper & Brothers Publishers, 1957.

Dellenbaugh, Frederick S. *The Romance of the Colorado River.* New York and London: G. P. Putnam's Sons, 1909.

Editors of Time-Life Books, with text by William H. Forbis. *The Cowboys.* New York: Time-Life Books, 1973.

Encyclopedia Americana. Volume 19. New York: Americana Corporation, 1968.

Encyclopedia Britannica. Chicago, London: Encyclopaedia Britannica, Inc., William Benton Publisher, 1968, vol. 15.

Explorations and Surveys for a Railroad Route from the Mississippi River to the Pacific Ocean. (The Pacific Railroad Surveys), vol. 11, Warren's Memoir.

Gottfredson, Peter. *History of Indian Depredations in Utah.* Salt Lake City: Press of the Skelton Publishing Co., 1919.

Hafen, LeRoy; and Hafen, Ann W. *Old Spanish Trails: Santa Fe to Los Angeles.* Glendale: The Arthur H. Clark Company, 1954.

Hastings, James, D.D., *et al.*, editors. *Dictionary of the Bible.* New York: Charles Scribners' Sons, 1943.

Hendricks, George D. *The Bad Man of the West.* San Antonio: The Naylor Company, 1859.

Henry, Will. *Alias Butch Cassidy.* New York: Random House, 1967.

Horan, James D. *The Wild Bunch.* New York: The New American Library, 1958.

Howard, Robert West, editor. *This Is the West.* Chicago: The New American Library, 1957.

Hunter, Milton R. *Brigham Young the Colonizer.* Salt Lake City: The Deseret News Press, 1940.

Jones, Daniel W. *Forty Years among the Indians.* Salt Lake City: Juvenile Instructor's Office, 1890.

334

Kelly, Charles. *The Outlaw Trail: A History of Butch Cassidy and His Wild Bunch.* Second edition. New York: Devin-Adair, 1959.

King, Murray E. *Last of the Bandit Riders.* New York: Bonanza Books, no date.

Lamar, Howard Roberts. *The Far Southwest 1846–1912: A Territorial History.* New Haven and London: Yale University Press, 1966.

Larsen, Gustive O. *Outline History of Utah and the Mormons.* Salt Lake City: Deseret Book Company, 1958.

Lavender, David. *One Man's West.* Garden City: Doubleday, 1956.

Lyman, Albert R. *Indians and Outlaws: Settling of the San Juan Frontier.* Salt Lake City: Bookcraft, 1962.

McElprang, Stella, compiler. *Castle Valley: A History of Emery County.* Emery County Company of the Daughters of Utah Pioneers, 1949.

McGregor, John C. *Southwestern Archaeology.* Urbana: University of Illinois Press, 1965.

Miller, David E. *Hole-in-the-Rock.* Salt Lake City: University of Utah Press, 1966.

Miller, J. Lane. *Harper's Bible Dictionary.* New York: Harper Brothers, Publishers, 1961.

Mould, Elmer W. K. *Essentials of Bible History.* New York: The Ronald Press Company, 1966.

New International Encyclopedia. Volume XVI. New York: Dodd Mead & Co., 1928.

Orr, James, *et al.*, editors. *The International Standard Bible Encyclopedia.* Grand Rapids, Michigan: Wm. B. Eerdman's Publishing Co., Volume 3, 1946.

Papers of the Michigan Academy of Science, Arts and Letters. Volume VII. Ann Arbor: University of Michigan, 1926.

Perkins, Cornelia Adams: Nielson, Marian Gardner; and Jones, Lenora Butt. *Saga of San Juan.* San Juan County Daughters of Utah Pioneers, 1957.

Pfeiffer, Charles F., editor. *The Biblical World: A Dictionary of Biblical Archaeology.* Grand Rapids, Michigan: Baker Book House, 1966.

Redd, Amasa Jay. *Lemuel Hardison Redd, Jr.* Salt Lake City: Privately published, 1967.

Redd, Lura; and Redd; Amasa Jay, editors. *The Utah Redds and Their Progenitors.* Salt Lake City: Privately published, 1973.

Revised Ordinances of Moab.

Riis, John. *Ranger Trails.* Richmond, Virginia: The Dietz Press, 1937.

Rockwell, Wilson. *The Utes: A Forgotten People.* Denver, Colorado: Sage Books, 1956.

Scorup, Stena. *J. A. Scorup: A Utah Cattleman.* Privately printed, 1944.

Stegner, Wallace. *The Sound of Mountain Water.* Garden City: Doubleday & Company, Inc., 1969.

Tanner, Faun McConkie. *A History of Moab, Utah.* Moab: Times-Independent Press, 1937.

Taylor, Raymond W.; and Taylor, Samuel W. *Uranium Fever.* New York: The Macmillan Company, 1970.

Warrum, Noble, editor. *Utah Since Statehood.* Volume I. Chicago and Salt Lake City: S. J. Clarke Publishing Co., 1819.

Wilson, Dick. *This Is Canyon Country.* Moab: Times-Independent Press, 1968.

Young, Levi Edgar. *The Founding of Utah.* New York: Charles Scribner's Sons, 1923.

Youngman, Bernard R. *The Lands and Peoples of the Living Bible.* Edited by Walter Russell Bowie. New York: Hawthorne Books, Inc., Publishers, 1959.

Dissertations and Theses

Baker, Arthur A. "Geology of the Moab District, Grand and San Juan Counties, Utah." New Haven, Connecticut: Yale University, 1931. Doctoral dissertation.

Brew, John Otis. "The Archaeology of Southeastern Utah and Its Place in the History of the Southwest." Cambridge, Massachusetts: Harvard University, 1941. Doctoral dissertation.

Gould, Laurence McKinley. "The Geology of the La Sal Mountains of Utah." Ann Arbor: University of Michigan, 1925. Sc.D. thesis.

Keeler, Daniel Albert. "Town on a Powder Keg: A Video Tape Production on the Industrial Emergence of Moab, Utah." Provo, Utah: Brigham Young University, 1966. MFA thesis.

Government Publications and Unpublished Papers

"Arches National Monument, Utah." National Park Service. Washington, D.C.: U.S. Government Printing Office, 1966.

Baker, Arthur A. "Geology and Oil Possibilities of the Moab District, Grand and San Juan Counties, Utah." U.S. Geological Survey Bulletin No. 841. Washington, D.C.: U.S. Government Printing Office, 1933.

Billings, Alfred N. "Memorandum, Account Book and Diary" (1885). Salt Lake City: Utah State Historical Society.

Bott, George F.; and Housely, Marian. "McClesky-Robinson Descendants." First edition. Alameda, California, 1968. Mimeographed manuscript.

Boutwell, J. M. "Vanadium and Uranium in Southeastern Utah." In *Contributions to Economic Geology, 1904.* Washington, D.C.: U.S. Government Printing Office, 1905.

Brew, John Otis. "Archaeology of Alkali Ridge, Southeastern Utah — With a Review of the Prehistory of the Mesa Verde Division of the San Juan and Some Observations on Archaeological Systemics." In *Papers of the Peabody Museum of American Archaeology and Ethnology.* Volume XXI. Cambridge: Peabody Museum, 1952.

Bunce, Winford. "Interview: Joseph Burkholder." Utah State Historical Society, January 30, 1937. Typescript.

————. "Interview: Robert G. Bryant." May 27, 1937. Utah State Historical Society. Typescript.

————. "Interview: Mary H. Wilcox Day." February 10, 1937. Utah State Historical Society. Typescript.

Chittenden, G. B. "Topographical Report on the Grand River District [and] On the San Juan District." In *Ninth Annual Report of the United States Geological and Geographical Survey of the Territories... 1875.* Washington, D.C.: U.S. Government Printing Office, 1877.

Christensen, Christian L. "Diary of Christian Lingo Christensen." Provo: Brigham Young University Library. Typescript.

"Echo." U.S. Department of Agriculture: La Sal National Forest, Form 406. (Publication of La Sal National Forest July–August 1911; January–April–July–December, 1912. Library of the U.S. Department of Agriculture. Part of a microfilm record of material on La Sal National Forest–695 pp. — personal property of Dr. Charles S. Peterson of History Department Utah State University, Logan, Utah.)

Heywood, Leland. "Historical Information about La Sal National Forest." 1940. Unpublished notes in possession of Charles S. Peterson, Utah State University, Logan, Utah.

Hill, J. M. "Notes on the Northern La Sal Mountains, Grand County, Utah." United States Geological Survey Bulletin 530-M. Washington, D.C.: U.S. Government Printing Office, 1912.

Holyoak, Arnel. "Interview: Delilah Jane Warner Peterson." March 9, 1937, August 1, 1938. Utah State Historical Society. Typescript.

Hunt, Charles B. "Structural and Igneous Geology of the La Sal Mountains, Utah." United States Geological Survey Professional Paper 294-I. Washington, D.C.: U.S. Government Printing Office, 1958.

Huntington, Oliver B. "Official Elk Mountain Mission Journal (1855)." Salt Lake City: L.D.S. Church Historian's Office. Typescript.

————. "Diary," Part II. 1847–1900. Copied by Brigham Young University Library, 1942. Typescript.

Jenson, Andrew. "History of Elk Mountain Mission." L.D.S. Church Historian's Office. Typescript.

————. "History of Moab Ward." Salt Lake City: L.D.S. Church Historian's Office. Typescript.

Jones, Kuman: "San Juan Mission to the Indians." Provo: Brigham Young University Library. Typescript.

Keeler, Daniel A. "The Journey of the Billings Party from Manti to Elk Mountain in 1855." 1964. Typescript.

King, Murray. "Introducing Matt Warner." Utah State Historical Society. No date. Typescript.

Lohman, S. W. "The Geologic Story of Arches National Park." United States Department of the Interior, Geological Survey Bulletin 1393. Washington, D.C.: U.S. Government Printing Office, 1975.

Macomb, J. N. "Report of the Exploring Expedition from Santa Fe, New Mexico, to the Junction of the Grand and Green Rivers." Washington, D.C.: U.S. Government Printing Office, 1876.

Morris, Earl H.; and Burgh, Robert F. "Anasazi Basketry: Basket Maker II through Pueblo III — A Study Based on Speciments from the San Juan Country." No. 533. Washington, D.C.: Carnegie Institution, 1941.

————. "Basket Maker II Sites near Durango, Colorado." No. 604. Washington, D.C.: Carnegie Institution, 1954.

Pace, William B. "Diary of the Elk Mountain Mission 1855–1856." L.D.S. Church Historian's Office; Brigham Young University Library. Typescript.

Silvey, Frank. Biographical sketches. January 14, 1936. Utah State Historical Society. Typescript.

————. "Early History and Settlement of Northern San Juan County, Utah." Utah State Historical Society. Typescript.

_____. "History and Settlement of Northern San Juan County and Paradox Valley, Just over the Line in Colorado." May 7, 1936. Utah State Historical Society. Typescript.

_____. "The Pinhook Indian Battle." May 14, 1938. Typescript.

Standifird, J. H. "Diary." 1873 to death at Moab, Utah in 1920s. Arizona Historical Foundation. Arizona State University, Phoenix, On microfilm.

Newspapers[1]

Arizona Republic, Phoenix, Arizona.

Denver *Post*, Denver, Colorado.

Deseret News, Salt Lake City, Utah.

Dolores News, Rico, Colorado.

Durango Daily Herald, Durango, Colorado.

Grand Valley Times, Moab, Utah (prior to 1919).

Moab *Independent*, Moab, Utah.

Moab *Times-Independent*, Moab, Utah.

Salt Lake *Daily Herald*, Salt Lake City, Utah.

Salt Lake *Herald-Republican*, Salt Lake City, Utah.

Salt Lake *Tribune*, Salt Lake City, Utah.

The Solid Muldoon, Ouray, Colorado.

The Monticello, San Juan Record, Monticello, Utah.

Pamphlets and Periodicals

Alexander, Thomas G. "From Dearth to Deluge: Utah's Coal Industry." *Utah Historical Quarterly* (Summer 1963), vol. XXXI.

Allred, B. W. "Cattle Roundup Mountain Style." *Corral Dust Potomac Corral of the Westerners*, Arlington, Virginia. (Winter and Spring 1966) vol. XI.

Armstrong, Burl. "Moab's Third Awakening." Salt Lake *Herald-Republican* (June 24, 1911).

Athearn, Robert G. "Utah and the Coming of the Denver and Rio Grande Railroad." *Utah Historical Quarterly* (July 1958), vol. XXVI.

---

[1]See footnotes throughout the book for various dates of publication.

Auerback, Herbert S. "Old Trails, Old Forts, Old Trappers and Traders." *Utah Historical Quarterly* (January-April, 1941) vol. IX.

Barnes, Fran. "An Arch, a Tunnel, Bridge — Or a Hole in the Rock: Experts Even Disagree on the Proper Definition." Moab *Times-Independent*, July 1, 1971.

————. "Canyonlands by Night." *Travel* (August 1970).

————. "Large Riverboat Now under Construction in Moab for Service on Colorado River Tour Excursions Here." Moab *Times-Independent*, December 30, 1971.

————. "Mine Operation Uncovers Puzzling Remains of Ancient Man." Moab *Times-Independent*, June 3, 1971.

————. "Petroglyphs in the Moab Area Attract Interest of Residents and Visitors Alike." Moab *Times-Independent*, September 3, 1971.

————. "The Best of the Southwest." Denver *Post*, August 2, 1970.

Bjarnason, Lofter. "The Geography of Utah." New York: The Macmillan Company, 1923. Pamphlet.

Breed, Jack. "Utah's Arches of Stone." *National Geographic* (August 1947), vol. 92.

Brooks, Juanita. "Indian Relations on the Mormon Frontier." *Utah Historical Quarterly* (January-April 1949), vol. XII.

Denver & Rio Grande Railroad. "Look to the Fertile Lands of Utah." No date. Pamphlet.

Ekker, Barbara Baldwin. "Freighting on the Colorado River, Reminiscenses of Virgil Ray Baldwin." *Utah Historical Quarterly* (Summer 1964), vol. XXXII.

————. "Son of Famed Western Outlaw Visits in Hanksville Area." Moab *Times-Independent*, July 9, 1970.

"Everyday Life in Bible Times." *National Geographic* (1968). Pamphlet.

"Exploration of the Colorado River and the High Plateaus of Utah in 1871-72." *Utah Historical Quarterly* (1948–49) vols. XVI and XVII.

"Exploration of the Colorado River in 1869." *Utah Historical Quarterly* (1947), vol. XV.

Fabian, Josephine. "Dead Horse Point in Rainbow Land." *Utah Historical Quarterly* (July, 1958), vol. XXVI.

Findley, Rowe. "Exploring Canyonlands National Park." *National Geographic* (July 1971), vol. 140.

————. "Realm of Rock and the Far Horizon Canyonlands." *National Geographic* (July 1971), vol. 140.

Hansel, Dave. "Ancient Fremont Indian Culture Now Studied at Paradox Valley." Moab *Times-Independent*, August 20, 1970.

Hansen, George H. "History of Exploration in Southeastern Utah." *Geology and Economic Deposits of East Central Utah.* Seventh Annual Field Conference of the Intermountain Association of Petroleum Geologists. Salt Lake City: Intermountain Association of Petroleum Geologists, 1956. Available at the Utah Geological and Mineralogical Survey, University of Utah.

Harline, Osmond L. "Utah's Black Gold: The Petroleum Industry." *Utah Historical Quarterly* (Summer 1963), vol. XXXI.

Hillinger, Charles. "Butch Cassidy's Sister Tells All." Los Angeles *Times*, April 3, 1970.

Hunt, Alice. "Archaeological Survey of the La Sal Mountain Area, Utah." *Anthropological Papers* No. 14. Salt Lake City: University of Utah Press, February 1953.

Hunt, Charles B. "La Sal Mountains." Moab *Times-Independent*, July 8, 1965.

Hussein, H. M., King of Jordan. "Holy Land, My Country." *National Geographic* (December 1964), vol. 126.

Jennings, Jesse D. "The Aboriginal Peoples." *Utah Historical Quarterly* (July 1960), vol. XXXIII.

Lambert, Neal. "Al Scorup: Cattleman of the Canyons." *Utah Historical Quarterly* (Summer 1964), vol. XXXII.

Maguire, Don. "Outline History of Utah's Great Mining Districts, Their Past and Present and Future as Producers of the Precious Metals." *Utah Mining Series* No. 4. Chicago: Rio Grande Western Railroad, 1899.

McConkie, Faun. "A History of Moab." Moab *Times-Independent* (Beginning April 26, 1934. Early manuscript asking for additional material and corrections.)

Melville, Bell Grosvenor. "Journey into the Living World of the Bible." *National Geographic* (October 1967), vol. 132.

"Moab, Utah, Modern Day Boom Town." *Intermountain Industry* (June 1961), vol. LXIII.

Naturalist (Summer 1970). Special issue on Canyonlands, vol. 1.

Nelson, ElRoy. "The Mineral Industry: A Foundation of Utah's Economy." *Utah Historical Quarterly* (Summer 1963), vol. XXXI.

Newell, Maxine. "Canyonlands." *Naturalist* (Summer 1970). Special edition, vol. 21.

"Outlaw's Death Still a Puzzler." *Arizona Republic*, January 21, 1973.

Roylance, Ward J. "Materials for the Study of Utah's Geography," 1962. (Revised, 1964). Pamphlet. XXII.

Rudy, Jack R. "Archaeological Excavations in Beef Basin, Utah." *Anthropological Papers* No. 20. Salt Lake City: University of Utah Press, March 1955.

Sharrock, Floyd W.; and Keane, Edward G. "Carnegie Museum Collection from Southeast Utah." *Anthropological Papers* No. 57. (Glen Canyon Series No. 16.) Salt Lake City: University of Utah Press, January 1962.

Snow, William J. "Utah Indians and Spanish Slave Trade." *Utah Historical Quarterly* (July 1929), vol. II.

Sorensen, Don. "Wonder Mineral: Utah's Uranium." *Utah Historical Quarterly* (Summer 1963), vol. XXXI.

Stewart, Omer C. "Culture Element Distributions: XVIII Ute-Southern Paiute," *Anthropological Records.* Berkeley and Los Angeles: University of California Press, 1942, vol. 6, no. 4.

Texas Gulf Sulphur Company. *Annual Report, 1962.* Houston, Texas (1963).

Tyler, S. Lyman. "The Yuta Indians before 1680." *Western Humanities Review* (Spring 1951).

"Utah's Land and Early People." Utah State Department of Public Instruction. State Capitol, 1947.

Valentine, Dan. "Nothing Serious." Salt Lake *Tribune,* June 1, 1973.

Walker, Don D. "The Carlisles: Cattle Barons of the Upper Basin." *Utah Historical Quarterly* (Summer 1964), vol. XXXII.

————. "The Cattle Industry of Utah 1850–1900." *Utah Historical Quarterly* (Summer 1964), vol. XXXII.

————. "Longhorns Come to Utah." *Utah Historical Quarterly* (Spring 1962), vol. XXX.

Wilson, Dick. "Moab's Spectacular Petroglyph Excites Imagination of Scientific Mind." Moab *Times-Independent,* June 13, 1968.

Woodbury, Angus M. "The Colorado River — The Physical and Biological Setting." *Utah Historical Quarterly* (July 1960), vol. XXXIII.

Young, Karl. "Wild Cows of the San Juan." *Utah Historical Quarterly* (Summer 1964), vol. XXXII.

Personal Interviews

Adams, Samuel
Allen, Hyrum
Bliss, Vern
Dalton, Bert
Dalton, Emma M.
Dalton, John
Darrow, Mary A. Lee
Day, Herbert H.
Day, Mary H. Wilcox
Doak, Edna House
Fish, Garnett L. Robinson
Goodman, Henry
Gould, Dr. Laurence M.
Green, Harry G.
Grimm, Louise Powell
Holyoak, John H.
Johnson, D. A.
Johnson, J. H.
Larsen, Lottie Johnson
Lemon, Libbie Larsen
Loveridge, J. T.
Maxwell, Addie Taylor
McConkie, Nora Johnson
McConkie, Oscar W.
McConkie, Wayne R.
McConkie, William R.
Peirce, June
Peterson, Dr. Charles S.
Peterson, Jane Warner
Peterson, John

Powell, Fred
Powell, Rene Kineson Berry
Ray, Neal
Redd, A. J.
Redd, Charles
Scorup, J. A.
Shafer, Essie
Shafer, F. M.
Shafer, John H.
Shafer, Will
Skewes, Lydia Taylor
Somerville, Andrew
Standifird, J. H.
Stewart, Mel
Taylor, Ada
Taylor, Arthur A.
Taylor, Don
Taylor, Hyrum
Taylor, Loren L.
Taylor, Lydia Ann Colvin
Taylor, Samuel J.
Trout, Tom
Westwood, Martha
Westwood, R. D.
White, Essie L.
Wilson, Ervin
Wilson, Joe
Wilson, Nicholas
Wilson, William (Billy)

Index:
Places, Events,
and Participants

Places and Events

Participants

THE FAR COUNTRY was composed in Baskerville by Twin Typographers. Editing, design, and suggestions for illustration were contributed by Sybil H. Clays. Layout and mechanicals were completed by Fran Clements of Bailey-Montague & Associates. The book was printed by Paragon Press, with binding by Mountain States Bindery. The book was printed on Patina II, supplied by Zellerbach Paper Company.

Full page photographs preceding chapters were made available through the courtesy of the Utah Travel Council and the Utah State Historical Society. The cover photo is by Bernard P. Lee.